THE EARLIEST BOOKS OF CANTERBURY CATHEDRAL

THE EARLIEST BOOKS OF CANTERBURY CATHEDRAL

Manuscripts and
Fragments to *c.* 1200

by

RICHARD GAMESON

LONDON
THE BIBLIOGRAPHICAL SOCIETY
THE BRITISH LIBRARY
THE DEAN AND CHAPTER OF CANTERBURY
2008

ISBN 978 0948170 166 (Bib. Soc.)
ISBN 978 07123 5008 2 (BL)

A CIP record for this book is available from
the British Library

Published by The Bibliographical Society

The British Library, 96 Euston Road
London NW1 2DB, England

The Dean and Chapter of Canterbury
(Canterbury Sources 4)

Printed by Henry Ling Ltd of Dorchester

Designed and typeset by Paul W. Nash

CONTENTS

PREFACE

A CATALOGUE OF THE earliest manuscript books of Canterbury Cathedral is long overdue. Notwithstanding the interest and importance of the items in question they are, as a whole, very little known: only a handful have ever been discussed in detail, while some of the group are virtually or indeed wholly unpublished. *Medieval Manuscripts in British Libraries*, hitherto the standard modern guide to the collection, treats only five of our items in depth; a further twenty-three receive summary notices of a couple of lines, while fourteen do not appear at all.[1]

The present volume is devoted to the items of pre-thirteenth-century date. The sheer number of high and late medieval manuscripts in the collection is such that to have continued beyond *c.* 1200 would have swollen the size of the present publication to unmanageable proportions, and would have postponed its appearance indefinitely. Correspondingly, restricting the scope to four centuries also meant that the relevant material could be treated in the detail it merits. Furthermore, whereas many of the items studied here were demonstrably, or very probably, in Canterbury at an early date – in some cases, indeed, being written there – this is very much more difficult to establish for a large number of the later manuscripts: the issues they raise are, to a significant extent therefore, distinct from those raised by our material which, for the most part, dates from the 'golden age' of monastic book production. Needless to say, the formidable body of later books and fragments might very usefully be the subject of separate volumes.

The manuscripts are arranged in the present catalogue in approximate chronological order. The account of each item is presented in the following sections.

A **heading** gives the item number in the present catalogue, the shelf-mark (or -marks), a summary characterisation of principal textual content, the place of origin, and the date-range, along with the reference for the accompanying illustration(s). The origin is stated with as much precision as the available evidence warrants, and may thus vary between the extremes of 'Saint Augustine's Abbey, Canterbury' on the one hand, and 'England or France' on the other. The date, which is almost invariably an estimate based on codicological, palaeographical and art-historical evidence, is expressed in terms of the formulae: ix/x; x^{in}; $x^{1/4}$; x^{1}; x^{med}, etc. (signifying turn of the ninth to tenth centuries, beginning of the tenth century, first quarter of the tenth century, first half of the tenth century, middle of the tenth century, and so on). In the rare instances where an item is datable on internal or external grounds, the formula is accompanied by a date in Arabic numerals ('after 987' etc.). Note that here, as throughout, 'x' (as in 987x1006) is used to indicate 'at an uncertain point between the given dates', whereas '–' (987–1006) means 'during the period that extends from the first date to the second'. Where applicable, the heading also supplies the secundo folio (2° folio) reference for the volume: i.e. the first words on the second folio, the standard means of identifying individual copies in medieval library catalogues.

Physical Description presents the codicology of the item: size, text-block, number of ruled lines, the space between them, the height of minims, the medium and nature of the ruling, the structure of the quires. All measurements are given in millimetres. Where, as is often the case, the item was subsequently re-used for another purpose, its present state is also described. With regard to fragments, an attempt is normally made to reconstruct as much of the original appearance of the book from which they come as the available evidence permits.

Content lists the texts, along with annotations and additions, following the order of the book. As some of the items are preserved as disordered fragments, mounted in different ways, others as flattened bifolia, and several bear various, sometimes incomplete or erroneous, series of folio or page numbers, it is impossible always to follow a single system for identifying the component leaves and pages. Folio references have been given wherever possible, but the state of certain items has sometimes required the use of other systems (these are explained in the relevant descriptions). References to folios (or pages or faces, etc.) are supplied within square brackets. For the identification of texts, reference is generally made (again within square brackets) to *Patrologia Latina*, often the only edition in Canterbury of the works in question. Where time and resources permitted, selected extracts were collated with other manuscripts and better editions held in libraries elsewhere, and these results are reported. In the case of the fairly extensive but terribly damaged liturgical items, it seemed worthwhile to present as full an account of the text as possible, making reference to widely-available editions.

In transcriptions, the following conventions were observed in so far as was practicable.

Capitals are used when they appear in the manuscript, but no attempt has been made to imitate their different grades. The exception is the concluding 'P[er]' at the end of prayers: sometimes lower case, sometimes a large or small capital in the manuscripts, this is always given a capital in the transcriptions. The choice of 'u' or 'v' follows the usage in the manuscript; e-caudata is simply represented by 'e'. Standard abbreviations are silently expanded; where there is a measure of doubt, the expansion is presented in brackets. A point (.) or stroke (´) is used to indicate an (ambiguous or unusual) abbreviation, the latter signifying the presence of some sort of tilde; no attempt has been made to expand such cases. Italic is employed to represent rubric. Punctuation is inserted only where it appears in the manuscript; however, no attempt is made to imitate the original marks: modern full-stop, comma and question mark signal major pauses, minor pauses and *punctus interrogativus*, however they be represented in the manuscript.

// indicates that the text begins or breaks off incomplete at this point.

/ represents a new line in the manuscript.

[...] enclose lost letters and words, an added '?' indicating uncertain restorations.

\.../ signal scribal insertions.

In collations [is used to separate the readings from different sources for a given passage.

Scribes and Script identifies the number of hands, characterising their writing and drawing attention to idiosyncracies, and indicates how these features lead to the date-range proposed.

Decoration describes and discusses major and minor ornament. It is hoped that the detail provided here and under **Scribes and Script,** in conjunction with the illustrations, may aid in the identification of sister leaves that have strayed into other collections.

History presents in chronological order such evidence as there is for the origin and provenance, the life and (in some cases) the later life, of the book.

Under **Commentary** observations are offered on the general significance of an item in relation to its historical context, where known. What may inform one reader will, of course, be well-known to another. As it is hoped that this publication will be used not only by specialists interested in a particular copy of a given text, but also by students of medieval book culture in general and those interested in Canterbury and Kent in particular, the Commentaries have been composed with the interests of a broad audience in mind.

The **Bibliography** cited for individual entries is confined to literature that specifically discusses (as opposed to merely listing or noting) the item in question. There seemed no value in including repeated references to Ker 1977, pp. 265–330, the most recent description of the collection, and which interested readers will doubtless have consulted anyway – except in relation to Lit. E. 42 (**no. 22**), the multi-volume passional which preoccupied Neil

Ker for many years and of whose complicated textual content he accordingly gave an exceptionally detailed and enduringly valuable account.

Each item is accompanied by one or more illustrations, carefully chosen to show representative and revealing features. They have been reduced to fit the standard page size. The pages in question are identified in the **Heading**.

The Introduction explores some of the general themes that are raised by the collection as a whole, and in particular, its importance for the bibliographical and cultural history of Canterbury in the earlier middle ages, at the end of the middle ages, and in the aftermath of the Dissolution of the monasteries and the English Reformation.

The text is supported by an Index of Manuscripts and an Index of People and Places. There is no Index of Incipits; however, as a large number of the items are more or less fragmentary and do not preserve their major incipits, whilst most of the others are common texts, such a tool would have served little purpose. Identifiable authors and the individuals commemorated in liturgical pieces naturally feature in the Index of People and Places.

In conclusion, it is appropriate to stress that this is still a growing collection. One of the most important manuscripts in the present catalogue, the late eleventh-century Canterbury copy of the Pauline epistles with Lanfranc's gloss (**no. 15**), was bequeathed to the cathedral in 1979. Equally, at a very late stage of the current work, the present writer identified a bifolium, offered for sale in London, as a companion to one already owned by the Cathedral: thanks to the prompt and energetic work of the archivist, Heather Forbes, and to the generosity of institutional and private benefactors, it was secured for the collection in 2005 (see **no. 14**). M. R. James, giant of English manuscript studies, concluded the Preface to one of his earliest catalogues (1895) with an appeal:

> I will freely confess that during the compilation of this book I have more than once been stimulated by the hope that some

> collector who should make use of my work might be led to think of [the institution where it was done] as a place where his manuscripts would be choicely valued, religiously preserved and minutely investigated. Now that the work is completed, the same hope recurs to me. I trust that in spite of its mistakes and defects, the books will be useful: and I think it can hardly fail to show that accessions to the collections of manuscripts would be as welcome gifts as any that could be made to us. There is no variety of ... medieval books which we should not prize ... fragments are often most precious ... Here too they are as secure as in the nature of things they can be from the accidents of fire, theft and dispersion by sale. The names of the donors are recorded and they are remembered with gratitude.[2]

I would wish to echo these sentiments in relation to Canterbury Cathedral, than which no finer nor more appropriate resting-place for donations of medieval manuscripts could be imagined. The best possible return for the present book would be the obligation to write a second!

Richard Gameson
Canterbury
The Feast of St Dustan 2005

NOTES

1 N. R. Ker *et al.*, *Medieval Manuscripts in British Libraries*, 5 vols. (Oxford, 1969–2002), II, pp. 265–330; V, p. 8. Its predecessor was C. E. Woodruff, *Catalogue of the Manuscript Books in the Library of Christ Church Canterbury* (Canterbury, 1911).

2 M. R. James, *A Descriptive Catalogue of the Manuscripts in the Fitzwilliam Museum* (Cambridge, 1895), p. xvii.

Henceforth all references are given in the form: author's surname plus date, the full details of each item being supplied in the Bibliography.

ACKNOWLEDGEMENTS

IT IS A PLEASURE to be able to record my gratitude to those who have helped in the realisation of this project. First and foremost, my thanks go to the Dean and Chapter, and to the ever-helpful and friendly staff of Canterbury Cathedral Library and Archives who have been so welcoming during the many years that I have been (intermittently) working on this catalogue – in particular to Michael Stansfield, the archivist under whom it was started, and Heather Forbes, under whom the typescript was finished. Preliminary study images were taken by David Pilcher; the final images used here are the work of Andrew Levison; they are reproduced by kind permission of the Dean and Chapter of Canterbury Cathedral and the Libraries and Archives Service of Kent County Council. The Canterbury Archaeological Society contributed a much-appreciated grant towards the cost of research trips to Brussels and Paris to study companion manuscripts in the Bibliothèque royale de Belgique and the Bibliothèque nationale de France. Help on particular points and comment on draft entries were kindly given by Bruce Barker-Benfield (manuscripts associated with Saint Augustine's Abbey), Martin Brett (**no.** 38) and Nicholas Orchard (**no.** 30). I am grateful to the Bibliographical Society for undertaking the publication of this complicated volume, and more particularly to David Shaw for shepherding it on its way in its early phases, and to Mirjam Foot for her care over its later stages, which included copy-editing that was exemplary both in its rigour and in its sensitivity. As ever, the last word is rightly reserved for Fiona and Christine Gameson, who not only gave invaluable help with the checking and proof-reading of Latin and English texts respectively, but provide the continuing moral support that, in an era inimical to such extremely time-consuming and 'old-fashioned' yet indispensable scholarly activities, makes such endeavours possible.

SUMMARY LIST OF MANUSCRIPTS

1 Add. 16, Bible; ix^{1}

2 Add. 127/19 and PRC 49/1/1–2, Priscian, *Institutiones grammaticae*; ix/x–x^{1}

3 PRC 49/24/1–7, Cassiodorus, *Expositio psalmorum*; x(?$^{2/3}$)

4 Add. 127/12, Homiliary; x$^{3/3}$

5 Add. 25, Werferth of Worcester, Old English version of Gregory's *Dialogi*; x^{ex}

6 Add. 32, Gregory, *Dialogi*; xi^{in}

7 PRC 49/2, Haimo of Auxerre, *Homiliarium*; xi^{in}

8 Add. 128/52, Missal (with notation); xi$^{1/4}$

9 Add. 127/1, Homiliary; xi^{1}

10 Add. 122, Opus incertum (homiletic fragment); xi^{1}

11 Add. 172, endleaf, Collectar; xi$^{3/4}$

12 Add. 20, Chrodegang of Metz, *Regula canonicorum*; xi$^{3/4}$

13 U4/20/2, Homiletic lectionary; xi$^{3/4}$

14 Add. 128/12 and 128/72, Gospel lectionary; xi^{2}

15 Add. 172, *Cantica Canticorum, Epistolae Pauli* (with Lanfranc's gloss); *Apocalypsis*; xi$^{4/4}$

16 Lit. B. 7, Canones; xi/xii

17 Lit. A. 8, Augustine, *Sermones*; xi/xii–xii^{in}

18 U3/162/28/1, Augustine, *Enarrationes in Psalmos*; xi/xii–xii^{in}

19 Add. 127/15, Ivo of Chartres, *Epistolae*; xii^{in}

20 X.1.11, flyleaves, Jerome, *In prophetas minores*; xii^{in}

21 Add. 127/20, Usuardus, *Martyrologium*; xii^{1}

22 Lit. E. 42 and Lit. E. 42A, part I, Passional; xii^{1}

23 PRC 50/20, Liturgica (with notation); xii$^{1\text{-}2/4}$

24 Add. 128/58, Augustine, *In euangelium Iohannis*; xii$^{2/4}$

25 Lit. D. 6, Gospel of Matthew, glossed; xii$^{2/4}$

26 U 102/6; Opus incertum (homiletic fragment); xii$^{2/4\text{–med}}$

27 SB B 232, final page; *membrum disjectum* from *Passiones* etc.; [xii^{med}]

28 PRC 50/17/1–3, Lectionary; xii^{med}

29 Add. 128/54, Lectionary; xii^{med}

30 Add. 127/24, Missal; xii^{med}

31 Add. 127/22, Breviary; xii^{med}

32 Add. 128/31, Breviary (with notation); xii$^{3/4}$

33 PRC 49/4/1–2, Gregory, *Moralia in Iob*; xii$^{3/4}$

34 Lit. A. 13, fols. 176–9, Canticles, glossed; xii$^{3/4}$

35 Add. 128/29, Missal (with notation); xii^{2}

36 Add 129/56 and PRC 49/3/3–5, Augustine, *In euangelium Iohannis*; xii^{2}

37 PRC 49/5/1–3, Peter Lombard, *Sententiae*; xii^{2}

38 PRC 49/6/1–2, Canones; xii$^{4/4}$

39 Add. 128/48, Officium/Inhumatio defuncti; xii^{ex}

40 Add. 128/10, Peter Comester, *Historia scholastica*; xii/xiii

41 Add. 127/17, Eusebius (Rufinus), *Historia ecclesiastica*; xii/xiii

42 Add. 128/14, Collectar; xii/xiii

CONDORDANCE

Shelf-mark	*Catalogue number*		
Add. 16	1	Add. 129/56	36
Add. 20	12	Add. 172	15
Add. 25	5	Add. 172, endleaf	11
Add. 32	6	Lit. A. 8	17
Add. 122	10	Lit. A. 13	34
Add. 127/1	9	Lit. B. 7	16
Add. 127/12	4	Lit. D. 6	25
Add. 127/15	19	Lit. E. 42	22
Add. 127/17	41	Lit. E. 42A	22
Add. 127/19	2	PRC 49/1/1–2	2
Add. 127/20	21	PRC 49/2	7
Add. 127/22	31	PRC 49/3/3–5	36
Add. 127/24	30	PRC 49/4/1–2	33
Add. 128/10	40	PRC 49/5/1–3	37
Add. 128/12	14	PRC 49/6/1–2	38
Add. 128/14	42	PRC 49/24/1–7	3
Add. 128/29	35	PRC 50/17/1–3	28
Add. 128/31	32	PRC 50/20	23
Add. 128/48	39	SB B 232	27
Add. 128/52	8	U3/162/28/1	18
Add. 128/54	29	U4/20/2	13
Add. 128/58	24	U102/6, cover	26
Add. 128/72	14	X.1.11, flyleaves	20

*INTRODUCTION**

IN THE EARLY SIXTEENTH CENTURY there were vast riches of medieval manuscripts in Canterbury. The books of Saint Augustine's Abbey and Christ Church Cathedral Priory numbered in the thousands; the town's Dominican and Franciscan friaries are both likely to have had substantial collections, as may its Augustinian priory (Saint Gregory's) and its nunnery (Saint Sepulchre's); in addition, the various hospitals and parish churches – not to mention a few private individuals – will all also have had book collections of some sort. The only general catalogue of Christ Church books to have come down to us, drawn up in the later years of Henry of Eastry's priorate (1285–1331), lists nearly 2000 volumes, and, notwithstanding losses and dispatches to Canterbury College (the *studium* in Oxford, founded in 1363), the total two centuries later will undoubtedly have been higher.[1] The incomplete, late fifteenth-century library catalogue of Saint Augustine's Abbey records a similar number.[2] On the eve of the Reformation, therefore, there is likely to have been in Canterbury a total of somewhere between 6,000 and 10,000 medieval books. To put these approximate figures in context, one should remember that a typical Oxbridge college collection in the later Middle Ages numbered between *c.* 200 and 600 volumes; at its recorded peak in 1473, the common library of the University of Cambridge possessed 330 books.[3] Thus it would be fair to claim that at the end of the Middle Ages, Canterbury had greater resources of books than any English town of comparable size; and if the variety and chronological spread of material is taken into account – because of the longevity of the two principal foundations, the volumes in question ranged in date from the sixth century to the sixteenth – it is doubtful whether any English town, except possibly London, could rival it.

A century later almost nothing of this remained. The Dissolution of the Monasteries and the Reformation of the English church had directly or indirectly caused the destruction of much. Around

350 books from Christ Church and some 280 from Saint Augustine's are still identifiable:[4] if these are respectable numbers in comparison with the survival rate from many other English medieval institutions, they represent but a fraction of what these two great houses once possessed. Moreover, the many other foundations in and around Canterbury have fared very much worse: only fifteen books are known from the local Franciscan collection, for example, and just one each from those of the Dominicans and Augustinians. Furthermore, the volumes in question have largely been alienated from the town. The mendicant manuscripts to which allusion has just been made, for instance, are now scattered between Hereford, Lincoln, London and Oxford: none remains in Canterbury.[5] The books of Christ Church and Saint Augustine's were carried away first by the 'salvaging' activities of a small number of influential collectors, most notably Matthew Parker (archbishop of Canterbury 1559–75); then, while those of the former abbey trickled away in dribs and drabs, those of the cathedral were depleted by large-scale appropriations – above all at the hands of John Whitgift (archbishop 1583–1604) and Thomas Neville (dean of Canterbury Cathedral 1597–1615). And whatever Neville's motives may have been, incidentally, for enriching his Cambridge College at the expense of his Cathedral Chapter, his actions were flagrantly in breach of the oath he will have sworn as Dean of Canterbury to 'guard, defend and keep ... all the goods, lands, tenements, rents, possessions, rights, liberties, privileges, and all other things as well moveable ... as immoveable ... of the same church'.[6]

Because so many Canterbury manuscripts are now elsewhere, those that are still in the town have tended to be overlooked or marginalized. Yet Canterbury still has a reasonable number of medieval books and, above all, fragments thereof. Tudor antiquaries and collectors focused their attentions, logically enough, on complete, non-proscribed volumes. By contrast, items that were already fragmentary, along with the leaves of outlawed service books, were left behind and – if not simply destroyed or lost – were re-cycled in bindings and as covers for court proceedings and other records. Such leaves, albeit fragmentary, are thus an extremely important complement to the better-known, complete volumes that survive in Cambridge, London, Oxford and elsewhere: not only do they, by and large, reflect different parts of the medieval book collections themselves, they also shed light on the different fates that could befall medieval books in the sixteenth century. Of the many manuscripts and fragments that are today in Canterbury, unquestionably the most important in this connection are the forty or so items dating from up to *c.* 1200: for many, indeed most of them, were certainly or probably owned in Canterbury or eastern Kent from a very early date (something that is much more difficult, if not impossible, to establish for later material); and some were demonstrably made there. Accordingly, this is the group that tells us most about book culture in Canterbury and Kent from the earlier Middle Ages through to the Reformation.

The early manuscripts and fragments studied here do not, of course, provide a basis for re-writing the history of Canterbury libraries from the Anglo-Saxon period to the sixteenth century; however, they do shed many interesting sidelights on that story.[7] These we shall explore under three broad headings: we shall first survey what the items reveal about the book culture of Canterbury during the period in which they were made; then, what they show about the use and re-use of older volumes in the later Middle Ages; and finally what they reveal about the history of medieval books and attitudes thereto during the Reformation and beyond.

* * *

Evidence for the first centuries of book collecting and making in Canterbury is exiguous in the extreme. Yet while it falls far short of revealing the nature of book culture in general in the region before the Viking Age, it does unquestionably show that Canterbury had access to a wide range of late Antique and early medieval continental manuscripts and that local scriptoria could produce books of an exceptionally high quality.[8] The swansong of this first phase of activity, curtailed by the general literary decline eloquently lamented by King Alfred and by the Viking raids of the ninth century,[9] is represented by the now-incomplete giant Bible, believed to have been made at Saint Augustine's Abbey, one leaf of which remains in Canterbury (**no. 1**).

From the tenth century onwards, extant manuscripts are far more numerous, permitting us – with due regard for certain imbalances in the sample – to perceive the book culture of Canterbury in some detail.[10] At Saint Augustine's Abbey texts were being collected and copied from a fairly early date in the tenth century, a phenomenon which intensified from the middle, and peaked in the second half of the century. The scriptorium of Christ Church, poorly represented for the first two-thirds of the tenth century appears to have burst into productivity in or around the long archiepiscopacy of St Dunstan (960–88), and maintained a vigorous output of books for study and *lectio divina*, along with some altar books, into the early eleventh century. If the texts that were acquired and copied at both centres were fairly conservative ones, the quality of in-house production was good and the resulting library books were remarkably handsome. The Latin manuscripts written at both Saint Augustine's and Christ Church in the tenth and early eleventh centuries were characterised by high standards of presentation with distinctive house-styles of ornamentation and script – be it the native square minuscule or the imported Caroline minuscule – implying a degree of scriptorium discipline which is difficult to parallel elsewhere in England at the time. The circumstances that the characteristic minuscule and display scripts in question are not observable in the items of appropriate date that are still in Canterbury (**nos. 4–7**) would tend to suggest that these were not produced locally, or – less likely – that they were made outside the confines of the two main foundations.

The sack of Canterbury in 1011 when, according to the Anglo-Saxon Chronicle, the Vikings overran the city and 'took all the ecclesiastics captive',[11] broadly coincides with, and may have caused or at least reinforced, the end of this phase of development. Although both scriptoria recovered from the débâcle – that of Christ Church particularly rapidly – the focus of their efforts appears then to have shifted. Less energy seems to have been devoted during the following generations to developing the library collections – whose already-conservative characters were thus effectively fossilised – while more was directed towards the production of liturgical and para-liturgical books, some of which were destined for 'export'.[12] The circumstance that the items in the present corpus which date from the couple of generations before the Conquest are homilies, liturgica and a Rule (**nos.** 7–10) – wherever they were written – might be regarded as a just reflection of the principal focus of interest at the time.

After 1066 the presence of Norman ecclesiastics and appointees in dominant positions gave a new stimulus and brought different priorities to book production and acquisition in Canterbury, as elsewhere.[13] English collections as a whole were rich in homilies, vernacular texts and altar books of various forms, but weaker in theology in general and patristics in particular, and much the same would seem to have been true of those at Canterbury. At Saint Augustine's, whose Anglo-Saxon library must have been outstanding and whose perceived deficiencies accordingly less severe, the period following the Conquest was characterised by a measured programme of copying patristic and other texts to supplement existing resources. This phase is represented in the present corpus by two fine manuscripts of Augustine and one of Jerome (**nos.** 17, 18, 20), along with a copy of the Pauline Epistles with Lanfranc's gloss (**no.** 15). Some of this work was still being written in the attractive and highly legible late standard Anglo-Caroline minuscule, a script that developed – arguably in Canterbury itself – at the beginning of the eleventh century (cf. **no.** 8); still flourishing around the time of the Conquest (**nos.** 9 and 11), this had its swansong at Saint Augustine's Abbey at the beginning of the twelfth century (**nos.** 17 and 18). At the same time, the manuscript of the Pauline Epistles (**no.** 15) illustrates the arrival of dramatically different styles of hand-writing from across the Channel in the wake of the Conquest, for the work of Norman scribes (probably from Mont Saint-Michel) is directly juxtaposed with that of Anglo-Saxons.[14]

At Christ Church, where a devastating fire in 1067 had depleted earlier resources and whose new archbishop, Lanfranc

(1070–89), is likely to have had particularly high scholarly standards, there was frenetic activity to remedy the losses and lacunae. Accordingly, the earliest post-Conquest Christ Church books tend to be physically unprepossessing, haste not taste being the driving force. However, a distinctive house style with a prickly minuscule script and a characteristic alphabet of coloured display capitals rapidly emerged.[15] In our corpus this is represented in its 'canonical phase' by an early twelfth-century copy of Ivo of Chartres' *Epistolae* (**no. 19**). The infiltration of such hand-writing into the scriptorium of Saint Augustine's Abbey in the early twelfth century is illustrated by a Jerome (**no. 20**) which, as it happens, was almost certainly copied from a Christ Church exemplar.

By the second quarter of the twelfth century both centres had accumulated good runs of patristic and post-patristic theology, often in handsome copies, and the main effort of transcribing library texts was winding down. This freed up time for grander projects, exemplified in the present corpus by the multi-volume Christ Church passional (**no. 22**). Made doubtless over an extended period of time around the 1120s, this must once have been a masterpiece; even in its incomplete and grievously mutilated state it remains a mighty testimony to Christ Church's scribal resources, and simultaneously advertises the continuity of traditions that had developed there in the late eleventh century. The volumes are still written in the prickly script, albeit of a slightly freer form; and the display capitals and decorated initials – some of which include foliate motifs with an unmistakable Anglo-Saxon pedigree, while one redeploys a figure-type first witnessed at Canterbury in the late tenth century – are likewise linked to earlier work.

The prickly script was also used for one of the early additions to the Christ Church passional,[16] and it is conceivable that the angularity of the writing in the mid-twelfth-century breviary (**no. 31**) represents an echo of the same style. Be that as it may, traces of this local script are barely perceptible in a slightly later addition to the passional.[17] The supercession of such distinctive regional types by more widespread late Romanesque, 'Transitional', and early Gothic book hands is illustrated by the broadly-contemporary glossed Matthew (**no. 25**), by the mid-twelfth-century lectionary (**no. 28**), the Canterbury missal (**no. 30**) and, above all, by the slightly later glossed Canticles (**no. 34**). By the time of the latest specimens in the present corpus – early Gothic book hands which range from the highly calligraphic (**no. 40**), through the formal (**no. 37**) and the hasty (**no. 41**), to the relatively informal (**no. 38**) and which are virtually impossible to localise on the grounds of their script alone – the hey-day of 'in-house' monastic manuscript production in Canterbury had passed. Christ Church and Saint Augustine's now acquired most of their books through gift, purchase and bequest. One would dearly like to know when, from where, and by which of these routes, the remarkably handsome over-sized copy of Peter Comestor's *Historia scholastica* (**no. 40**), dating from *c.* 1200, reached Canterbury; however, in the absence of documentation, it is impossible to find out.

Several items, which are intimately linked to books that have migrated elsewhere, illustrate the importance of the material described here for understanding broader patterns of scribal and literary culture at Canterbury during the 'golden age' of local book production. The endleaf of Add. 172 (**no. 11**), for instance, is a rejected bifolium from a collectar that was written in the third quarter of the eleventh century and was re-used as a guard-leaf at Saint Augustine's Abbey within a generation. Now, the highly talented scribe who was responsible for this leaf also wrote a copy of Chrodegang of Metz's *Regula canonicorum*, known only from a fragment which is also still in Canterbury (**no. 12**), as well as a complete pontifical which has migrated to Cambridge.[18] Where in Canterbury was this distinguished calligrapher based? A pontifical is by definition an episcopal book – it has been suggested that this particular one was made for the notorious Stigand (archbishop from 1052 until his deposition in 1070) – and is therefore more easily associable with Christ Church than with Saint Augustine's Abbey. Equally, a Rule for secular canons is more intelligible in relation to an archbishop in whose archdiocese was Rochester (which until *c.* 1080 was staffed by canons) and who (in the person of Lanfranc) founded a house in Canterbury that was probably served by regular canons *ab initio* (Saint Gregory's).[19] Furthermore, there is a reasonable chance that this manuscript is the 'Regula canonicorum a' that appears on the list of *libri anglici* in the early fourteenth-century Christ Church library catalogue.[20] On the other hand, the collectar leaf was certainly at Saint Augustine's Abbey at the end of the eleventh century; moreover, the pontifical was glossed by a known Saint Augustine's Abbey scribe – who was responsible, *inter alia*, for another book that is still in Canterbury (**no.** 17). There is no easy way to cut this Gordian knot. However, the conundrum might itself be held to reflect the connections that existed between the principal foundations in the town during the second half of the eleventh century; more speculatively, it may even afford us a glimpse of a scribe who worked (at least some of the time) at the specific behest of the archbishop.

Other items in the present corpus provide less ambiguous evidence for connections between Christ Church and Saint Augustine's. The main body of Add. 172 (**no.** 15), which includes a copy of the Pauline Epistles with Lanfranc's gloss, was written at Saint Augustine's Abbey in the last quarter of the eleventh century and remained there, as medieval *ex libris* and shelfmarks attest. The book itself illustrates something of the cultural mix in that community in the aftermath of the Norman Conquest, since, while a couple of the scribes have archetypical English hands, one is conceivably Flemish (and we know, incidentally, of at least one Fleming, Goscelin of Saint-Bertin, who was at Saint Augustine's at the time),[21] a couple of others are certainly Norman, and yet others 'Anglo-Norman'. Now, the first Norman abbot of the community, Scollandus (1070x2–87), came from Mont Saint-Michel – where, incidentally, we know he had worked as a scribe.[22] The Norman script of one part of this book and, to a lesser extent, the Norman-style minor initials therein, reveal the participation of Norman personnel (probably from Mont Saint-Michel) in book production at Saint Augustine's in the late eleventh century. Furthermore, we know that the exemplar for part of the text had very recently been imported from Normandy, more particularly from Le Bec. A letter from Anselm, then prior of Le Bec, to Archbishop Lanfranc shows that, around 1076, the latter had asked to be sent the Le Bec copy of his gloss on the

Pauline Epistles; this was duly done – with the expressed hope that a new copy of the work might be returned in due course.[23] The present manuscript, made at Saint Augustine's Abbey and now the oldest version of the work to survive, must have been copied shortly after 1076 either directly from the Le Bec original or from a Christ Church intermediary: either way the exemplar must have been loaned to the abbey by the cathedral.

Another such instance, which shows that exchange of bibliographical resources continued a generation later, is provided by a pair of leaves from an otherwise lost manuscript of Jerome's *In prophetas minores* that was made at Saint Augustine's Abbey in the early twelfth century (**no. 20**), for its exemplar was very probably the slightly older Christ Church copy of the text now in Cambridge.[24]

The present corpus also includes an item which attests to the bibliographical relations between Christ Church and Rochester a couple of generations after the Norman Conquest.[25] The early twelfth-century Canterbury leaves from a copy of the letters of Ivo of Chartres (**no. 19**) include a major anomaly – the omission and subsequent insertion of one particular line of text – which was echoed in the slightly later Rochester copy of the same work.[26] Minor discrepancies between the texts of the two manuscripts in other respects make it unlikely that the Christ Church copy was itself the immediate source for the Rochester one: it is more probable that both descend from a common exemplar. One might hypothesise, then, that Christ Church acquired a continental manuscript of the work which, having been copied in Canterbury, was subsequently loaned to Rochester, where it was transcribed again.

An item which alludes to the ties between all three Kentish foundations we have considered is the multi-volume passional that was made at Christ Church in the 1120s, many leaves of which remain in Canterbury (**no. 22**), for the set was clearly related to the comparable collections that were transcribed at Saint Augustine's Abbey and at Rochester around the same time (now represented respectively by London, British Library, MS Arundel 91 plus Oxford, Bodleian Library, MS Fell 2, and by Oxford,

Worcester College, MS 273).[27] Here again the loss of crucial pieces of the puzzle – all three sets are seriously incomplete, above all that of Rochester, from which but one fragment of a single leaf survives – foils attempts to reach definitive conclusions about the nature of the interrelations between these sets and their antecedents. Such work as has been done on texts that the surviving portions of different sets have in common, has been seen to fit the theory that the Christ Church copy was the exemplar for those of Saint Augustine's and Rochester.[28] However, given that on palaeographical and art-historical grounds one would incline to date the Saint Augustine's volumes before the Christ Church ones, while the Rochester copy is very probably datable to before 1123[29] and is thus almost certainly anterior to them, this seems doubtful. The alternative hypothesis – which is also compatible with the textual evidence – that two or even all of them descend independently from (lost) common exemplars, thus has more to recommend it. Yet whatever the exact nature of their interconnections, the fact that the three sets are related is not in doubt, nor that in some way or other they attest to the sharing of bibliographical resources between the two great Canterbury houses and Rochester.

A final case worth mentioning makes the complementary point that on some occasions the three Kentish houses had access to different exemplars for the same texts. Lit. A. 8 (**no.** 17), a substantial volume written at Saint Augustine's Abbey around 1100 by a scribe who appears in several other manuscripts from the abbey (and who was also the afore-mentioned glossator of the Canterbury pontifical),[30] is the earliest extant English copy of a common collection of the sermons of Augustine of Hippo known as *De uerbis domini et apostoli* which was here augmented (from the outset) by a couple of additional sermons. The circumstance that a manuscript of the core collection had been made at Mont Saint-Michel about a generation earlier (Avranches, Bibliothèque municipale, MS 82) would seem to invite the speculation that this (or an immediate relative of it) was the basic exemplar, obtained through the agency of Scollandus, and that it was then supplemented in Canterbury from other sources; however, it is clear – despite fire damage – that the Avranches manuscript contained a different version of the collection. A slightly later Rochester copy of the collection does have the additional sermons that are found in Lit. A. 8; however, as it presents the main run of sermons in a slightly different order, it is unlikely to descend from it.[31] Nor does the content of the lost Christ Church copy that is described in Henry of Eastry's library catalogue correspond exactly to that of our manuscript.[32] The logical inference, therefore, is that in this case Saint Augustine's, Christ Church, and Rochester used different exemplars, suggesting that multiple versions of this popular collection circulated in Kent in the aftermath of the Conquest. This shows that, while the three houses could pool bibliographical resources, equally each could have recourse to sources of its own – and hence that the case of every text must be examined individually.

To sum up: these and other items dovetail into the picture of book production in Canterbury and Kent before and, especially, after the Conquest that is offered by other sources, while at the same time enlarging our understanding of the complex patterns of literary exchange between the major foundations in Kent on the one hand, and between England and Normandy on the other.

* * *

In the first half of the fifteenth century, thanks to the sponsorship of Archbishop Chichele (*sedit* 1414–43), Christ Church invested in a new, purpose-built library room, which was erected as an extra storey above the prior's chapel (itself above the infirmary cloister).[33] A document of 1508, compiled by William Ingram (the *custos* of Becket's shrine) and inspired by a comprehensive renovation of the collection, lists some 300 books that were kept on – most probably chained to – sixteen lecterns therein.[34] Many of the volumes in question contained standard patristic texts and were certainly or probably manuscripts that dated from the later eleventh or the earlier twelfth century, and which had been given a new and prestigious lease of life in the new facility. The final book on the lower shelf of the first side of the sixth desk, for instance, was the volume of Jerome, *In prophetas minores* that was mentioned above in connection with its role as the exemplar for a manuscript made at Saint Augustine's Abbey which remains in Canterbury (see **no. 20**).

Correspondingly, a good number of the items described here bear additions and annotations which show that they continued to be used long after they were made – sometimes, indeed, throughout the entire Middle Ages.[35] The late tenth-century copy of the homiliary of St Père de Chartres (**no. 4**) was extensively revised *in rasura* in the first half of the twelfth century; moreover, its punctuation was comprehensively overhauled and regular breaks inserted – doubtless to suit it to the expectations of a different generation for the presentation of a book to be used for public reading. Similarly, the manuscript of Gregory's *Dialogues* (**no. 6**), copied (rather negligently) soon after the millennium, received some corrections in the second half of the eleventh century and others in the twelfth century or later, indicating a two-hundred-year period of use. Even longer was the working life of an eleventh-century homiliary (**no. 9**) which, an interlinear annotation implies, was still seeing active service in the later Middle Ages. Equally, the mid-twelfth-century missal (**no. 30**) bears notes dating from the thirteenth or fourteenth century, while a later twelfth-century breviary (**no. 32**) has fourteenth- or fifteenth-century ones. More dramatically, the early eleventh-century missal (**no. 8**) was comprehensively re-worked in the fourteenth or fifteenth century by at least three different hands to suit the changed needs of a new era.

A sequence of substantial supplements shows that the seven-volume passional from Christ Church (**no. 22**) was gradually augmented over a long period of time. As noted above, the initial collection was copied in the 1120s. A first addition, made a generation later (in the mid-twelfth century), includes a miracle of St Ouen that was reputedly witnessed by Elmer, prior of Christ Church from 1128 to 1137; soon afterwards, in the third quarter of the century, a Life of St Gregory was added, followed by a verse epitome of the Life of St Anselm – a text composed after 1163. Additions were still being made three centuries later: Ailred of Rievaulx's Life of Edward the Confessor and an abbreviated version of William of Malmesbury's Life of St Wulfstan of Worcester were inserted into volume I, and a passion of the Seven Sleepers into volume IV by the hired scribe, Theodoric Werken, whose other work for Christ Church is dated to the 1470s.[36] Subsequently, a Life of Augustine of Canterbury was added to volume II by a scribe who was demonstrably active under Prior Goldwell (1517–40).[37] If the collection had been preserved in a complete, as opposed to a highly fragmentary state, more such supplements – and further phases of augmentation – would probably be apparent.

The insertion of extra leaves that some such additions required must sometimes have involved pulling and rebinding. Correspondingly, it was perhaps in response to similar expansion, and not merely for repair, that an 'old book of readings' (*liber uetus collacionum*) appears on a list of Christ Church books that were sent to the binder in the early sixteenth century.[38] Yet whatever the precise circumstances and motive, this venerable volume, like so many others, was being reconditioned for continuing service.[39]

The collection of sermons by Augustine of Hippo (**no. 17**) received no substantial additions or annotations. However, interest in and use of the manuscript at the end of the Middle Ages is indicated by the fact that it was fully 'reconditioned' then: the volume was foliated, the individual sermons were numbered (and cross-referenced), and running headings were added (moreover, picking up the point made in the previous paragraph, the extent and neatness of the writing throughout suggest that it was pulled and then rebound as part of this house-keeping process). It was thus equipped for use for reference purposes as well as for the continuous, sequential meditative consumption of *lectio diuina*. Precisely the same happened to other such works around the same time – indeed through the activity of the same hands: the fragmentary copy of Gregory's *Moralia* (**no. 33**) is a case in point. If such interventions reveal individual items being 'revitalised' internally in the later Middle Ages, Lit. A. 8 (**no. 17**) and a couple of other manuscripts from Saint Augustine's Abbey that are in our corpus, Add. 172 and Lit. D. 6 (**nos. 16** and **25**), simultaneously attest, via the sequence of *ex libris* inscriptions and shelf-marks that they bear, to the ordering and re-ordering of the collection as a whole across the centuries. All three books received a note of their content in the twelfth century. Then in the thirteenth century the title in Lit. A. 8 was given additional precision through an extra note to the effect that it was glossed, while that in Lit. D. 6 was erased and re-written. In the (?later) fourteenth century, *ex libris* and shelf-marks were added to all three books; Lit. D. 6 appears to have been reshelved (possibly more than once) shortly thereafter, since both its *distinctio* and it *gradus* numbers were changed – a phenomenon which can, of course, be paralleled in other volumes from the collection.[40] Finally, at the end of the Middle Ages, supplementary reference letters were added to the inscriptions in Add. 172 and Lit. A. 8 ('cum B', 'cum C') to distinguish them from other copies of the same work. In all three cases the final state of the title and shelf-mark corresponds to that given in the late fifteenth-century house library catalogue (Lit. D. 6: 'Matheus glo' cum C ... d. III, G.I'; Add. 172: 'Epistole pauli glo' et in eodem libro Cantica canticorum et apocalypsis Iohannis sine glo' cum B ... d. III. G. II'; Lit. A. 8: 'Augustinus de uerbis domini in Euang cum B ... d. IIII, G. III'). The broader history of the development and use of the library as a whole falls outside the scope of the present study.[41] Suffice it to say that the shelf-marks in these and other manuscripts, along with the catalogue and other evidence, show that a series of librarians (the most famous and attentive of whom was Clement of Canterbury)[42] laboured to keep the collection as a whole – including the very many older books – ordered and serviceable up to the end of the Middle Ages. And it will be remembered that the fourteenth-century Custumal of Saint Augustine's Abbey specifies that the Cantor should have his seat in front of the book-cupboard in the cloister, his carrel next to it, with the Succentor positioned nearby, so that one or both of them should always be on hand to respond to the reading requests of the brothers. Their role, it is clearly implied, was to oversee and guard the collection in perpetuity.[43]

Physical and documentary evidence shows similar activities going on at Christ Church in the late fifteenth and early sixteenth centuries, when hired scribes – such as the aforementioned Theodore Werken, along with Jacques Nele (who features in the prior's accounts for 1492, being remunerated 'for various writing-tasks for the Lord Prior') – might be set to reconditioning or even re-transcribing old volumes.[44] Repairs specifically to altar books or precious bindings are also occasionally recorded. Thus the Christ Church sacrist's accounts for 1473–4 include a payment of 3*s*.4*d*. for the repair of two gospel books, and those for 1493–4 note the expenditure of 4*s*.8*d*. for the binding of two missals (both associated with particular altars).[45] A short list of Christ Church books that were at the binders in the early sixteenth century has come down to us: the nature of the texts in question – which were evidently from different collections and stores, and include 'the epistle-book of St Thomas' – leaves little doubt that this referred to the re-binding and repair of older volumes rather than the initial binding of new ones.[46]

The latest example in this corpus of revision in response to changing needs is provided by the collectar fragment, **no. 42**. The fact that the reference to Thomas Becket was expunged, as required by Henry VIII's proclamation of 16 November 1538,[47] shows that this book dating from around 1200 was still, in some sense, in service during the second quarter of the sixteenth century, as the storm-clouds of the Reformation were gathering.

If the evidence we have surveyed demonstrates that some of the items treated here were being read long after the period when they were written, annotations in another twelfth-century volume, a glossed Gospel of St Matthew (**no. 25**), indicate that by the middle of the thirteenth century it was being put to an altogether different use. A series of notes in Hebrew reveals that the manuscript was pawned at least three times by several individuals, all with Kentish names – Adam of Sandwich, Hugh of Canterbury, and Hugh of Monigham (i.e. Mongeham). The script of an early correction suggests that the book was in Kentish hands by the second quarter of the twelfth century and it bears the medieval shelf-marks and *ex libris* of Saint Augustine's Abbey; it is likely, therefore, that the volume belonged to the abbey at the time when it was being pawned, and that the two Hughs, along with Adam of Sandwich, were members of that community. Furthermore, one of the Hebrew notes records that copies of the Epistles and of Mark's Gospel were pawned on the same occasion. The comparatively modest sums that were thereby raised, and the repetition of the act suggest that, rather than a desperate response to deep financial crisis, this was instead merely an expedient way of raising petty cash to meet a particular, short-term need. Given that the inscriptions are in Hebrew, the book was patently pledged to a Jew, presumably in Canterbury. Assuming that this was indeed the act of members of Saint Augustine's Abbey, it was a modest counterpart to the activities of contemporary Christ Church, whose monks are documented as borrowing more substantial sums of money from the Canterbury Jews in the thirteenth century.[48] By this date, a twelfth-century glossed book whose apparatus predated the *glossa ordinaria*, may have seemed expendable for such purposes; the late fifteenth-century library catalogue of Saint Augustine's Abbey lists seven glossed copies of Matthew's Gospel, along with six of Mark's and no fewer than eighteen of the Epistles.[49] At the same time, the irony of pawning books of the New Testament to Jews may not have been disagreeable to a venerable Benedictine community!

Some of the items were patently recycled in more drastic ways at an early date. What type of circumstances could lead to this? Certain items were or may have been defective *ab initio*. The eleventh-century collectar fragment (**no. 11**) is a case in point. Doubtful and erroneous readings along with physical anomalies (above all, the fact that its conjoint folio was left blank) suggest that this bifolium is unlikely ever to have been part of a complete book; on the contrary, it was presumably 'rejected' as soon as it had been written, kept as scrap, and was eventually re-employed as an endleaf plus paste-down. The case of the mid-twelfth-century glossed canticles (**no. 34**) is less clear-cut. Its idiosyncrasies need not have prohibited use; indeed a supplementary gloss made at least half a century after the leaves were originally written, and the insertion of an omitted minor initial at some point thereafter would seem to imply a fair period of service. Nevertheless, they may have made it a candidate for recycling in due course, and its pages were certainly re-used as endleaves by the later Middle Ages. In both cases, ironically, these items have come down to us precisely because they were set aside, or abandoned as reading matter, and used for other purposes.

Certain books might simply have worn out or gone out of date. If one looks at survival rates as a whole from our period, there is a disproportionately low representation of grammatical and pedagogical texts – doubtless in part because many copies were literally used to death, while those that survived then fell from fashion and were abandoned.[50] The intense glossing, in several layers, to which the Canterbury Priscian fragments (**no.** 2) were subjected, illustrates the first point. Multiple copies of the work (or parts thereof) are recorded in the library catalogues of Saint Augustine's, Christ Church, and Rochester, and we may note that two of those listed in the later twelfth-century Christ Church catalogue and two of those in the 1202 Rochester one were already said to be incomplete.[51] Moreover, one of Christ Church's five copies of 'Priscianus magnus' and four of its five 'Priscianus constructionum' are recorded to be in parchment wrappers ('in pargameno' [sic]) as opposed to robustly bound with wooden boards ('in asseribus'), and were thus all the more vulnerable to wear and tear (both of the aforementioned imperfect copies were, we may note, 'in pargameno'). More generally, seven of the titles that appear on the later twelfth-century Christ Church list – a fragment that focuses on pedagogical/*artes* texts – were recorded as incomplete. In a different era with other pedagogical demands and resources, such volumes were particularly vulnerable to cannibalisation if the need arose.

Service books were equally prone to being worn out by daily use, or going out of date. The general paucity of pre-Conquest service books and the fact that most of what we have is highly fragmentary, is not just a consequence of the Reformation, charnel house of early English liturgical books though that was, but also of the many liturgical revisions that preceded it. The missal, Add. 128/52 (**no.** 8), written in the earlier eleventh century was, as remarked before, still in service in the fourteenth to fifteenth century. However, it bears offsets of fifteenth- to sixteenth-century script running at right-angles to the main text which, while they might reflect re-use in a binding after the Reformation, are also compatible with recycling as endleaves a generation or so before it.

The same could even apply to Bibles, the text of which was also subject to periodic revision and reorganisation, above all in the early thirteenth century. The oldest manuscript fragment at Canterbury Cathedral (**no. 1**) is a *membrum disjectum* from an early ninth-century pandect that was owned by, and probably made at Saint Augustine's Abbey; yet by the thirteenth century at the latest, it had been subdivided and parts of it were being recycled. But then, as the library catalogue shows, Saint Augustine's steadily accumulated Bibles, and by the late fifteenth century had a total of over fifty, several of which were demonstrably acquired as 'new copies' in the thirteenth century. The specimen given by Nicholas de Thorne (abbot 1273–83), for instance, is specifically described as a revised Paris Bible ('correcta Parisius') which presumably implies that it was one of the popular 'second-generation' Bibles that were produced in Paris from *c.* 1230;[52] while the still-extant example that was offered by Robert of Battle incorporates his name in the original work (fol. 2r), dating it to his abbacy (1225–53).[53] In such circumstances, one could afford to 'sacrifice' earlier, partly superceded, possibly damaged or now incomplete copies (or at least parts thereof) – unless they had important historical or spiritual associations. (The supremely resonant copy at Saint Augustine's was the now-lost, two volume *Biblie sancti Gregorii* – associated rightly or wrongly with Pope Gregory the Great – which had pride of place at the very head of their library catalogue.)[54] The point is underlined by Christ Church, which had a large communal Bible by the late eleventh century if not before,[55] yet in the mid-twelfth century (in accordance with fashion) commissioned a fine, new, large-format copy – which in turn, two centuries later, it was happy to pass on to its daughter house, Dover Priory.[56] The de-accessioning, redistribution or even loss of high-grade books is illustrated more generally by the Christ Church inventory of 1315. This enumerates a total of twenty-two treasure bindings of the sort that adorned gospel books and psalters, two of which are specifically recorded to be without books in them.[57] Correspondingly, the fact that part of a venerable eighth-century gospel book of Northumbrian origin but probable Saint Augustine's Abbey provenance, came into the hands of Cardinal Wolsey who died in 1530, suggests that the volume in question had been subdivided and alienated before the Dissolution.[58]

The present corpus provides striking examples of the uses to which rejected leaves and the pages of obsolete books were put during the Middle Ages. Whole sheets could be deployed at the fronts and backs of newer volumes: as we have seen, the rejected bifolium from the eleventh-century collectar was deployed as the endleaf and paste-down in the original binding of a volume of late eleventh-century date (**nos. 11** and **15**). Parts of the above-mentioned ninth-century Saint Augustine's Abbey Bible – from which **no. 1** comes – were being used for similar purposes by the thirteenth century: one sheet, folded in half, was redeployed as the front guard-leaf of a late tenth-century copy of John the Deacon's *Vita Gregorii*, as the inscription that was then added to it attests.[59] And the mid-twelfth-century Canterbury Canticles (**no. 34**) became endleaves for a fourteenth-century copy of Duns Scotus on the *Sentences* of Peter Lombard, a volume acquired by the Christ Church monk and scholar, James de Oxeney († 1361).[60]

Whole sheets could equally be used to form bindings, covers or wrappers for memoranda of various sorts. The early twelfth-century liturgical fragments PRC 50/20 (**no. 23**) were used thus for the cover of a register of wills from the consistory court for the period 1459–84; while the late twelfth-century Office of the Dead 128/48 (**no. 39**) reputedly came from the binding of a register of 1468.[61] Alternatively, the leaves might be cut into thin strips or small squares and used to reinforce joints or line spines. The tenth-century Cassiodorus fragments (**no. 3**) were used as spine-liners in the register of wills from the Archdeaconry Court for 1567–70. If this last example dates from a generation after the Dissolution of the Monasteries, the others all predate it; and it is worth stressing that such recycling went on as a matter of course throughout the Middle Ages.[62]

* * *

Yet if scrapping and recycling were part of the natural life-cycle of medieval books, the middle decades of the sixteenth century were nevertheless, in protestant countries, a period of holocaust for manuscripts. The details of this tragic phenomenon are well known and need not detain us here.[63] Suffice it to say that a series of factors, each of which by itself would have been extremely injurious – fanatically enforced liturgical and ecclesiastical change, equally strict reform of the universities, an increasing availability of printed books, and the dissolution of the religious institutions that had harboured medieval libraries – now coincided to devastating effect.[64] Thus in addition to the countless liturgical volumes that were proscribed, very large numbers of library texts became obsolete and homeless. In some cases oblivion seems to have followed fairly rapidly. From Dover Priory, for example, whose celebrated library catalogue of 1389 records a book collection of over 400 volumes, only twenty manuscripts would seem to survive; from the royal abbey of Faversham, fewer than ten are known to remain; Saint Gregory's (Canterbury), Malling, and Tonbridge are now represented by but a single volume each; while from Saint Radegund's, Bradsole (near Dover), whose late thirteenth-century catalogue lists some 150 items, not a single library book is known to have come down to us.[65]

At the cathedral priories of Canterbury and Rochester, by contrast, along with Saint Augustine's Abbey, quite different turns of events resulted in comparatively high rates of survival – albeit in other hands. As is well known, a substantial number of Rochester manuscripts were appropriated for the library of King Henry VIII, descending thence to the royal *fonds* of the British Library. It has reasonably been conjectured that the large-scale absorption of this qualitatively modest collection was indirectly due to the person of John Fisher, bishop of Rochester from 1504 to 1535:[66] for his own work, Fisher is likely to have borrowed Rochester Cathedral books which, after his arrest (1534) and execution (1535), may have been sequestered by the Crown from his palace at Rochester. If the medieval books of Christ Church became over-night the library of the New Foundation of Canterbury Cathedral, they were then pilfered by a series of high-placed church office-holders, starting with Nicholas Wotton (dean of Canterbury 1541–67) and reaching a climax in the persons of John Whitgift (archbishop 1583–1604) and Thomas Neville (dean 1597–1615) at the turn of the century.[67]

The dispersal of the library of Saint Augustine's Abbey seems to have been a particularly piece-meal and leisurely process. The foundation surrendered to the Crown on 30 July 1538; but while demolition of the abbey church started in 1541, the creation of the New Lodgings (an adaptation of the buildings around the great court) had begun in October 1539: thus far from being abandoned, the site was to have a series of distinguished tenants. Many of the books seem to have remained in situ, essentially safe, only to be alienated in dribs and drabs by interested – or just conveniently placed – parties. Among the earliest volumes to be removed was probably the above-mentioned Bible of Robert of Battle which, inscriptions record, was taken by Sir Anthony St Leger (1496–1559), a Crown agent responsible for overseeing the surrendered site.[68] Illustrative of the fact that much humbler men were also able to profit from the collection is the Homer which passed into the hands of a Canterbury baker, from whom it was then acquired – presumably saving it from an ignominious fate wrapping pies – by Archbishop Parker.[69] If significant caches found their way into the greatest collections of the time – nearly thirty books ended up in the royal collection, for example, a similar number in the hands of Matthew Parker, and some forty in those of John Dee – while smaller numbers gravitated towards lesser collectors, such as Walter Cope († 1614), a good number were still at the abbey site at the end of the sixteenth century. For in 1602 the then-tenant, Henry Lord Cobham, could promise some of them to Thomas Bodley and the University of Oxford. Writing to his librarian, Thomas James, in June 1602, Bodley recorded that 'My Lord Cobham hath given £50 to the librarie and promiseth divers MS. out of St Augustines librarie in Canteb. whiche I will call for heerafter'.[70] Unfortunately, because of Cobham's fall – on account of plotting against King James I – this came to nothing, and such of the residue as has survived seems to have migrated in small caches, directly and indirectly, into the hands of subsequent collectors, great and small. Of the five, for example, that ended up in the possession of William Laud (1573–1644/5, archbishop from 1633), passing thence to their final resting place in the Bodleian Library, one had been owned (in 1599) by the collector Jasper Gryffyth († 1614), sometime chaplain to Archbishop Bancroft, another first by Henry Elsynge (the elder), clerk of the Parliaments from 1621, then perhaps by Sir William le Neve (*c.* 1600–61).[71] While Laud exemplifies the great collector (though principally of continental rather than English material), the volumes that are still in Canterbury reflect the activities of more modest and even lowly men.

Of the three complete Saint Augustine's Abbey books in the present corpus, two (**nos.** 17 and 25) were given to the cathedral in the seventeenth century through the agency of a William Kingsley – presumptively Canon William Kingsley, grandson of the Archdeacon of Canterbury of the same name. Kingsley junior, so inscriptions in the relevant books inform us, acquired these – and two other manuscripts – in 1667; where he obtained them is, unfortunately, not stated, but it is likely that they had never moved very far from their medieval home. The third complete Saint Augustine's Abbey manuscript (Add. 172; **no.** 15) was acquired in the sixteenth century by a certain Thomas Wylde, as an *ex libris* attests. It seems likely that the individual in question was connected to the Wilde/Wylde family (or families) who are documented on Thanet from the late Middle Ages: an earlier Thomas Wilde, for example, is recorded as churchwarden of St Peter's, Thanet, in the archidiaconal visitation of 1502,[72] while a later man of the same name is documented as a modest landholder at Minster in 1626–7.[73] The plausibility of the association is enhanced by the fact that our man also possessed two further manuscripts from Saint Augustine's Abbey, one of which ended up in Cambridge, the other in Oxford.[74] Add. 172, after extensive wanderings and having passed through the hands of some of the most famous English manuscript collectors of the nineteenth and twentieth centuries – Walter Sneyd († 1888), George Dunn († 1912), Charles St John Hornby († 1946) and John Roland Abbey († 1969) – finally returned to Canterbury in 1979.

Yet for every Kentish book that has survived, at least twenty have not. As very large numbers of manuscripts became homeless, many, above all liturgical ones, were scrapped. So copious was the quantity of parchment thus 'released' by the Dissolution and Reformation that it was still being used up by binders and others in the second half of the seventeenth century: the half-leaf in the present corpus that was deployed to form the cover of a paper note-book dating from that period illustrates the point (**no. 26**). However, the most intense period of re-use was, as one would expect, the half-century from *c.* 1540 to *c.* 1590 when parchment leaves were re-deployed for everything from stuffing scarecrows, lining pie-cases and cleaning boots, through making envelopes, to forming wrappers and covers for school exercise books, business accounts, parish documents and court records.[75] One of our items (**no. 18**) ended up covering a Kentish parish register, while many of the early fragments which survive at Canterbury were used as wrappers for the records of one or other of the various local courts. As the leaves are generally inscribed with the year(s) of the proceedings in question, the precise period of their re-use is documented. The earliest such date associated with one of the fragments was – reputedly – 1541–2.[76] The latest 'starting date', on a Peter Lombard, is 1586–91;[77] while the latest date of all is 1584–1606.[78] Recycled fragments might sometimes see multiple re-use – as is implied, for example, by the circumstance that the label of PRC 49/3/3–5 (**no. 36**) was overwritten, suggesting an initial re-deployment prior to the earliest legible date of 1565. The bifolium Lit. E. 42A, fols. 77 and 78 (**no. 22**) was originally employed to cover records of 1586–88 but was then used for the next four-year period, as is indicated by the '=1592' that was added by a different hand at the end of the original 'title'.[79] In other cases, such as Add. 128/54 (**no. 29**), the first label simply faded and was subsequently repeated in a more durable ink.[80] As noted above, one of the liturgical items, the collectar (**no. 42**), was demonstrably still in service in 1538; however, the added dates show that its leaves were being recycled for covers by 1556. The logical deduction, therefore, is that it was one of the countless casualties of the Acts of Uniformity

(1549) and the closely related Act Against Superstitious Books and Images (1550).[81]

The ways in which such leaves might be treated may be illustrated by the pair from Jerome's *In prophetas* (**no. 20**) and the bifolium from a handsome mid-twelfth-century lectionary (**no. 27**) which, as the dates written on them indicate, were recycled in the early 1570s and 1580s respectively. The former seems to have served as lining for a cover which was formed principally from the leaf of a late medieval antiphonal: this was turned sideways and folded around the new volume while the folios from the Jerome were inserted as liners. The lectionary bifolium was inverted and its four corners cut off in order to facilitate the turning in of its edges: a strip about 70 mm wide was turned over along each edge of the leaf in order to make a smaller stiffer cover, within which documents were secured by being sewn on four cords, which were then laced through pairs of holes pierced in the new 'front' and 'back' of our sheet. The new assemblage was labelled both on the 'spine' and on the new 'front': as the bifolium was now upside down, the former large lower margin offered a blank space at the top of the cover which was well suited for taking a new title, while the intercolumnar space provided a long blank vertical column below it, ideal for a series of dates.[82]

If fanatical legislation and the allied penalties for non-compliance account for the destruction and re-use of service books on a massive scale, while conversely the importance of such liturgical volumes to recusants, not to mention the visual beauty of some of them, could enhance their chances of survival, it is often difficult if not impossible to discover what led to the preservation or destruction of particular groups of ordinary library books. Doubtless many such volumes simply paid the price for being in the wrong place at the wrong time; however, in relation to the library of Saint Augustine's Abbey (where a significant number of books did evade destruction, despite being 'available' for a long period), other factors must have come into play. One important variable was the physical condition of the individual manuscripts themselves. If a book was already imperfect and its text a common one, readily available in better copies (not to mention printed editions), it was unlikely to have appealed to antiquaries or collectors, and offered a ready-made quarry for busy notaries. Volumes such as the duplicate copies of Gregory the Great's works that were already listed as 'imperfect' in the library catalogue of Saint Augustine's, along with volumes that were technically complete but very tatty, were particularly vulnerable.[83] Beyond this, the accident of where a particular volume was stored, even whether it was at the top or bottom of a given pile, may have made a crucial difference to its chances of survival. Some manuscripts may in fact have passed intact into a first pair of private hands, but then either have been damaged in their new home, or were regarded with less interest – even positive distaste – by the collector's descendants, and hence ended up as fodder for bindings and wrappers a couple of generations later: of the items in the present corpus, **no.** 18, with its early modern sketches and doodled names, seems the most likely to have followed this type of route to the scrap heap.[84]

The largest single source of the early Canterbury leaves that have come down to us was the multi-volume passional written at Christ Church in the 1120s (**no.** 22). The grand dimensions of the volumes (whose pages measure *c.* 390 × 275mm, and a bifolium from which is therefore 390 × 550 mm) made their leaves particularly useful as wrappers, while the considerable number of pages in the set as a whole meant that it offered an exceptionally rich fund of them. Much the same was true of the large-format lectionaries in the present corpus, **nos.** 28–9, but only a handful of their pages have survived. The dates written on the bifolia scavenged from the passional show that the series was being systematically cannibalised over a period of at least twenty-five years, from 1572 to 1596; a particularly vivid witness is the bifolium 60–61 on which, in 1573, several sets of labels were boldly inscribed by at least two hands, the letters of one set of titles being up to 50 mm high. Yet even in this case, the vagaries of fortune can be perceived. When complete, the passional comprised a set of seven volumes. The history of the set in the third quarter of the sixteenth century remains obscure, despite several inviting but probably false trails.[85] Thereafter, six of the volumes were evidently scrapped, and their leaves – over eighty of which have been recovered and regrouped since the late nineteenth century – used to wrap court and other records.[86] By contrast, the remaining volume, split into three reasonably intact parts, passed into private hands; individual portions belonged to John Dee, Robert Cotton and Lord Harley, before finally coming to rest in the British Library.[87]

The fate of the Christ Church passional may usefully be compared with that of the similar sets which belonged to Saint Augustine's Abbey and Rochester Cathedral. Rochester's medieval library catalogues reveal that its passional comprised four volumes.[88] Of these, only one fragment from a single leaf is currently known to survive: it comes from a page which seems to have been re-used first as a book cover by Thomas Willoughby, dean of Rochester from 1574 to 1581, and was then subsequently re-deployed in the binding of a copy of B. A. Montanus, printed in Antwerp in 1572 but presumably bound in England.[89] Of the presumed seven volumes from Saint Augustine's, two have come down to us. One, which in the sixteenth century seems to have passed through the hands of a certain John Lucas, was purchased in 1652 by the Bodleian Library (where it was confusingly 'misfiled' among the 'Fell' *fonds*).[90] The other gravitated, along with a clutch of manuscripts from Saint Augustine's, into the possession of Thomas Howard, second earl of Arundel (1586–1646), whose library was presented in 1681 by his grandson, Henry Howard, to the Royal Society, being bought therefrom by the British Museum in 1831.[91] Whilst this latter volume is essentially intact, the former was despoiled of many of its decorated initials – a reminder that surviving the Dissolution and Reformation did not necessarily mean transmission unharmed.

In addition to the traumas of dismemberment and the rigours of life as paste-downs or wrappers, some of the Canterbury fragments likewise bear the scars of further adventures, be it trial by fire and water, or human mischief. Liquid damage to one page of the mid-twelfth-century breviary (**no. 31**), which clearly occurred after the leaf had been turned inside out, illustrates the former; the mug-stain and doodled heads on the bifolium, U3/162/28/1 (**no. 18**), along with the circles drawn with a compass on Lit. E.

42, fols. 56v and 46r (**no. 22**), the latter. Equally telling is the difference in the state of the last bifolium of Add. 127/1 (**no. 9**) in comparison with the first three. Fols. 1–6 were cut down to be used as wrappers for documents and bear re-use dates in the 1580s and 90s (in fact the first bifolium, 1–2, may have been re-used twice since it has a faint '1580' on 1r, seemingly superseded by a bold '1594–5' on 2v). By contrast, the bifolium 7-8, which was used as a wrapper in 1587–9, seems first to have served as a blotting sheet or writing surface, for in addition to large ink blots it is covered on all sides with innumerable pen-trials, doodles, names and phrases jotted by divers late sixteenth-century hands.[92] The most extreme illustration of the traumas to which such recycled fragments could be exposed is Add. 122 (**no. 10**), which has been rendered so fragmentary and fragile by the combination of re-use in a binding and damp damage that hardly anything now remains.

Alongside such brutal re-use and casual abuse in the aftermath of the Reformation, one also finds intelligent use. One thinks, for instance, of how the late fourteenth-century cartulary of Dover Priory was produced as evidence in the Court of Wards at the very end of the sixteenth century – as the notes on added preliminary leaves record.[93] The best example of the phenomenon within the present corpus is provided by the collection of Canons (**no. 16**). Written around 1100, and supplied with running headings and rubrics in the thirteenth century, the book was extensively annotated in the sixteenth century by several cursive hands, one of which also practised a neat italic. The annotations identify the content of sections, provide cross-references, name the sources of passages, flag particular themes, and occasionally even comment on the text. From the issues that inevitably feature in such a collection, those that seem particularly to have interested the annotators include the nature of papal and episcopal power, the hierarchy of the church, the sacraments, the laity and their relationship to the church. Individual highlighted themes include, 'that the eucharist ought not to be reserved', 'for what reasons a child ought to be immersed thrice at baptism', 'concerning predestination and free-will', and that meat 'should not be eaten on the sabbath'; while comments include the sharp note, 'Accursed gloss which corrupts the text'. On three occasions, following a short passage devoted to the judicious memorialisation of martyrs and accompanying Pope Gregory VII's strictures against those who might fail to respect ecclesiastical jurisdiction and then freedom of investiture, is the splendid vernacular exclamation: 'good stuff'![94] By contrast, many canons attracted no comment; cases such as the stipulation that eunuchs who entered that condition for medical reasons or through barbarian attack might remain clerics, but self-mutilators should not,[95] whatever their intrinsic or historical interest, were irrelevant to contemporary concerns and were simply passed over.

Now, the most celebrated collector of medieval manuscripts in England in the sixteenth century was, of course, Matthew Parker (1504–75), archbishop of Canterbury from 1559 to 1575, one of whose chief concerns was to demonstrate the extent to which the Elizabethan church settlement that he was required to enforce echoed the best practices of primitive Christianity and of the early church in England. Many of the manuscripts that he 'salvaged' with more or less legality were, in part at least, tools to this end.[96] The careful scrutiny of church canons and their implications with consideration of their acceptability or otherwise from a sixteenth-century protestant perspective that we see in **no. 16**, is precisely what one would expect from Parker and his circle; and the hands responsible can be paralleled in other manuscripts that certainly belonged to him. How and why this volume remained in (or ended up at) Canterbury while the vast majority of manuscripts that came into his possession were lodged in Cambridge is unclear; however, the book provides a fascinating insight into the role of medieval manuscripts – and of the ecclesiastical past in general – in the formation of the fledgling Anglican church.

To conclude: the loss and alienation of the thousands of manuscripts that were in Canterbury in the Middle Ages is a tragic occurrence, yet it should not lead us to overlook those that are still there. They include some extremely important items – the earliest English copies of the homiliaries of St Père de Chartres (**no.** 4) and Haimo of Auxerre (**no.** 7), of the Old English translation of Gregory the Great's *Dialogi* undertaken under the aegis of King

Alfred the Great (**no. 5**), of Lanfranc's gloss on the Pauline Epistles (**no. 15**), and of the letters of Ivo of Chartres (**no. 19**) – along with some exceptionally handsome ones, most notably the copies of Chrodegang's *Regula canonicorum* (**no. 12**) and Peter Comestor's *Historia scholastica* (**no. 40**). Several items are crucial pieces of evidence for understanding the scribal and intellectual history of east Kent in the earlier Middle Ages, which underline, more generally, the key importance of Canterbury and its libraries in the cultural life of late Anglo-Saxon and early Anglo-Norman England as a whole. Futhermore, paradoxical though it may seem, part of their particular interest is the vicissitudes that they have suffered. The destruction of books and the recycling of parts of them, however distressing it may be, is and always will be an integral part of the history of libraries, texts, and of attitudes to them. Whilst we have undoubtedly lost huge amounts of irreplaceable material through this process, ironically it has also saved certain items that would otherwise have vanished utterly. It is only because pages were re-used for endleaves and paste-downs in the Middle Ages that we have some of the items we have considered; it is only because leaves from proscribed liturgical books and other manuscripts were systematically used to cover sixteenth-century documents that we have any part of them at all. Correspondingly, while the complete manuscripts that slumbered safely in the libraries of Catholic countries during the Reformation offer much better, fuller insight into their medieval contexts, they are often mute about the early modern period. Our damaged books and dismembered fragments still shed some light on their original contexts, and are simultaneously eloquent witnesses to the upheavals of the sixteenth century and beyond. Many of them document indirectly – sometimes, indeed, directly – the activities of those men and their functionaries who destroyed the institutions that had made, bought, and protected the manuscripts, providing graphic illustration of the brutal effects of proscription, dissolution, and appropriation. One or two items may echo the activities of recusants, while a few let us glimpse Tudor and Stuart bibliophily and antiquarianism, along with English attitudes to the church at large.

NOTES

* Many of the generalisations in the present essay are based on evidence presented and literature cited in the individual catalogue entries, to which reference should be made for further details.

1 London, British Library, MS Cotton Galba E. iv: printed in James 1903, list II; overview: Ramsay 1995, pp. 355–61. For the books in Oxford see Pantin 1947, I, pp. 3–76; also de Hamel 1997.

2 Dublin, Trinity College, MS 360: James 1903, list VIII, with description at pp. lvii–lxiii; reproduction: Emden 1968, pl. I. A new edition by Bruce Barker-Benfield for CMBLC is at an advanced state of preparation.

3 Clarke and Lovatt (ed.) 2002, list UC3.

4 Listed in Ker 1964, pp. 29–48, with Watson 1987, pp. 10–13.

5 Listed: Ker 1964, p. 48; Watson 1987, p. 13.

6 'I ... do call God to witness, and by these God's holy gospels do swear that to the best of my power I will well and faithfully rule and govern in this church according to the Ordinances and Statutes of the same; and that all its goods, lands, tenements, rents, possessions, its rights, liberties, privileges, and all other things as well moveable ... as immovable, and all other interests of the same church I will well and profitably guard, defend and keep, and I will take care, as far as in me lies, that the like be done by others ...': *Statuta ecclesiae cathedralis et metropoliticae Christi Cantuariae*, c. 3 ('Juramentum Decani'): ed. and trans. *Statutes* 1925, pp. 6–9. Drawn up under Henry VIII, these statutes were revised and confirmed by Charles I and endorsed by Act of Parliament (*ibid.*, p. v).

7 For general accounts with differing emphases see James 1903, pp. xix–xc; Emden 1968; Ramsay 1995; and de Hamel 1997. The Introductions to the forthcoming CMBLC volumes for Christ Church and Saint Augustine's will doubtless provide authoritative overviews based on much new information.

8 See further Gameson 1999a and 2001–2. For the speculation that the pre-Viking Age book-list in Vatican City, Biblioteca Apostolica Vaticana, Pal. lat. 210 might conceivably be a copy of an early Canterbury list see Gorman 2004, esp. pp. 56–60.

9 Preface to the Old English *Regula pastoralis*: Sweet (ed.) 1871, pp. 2–9.

10 See further Gameson 2000.

11 *ASC* (C): O'Brien O'Keefe (ed.) 2001, p. 96.

12 York Minster Library, MS Add. 1 (went to York); British Library, Add. MS 34890 (to Winchester); Hanover, Kestner-Museum, MS W. M. XXIa, 36 (to Hersfeld).

13 Gameson 1995 and, more generally, 1999b.

14 The starting point for modern discussion of the phenomenon in general is Ker 1960, pp. 22–32; refined for Canterbury by Webber 1995 and Gullick 1998.

15 Webber 1995; Gullick 1998.

16 Lit. E. 42 (**no. 22**), fols. 62–3 and 75.

17 Lit. E. 42, fol. 16v (s. xii$^{3/4}$).

18 Cambridge, Corpus Christi College, MS 44: Budny 1997, I, no. 46; Orchard (ed.) 2002, I, pp. 76–7.

19 Woodcock (ed.) 1956, pp. ix–x.

20 James 1903, list II, no. 317 (p. 51).

21 Talbot 1955, 5–10 and Barlow (ed.) 1962, pp. xlv–xlviii for summaries of his career.

22 *Teste* the colophon in Avranches, Bibliothèque municipale, MS 103 (Gregory), fol. 220v; printed: Alexander 1970, p. 222.

23 'Epistolas beati Pauli vestro mandato libenter parentes vobis mittimus; sed quoniam quod in eodem codice de vestro opere est, alibi non habemus, satis scire potestis quid vos aliquando factum ire desideremus': ep. 66: Schmitt (ed.) 1946–61, III, pp. 186–7.

24 Cambridge, Trinity College, MS B. 3. 5: see Ker 1979.

25 On Rochester books in general during this period, with many comments on connections with Christ Church, see Richards 1988.

26 London, British Library, MS Royal 6 B. vi.

27 Kauffmann 1975, ills. 40–1, 43–4; Watson 1984, I, no. 882, II, pl. 42.

28 Ker 1977, pp. 294–5 with n. 1; Love (ed.) 1996, pp. clxxiii–iv, clxxvi–viii, clxxxiii–vi.

29 Appearing in an original entry in the house library catalogue of that date: Sharpe *et al.* (ed.) 1996, p. 490 (B77, no. 82).

30 Cambridge, Corpus Christi College, MS 44.

31 London, British Library, MS Royal 5 C. viii.

32 James 1903, p. 14, no. 16.

33 Ramsay 1995, p. 364; a fuller account by Margaret Sparks is in preparation.

34 Canterbury Cathedral A&L, Lit. C. 11: James 1903, no. VI.

35 For comments on the use and reconditioning of older books at Saint Albans in the later Middle Ages see Clark 2004, esp. pp. 94–5, 120 and 135.

36 For Werken: Mynors 1950; de la Mare 1976; Robinson 1988, I, nos. 326 and 359; II, ills. 312, 316. The manuscripts he copied for Christ Church are now Cambridge, Trinity College, MS B. 3. 21 with Cambridge University Library, MS Ff. 3. 10; and Cambridge, Trinity College, MSS R. 17. 4 and R. 17. 5.

37 See Parkes 1997, esp. p. 122.

38 James 1903, p. 163.

39 The high number of sewing holes visible in the folds of the bifolium from our mid-twelfth-century breviary (**no. 31**) strongly suggests that the volume was resewn and rebound on several occasions during a long working life.

40 To cite but one of many examples: Oxford, Trinity College, MS 4 (Augustine; Gregory Nazianzenus).

41 It will doubtless be authoritatively treated in the Introduction to Bruce Barker-Benfield's forthcoming edition of the library catalogue.

42 On whom see Barker-Benfield 1980. One of the books most intimately associated with him remains at Canterbury: Lit. D. 16 (described: Ker 1977, pp. 281–2).

43 Thompson (ed.) 1902–4, I, pp. 202–3.

44 Parkes 1997.

45 Printed: Wickham Legg and St John Hope 1902, p. 120.

46 James 1903, pp. 163–4.

47 Printed: Borenius 1932, Appendix I (pp. 109–10).

48 Urry 1967, p. 120.

49 James 1903, p. 206.

50 See further Gameson 1999b, pp. 20–44, for an overview of survival rates of individual texts and authors as reflected in manuscripts of English provenance dating from between *c.* 1066 and 1130 (grammatical texts in particular are considered on pp. 27–9).

51 James 1903, p. 7; Sharpe *et al.* (ed.) 1996, list B79, entry 173 (p. 518).

52 James 1903, p. 197 (no. 7). On the emergence of the Bibles in question see, in general, Light 1987 and 1994.

53 London, British Library, MS Burney 3: Morgan 1982, cat. 63, ills. 219–222; colour plate: Alexander 1978b, pl. 28. Cf. James 1903, p. 197, item 10.

54 James 1903, p. 197, items 1–2. See further Budny 1999.

55 London, British Library, MS Royal 1 E. vii and viii: see Marsden 1994.

56 Cambridge, Corpus Christi College, MSS 3 and 4: Kauffmann 1975, no. 69. The date of the transfer from Christ Church to Dover is uncertain; however, assuming (following Dodwell 1954, p. 48) that the manuscript is identical with the 'Biblia Edwini' in Henry of Eastry's Christ Church catalogue (James 1903, p. 51, no. 321), and given that it features as 'A.I' in the Dover library catalogue (Stoneman (ed.) 1999, p. 48 *et alibi*), this would seem to have occurred between *c.* 1326 and 1389, the respective dates of these two documents.

57 Wickham Legg and St John Hope 1902, no. II (p. 79).

58 London, British Library, MS Royal 7 C. xii (offsets). The other portions are Cambridge, Corpus Christi College, MS 197B and British Library, MS Cotton Otho C. v. For the manuscript as a whole and the provenance of its constituent parts see Budny 1997, I, no. 3.

59 Oxford, Bodleian Library, MS Lat. bib. b. 2 (P).

60 Such practices were universal, as is underlined by the many recycled fragments that are still in situ as endleaves and paste-downs within groups of manuscripts that have fortuitously retained medieval bindings (e.g. the Romanesque books from Anchin, Marchiennes and Saint-Amand in Northern France/Flanders). A complementary case comes from Tynemouth, a dependency of Saint Albans, where in the 1440s the sub-prior, John Bamburgh, re-used the leaves of a *s.* xiii missal to copy an anthology of literary texts: Clarke 2004, p. 111.

61 Recorded thus by Ker 1977, p. 321 (presumably on the basis of information supplied by William Urry), this is now seemingly impossible to verify.

62 See further Gameson 2005. Of later examples still at Canterbury, it will suffice to cite Add. 129/39, a bifolium from a *s.* xiv missal which is still attached to the remnant of a late medieval binding.

63 See, e.g., Wright 1958; Coates 1999, ch. 8; Ramsay 2004; and Gameson 2005.

64 Extracts from relevant royal legislation are conveniently collected in Tanner 1930, esp. pp. 58–68 (Acts for the Dissolution of Lesser and Greater Monasteries, respectively 1536 and 1539) and 107–15 (First Act of Uniformity, 1549; Act against Superstitious Books and Images, 1550).

65 Surviving manuscripts listed in Ker 1964 and Watson 1987. Editions of the catalogues of Dover and St Radegund's: Stoneman (ed.) 1999, and Bell (ed.) 1992, inventory P2.

66 Carley (ed.) 2000, pp. xl–xli; also Carley 2004, esp. pp. 89–92.

67 Ramsey 1995, esp. pp. 373–5; de Hamel 1997, esp. pp. 271–4.

68 London, British Library, MS Burney 3; see note 53 above.

69 Cambridge, Corpus Christi College, MS 81; as recorded in a contemporary note on the front leaf, printed: James 1912, I, p. 165.

70 Wheeler (ed.) 1927, letter 8.

71 Oxford, Bodleian Library, MSS Laud lat. 65; Laud misc. 225 (ex Gryffyth), 296, 330 (ex Henry Elsynge), and 385.

72 Woodruff 1935, p. 40.

73 Hussey 1909, p. 78.

74 Cambridge University Library, MS Kk. 1.17; Oxford, Bodleian Library, MS Lat. th. b.2. The inscription in the former is reproduced in Gameson 1999b, pl. 19.

75 Rare examples of reproductions that actually show the forms of re-use themselves (as opposed to details of extracted and reconditioned fragments) include: Rawcliffe 1999, ill. 42; Abukhanfusa 2004, esp. ills 1, 7–10, 36, 39–40, 67, 71, 76, 78, 84, 87, 89; Gameson 2005, ills. 1 and 4.

76 Add. 128/10 (**no. 40**), Peter Comestor.

77 PRC 49/5/1–3 (**no. 37**).

78 PRC 50/17/3 (**no. 28**).

79 The effaced notes on Lit. E. 42, fols. 69 and 74 (**no. 22**) might reflect the same phenomenon, implying a first re-use prior to the currently inscribed date of 1576.

80 Also retraced was Lit. E. 42A, fol. 79 (**no. 22**).

81 For the legislation see note 64. For a convenient overview of the doctrinal and liturgical changes: Dugmore 1958, pp. 111–75; and of their implementation and implications: Duffy 1992, pp. 448–503.

82 See further in general Ker 1977, pp. 312–15.

83 James 1903, pp. 232–3: nos. 387 ('Prima pars moralium eiusdem super Iob imperfecta cum B, quia deficiunt vj libri'), 391 ('Gregorius super Ezechielem imperfectus quia deficiunt viii omelie de extrema parte cum B'), 396 ('Registrum Gregorii vetus cum B imperfectus'), 402 ('Dialogus Gregorii vetus et debilis cum C'). In each case the 'A' copy of the same text (nos. 385, 390, 395, 400), with no such comment, was presumably complete.

84 The workaday Anselm – so neither a rare text, nor a handsome manuscript – that is one of the rare survivals from the collection of the Canterbury Franciscans (their *ex libris* on fols. 1r and 5r) owed its exceptional fortune to the chance of having passed (by unknown means) within about a decade of the Dissolution into the hands of Thomas Pope (his signature on 2v and 5r) who promptly left it to the Oxford College he founded in 1555, where it was then preserved (Oxford, Trinity College, MS 37).

85 See **no. 22** (History).

86 While a fair number of sheets survive from several of the volumes, only a couple of late medieval supplementary folios are currently known from vol. IV. It is difficult to know what, if any, weight to place on such discrepancies.

87 London, British Library, MSS Cotton Nero C. vii, fols. 29–78; Harley 315, fols. 1–39; Harley 624, fols. 84–143.

88 Sharpe *et al.* (ed.) 1996, p. 490: B77, no. 82 ('Passionalia in iiii uoluminibus'); also B 79, no. 56.

89 Oxford, Worcester College, MS 273: Watson 1984, I, no. 882; II, ill. 42.

90 MS Fell 2: 'Johannes Lucas' p. 465. Pächt and Alexander 1973, no. 68.

91 London, British Library, MS Arundel 91: Kauffmann 1975, cat. 17.

92 Lit. E. 42A, fols. 76–77 and 44–45 (**no. 22**) were liberally spattered with ink at some point.

93 London, Lambeth Palace Library, MS 341: James 1932, pp. 393–7; Robinson 2003, I, no. 68; II, pl. 60.

94 See the commentary on **no. 16** for the relevant folio references. The last is reproduced: Gameson 2005, ill. 2.

95 Lit. B. 7 (**no. 16**), fol. 48v.

96 See in general Page 1993 and, for a specific case directly related to Canterbury, Gameson and Gameson 2005, esp. pp. 34–8.

THE CATALOGUE

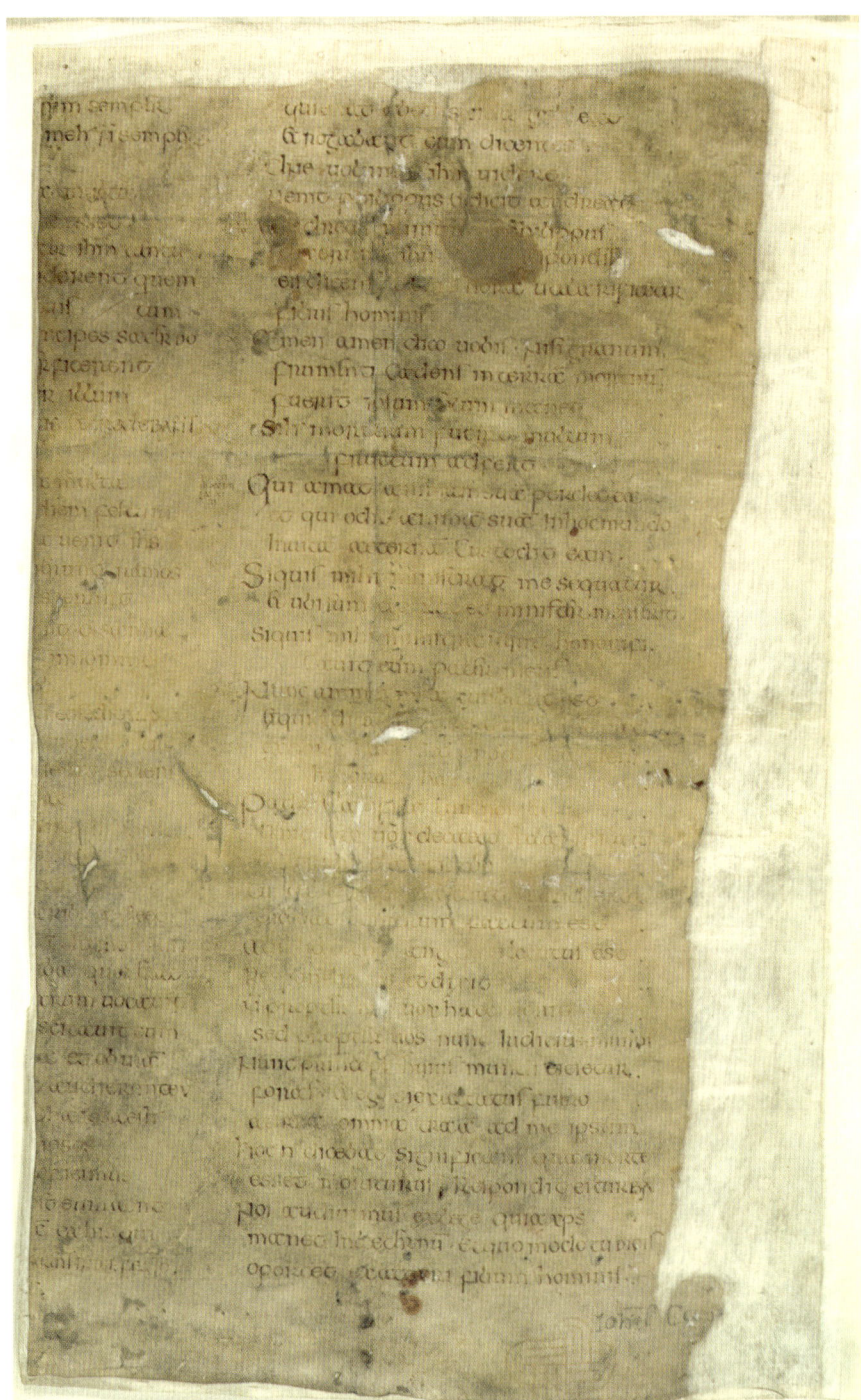

1 Add. 16.

Bible
Canterbury, Saint Augustine's Abbey; *saec.* IX[1]
Illustration: verso of leaf

Physical Description

Part of one leaf, in very poor condition. The recto is severely weathered, stained, darkened and perforated, and bears the scars of folding; the verso is damaged in the same ways but to a lesser extent. Both sides of the leaf include most of one column of text plus a vertical slither from a second – though on the recto, the areas in question are so damaged as to be largely indecipherable. The fragment is set in a modern parchment surround, and mounted within a stiff cover.

Maximum dimensions: 390 × 200 mm. Two columns (width: *c.* 120 mm). Number of written lines: 41 survive (from an original 42). Space between lines: 9 mm. Height of minims: 3 mm. A few prickings (to guide the vertical rulings) survive in the lower margin; a line of round pricking holes (to guide the horizontal rulings) runs down the outer boundary of the near-complete column of text.

The leaf was once part of the so-called 'Royal Bible', the other surviving portions of which are London, British Library, MS Royal 1 E. vi and Oxford, Bodleian Library, MS Lat. bib. b.2 (P).

Content

Gospel of St John, 11.38–12.34 (with lacunae, owing to lost areas; substantial portions of what survives are effectively illegible). The text is set out as follows.
[Fol. 1r, col. 1] // Ihesus ergo rursum [John 11.38] ... [most of the lower portion of the column is illegible] **[Fol. 1r, col. 2]** [top line lost; second line:] ut interfice[runt] [John 11.53; only a strip from this column remains, and its text is largely illegible].
[Fol. 1v, col. 1] //[e]nim semper [–lost–] me autem non semper [John 12.8; only a strip from this column remains] ... [ador]arent in die festo [John 12.20]. **[Fol. 1v, col. 2]** [top line lost apart from

the bottoms of a few descenders, then:] // qui erat a bethsaida galileae [John 12.21] ... oportet exaltari filium hominis [John 12.34].

Collation of the only portion that is relatively complete and legible (fol. 1v, col. 2: John 12.21–34) against Weber (ed.) 1983 revealed no variants (aside from the Insular orthographic preference for 'u' in place of 'b').

Scribes and Script

The fragment was written by a single scribe in an elegant, spacious and highly formal Insular minuscule. There are generous spaces between words, but within them many letters 'bite' their neighbours. As a whole, the script is characterised by beautifully rounded curvilinear forms and triangular serifs; notable individual letter-forms include a curvilinear 'l' (like an upside-down question mark without the dot), a similarly conceived 'b' (effectively a little circle with a stem on top), and an 'x' whose straight left leg bifurcates at the end. Punctuation: medial point (minor pause), low point (major pause). A different, much squarer, laterally compressed alphabet was used for the (only partially preserved) final line of fol. 1v, col. 1, doubtless as a device to save space; though less ornate, the letter-forms can be compared with those of the display capitals used elsewhere in the volume (see, e.g., Brown 1990, pl. 17).

The surviving parts of the manuscript as a whole have been ascribed to five scribes (Budny 1999, p. 243). For analysis of the script of the much better preserved London portion, see Lowe 1972, no. 214.

Decoration

Each verse is headed by an enlarged (one-line-high) pen-drawn initial, outlined in red dots.

On the verso in the lower margin are drawn a couple of fairly crude interlace designs (one has been largely cut away); they are impossible to date, but do not look Anglo-Saxon. (For a summary account of the extensive decoration in the London portion – which included canon tables, purple title pages, and miniatures – see Alexander 1978, no. 32.)

History

Attributed to the scriptorium of Saint Augustine's Abbey, Canterbury, on palaeographical, artistic and other circumstantial grounds, this was certainly the medieval, indeed pre-Conquest, provenance of the Bible. Interest and investment in the volume in the late Anglo-Saxon period is indicated by the fact that a portrait of St Mark was added in the early eleventh century (see Temple 1976, cat. 55, ill. 172). However, a more casual attitude appears later in the same century when a Viking-style motif and the inscription 'P ego' were added to the same page; the doodle has been credited to the Saint Augustine's Abbey scribe responsible, amongst other things, for Lit. A. 8 (**no.** 17) (Budney 1997, I, p. 255), though with such a small sample of script, it is difficult to be certain. Whether or not the doodle reflected a change in the status or condition of the volume in the aftermath of the Norman Conquest, it was partly dismembered by the thirteenth century at the latest (as is attested by the title, 'Quatuor evan' vetera cum A' that was added to the front of the gospel portion at that date), and some pages were being recycled for binding material. The Oxford folio was used, folded in half, as the front endleaves of a late tenth-century copy of John the Deacon's *Vita Gregorii*: it bears a fourteenth-century Saint Augustine's Abbey *ex libris* for that volume (NB: the Bible folio was removed from the main manuscript – Bodleian Library, MS Bodley 381 – in 1897 and is now MS Lat. bib. b.2 (P).) The Canterbury leaf may have been put to similar use: running across the middle of the recto (upside down in relation to the original script) are traces of what might have been a medieval inscription; though now illegible and virtually obliterated, the initial capital 'D' remains easily discernible, raising the possibility that it was once a shelf-mark plus title (D[istinctio] ...). One can only speculate as to why this handsome volume was dismembered in or by the thirteenth century. However, it may already have been damaged and imperfect, and in the wake first of the new giant Bibles of the twelfth century and then of the reformed Parisian ones of the thirteenth, an elderly copy in outdated script may have seemed expendable – particularly in a community that may also have had more venerable ones, notably a (now lost) presumably late Antique Bible associated with Gregory the Great. It seems likely – as suggested by James (1903, pp. lxv and 516) and supported by Barker-Benfield (forthcoming) – that the gospel-book portion of the volume may be identified with item 190 in the late medieval library catalogue of Saint Augustine's Abbey: 'Quatuor Euangelista glo' cum A ... D' 3ª Gª 1º'. Certainly, the title on its flyleaf, 'Quatuor euan' vetera cum A' and the final (altered) form of its shelf-mark, 'D.III. G.I' are consonant with this hypothesis. Yet even this much-reduced portion may have been incomplete, for if the vestigial inscription on the Canterbury fragment was indeed a late medieval shelf-mark, then this leaf – and those that once followed it – must have strayed from the rest of the gospels by the time the catalogue was compiled.

The London portion is next documented as the property of John Lord Lumley (*c.* 1534–1609), from whom it passed into the Royal collection and thence to the British Museum; while the Oxford part emerges in the hands of Thomas Allen (1540–1632), who gave it to the Bodleian Library at its foundation in 1601. Our folio has probably always remained in Canterbury or its environs. It was discovered in a box of fragments in the Cathedral Library in 1946: this collection is believed to have been assembled in the late nineteenth century by Joseph Brigstocke Sheppard; unfortunately, the contexts from which the individual items therein had been recovered were not recorded and hence their early modern provenances are lost. At some point following its recognition, 'Ioh[ann]is Cap//' was written in pencil in the lower margin of the verso. The truncation of the phrase suggests that in the period between the initial discovery of the leaf and its modern conservation, some part of it has perished.

Commentary

This leaf, the oldest manuscript fragment now in the Cathedral collection, was part of a large format Anglo-Saxon Bible, of which all that now remains is a substantial portion of the gospels plus a single folio from the Acts of the Apostles. London, British Library, MS Royal 1 E. vi ends on fol. 77v with, 'facere ut et hic non moreretur'; the Canterbury folio begins with the next words,

'Ihesus ergo rursum fremens'. The final page of MS Royal 1 E. vi is signed 'LXXXVIII'; the present fragment was evidently the first leaf of the next quire.

The quire signatures in the London portion, which run from 'LXXX' at the beginning of the gospels through to the above-mentioned 'LXXXVIII' on fol. 77v, show categorically that this was once a complete Bible – which, it can be calculated, must originally have had over 1000 leaves. The maximum size of the surviving leaves is *c.* 471 × 348 mm. As only one bifolium of such proportions could have been acquired from an animal skin, the project as a whole must have required the skin of at least 500 animals – a very considerable outlay.

The text was set out two columns to the page, generally with forty-two lines. In the surviving portion, the work of five scribes has been distinguished, the most important of whom has also been credited with adding the interlinear gloss to the Vespasian Psalter (British Library, MS Cotton Vespasian A. i), a Canterbury manuscript of a century earlier, and with contributing to a gospel book of which only fragments now remain, divided between Worcester and Oxford (Worcester Cathedral Library, MS Add. 1; Oxford, Bodleian Library, MS Lat. bib. d.1 (P)). The Worcester-Oxford gospel text is very close to that of the present manuscript, which it probably predates; and the two volumes may have been copied from the same exemplar.

The Royal Bible fragment still has impressive decorated canon tables and four purple-dyed leaves – three bearing *tituli*, written in monumental gold and silver capitals, that describe lost picture pages, and one bearing the start of Luke's Gospel, presented in decorated script under an ornamental arcade. The evidence of the surviving *tituli* pages, plus offsets and other traces show that the gospels once included a series of illustrations.

The scale and opulence of the project bear witness to the considerable resources of Saint Augustine's Abbey in the earlier ninth century, a period when Viking raids were beginning but had yet to take a devastating toll. With its extensive use of precious materials, the volume represents the swansong of a Canterbury and Minster-in-Thanet tradition of luxury book production that dated back at least as far as the earlier eighth century. It should probably also be seen in relation to the fact that during the first half of the ninth century Canterbury still had the primary mint south of the Humber, reflecting relatively easy access to precious metals from the Continent. In the troubled second half of the century, the importance of the mint declined – by which time Kentish book production, deluxe or otherwise, had seemingly stopped.

Complete Bibles were extremely rare in England prior to the eleventh century (biblical books generally circulated individually or in small groups). Three pandects (single-volume Bibles) were produced at Wearmouth-Jarrow in Northumbria before 716, the last of which survives complete (Florence, Biblioteca Medicea-Laurenziana, MS Amiatino 1: the 'Codex Amiatinus'), while a few pages survive from one of the other copies. A two-volume Bible of Christ Church, Canterbury provenance that was produced in the late tenth century has come down to us intact as British Library, MS Royal 1 E. vii–viii; and the dimensions of a coeval fragment of the Minor Prophets at Columbia (University of Missouri, Ellis Library, F.M. 4) suggest that it too was once a full Bible. Our manuscript is the only other English example dating from before the millennium; and even though a few other examples may have vanished without trace, we can be certain that it was always a member of a small, select group. The fact that it was the only one to have had extensive illumination adds considerably to its importance. The Canterbury fragment, though in poor condition, remains a vital witness to one of the great book-producing endeavours of Anglo-Saxon England.

Bibliography

Lowe 1972, no. 214; Alexander 1978, no. 32; Brown 1996, esp. pp. 93–5 and 171–8; Budny 1999; Marsden 1999.

2 Add. 127/19 and PRC 49/1/1–2

Priscian, *Institutiones grammaticae*
France (?north); *saec.* IX/X–X[1]
Illustration: Add. 127/19, fol. 1r

Physical Description

Four leaves from one quire (or possibly two adjacent quires) at the start of the book; the text on two of them is consecutive; the disjunctions between the others are the equivalent of lost single leaves. Their original order was as follows (the disposition of the hair and flesh sides of each leaf is indicated in brackets): Add., fol. 2 (FH); lost leaf; Add., fol. 1 (FH); lost leaf; PRC, fol. 2 (FH); PRC, fol. 1 (HF). It is possible that Add., fol. 2 and PRC, fol. 1 once formed a bifolium, in which case, our pages would be the remains of the three inner sheets of a single quire. If, alternatively, PRC fols. 2 and 1 once formed a bifolium, this could represent the centre either of a quaternion that started with the lost leaf 1 (Add. fol. 2 then being the final leaf of the previous quire) or – conceivably – of a larger gathering (of twelve leaves, in which Add. fol. 2 was leaf 2).

Though cut down, the leaves are in generally good condition, the state of Add. 127/19 being slightly better than that of PRC 49/1/1–2 (which is marked by fold lines and perforated by a scattering of small non-original holes). Parchment: moderate quality (the follicles are readily visible on the hair sides). Maximum page size (based on Add. 127/19): 282 × 213 mm. Written area: 200 × 144 mm. Lines per page: 24. Space between lines: 9 mm. Height of main text minims: 1.5–2 mm. Height of marginal gloss minims: 0.75 mm. Ruling: hard point.

Content

Priscian, *Institutiones grammaticae* (CPL, 1546), Book I, sections 21–5, 27–31, and 33–40. The distribution of this text across the leaves is as follows (note that both sets of leaves have been mounted and numbered in reverse order – the 'second' leaves should come first).

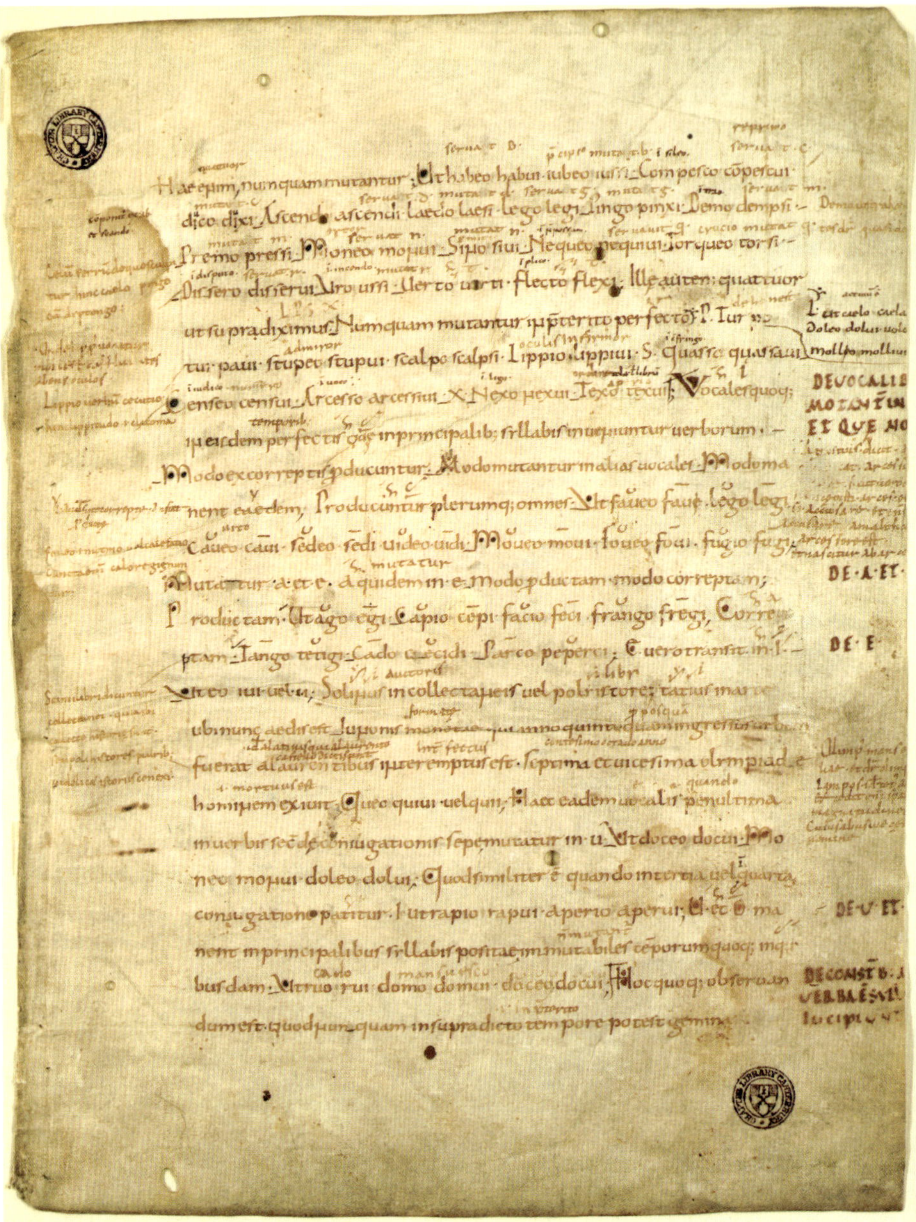

[**Add. 127/19, fol. 2r**] // protulit in epodo hoc uersu ... [**fol. 2v, end**] In latinis tamen dictionibus nos quoque pro Ph coepimus .F. // [Keil 1855–80, vol. II, p. 16, line 8–p. 19, line 9].
[One folio lacking.]
[**Add. 127/19, fol. 1r**] // Hae enim numquam mutantur. Ut habeo habui, iubeo iussi ... [**fol. 1v, end**] Alia eiusdem speciei ut inuo-// [Keil, vol. II, p. 21, line 15–p. 23, line 21].
[One folio lacking.]
[**PRC 49/1/2r**] // a patre. Ergo si est a pari .R. euphonie causa additur, [Keil, vol. II, p. 26, line 8] ... [**PRC 49/1/1v, ends:**] R sine aspiratione ponitur in latinis, in grecis // [Keil, vol. II, p. 31, line 15]

Although the original transcription was unintelligent (see **Scribes and Script** below), it was soon corrected, and in this emended form the departures from the text printed by Keil are generally modest.

There is regular interlinear glossing (in several layers), generally providing synonyms or definitions for individual words (e.g. *clausula* to *epodo* at Add., fol. 2r, line 1; *delicatus* to *lautus* at Add., fol. 2r, l. 8; *uitantes* to *effugientes* at Add., fol. 2r, l.15; *affirmat* to *testat* in PRC, fol. 2r; *impingo* to *impello* at PRC, fol. 1v, l. 15, etc.), but also explanations (e.g. *lapis* for *smaragdus* on Add., fol. 1v, l. 20; *nom insule* to ΚΥΠΡΟΣ at PRC, fol. 2r) or cross-references (e.g. PRC, fol. 2r, l. 5, where *Pauca sunt quae hanc non seruant regulam* attracted the note *supra dicta*). In addition, almost all the Greek words that are not followed in the main text by a Latin transliteration or translation were supplied with one between the lines.

The (originally wide) side margins were intermittently used for notes (now often rather worn and/or partly lost through trimming), which generally expand or illustrate points mentioned in the main text; a few are keyed in to place by a symbol. The aforementioned *epodo* (Add., fol. 2r, l. 1), for instance, attracted the short comment, *Epos clausula in epodo*; while ... *acherunte pro acheronte profundo* (PRC, fol. 2r, l. 20) received the gloss *Acheron interpraetatur sine gaudio, est enim fluuius infernalis* (partly duplicating a shorter, less formally written interlinear gloss on the same phrase: *fluuius infernalis*). A few marginal glosses, like the interlinear ones, are short notes or synonyms: thus beside *Lux quoque lucis Lucifer* (PRC, fol. 2r, l. 3) an early hand wrote 'Φosforos luc//' in a hybrid of Latin and Greek. Some such notes were subsequently erased.

Scribes and Script

The main text is the work of a single scribe, writing a moderately neat, continental Caroline minuscule. The basic matrix is fairly square, but the ascenders, descenders and sentence capitals are relatively tall. While the down-strokes of most minims generally terminate in a small upward curl or a rising terminal, those of m, n and r, along with the leg of h tend to taper to a 'spike'. The ink is (now) very brown. Word division within sense units is often minimal, even non-existent, while some of the divisions the scribe did introduce were incorrect; he also occasionally misconstrued what he was copying – all suggesting that he was working directly or indirectly from an exemplar without word division. His mistakes were then carefully rectified by a corrector who erased letters, inserted commas to indicate word division, and drew lines to link parts of words that had been erroneously separated. Thus on Add., fol. 2r, l. 14 where the original scribe had written 'di uli gatam' (for 'diu ligatam'), the corrector added lines between the first i and u, and the second i and the g, and inserted a comma between the u and the l in order to achieve the correct reading. The Greek phrases on Add., fol. 2r, and PRC, fols. 1r and 2v were also rewritten *in rasura* at a very early date; individual Greek words, by contrast, were left in their original state. Ironically, the rewritten phrases are frequently garbled, whereas the untouched words are, in general, reasonably sound.

The punctuation seems originally to have consisted of low and medial point, 'semi-colon' and *punctus elevatus*, but it is difficult to describe their use in this phase since some, possibly many, of them were subsequently modified. The diacritics used to indicate long and short vowels on Add. 127/19, fol. 1r ('-' and 'u') are by the original scribe, who may also have been responsible for the other interlinear symbols that occasionally appear (above all on

Add. 127/19, fol. 2). Sentence capitals are a hybrid alphabet in which stylised square capital, uncial, half-uncial and rustic forms were all used; on Add., fol. 1r, their counter-spaces were ornamented with a red dot.

The great majority of the glosses, written with varying degrees of formality in a more cursive version of the same basic script, are the work of several continental hands, broadly contemporary with, indeed including, the scribe of the main text. Some were erased – a few of which were then rewritten.

That the volume continued to see active service for more than a century and a half after it was made is indicated by further glosses in later hands. Four interlinear glosses on PRC, fol. 2r, between lines 5–6 and 6–7 (*non auiceps*, *non menaceps*, *augur*, and *ut res publica*) are of indeterminate *s.* x or possibly even xi date. One interlinear correction on Add. 127/19, fol. 1 (hair side) (line 18 *fluctum* for *illum*) is the work of a slightly later Caroline hand, probably of *s.* xi date. Also probably *s.* xi are two interlinear glosses and one correction on the flesh side of Add. 127/19, fol. 2 (*potest* glossing *possit* at the end of line 5; *l[icet] uet[er]es* glossing *uetustissimos* in the middle of line 11; and *q[u]oq[ue]*, an insertion near the start of line 19), however, these are done in a much darker ink, and are possibly the work of an English hand; unfortunately, the sample is too small to be certain. The word *menceps* on PRC 49, fol. 2r, line 6 was rewritten *in rasura* by a hand which, though tailored to the scale and aspect of the original script, nevertheless looks to be of *s.* xi^{2} date.

Decoration

There is no decoration in the surviving fragment; it is doubtful whether the original manuscript would have had much, if any. As noted above, rubrics in rustic capitals were supplied in the margin; on Add 127/19, fol. 1 they are in red; on PRC in ordinary ink.

History

Written in (?northern) France at the very end of the ninth or in the earlier tenth century, the manuscript continued in active use for at least a century and a half, as the interventions by different glossing hands (detailed under **Scribes and Script**) reveal. Though conceivably in English hands a generation or so before 1066, the volume most probably crossed the Channel in the aftermath of the Conquest (see **Commentary**). There is no evidence bearing on its later medieval history. The manuscript would appear to have been dismembered in s. xvi: PRC 49/1/1–2 was the wrapper of PRC 10/15, a register of inventories of the archdeacon's court from 1583–7 (both its leaves have 'A. INV. 15' pencilled on them). The context from which Add. 127/19 was recovered is seemingly unrecorded.

Commentary

Priscianus Caesariensis (whose exact dates are unknown, but who taught at Constantinople in the reign of Anastasius, 491–518) was the most prolific and influential late Latin grammarian. Originally written to teach Latin to native Greek speakers, his *Institutiones grammaticae* became, from the ninth century onwards, a standard text for studying and teaching Latin grammar in the medieval west. Even making allowance for huge losses and for the imbalance of the surviving sample, the fact that we have only four pre-ninth-century copies and more than seventy ninth-century ones, attests to its enshrinement in the curriculum during the Carolingian period. The first of its eighteen books (from which the Canterbury fragments come) is the prolegomenon to tackling the individual parts of the language in more detail. As a study and teaching tool, copies of the work are likely to have been particularly exposed to wear and tear; and the number of surviving manuscripts, though very considerable, gives a wholly inadequate guide to its circulation. The strain placed on such study books from the mid-ninth century is revealed by the burgeoning glossing to which they were subject – which, at the same time, shows individual teachers and readers interacting with the text. The majority of the commentary in question sprang from individual words (as in the present copy).

Judging by the exiguous manuscript evidence, Priscian's *Institutiones* does not seem to have been much used in Anglo-Saxon England. An 'Excepciones de Prisciano, a' appears among the *Libri Anglici* section of Prior Eastry's Christ Church library catalogue (James 1903, p. 51, no. 320) and might, therefore, be presumed to have been in Old English and of pre-Conquest date; however, the volume in question may have resembled Antwerp, Plantin-Moretus Museum, MS 47 and Paris, BnF, n.a.l. 586, where the Latin *Excerptiones de Prisciano* is accompanied by some Old English glosses; alternatively, it might have contained Ælfric's *Excerptiones de arte grammatica anglice*, a distillation in Old English of this same text. Whatever the truth of this particular case, the popularity of the *Institutiones* itself undoubtedly rose in the wake of the Norman Conquest, and English manuscripts of the work – along with imported continental copies – start to appear in greater numbers. It is also at this time that it first features on an English book list (Lapidge 1985, no. XI). The coincidence with the Conquest was partly fortuitous: Priscian's stock rose in northern Europe in general from the mid-eleventh century thanks to renewed attention from various masters, increasingly interested in the philosophical implications of language. However, given that one of the scholars in question was Lanfranc of Bec (some of whose thoughts on Priscian have come down to us (see Hunt 1943)), the coming of the Normans may indeed have helped to further the cause of the *Institutiones* in late eleventh-century England. Certainly, Lanfranc's impact in this respect at Canterbury can still be perceived. He gave a copy containing Books 1–16 (the section dealing with accidence, which was commonly separated from Books 17–18 that treated syntax) to Christ Church: the first item on the imperfect late twelfth-century Christ Church book-list is 'Priscianus Magnus Lanfranci in asseribus' (James 1903, p. 7, no. 1), presumably reappearing at the head of the relevant section in Henry of Eastry's catalogue as 'Priscianus Magnus Lanfranci Archepiscopi libri xvi' (James 1903, p. 53, no. 389). Moreover, the fact that his manuscript was consulted at Canterbury *c.* 1100 is attested in a handsome copy of the work that was made there around this time (Cambridge University Library, MS Ii. 2.1). In the margin of fol. 100v of this volume, the scribe himself noted that the section in question was lacking from the archiepiscopal copy ('... omnino deest in libro arch[iepiscopi]');

while on fol. 38v a different but coeval hand recorded that the final paragraph of Book V was likewise lacking from the archbishop's Priscian ('hoc totum in isto loco omnino deest in prisciano archiepiscopi usque ad breuiter regulas' [i.e. up to the start of the prefatory letter to Book VI]). For what it is worth, we may note that the manuscript from which the Canterbury leaves came was not the exemplar for CUL, MS Ii. 2. 1: aside from numerous and repeated differences of spelling (aelos/eoles; nichilo/nihilo; sillabae/syllabe; etc.) and dramatically different treatment of the Greek, there is one occasion of divergent readings (for Keil 1855–80, vol. II, p. 18, l. 9 ff., our fragment has 'Apud nos quoque est inuenire quando pro u consonante B ponitur' while CUL, MS Ii. 2. 1 reads 'Apud nos quoque inuenitur quod pro v consonante b ponitur').

CUL, MS Ii. 2. 1 is also notable as an early copy of the work that was specifically designed to accommodate glosses, having wide outer margins (*c.* 92 mm; general size: 350 × 262 mm; main text-block, 268 × 134 mm). Ironically, notwithstanding its design and the intensity of the glossing on a few pages, overall it is quite lightly glossed, is in a generally fresh condition, and, unlike our fragment, shows little sign of academic or pedagogical use. (Subsequent pointing 'nota' hands suggest that in the later middle ages its second part, the 'Ars minor', received more attention than its first, the 'Ars maior'.)

A broadly contemporary copy associated with Saint Augustine's Abbey has also come down to us: Cambridge, Trinity College, MS O. 2. 51, part II. Economically conceived in terms of size and density of text (it was written to a smaller gauge, with more extensive use of abbreviations), it nevertheless had wide margins, now drastically trimmed, which received glossing at a much later date, and was adorned with a series of spirited and colourful decorated initials. Once again, divergent readings (e.g. Keil 1855–80, vol. II, p. 17, ll. 1–2: Canterbury, 'inuenitur pro nihilo' [Trinity, 'pro nichilo inuenitur'; Keil, p. 17, l. 5: Cant. '[i]ambicum trimetrum' [Trin., 'trimetrum iambicum'; Keil, p. 17, l. 25: Cant., 'causa solet fieri' [Trin., 'causa fieri solet'; Keil, p. 18, l. 1: Cant. 'Sicubi nuncubi' [Trin., 'nuncubi sicubi'; Keil, p. 18, l. 8: Cant.,

'Apud nos quoque est inuenire quando' [Trin., 'Apud nos quoque inuenitur quando'; etc.) show that our manuscript cannot have been its exemplar. It may be noted, however, that the treatment of the Greek in these two manuscripts (and in contradistinction to CUL, MS Ii. 2. 1) is very close.

The subsequent accumulation of copies of Priscian's *Institutiones* in Kent is illustrated by the 1202 Rochester library catalogue, which lists five of them, by Henry of Eastry's Christ Church catalogue, which includes seven in a block with others elsewhere, and by the late medieval Saint Augustine's Abbey catalogue which records a similar number. One of these last, we may note, is described as an old book ('Prescianus maior et minor cum B liber uetus': James 1903, p. 356, no. 1352); if there is an outside chance that our fragments, given their antiquity, come from this copy, there is sadly no way of investigating the matter further.

Bibliography

Passalacqua 1978, nos. 97 and 344; Bischoff 1998, no. 853; Gameson 2002, p. 182; Gameson 2005, ill. 3 (showing PRC).

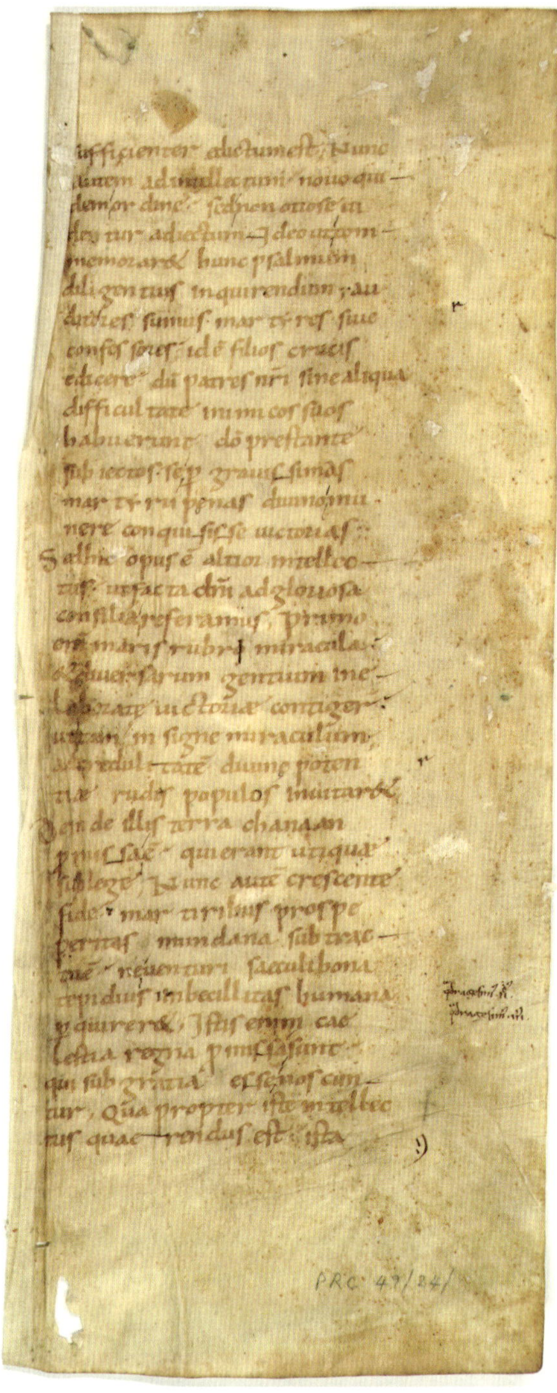

3 PRC 49/24/1–7

Cassiodorus, *Expositio psalmorum*
'France'; *saec.* X(?$^{2/3}$)
Illustration: PRC 49/24/2 recto

Physical Description

Seven fragments. **PRC 49/24/3–7** are five small squares, each measuring *c.* 58 × 60–65 mm; all are severely damaged (seemingly from glue), one side in each case being darkened, the other whitened (the text on the former remains legible, that on the latter has been almost totally effaced). These were presumably used to line the spine compartments of the host volume. **PRC 49/24/1** and **2**, by contrast, are substantial strips (measuring 363 × 148 and 360 × 135 mm respectively), representing approximately half a folio in each case. Both are very weathered, marked with glue, have fragments of paper adhering to them, and bear turn-in stains – reflecting their subsequent use within the covers of PRC 17/40 (see **History**). Nevertheless, they preserve generous outer margins on all three sides and their text remains substantially legible. Each bears a single column of text on recto and verso (from an original two-column layout). Column width: 90 mm. Lines: 35. Space between lines: 7 mm. Height of minims: 2–3 mm. Ruling: hard point. The page size of the original volume can be estimated as *c.* 375 × 300 mm, the written area as *c.* 265 × 210 mm.

PRC 49/24/1 and 3–7 are all from one leaf; PRC 49/24/2 comes from the next leaf but one (see **Content**).

Content

Cassiodorus, *Expositio psalmorum* (CPL 900), portions of the commentaries on psalms 41, 42 and 43. The exact content of the fragments is as follows.

[PRC 49/24/1, recto] //commotum se ad continuas lacrimas [PL 70, col. 306C] ... Psalmus ergo sicut sepe dictum est [PL 70, col. 307 A, continuing immediately on the verso:] significat melos ... Iudica me, deus, et discerne causam meam de gente non sancta // [col. 307B end].

The small fragments all come from the second column of the same page as the previous strip and collectively contain most of PL 70, col. 307 B/C–D; the first portion (number '3') includes part of the upper margin. They should be ordered as follows: 1) (fragment 3), // [fi]delis saeculi huius iniquita[tibus] ... Ut in iudicio domini ca[usa] [PL col. 307B-C]; 2) (fragment 6), [seques]traretur ab impiis quando ... discerne causa[m] [col. 307C]; 3) (fragment 4), [di]uide permixtionem me[am quam] in saeculo ... contueri po[terat] [col. 307C]; 4) (fragment 5), praeceptis probabantur ... fidelibus inuenitur [col. 307 C-D]; 5) (fragment 7) [first line illegible apart from 'mori[bus]', then:] aliqua prauitate uitiar[i] ... grassatur ut su[nt] [col. 307D].

[PRC 49/24/2, recto] // sufficienter edictum est. Nunc autem ad intellectum [PL 70, col. 309D] ... [bottom:] quaerendus est ista [PL 70, col. 310A, continuing on the damaged verso:] gratia contuenda quoniam [–effaced–] ... Deus auribus NOSTRIS audiuimus patres NOSTRI ad- [corrected to: an-]// [col. 310A–310C].

The equivalent of five manuscript columns is missing between fragments 1 plus 3–7 on the one hand, and 2 on the other – i.e. one whole leaf and the first column of the next.

Scribes and Script

The fragments are probably all the work of a single scribe. The difference in weight between the writing on the two substantial strips is better accounted for by the assumption of a different, or re-cut pen than by postulating a change in hand; the basic letter forms and the way they are drawn remain the same. The ink is (now) very brown. The script is a rather rough late Caroline minuscule, which seems to have been hastily written. Notable features include clubbed ascenders, a 'g' with an open bowl, a 'p' with a rather pinched one, and a capital 'I' which starts with a generous horizontal stroke to the right of the upright (resembling an inverted 'L'). Word separation is generous. Punctuation: semicolon or two points and a comma (major pauses); *punctus elevatus* (minor ones). The general aspect of the hand suggests production in West Francia, north of the Loire, during the tenth century (perhaps the second third). Quotations from the psalms are written in ordinary ink in a hybrid display script which encorporates some uncial-based forms. The rubric introducing a new psalm is presented in hybrid uncial-based capitals in ordinary ink.

The original transcription was rather negligent: in particular, the scribe regularly broke words incorrectly (presumably implying that his exemplar had little or no word division). Subsequently, the text was carefully corrected by a different hand (using a much darker ink) which joined together with lines the syllables that had been incorrectly separated, and inserted 'ticks' to indicate the divisions between words that had been overlooked. Some of the punctuation was reworked at the same time, and 'quotation marks', signalling extracts from the psalter text, were added. A few letters were retraced or corrected (e.g. 'rubro' to 'rubri', and 'inbecillitas' to 'imbecillitas', both on fol. 2r).

Rubrics identifying the psalm in question ('quadragesimus primus', 'quadragesimus secundus' (twice), 'quadragesimus tertius') were added in the margins in dark ink in a compressed and fairly informal late Caroline minuscule. In so far as one can judge from such a small and abbreviated sample, this scribe was of 'French' rather than English origin, and was probably active in *s.* xi[2] or xii[1].

Crosses were added to the margins, marking the first verses of psalms 42 and 43 – presumably echoes of the *crux ansata* that Cassiodorus placed beside the first verse of each psalm for the convenience of the reader. They are crudely drawn in an ink that is darker than that of the original scribe but lighter than that of the corrector, and it is difficult to gauge when they were added.

Decoration

None in the surviving portions.

History

The manuscript was written on the continent in the tenth century. The continental correcting hand – though possibly that of a foreign scribe working in England in the generation after the Norman Conquest – would seem to imply that it was still there *c.*

1100. Presumably in England before the Dissolution (see further **Commentary**), it was seemingly broken up by s. xvi$^{3/4}$ being used for the binding of PRC 17/40, the register of Wills from the Archdeaconry Court for 1567–70.

Commentary

Flavius Magnus Aurelius Cassiodorus (*c.* 495–after 580) started his compendious commentary on the Psalms at Ravenna between 538 and 540, completing a first version in Constantinople around the middle of the century; he subsequently revised it at his own foundation of Vivarium in southern Italy between 560 and 570. Apart from Augustine's *Enarrationes in psalmos* (Cassiodorus's principal source), this is the only 'ancient' commentary to treat every psalm; moreover, it ranges well beyond its immediate subject, including – *inter alia* – refutations of all known heresies, and outlines of every known science. Nonetheless, it is logically arranged with each section following the same formula: after consideration of the title of the psalm, its divisio and construction, Cassiodorus embarks upon a verse by verse commentary, in which he elucidates matters of style and grammar as well as content and meaning; he then sums up the implications of the psalm in question for Christian life. The result was a very long work: the copy represented by the Canterbury fragments will originally have occupied about 700 folios, and it was probably, therefore, presented in three volumes, as was commonly the case (the extant fragments come from Volume I).

Notwithstanding its great length, the work enjoyed significant popularity and, although no very early copies have come down to us, there are parts of at least ten from the eighth century – at which time, Northumbria and northern Francia emerge as the principal centres for its transmission. As with many other texts, copying peaked first in the ninth century and then again in the twelfth (Halporn 1981); however, in contrast to the case of most other texts, the number of copies transcribed in the tenth and eleventh centuries remained comparatively high. The present fragments are further evidence of this phenomenon. The fact that the subject of the work was the Psalms, of which it offered a comprehensive and orderly treatment, doubtless recommended it to the monastic communities that were then the main, if not only, centres of scribal activity.

England seems to have been one of the exceptions to this general pattern. Whilst England participated, albeit belatedly, in the tenth-century monastic reform movement, and although the English reformers were in close contact with centres such as Fleury and the Low Countries where Cassiodorus's text was then being actively copied, no copies of the work are known to have been written or owned in England in the tenth or eleventh centuries. Nor, unlike many patristic works, does it seem to have been particularly popular in the aftermath of the Conquest – only one, or possibly two, English copies survive from the first third of the twelfth century. The evidence of book lists reveals that Glastonbury acquired a copy during the abbacy of Henry of Blois (1126–71) and that Reading had obtained one by 1192, but Rochester never seems to have had the work.

Bearing in mind both this general pattern and the evidence of the 'French' annotating hand, the most likely time for the Canterbury manuscript to have travelled to England is the twelfth century. Both Christ Church and Saint Augustine's owned three-volume copies of the work by the later Middle Ages as their library catalogues show; and the circumstance that the Christ Church copy (James 1903, p. 51, nos. 328–30) appears among the *Libri de armariolo claustri*, which were predominantly volumes of twelfth-century date or earlier, adds to the likelihood that this copy at least was acquired before 1200. It is a reasonable assumption, therefore, that our item is the remains of one of these two sets. In point of fact, the vestiges of two separate copies of the work of Canterbury provenance are known – though they have seemingly never been seen together. Neil Ker, who did not apparently know the present fragments, saw in Canterbury in 1949 a single leaf of twelfth-century date from the beginning of volume two of the work. On his MLGB record card for this lost item (kept in the Bodleian Library) he noted: 'Canterbury Cath. Box ABC. Cassiodorus in Pss. 51– (1 leaf only) s. xii. [Secunda] Pars Cassiodori [...] at top (s.). 2 cols. 32+ ll. Script in general like

Canterbury. Evidently the 2nd leaf of the MS: beg. Anticristus [...] non in merito deputatur. Doan autem = PL 70, col. 373, line. 2. ?Is/cf. ALCD [ie. James 1903], no. 329'. In *Medieval Manuscripts in British Libraries* (Ker 1977, p. 312), recording that it was, 'marked at the head on the recto "Secunda Pars Cassiodori"', he again suggested that the leaf might have come from the Christ Church copy. Why he associated it with Christ Church in particular is, unfortunately, not explicitly recorded, and as the leaf, unlocatable when Ker returned in the 1970s, is still lost, it is currently impossible to know whether the appearance of the original script or of the added title favoured this precise attribution. Be that as it may, it is clear from the information Ker noted on the record card that the lost leaf cannot have come from vol. II of the set of Cassiodorus described in the late medieval library catalogue of Saint Augustine's Abbey (James 1903, p. 235, no. 413) since the *secundo folio* reference of that manuscript was 'aperiat' – not 'anticristus' as on the lost leaf. Thus, given that the lost leaf cannot have belonged to this set but may have come from the Christ Church one, and given further that, in view of the difference in date, it is unlikely to have been from the same set as the present item, one might then be prepared cautiously to entertain the hypothesis of a Saint Augustine's provenance for the copy represented by the present fragments (James 1903, p. 234, nos. 412–14).

4 Add. 127/12

Homiliary
England; *saec.* X$^{3/3}$
Illustration: fol. 1r

Physical Description
One incomplete bifolium (originally the centre of a quire), mounted in a modern guard-book. It has been drastically cut down, with the loss of much of the outer column of fol. 1. A deep fold-line runs horizontally across the middle of the sheet as a whole; below this line on fol. 1r and, above all, fol. 2v, the parchment is significantly more weathered and discoloured than elsewhere. Maximum page size as it survives: 336 × 262 mm (probable original size: *c.* 355 × 270 mm or more). Written area: 263 × 186 mm. Two columns per page (column width: 90 mm). Lines: 32. Space between lines: 8 mm. Height of minims: 3 mm. No prickings are preserved. Ruling: hard point (the impression is strongest on fol. 1r, but even this seems to be a transmitted, as opposed to direct, impression, suggesting that the quire was made up, folded, and then ruled). Sewing holes survive in the gutter at *c.* 18, 40, 58, 77, 100, 162, 217, 255, 268 and 305 mm from the top of the leaf.

Content
Two items (both incomplete) from the homiliary of Saint-Père de Chartres:
[Fol. 1r] *XV. OMELIA IN PVRIFICATIONE SANCTAE MARIAE.* CONVENIENDUM est in unum fratres karissimi ad huius diei solemnitatem, quia hodie christus cum substantia nostrae carnis in templo est dignatus [–erasure–] praesentari, … [a large portion of the middle is imperfect owing to the loss of much of the outer column of the leaf] … **[fol. 2r]** … qui cum eo semper uiuit, dominatur et regnat per omnia secula seculorum. Amen [Barré 1962, p. 19, no. 15].
[Fol. 2r-v] [No rubric.] Inquirendum est, fratres karissimi, et subtiliter discutiendo inuestigandum, quid misterii continetur in officiis quae scripta sunt in antiphonario et misali libello. Ardor

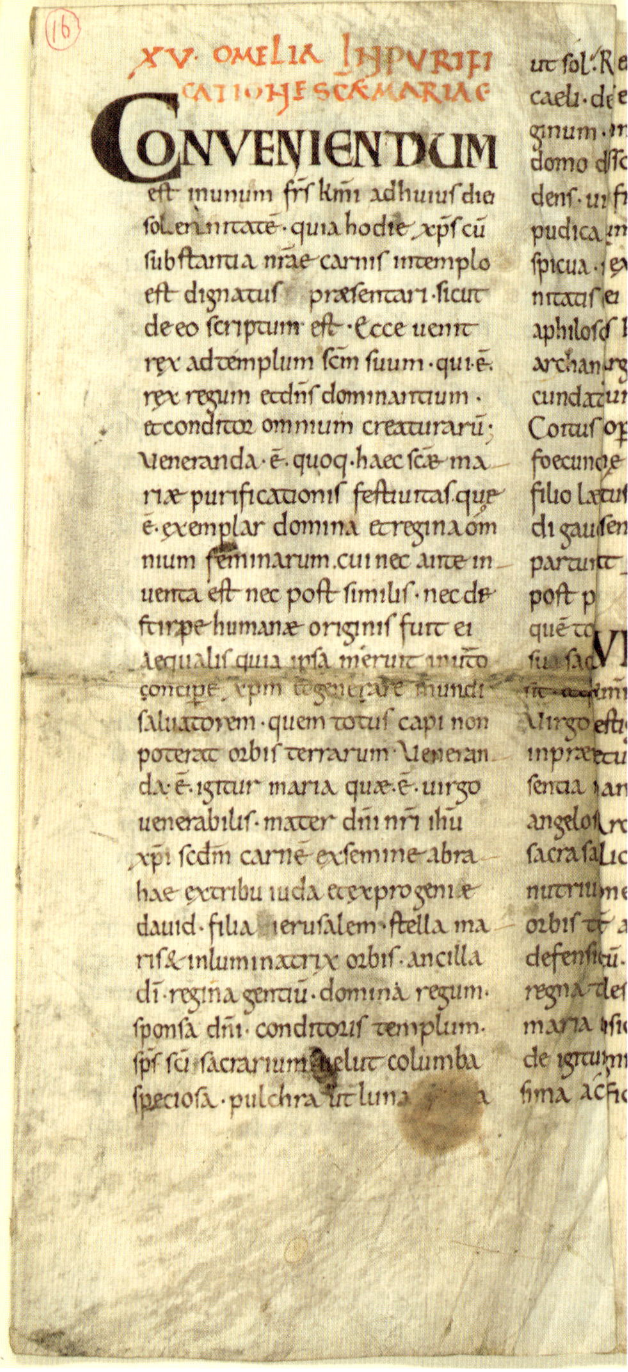

XV· OMELIA INPURIFI
CATIONE SCAE MARIAE
CONVENIENDUM
est inunum frs karmi adhuius die
sollemnitate· quia hodie xps cū
substantia nrae carnis intemplo
est dignatus praesentari· sicut
de eo scriptum est· Ecce uenit
rex adtemplum scm suum· qui ē·
rex regum etdns dominantium·
etconditor omnium creaturarū;
Ueneranda· ē· quoq· haec scae ma
riae purificationis festiuitas· quae
ē· exemplar domina etregina om
nium feminarum. cui nec ante in
uenta est nec post similis· nec de
stirpe humanae originis fuit ei
Aequalis quia ipsa meruit initio
concipe xpm regenerare mundi
saluatorem· quem totus capi non
poterat orbis terrarum· Ueneran
da ē· igitur maria quae ē· uirgo
uenerabilis· mater dni nri ihu
xpi scdm carne exsemine abra
hae extribu iuda etexprogenie
dauid· filia ierusalem· stella ma
ris& inluminatrix orbis· ancilla
dī· regina gentiū· domina regum·
sponsa dni· conditoris templum·
sps sci sacrarium· uelut columba
speciosa· pulchra ut luna [illegible]

enim ... et opus domini non respicitis // [end of the leaf] [Barré 1962, p. 19, no. 16].

Scribes and Script

In its original form, the surviving portion was the work of a single scribe with a distinctive and fairly consistent if rather unappealing hand. If his script is technically a Caroline minuscule, numerous elements therein – ranging from general features (e.g. the angled triangular serifs, and the tendency to weight strokes irregularly) to the treatment of particular letters (notably the 'e' with a long tongue and the 't' with a long tapering head-stroke) – echo indigenous Anglo-Saxon writing, favouring a date in the generation before the millennium. (The fact that the quire seems to have been ruled folded – a common practice in England before *c.* 1000 but rare thereafter – is consonant with this dating.) Tildes and the (standard) abbreviation marks for 'ur', 'us' and 'orum' tend to be of generous proportions; 'et', though sometimes represented by an ampersand, is often written in full; 'est' is generally represented by an 'e' flanked by two dots, under a tilde. Original punctuation: high and low points (not always perfectly distinguished), the former indicating a stronger pause than the latter; some were converted into *punctus elevati* at a later date. A hybrid alphabet was used for sentence capitals.

The text was extensively corrected *in rasura* by a flowing but quite angular hand of *s.* xii^{1}, which is possibly a mature version of the Kentish prickly script. Corrections, which are particularly numerous on fols. 1v and 2r, ranged from emending the ends of words (e.g. larg*iter* and antiqui*tatem*, both fol. 2r, col. ii) to replacing whole passages (e.g. fol. 1v, ll. 18–20 and 27–33). The same scribe also changed some of the medial points to *punctus elevati* and added dashes to signal the (many) line-breaks; occasionally, too, he added a 'comma' to mark off 'et's that the original scribe had joined to the following word.

Decoration

None survives; there is unlikely to have been much, if any. Bastardised rustic capitals were used for the orange-red rubric on fol. 1r (no rubric was supplied on fol. 2r). Both homilies are introduced by a row of enlarged (one-line-high) ordinary ink display capitals of slightly irregular form, headed by a still larger (two- or more-lines-high) ink initial. (Similar capitals appear in, e.g., Oxford, Bodleian Library, MS Bodley 155, a slightly younger gospel book of Barking provenance.)

History and Provenance

Written in southern England in the last third of the tenth century, the volume was still being used 150 years later. In the first half of the twelfth century, certain passages were re-worked and the punctuation and line-breaks were comprehensively re-done, which strongly suggests that it was being fully reconditioned for continuing service in a new milieu with different expectations about the presentation and pointing of texts for public reading. The hand responsible could be, though is not necessarily, Kentish. The sheet was evidently recycled as, or in, some sort of wrapper in the early modern period, and there are four lines of scrawl in a ?*s*. xvi–xvii hand at the lower edge of the outer margin on fol. 2v (the most weathered portion of the sheet), running at right-angles to the original text. This is largely illegible; however, the first three lines all end with a number (3, 6 [crossed through] and 2), while the first word of the last line may be 'court'. Subsequent Kentish provenance is confirmed by the annotation 'Godmersham' boldly written higher up on fol. 2v in a fairly modern hand (?*s*. xviii–xix).

Commentary

The homiliary of Paul the Deacon (see **no. 9**) was followed in the ninth century by other collections with similar or complementary functions. Some provided liturgically-arranged material for meditational reading, others homilies appropriate for public preaching. The homiliary of Saint-Père de Chartres (named after a copy of the work from that foundation) is one such collection, suitable for use in preaching to the laity. Internal evidence indicates that it is unlikely to have been drawn up before the second quarter of the ninth century. In contrast to Paul the Deacon, the compiler of this collection (like that of others from the period) rarely included texts intact: rather they were subjected to greater or lesser adaptation and combination. Thus the first of the two homilies in our fragment combines portions taken from works by Pseudo-Hildefonsus, Pseudo-Gregory, and Ambrose (the second, by contrast, is largely derived from Amalarius) (Cross 1987, p. 25).

The eponymous manuscript from Saint-Père de Chartres (Chartres, Bibliothèque municipale, MS 25 (*olim* 44), fols. 119–62; ?s. x), already imperfect by the nineteenth century (when it was described in the *Catalogue général*), was burned in 1944 and is now in a very fragmentary state. The earliest usable manuscript of the collection is a late eleventh-century English copy of Bury St Edmunds provenance, now Cambridge, Pembroke College, MS 25, fols. 3r–180v. The Canterbury fragment, which predates Pembroke MS 25 by about a century, is the oldest extant direct witness to its circulation in England; the circumstances that its first surviving item, which corresponds to homily 15 in Pembroke MS 25, is actually numbered 'XV', and that the homily which follows is Pembroke's number 16, underline the correlation between the two copies. Further evidence that the collection, or derivatives thereof, were known in England by the second half of the tenth century at the latest is provided by the 'Vercelli Book' of that date (Vercelli, Biblioteca Capitolare, MS CXVII), for four of the anonymous Old English homilies that are preserved therein echo passages from its sermons.

Bibliography

Clayton 1985, esp. p. 218; Cross 1987, esp. pp. 1 and 49; Cross 1991, esp. p. 205.

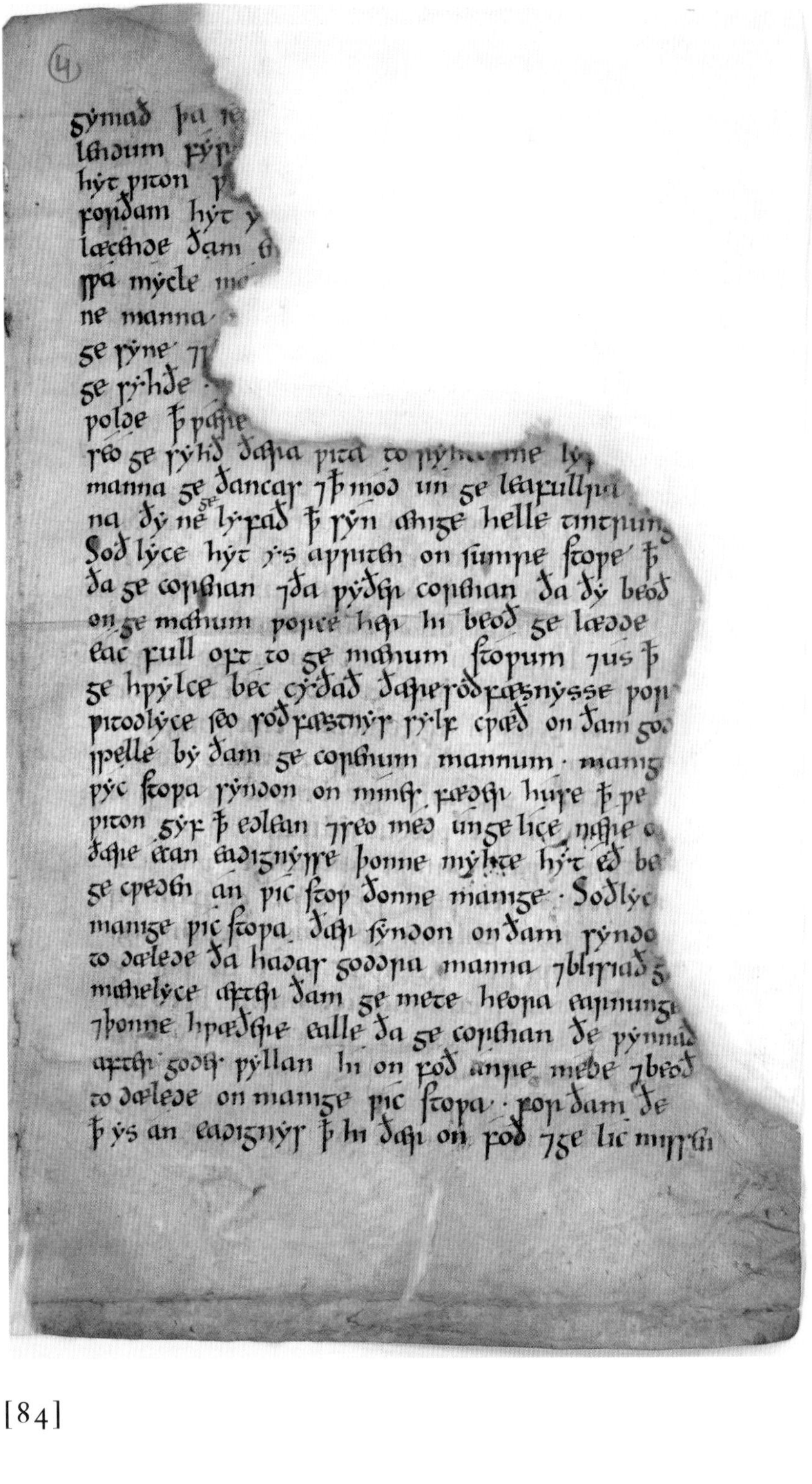

5 Add. 25

Werferth of Worcester, Old English version of Gregory's *Dialogi*
England; *saec.* X[ex]
Illustration: fol. 4r

Physical Description
Fragments of two adjacent bifolia, now repaired and recomposed within parchment surrounds. (The gap in the text between fols. 2v and 3r is the equivalent of two folios – one bifolium, which was presumably, then, the centre of this quire.) Much of the top and outer edges of each leaf have been destroyed, with substantial loss of text, especially on fols. 2 and 3. The sections that remain bear the scars of folding, and are stained and damaged (particularly fols. 2 and 3). Sufficient remains of the bifolium fols. 1 and 4 to establish the approximate original dimensions. Probable page size: *c.* 320 × 192 mm. Written area: 246 × 140 mm. Long lines. Lines per page: 31. Space between lines: 8 mm. Height of minims: 3 mm. Ruling: hard point.

Content
Werferth of Worcester's Old English translation (original, not revised, version) of Gregory the Great's *Dialogi*: parts of Book IV, chs. 32–4 and 36, imperfect.
[Fol. 1r] //he ge læd[ed] [–] ... and feded **[Fol. 1v]** // [r]odne [–] ... ac hwæðere he ðær on g[a]n swyðe byfi// **[Fol. 2r]** // swyðe bli[ð] [–] ... hwæt seo sawul ðrowað// **[Fol. 2v]** //[æ]ggen on [–] ... ytemyste lyð hys **[Fol. 3r]** // e of lic[h] [–] ... swa hys hlaford hyne het, and ða **[Fol. 3v]** // m. com [–] ... ofer ealle oðru land. **[Fol. 4r]** gyniað þa se [–] ... ge lic missen **[Fol. 4v]** // þe hi ða eadig [–] ... and heora ge hwylc sægð þæt he//

The text of the fragment (which corresponds to Hecht 1900, p. 307, line 16 – p. 310, l. 13 and p. 313, l. 20 – p. 316, l. 16) is printed in full by Yerkes 1977; the relationship between all the extant copies is considered there and in Yerkes 1986.

Scribes and Script

What survives is the work of a single scribe. The hand is regular and eminently legible though not particularly calligraphic. Despite long ascenders and descenders, the basic matrix is fairly square and individual strokes are thick. Most vertical lines are headed with wedge-shaped serifs and terminated with wedge-shaped or rising feet; horizontal strokes (e.g. at the top and bottom of the bowl of 'a', along with the 'bridges' of 'h', 'm' and 'n') generally rise from left to right. Word separation is very generous, but there is intermittent biting of letters within words. 'Y' is invariably dotted; the Tironian 'et' is invariably used. Apart from þ with a tilde for 'þæt', there is hardly any abbreviation. Punctuation: medial point (for major and minor pauses). There are regular, original 'acute' accents. The counter-spaces of sentence capitals are coloured in red.

Decoration

None survives; the original volume is unlikely to have had much, if any.

History and Provenance

There is no evidence bearing on the origin of the manuscript. In view of its modern provenance, it is tempting to assume that these leaves are the remnant of the *Dialogus beati Gregorii* which appears among the *libri anglici* in the catalogue of Christ Church books made in the time of Henry of Eastry (James 1903, list II, p. 51, no. 306). Apparently discovered in *s.* xix (though the precise context and circumstances are seemingly unrecorded), these leaves were first listed by Woodruff (1911) as 'Fragments of Treatises' no. XIX (at which stage, presumably, the '19' in red pen was added to fol. 1r); they were transferred to their present context and classification by William Urry *c.* 1950.

Commentary

For Gregory's *Dialogi*, see **no. 6**. The chapters in the present fragment (in common with much of Book IV) recount miraculous incidents that illustrate the relationship between life and afterlife.

At the end of the ninth century, the *Dialogi* were included in King Alfred the Great's programme of translation into Old English; Alfred's biographer, Asser († 908/9), ascribes the translation to Bishop Werferth of Worcester (*sedit* 869x72–907x915). Subsequently, a revised version was produced. Four manuscripts of the Old English versions have come down to us: the present fragment (which is the oldest surviving witness); Cambridge, Corpus Christi College, MS 322 (xi^{2}; Worcester); London, British Library, MS Cotton Otho C. I, vol. 2 (xi^{in}; Worcester); and Oxford, Bodleian Library, MS Hatton 76, fols 1–54 (xi^{1}; Worcester). Canterbury, Corpus, and Otho are all independent descendants of an exemplar containing Werferth's original translation (none was directly copied from one of the others); Hatton, by contrast, contains a different version and its exemplar had evidently been revised through careful comparison with the Latin text.

A prose preface in Alfred's name, which is found in Corpus and Hatton, states that the work was designed to help the king reflect on heavenly matters amidst earthly tribulations. Be that as it may, it is clear from the poetic preface which replaces this in Otho that Alfred had sent a copy of the translation to Wulfsige, bishop of Sherborne (*sedit* sometime between 879 and 900); and other copies may likewise have been distributed at the royal command.

The three better-preserved manuscripts, Corpus, Otho and Hatton, all have early associations with Worcester; the Canterbury fragment is of unknown origin and early provenance. Its appearance presents no telling similarities to the many, admittedly mainly Latin, volumes produced at Saint Augustine's Abbey and Christ Church in the later tenth century, so there is no evidence to support a case for a Canterbury origin. That a copy of the work should have found its way to Canterbury at an early date is, however, highly likely. Whatever its early history, as one of fewer than thirty manuscripts written principally in Old English to have come down to us from the tenth century and, as the earliest witness to an Alfredian text, its importance remains considerable.

Bibliography

Ker 1957, no. 96; Yerkes 1977, 1979, 1986; Doane and Pulsiano 1997, no. 110.

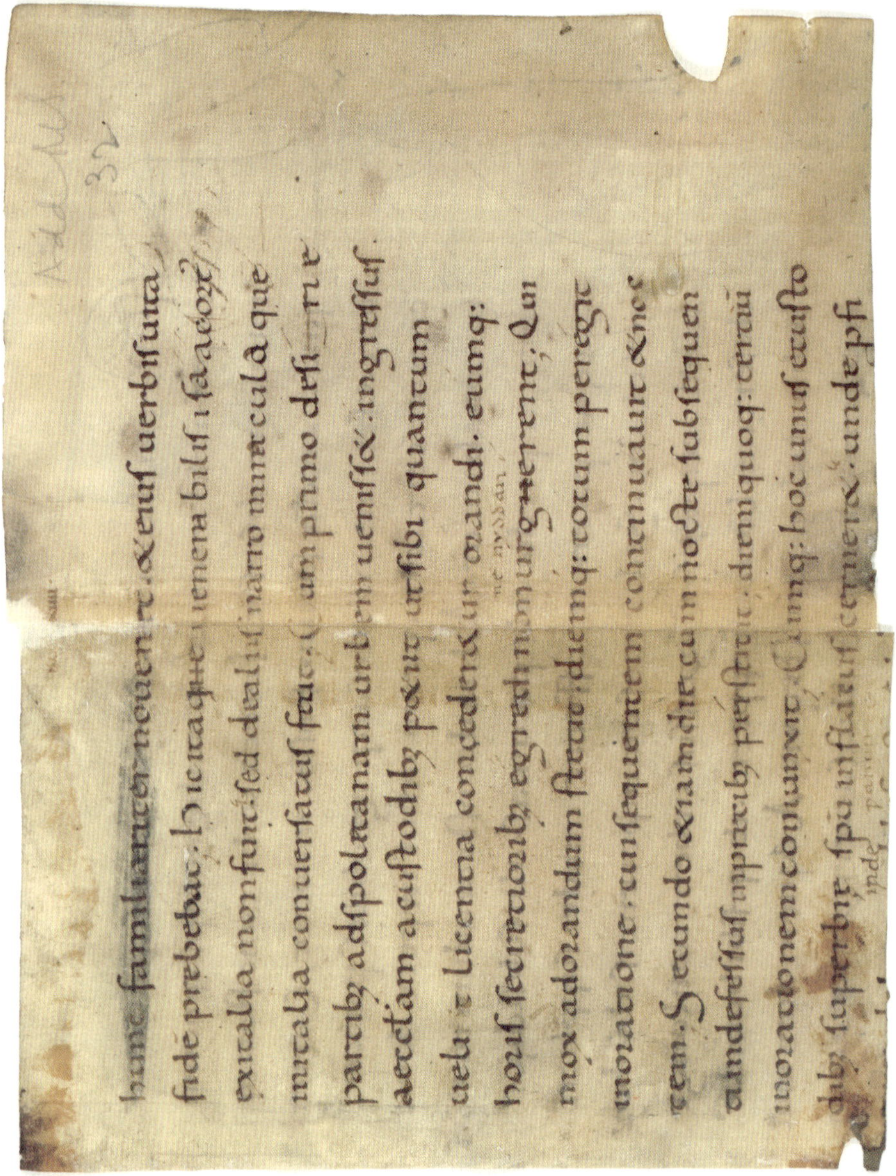

6 Add. 32

Gregory, *Dialogi*.
England; *saec*. XI^{in}
Illustration: recto of leaf

Physical Description
Two adjacent fragments from a single leaf which have been rejoined (with a slight widening effect). The surfaces are generally weathered and stained from re-use in a binding (see **History** below), but the text is clear and legible, except at the join. The parchment includes two original flaws. Size of reconstructed fragment: 140 × 180 mm. Width of text block: now 130 mm (probably originally 128–9 mm). The outer margin (which is well preserved) measures 36 mm. Lines: 14 (plus the tips of the ascenders from the 15th) survive. In view of the amount of text that is missing, the number of lines per page was probably originally 25. The size of the full text block would then have been *c*. 210 × 128 mm. Space between lines: 8 mm. Height of minims: 2 mm. Ruling: hard point.

Content
Gregory, *Dialogi*, III, 14 (incomplete).
[Recto] // hunc familiariter nouerat, et eius uerbis uita fidem prebebat. Hic ... superbie spiritu inflatus cerneret, unde profi// [PL 77, col. 244, B–C; Moricca (ed.) 1924, p. 164, ll. 10–20].
[Verso] // posse eici clamauit. Mox autem ... aeterne uite accen// [PL 77, col. 244, D–col. 245, A; Moricca (ed.) 1924, p. 165, ll. 9–19].
On both sides of the leaf, the ascenders of (and the gloss and correction to) the following line – though nothing more of it – are preserved. The quantity of text that is missing between the truncated end of fol. 1r and the beginning of fol. 1v is the equivalent of 11 lines (or conceivably ten, if the scribe compressed his work slightly more towards the bottom of the page than at the top).

The upper margin of the recto has the contemporary heading, '[–obliterated–] xiiii'. The recto also has the Old English glosses, 'ne nyddan' (to 'non urg[u – deleted]erent'), and 'wanunge' (to ['defectus']).

Significant departures from the text printed by Moricca 1924 (M) are as follows (the reading in the Canterbury fragment (C) is always presented first). [**Recto**] C: sed de aliis narro [M, p. 164, l. 12, sed ea illius narro; C: ad spolitanam urbem uenisset [M, p. 164, l. 13, ad spolitanam orbem uenissit; C: concederet [M, l. 15 concideretur; C: non urguerent, corrected to urgerent [M, l. 16 urguerent; C: Qui mox adorandum [M, l. 16, qui mox ad orandum; C: in orationem [M, l. 19, in oratione; C: cerneret [M, l. 21, cernerit. [**Verso**] C: corpus uir sanctus [M, p. 165, l. 9, corpus uir Dei; C: inuaserat [M, l. 10, tenuerat; C.: urbe [M, l. 10, orbe; C: omnipotentis domini [M, l. 16, omnipotentis Dei; C: urbem [M, l. 16, orbem; C: humile [M, l. 17, humilem.

Scribes and Script

The main text is written in a neat, slightly squat Anglo-Caroline minuscule, characterised by a gently curling ductus: minims start with a serif to the left of the letter-form and end in a foot to the right, giving them a slight, back-to-front 's'-curve. Word separation is pronounced, but within words letters are frequently touching or even joined. Sentences are headed by a rustic capital or a stylised uncial. The original punctuation seemingly comprised low and medial points (for major and minor pauses respectively); however, this was subsequently re-worked, the former being altered to semi-colons, a couple of the latter being changed to *punctus elevati* or *interrogativi*.

The initial transcription was very careless, and even within this tiny fragment there are several corrected errors, not to mention dubious readings that were allowed to stand. A couple of the errors were rectified by the text scribe himself (e.g. the **u** crossed through on the recto, l. 8; the adapted **n/g** [innobiles > ignobiles] on the verso, l. 5); others were corrected by different contemporary hands (e.g. recto l. 4, the emendation of 'desi––ri–e' (where the dashes represent irrecoverably obliterated original letters) to 'de sirie'; verso, l. 4, the addition of 're' to 'curre'; l. 13 the changing of 'At-quem' to 'Adquem').

A different hand was responsible for the interlinear Old English glosses.

Another, later (? xi^{2}) hand effected several corrections *in rasura* (e.g. 'sed', recto, l. 3; and 'sed' verso, l. 10), inserted 'inde' above the lost bottom line on the recto (which should have read, '–cere debuit inde ad defectus …'), and may also have been responsible for re-working the end of recto, l. 2.

A still later (*s*. xii^{+}) hand supplied 'ad' as an interlinear addition over l. 9 on the recto.

It is difficult to ascertain which of the annotators/correctors was responsible for emending the punctuation.

History

Written in England, where it was read and glossed at an early date, its subsequent history is largely a blank. The fragment was removed in August 1956 from the binding of Z.19.9, Io[hannes] Foucherius, *Formulae exercendarum causarum* … (Paris, 1543). Whether this was a first or second phase of re-use is unclear, and so is where it happened (the panels on the binding of the volume are of Netherlandish origin, but it is not impossible that casts were used in England.)

Commentary

Pope Gregory the Great († 604), initiator of the Roman mission that arrived in Kent in 597, was effectively regarded by the Anglo-Saxons as their patron saint; his writings enjoyed considerable authority and seem to have had a reasonable circulation in early England. Written in 593–4 at the instigation of the *fratres* of his *familia* (cf. his ep. III, 50), the *Dialogi* are presented in the form of a dialogue between Gregory himself and his interlocutor, Peter. They provide accounts of the miracle-working holy men of early Italy, and include (Book II) the earliest biography of St Benedict of Nursia, the father of Benedictine monasticism. The Canterbury fragment comes from the chapter devoted to Isaac of Spoleto, an exemplary monastic who despised wealth and was able to prophesy and exorcise. He was also credited with a strong sense of humour.

Three fragmentary manuscripts of the *Dialogi* of eighth-century date are sometimes ascribed an origin in England (Münster in Westfalen, Universitätsbibliothek, Fragmentenkapsel 1, no. 2; Stuttgart, Württembergische Landesbibliothek, Theol. et Philos. Q. 628; and Wroclaw (Breslau), Biblioteka Uniwersytecka, Akc. 1955/2 and 1969/430); however, as the palaeographical evidence is ambiguous and their demonstrable provenance continental, one should avoid making too much of them. Nevertheless, the work was clearly known in England at an early date, as allusions to, and echoes of it in the works of Aldhelm and Bede, as well as in the Whitby Life of Pope Gregory (comp. *c.* 700), show. Bede well summed up its purpose in the encomium on Gregory that he included in his *Historia ecclesiastica* (II.1): 'he collected the virtues of the most famous saints he knew or could learn of in Italy, as an example of life to posterity: just as in his expository works he taught what virtues men ought to strive after, so, by describing the miracles of the saints, he showed how glorious those virtues are'.

Four copies of the Latin text survive from late Anglo-Saxon England, all dating from shortly before or soon after the millennium: the present fragment; Lambeth Palace Library, MS 204 (origin, ?Canterbury, Christ Church; provenance, Ely); Oxford, Bodleian Library, MS Tanner 3 (provenance, Worcester); and Rouen, Bibliothèque municipale, MS A. 337 (origin, Canterbury, Christ Church; provenance, Jumièges). The text also circulated in Werferth of Worcester's Old English translation (represented by Add. 25: **no. 5**) and its revision. Incidentally, the suggestion that the Canterbury copy of the Old English version may have been the source of the glosses in the present fragment (Yerkes 1986, p. 336) overlooks the fact that there is no evidence that the latter was at Canterbury prior to the acquisition of the printed book from whose binding it was recovered. The copies of the Latin text at Lambeth, Oxford and Rouen are handsome books, and all have decoration of some sort. If their appearance attests to the high regard in which Gregory's text was held, the Canterbury fragment, with its evidence of use, implies that the work was indeed much read in late Anglo-Saxon England. The paucity of manuscripts of the *Dialogi* made in England in the couple of generations after the Conquest suggests that copying the text was not seen as a priority by the Normans; but then it was one of the few works by a father of the church of which there were already multiple copies. The present manuscript shows that at least one Anglo-Saxon copy continued to see active service well after the Conquest.

Bibliography

Ker 1957, p. lxiii (no. 97*); Doane and Pulsiano 1997, no. 111.

7 PRC 49/2

Haimo of Auxerre, *Homiliarium*
England; *saec.* XI[in]
Illustration: fol. 1v

Physical Description
A single bifolium (as the two inner pages are consecutive, it originally stood at the centre of its quire). The whole sheet has been brutally cut down, with the loss of about six lines of text from the top of all its faces, and of a large part of the outer column of text on fol. 1. All the surviving surfaces are rubbed, stained, sliced and extensively discoloured from subsequent re-use as a wrapper; they have also suffered liquid, ink and ?wax damage; while a harsh rub or fold-mark runs horizontally right across fols. 1r and 2v – all of which has obliterated text. Maximum dimensions of the better preserved half-sheet: 306 × 255 mm. Written area: 258 × 190 mm. Two columns of 84 mm. Lines: now 28 (out of a probable original 34). Space between lines: 10 mm. Height of minims: 3 mm. Ruling: hard point.

Content
Haimo of Auxerre, *Homiliarium … ad plebem in euangelia de tempore et sanctis*, including much of homily 89, all of homily 90 (though imperfect because of lost lines), and the start of homily 91.
[Fol. 1r, col. 1, line 1] //petetis tale est ac si diceret, cum spiritus … **[fol. 1r, col. 2, bottom]** naturam diui[nam scilicet et humanam nobis] commendauit, // [Haimo, Homilia 89, Dominica quinta post Pascha: PL 118, cols. 525D–526D].
[Fol. 1v, col. 1, line 1] //[Se]rui accipi[ens] … **[1v, col. 2, line 12]** … cogitationes meas de longe [Psalm 138.3 ; Haimo, Homilia 89, Dominica quinta post Pascha: PL 118, cols. 526D–527C].
[Fol. 1v, col. 2, line 12] cap. ?*UII* [or *XIII*]. *SERMO* [?*E*]*ROGATION*[*IS*] … *SUMPSERUNT*. SED QUIA DIES LETANIARUM … **[2v, col. 1, l. 2]** agnitionem ueritatis [–erasure–] uenire [I Timothy, 2.4; Haimo, Homilia 90, De litaniis:

PL 118, cols. 527C–528D (complete bar losses at the tops of the folios)].
[Fol. 2v, col. 1, l. 3] *ITEM UNDE SUPRA. LECTIO EPISTOLAE SANCTI IACOBI APOSTOLI.* Karissimi. Confitemini alteruterum peccata uestra, et orate pro inuicem ut saluemini et cetera [James 5.16]. Ad optimum salutis nostre remedium ... **[2v, col. 2, ends:]** dedit plu[uiam et] terra dedit, fructum suum // [James 5.18; Haimo, Homilia 91, Feria secunda post Vocem jucunditatis, in Litaniis majoribus: PL 118, cols. 529A–529D].

Scribes and Script

The surviving portion is the work of a single English scribe, writing a bold, upright Anglo-Caroline minuscule. In terms of its rectilinear matrix and general aspect it may be related to types of hand that were practised at Canterbury in the late tenth and early eleventh centuries – though it is distinguished from most of them by the regular use of clubbed ascenders. Other notable features include an 'a' with quite a high back, and an ampersand with a fat body, a squashed head and a long upper limb that ends in a wedge-shaped serif. The writing is spaciously set out, use being made of the most common suspensions and contractions in individual words. Sentence capitals are a mixed alphabet. Punctuation: medial point (minor pause), *punctus elevatus* (minor pause), and 'semi-colon' (major pause).

At early dates (s. xi) an originally lower-case 'u' on fol. 1v was capitalised; 'nota' was added beside the last line of the first column on fol. 1r; and a different, less formal hand made a short insertion between homilies in the intercolumnar space at the top of fol. 2v (although the first line of the addition is now very difficult to decipher – ?res[tet] i[n] glo[ria] – the next three lines clearly say 'in secula seculorum amen', implying a concluding imprecation).

Decoration

None survives, and it is unlikely there was ever very much – if any. Individual items are headed by enlarged (three- to four-lines-high), plain red capitals, with a rubric in red rustic capitals.

History

There is seemingly no direct evidence for the early history of the book from which the present bifolium comes, and which was presumably broken up in *s.* xvi. Certainly, our sheet is marked in the margins and intercolumnar spaces, inside and out, with casual jottings in several *s.* xvi hands. Often rubbed and otherwise partly obliterated, these include the words and names: 'Chrisy', 'Faculty', 'Robertus', 'Crammere?/tempore', 'Stringer', and 'postremo'.

Commentary

Haimo was school master at Saint-Germain, Auxerre, from *c.* 840 and would seem to have produced his literary works, an impressive series of scriptural commentaries along with his homiliary, between then and *c.* 860; he ended his career as abbot of Cessy-les-Bois, probably between 865 and 875. His achievement as a homiliarist was the creation of a coherent series of systematic exegetical commentaries on the relevant readings from Scripture, editing, combining and augmenting patristic sources to that end. As a whole, his homiliary provided a comprehensive sequence in liturgical order for the cycle of Sundays and feast days of the night office. The collection, which was re-worked around the end of the ninth century, enjoyed a reasonable circulation both in its original and its revised state, its popularity being reflected in the survival of some forty copies. The only extant manuscript of ninth-century date belonged to the cathedral of Cambrai (Cambrai, Médiathèque, MS 307); the handful of tenth-century manuscripts include copies from Saint-Germain-des-Prés and Saint-Pierre de Malmédy (BnF, MSS lat. 12305 and lat. 8568).

The homiliary, which was known to Ælfric of Eynsham († *c.* 1010) (who cites Haimo as a source on three occasions), had evidently reached England by the late tenth century, presumably in the wake of the monastic reform movement. The Canterbury fragment is, nonetheless, the oldest material witness to its presence in England – indeed it is the only pre-Conquest copy to have come down to us. The next witness (Durham Cathedral Library, MS B. III. 11, fols. 1–135, which includes a selection of Haimo homilies alongside Gregory the Great's *Homiliae in Euangelia*) is at least 50 years younger; written on the continent in the later eleventh century, it reached Durham shortly thereafter.

As the Canterbury fragment was once believed to have been part of the collection represented by Add. 127/1 (**no. 9**) (Ker 1977), and was then held to have belonged to a companion volume (Cross and Hall 1993), it is worth clarifying the nature of the 'relationship' between the two sets of fragments. The volumes they represent were clearly of similar layout and conception – though no more so than one might expect for broadly contemporary copies of comparable collections. However, contrary to previous claims, they do not share a scribe: there is thus no direct link between them. Moreover, the hand of the scribe of the present fragment belongs to a different, slightly older tradition than those responsible for Add. 127/1. Whilst this may reflect a difference in date – or even the variations that were possible within a large scriptorium – proof positive for a connection between the two collections is lacking. The script of the present fragment is not incompatible with an origin at Canterbury; the same cannot so easily be said of Add. 127/1. Be that as it may, with the present manuscript, Add. 127/1, and Add. 127/12 (**no. 4**), not to mention the enigmatic Add. 122 (**no. 10**), Canterbury possesses the relics of at least three different, substantial homily collections that were copied in England during the generations on either side of the millennium.

Bibliography

Cross and Hall 1993.

8 Add. 128/52

Missal (with notation)
England; *saec.* XI$^{1/4}$
Illustration: fol. 3v

Physical Description
Three separate leaves, now mounted within a folder. Fols. 2 and 3 are sequential; one (lost) leaf originally stood between fols. 1 and 2. All the surfaces are darkened and weathered, and a fold-scar (punctuated with sewing holes) runs vertically down the centre of each leaf; nevertheless, the three folios are substantially intact with reasonably wide margins. The parchment includes some original holes. Size: 300 × 198 mm. Written area: 232 × 140 mm. Lines: 33. Space between lines: 8 mm. Height of minims: 2 mm. Ruled in hard point on the hair sides (fols. 1v, 2v, and 3r). The ruling pattern is asymmetrical: the written area is framed by double upper and outer boundary lines, but by single ones at the bottom and inner edge.

Content
Portions of the Temporale from a missal (Feria IV post dominicam III quadragesime – Dominica IV quadragesime (imperfect)).
NB: large portions of the text, above all the chants, were either replaced or rewritten between the lines to a larger gauge in the later middle ages; much of the original rubric is now either obliterated or extremely faded. References are provided to the printed editions of the Leofric Missal (Orchard (ed.) 2002: L, cited by item number) and the Westminster Missal (Wickham Legg (ed.) 1891–3: WM, cited by column).
[Fol. 1r] //et a cunctis erroribus expiatos, supernis promisionibus reddat acceptos. Per. [L 632; WM 166, acephalus].
Super populum. Concede quesimus omnipotens deus, ut qui protectionis tue gratiam querimus ... seruiamus [L 633; WM 166]
[Original rubric obliterated; '*Officium*' subsequently supplied.] Salus populi ego sum ... in perpetuum [same written between the lines in the later middle ages; L 634, A; WM 166–7].

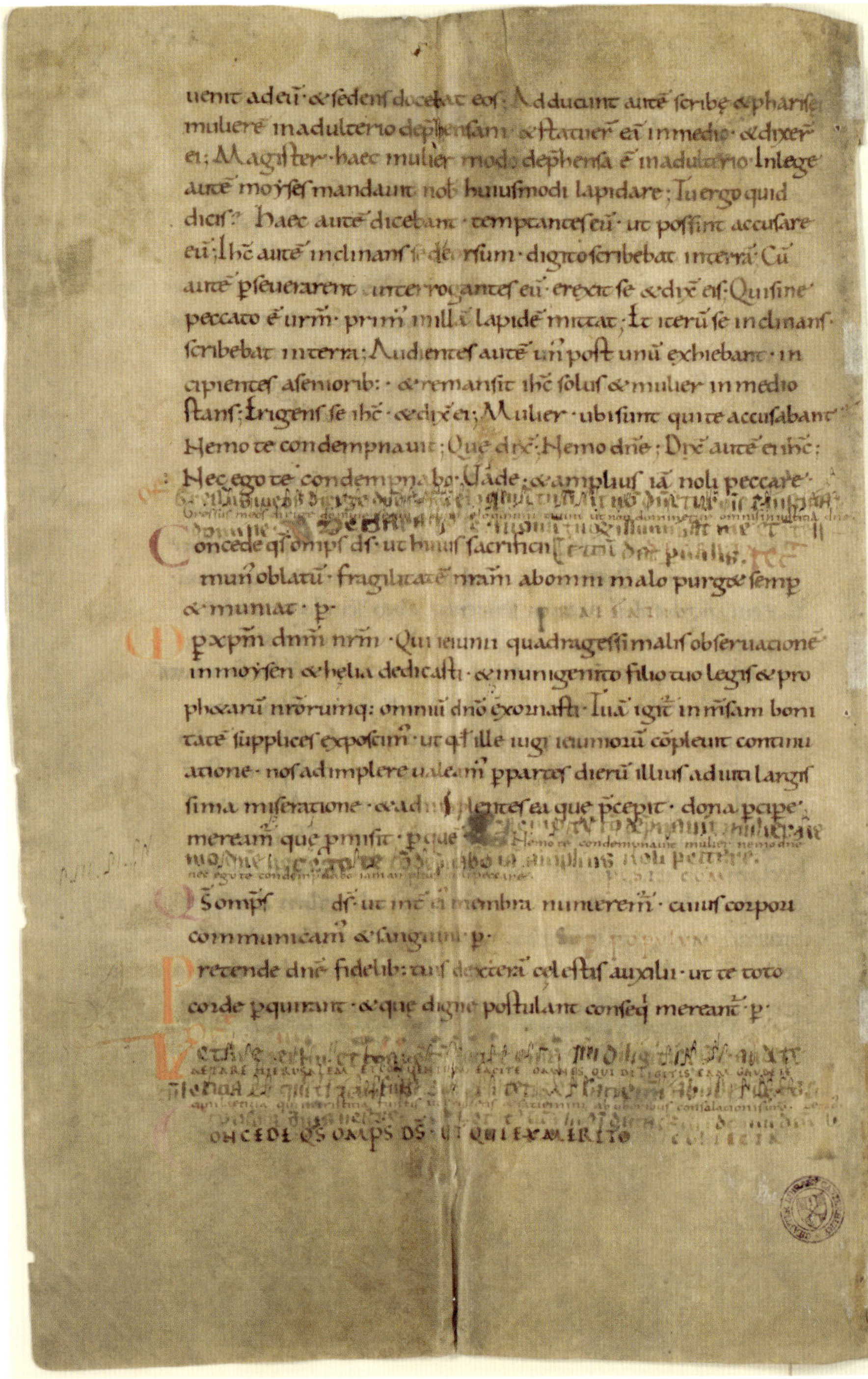

Ps. Adtendite [L 634; WM 167]
[Original rubric obliterated; '*Oratio*' subsequently supplied.] M [the text that followed was thoroughly erased and replaced in the later Middle Ages by:] Concede quesumus omnipotens deus ut ieiuniorum ... acceptos [WM 167]. [At a still later date, added to the outer margin was:] *Ps.* Attendite popule meus ... oris mei [WM 167].
[Original rubric obliterated. Marginal late medieval note:] Ieremie prophete.
In diebus illis. Factum est uerbum domini ad me dicens, Sta in porta ... Dicit dominus, omnipotens [Jeremiah 7, 1–7: WM 167].
GR. Oculi omnium ... opportuno [same written to a larger gauge in the later middle ages; L 634; WM 167].
V. Aperis tu manum tuam ... benedictione [same written to a larger gauge in the later middle ages; L 634].
Secundum Marcum. In illo. Surgens autem iesus de si\na/goga introiuit in domum symonis ... in synago – **[fol. 1v]** – gis galileae [NB: despite the rubric, this is not Mark's version (1.29–31) but Luke's: 4.38–44, cf. L 634*]. [Added in the lower margin in a late medieval hand – and partly retraced at an even later date – is:] // facis singnum [sic for 'signum'] ut uideamus et credamus tibi? Quid operaris? Patres nostri ... Ego sum panis uite, qui uenit ad me non esuriet et qui credit in me non siciet// [John 6, 30–35, acephalus and incomplete (the reading as in WM 168 is John 6, 27–35): the missing portions were presumably either written in the lost outer margin or on a separate inserted slip].
Of. Si ambulauero ... dextera tua [same written to a larger gauge in the later middle ages; WM 168]
[Total erasure of original text; replaced by late medieval:] Fac nos domine quesumus ad sancta misteria ... obsequium. Per [WM 168–9].
VD aeterne deus. Et tuam inmensam ... mereamur. Per christum [L 637].
Co. Tu mandasti [same written to a larger gauge in the later middle ages; L 634; WM 169]
Postcom. S [remainder of original wholly erased. Late medieval replacement:] Sacramenti tui ... defendat. Per [WM 169].

[Original rubric erased; *Super populum* supplied in late middle ages]. Subiectum tibi populum ... mandates. Per [L 639; WM 169].
Feria VI ad sanctum Laurentium [late medieval addition: *Officium*]. Fac mecum domine signum ... me [same written in late middle ages; L 640; WM 169].
Ps. Incline domine [same written in later middle ages; L 640; WM 169].
Oratio. Ieiunia nostra quesumus domine benigne fauore ... in mente. Per [L 641; WM 169].
Lectio libri numeri [repeated by late medieval hand]. In diebus illis. Conuenerunt filii Israel ad moysen et aaron, ... egressae sunt aquae // [Numbers 20.1–5 (edited), 6–11, breaking off incomplete; cf. L 640*; WM 169–70].
[Leaf lacking]
[Fol. 2r] // accenderet. Imploramus itaque ... tibi placeamus. Per quem. [L 643, acephalus Preface].
[Late medieval rubric: *Com*]. Qui biberit aquam ... eternam [same written to a larger gauge in the late middle ages; L 640; WM 173]
Postcom. Huius nos domine perceptio ... perducat. Per [L 644; WM 173].
Super populum. Praesta quesumus omnipotens deus, ut qui in tua protectione ... uincamus. Per [L 645; WM 174].
SABBAT?US AD SANCTAM SUSANNAM. Verba mea auribus [same written to larger gauge; L 648; WM 174].
Ps. Rex meus et deus meus [same written to larger gauge; L 648].
Collecta. Praesta quesumus omnipotens deus, ut qui se affligendo carnem ... ieiunent. Per [L 646; WM 174].
Lectio Danielis Prophete. In diebus illis. Erat uir in babylone, et nomen eius ioachim ... [continues across **fol. 2v**, and ends on **fol. 3r**:] ... eos. Et saluatus est \in/noxius sanguis, in die illa [Daniel 13.1–62; L 648*; WM 174–8].
GR. Si ambulem in medio umbre mortis ... domine [same written to larger gauge; L 648; WM 178].
V. Uirga tua ... consolata sunt [same written to larger gauge; L 648; WM 178].

[Original rubric faded to illegibility; 'Iohannem' supplied twice by different late medieval hands.] In illo. Perrexit ihesus in montem olíueti ... **[fol. 3v]** ... et amplius iam noli peccare [Jn 8.1–11; L 648*; WM 178–9].
Of. Gressus meus ... iniustitia domine [same written to larger gauge; WM 179].
Secretum [repeated by late medieval hand]. Concede quesumus omnipotens deus, ut huius sacrificii ... semper et muniat. Per [L 647].
Praefatio. VD per christum dominum nostrum. Qui ieiunii quadragesimalis ... dona percipere mereamur que promisit. Per quem [L 649].
[Rubric obliterated.] Nemo te condempnauit mulier ... noli peccare [same written to larger gauge; L 648; WM 179]
Postcom. Quesumus omnipotens deus, ut inter eius membra numeremur ... et sanguini. Per [L 650; cf. WM 179].
Super populum. Pretende domine fidelibus tuis dexteram celestis auxilii, ... postulant consequi mereantur. Per [L 651; cf. WM 179–80].
[Rubric largely illegible] *Dominica IIII* [–?–]. Laetare Hierusalem ... consolacionis uestre [the first line written in small rustic capitals; the whole repeated by late medieval hand; L 653; WM 180].
Ps. Letatus.
Collecta. Concede quesumus omnipotens deus ut qui ex merito // [end of page; all in rustic rapitals; repeated by late medieval hand; L 652; WM 180].

Scribes and Script

The original stratum (main text and chant alike) is the work of a single scribe who wrote a fine, well-controlled Anglo-Caroline minuscule. Whilst the general proportions of the hand echo some good English Caroline writing of the late tenth century, the individual letter-forms are best paralleled in work of the early eleventh century. This is arguably the sort of writing which provided the context for, and from which emerged – by the second and third decades of the eleventh century – the late standard Anglo-Caroline minuscule (see further **nos. 11–12**).

There is moderate use of the most common abbreviations. Punctuation: medial point (for minor and occasionally also major pauses), 'semi-colon' (for major pauses and introducing direct speech), plus *punctus interrogativus*. Rustic-related forms are used for sentence capitals. There are occasional 'acute' accents. The chant texts are written in the same script but approximately half the size of the normal text – thereby leaving space above the words for notation. They are accompanied by 'Insular' neumes – most of which, however, have been obliterated in whole or part by the late medieval additions. The notation itself, though contemporary with the original text, was done in a different ink, and may be the work of another hand; although some effort was made to space key words with the needs of the notator in mind, the latter was often still squeezed for space.

At least three s. xiv–xv hands, two fairly formal in grade, one cursive, none very tidy, made extensive interventions, principally to the chant cues. One hand re-copied these to a larger gauge – but very untidily – above the originals (across the Anglo-Saxon neumes), re-doing some of the rubrics and initials. In addition, on fol. 1r the same hand replaced the original prayer before Jeremiah 1.1–7 with 'Concede quesumus omnipotens deus ut ieiuniorum nobis sancta deuotio et purificationem tribuat \et maiestati/ tue reddat acceptos. Per', and supplied the reading from John 6 in the lower margin. A second and later hand inserted the omitted 'et maiestati' in the new 'Concede quesumus', and added in the margin the corresponding Psalm ('Attendite popule meus legem meam, inclinate aurem uestram in uerba oris mei' (77)), plus the rubric, 'Ieremie prophete' (cf. Hughes (ed.) 1963, pp. 42–3). A third, less formal hand retraced part of the added reading from John 6.

Decoration

None survives (the volume is only likely to have had significant decoration at the Common Preface and the Canon of the Mass). The initials in the fragment are all plain, single-colour, red-orange (now faded) or purple, and are one to two lines high. One-line-high red rustic capitals were used for rubrics (very faded). The late medieval, rewritten chant texts were supplied with plain red initials of similar scale to (though of newer type than) the originals. There is an early sketch/doodle of a plant in the outer margin of fol. 3v, and a rather later doodle based on a fleur-de-lys form in the lower margin of fol. 1v.

History

Written in the early eleventh century, the book was still seeing active service over 300 years later when the chant texts were laboriously rewritten. Faint offsets on fol. 3r of *s.* xv–xvi script, arranged in two columns and running across the right hand half of the page at right angles to the primary content, may indicate that the sheets were re-used as guard-leaves a generation or so before the Reformation; however, it is equally likely that these stains date from a phase of post-Reformation re-use when the present sheets seem to have formed some sort of cover lining in a binding structure, with the late medieval sheet as a flyleaf or paste-down. Faint pencil notes, identifying the subject of the readings, were added to the margins in pencil by a modern (?*s.* xx^{med}) hand. A fragmentary piece of paper kept with the item includes the note, 'Box AB\c/ [ser]vice books. XYZ. Bundle M. 3 folios', which, however, is insufficiently specific to indicate the early modern context from which it was recovered.

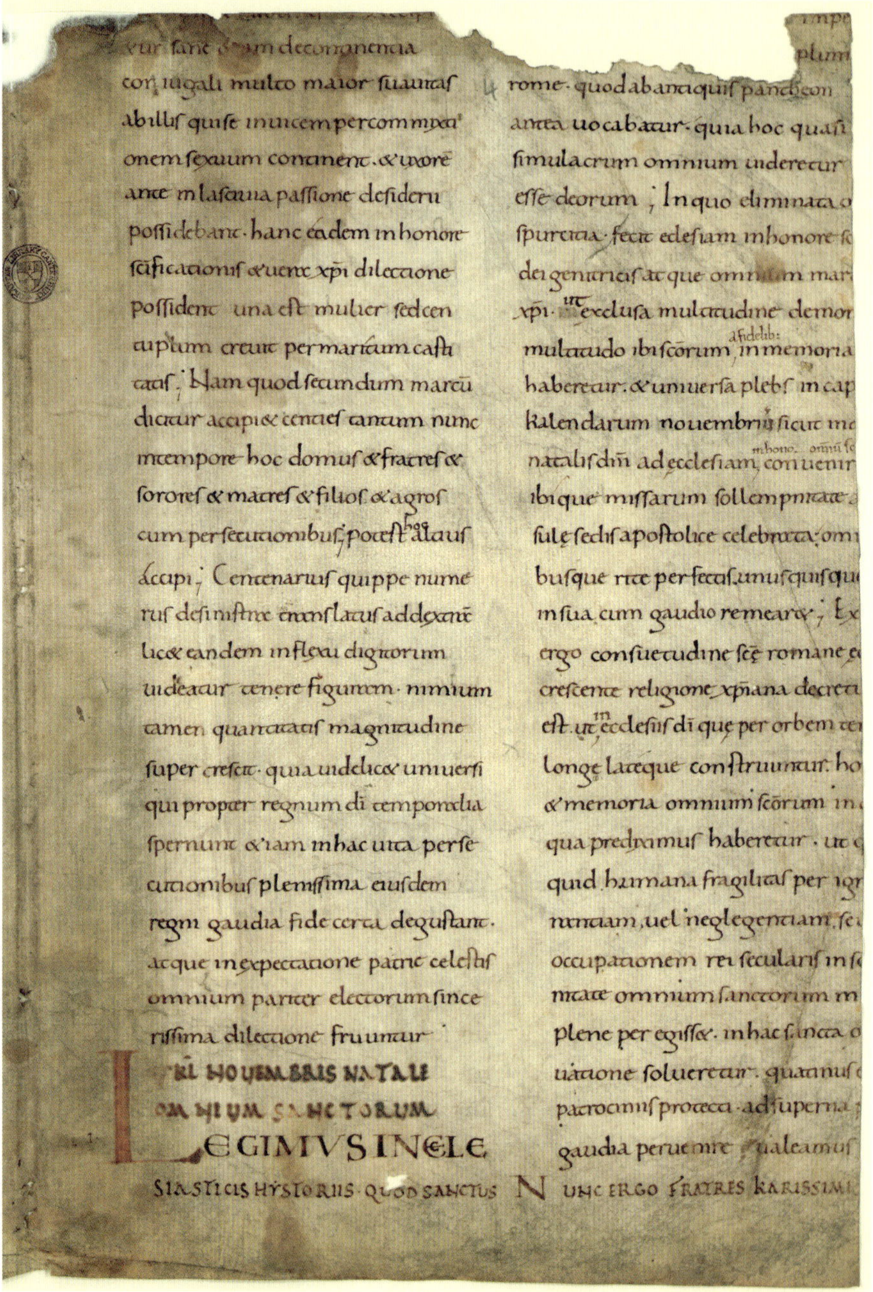
conjugali multo maior suauitas
abillis quisc inuicem percommixti
onem sexuum continent. & uxore
ante in lasciuia passione desiderii
possidebant. hanc eadem in honore
scificationis & uenit xpi dilectione
possident una est mulier sed cen
tuplum creuit per maritum casti
tatis; Nam quod secundum marcu
dicitur accipiet centies tantum nunc
in tempore hoc domus & fratres &
sorores & matres & filios & agros
cum persecutionibus; potest aliaus
accipi; Centenarius quippe nume
rus de sinistra translatus ad dextera
lic& eandem in flexu digitorum
uideatur tenere figuram. nimium
tamen quantitatis magnitudine
super crescit. quia uidelic& uniuersi
qui propter regnum di temporalia
spernunt & iam in hac uita perse
cutionibus plenissima eiusdem
regni gaudia fide certa degustant.
atque in expectatione patriae celestis
omnium pariter electorum since
rissima dilectione fruuntur
KL NOUEMBRIS NATALE
OMNIUM SANCTORUM
LEGIMUS IN ECLE
SIASTICIS HYSTORIIS. QUOD SANCTUS

rome. quod ab antiquis pantheon
antea uocabatur. quia hoc quasi
simulacrum omnium uideretur
esse deorum; In quo eliminata o
spurcitia. fecit eclesiam in honore sc
dei genitricis atque omnium mar
xpi. ut exclusa multitudine demon
multitudo ibi scorum in memoria
haberetur. & uniuersa plebs in cap
kalendarum nouembris sicut in
natalis dni ad ecclesiam conuenir
ibique missarum sollempnitate
sule sedis apostolice celebrata. omn
busque rite perfectis unusquisqu
in sua cum gaudio remear&; Ex
ergo consuetudine sce romane ec
crescente religione xpiana decret
est. ut in ecclesiis di que per orbem te
longe lateque construuntur. ho
& memoria omnium scorum in
qua predramus haberetur. ut q
quid humana fragilitas per ig
norantiam, uel neglegentiam, se
occupationem rei secularis in s
nitate omnium sanctorum m
plene per egiss&. in hac sancta o
uatione solueretur. quatinus
patrociniis protecta. ad superna
gaudia peruenire ualeamus
NUNC ERGO FRATRES KARISSIMI

9 Add. 127/1

Homiliary
England; *saec.* XI[1]
Illustrations: fols. 4r, 5v, 7r

Physical Description

Four non-consecutive bifolia. They are mounted separately within a guard-book but their leaves are foliated sequentially in a modern hand, '1'–'8'. The sheets are all more or less incomplete, cut down, and damaged, their surfaces weathered, stained and written on, as a result of re-use in *s.* xvi: more particularly, fol. 1 has lost much of its outer column; fol. 2 lacks large areas within its inner column and is badly damp damaged; the outer columns of fols. 3 and 4 are cropped; fol. 5 (the edges of which were turned in rather than sliced off) has lost portions at the top of its outer column, seemingly through damp; of fol. 6 only a slither of the inner column survives; fols. 7 and 8 were extensively scribbled on and ink-stained in the early modern period, and part of the outer column of the latter has been cut off.

The original parchment included holes and flaws (especially fols. 7 and 8). Maximum surviving page size: 410 × 266 mm. Written area: 310 × 200 mm. Two columns per page (column width: 90 mm). Lines: a maximum of 34. Space between lines: 9 mm. Height of minims: 2 mm. Ruling: hard point on each hair side (there are double boundary lines to either side of both columns, but seemingly only the first and last horizontal rulings were extended). At the joint of fols. 5 and 6, holes for sewing appear at 20, 30, 50, 95, 130, 160, 190, 200, 250, 260, 290, 340, 350, 360 and 370 mm from the upper edge.

Content

A homily collection descended from the Homiliary of Paul the Deacon (summer portion). The individual items (more or less imperfect) are as follows:

a) **[Fol. 1r, col. 1;** starts imperfect] // iohannes quidem … **[fol. 1r, col. 2]** sunt basilice [–part of line lost–] honore sancti io[hannis –

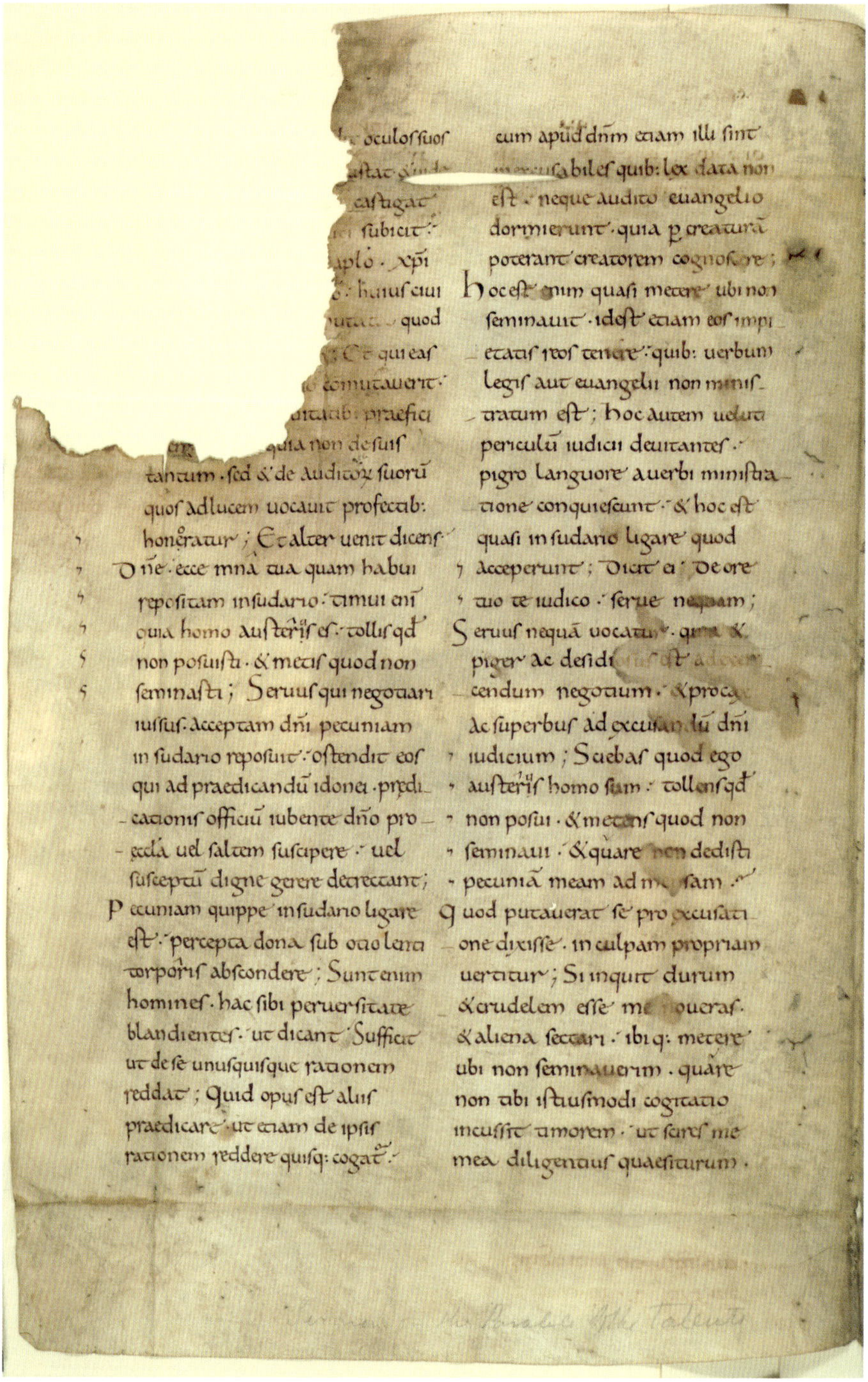

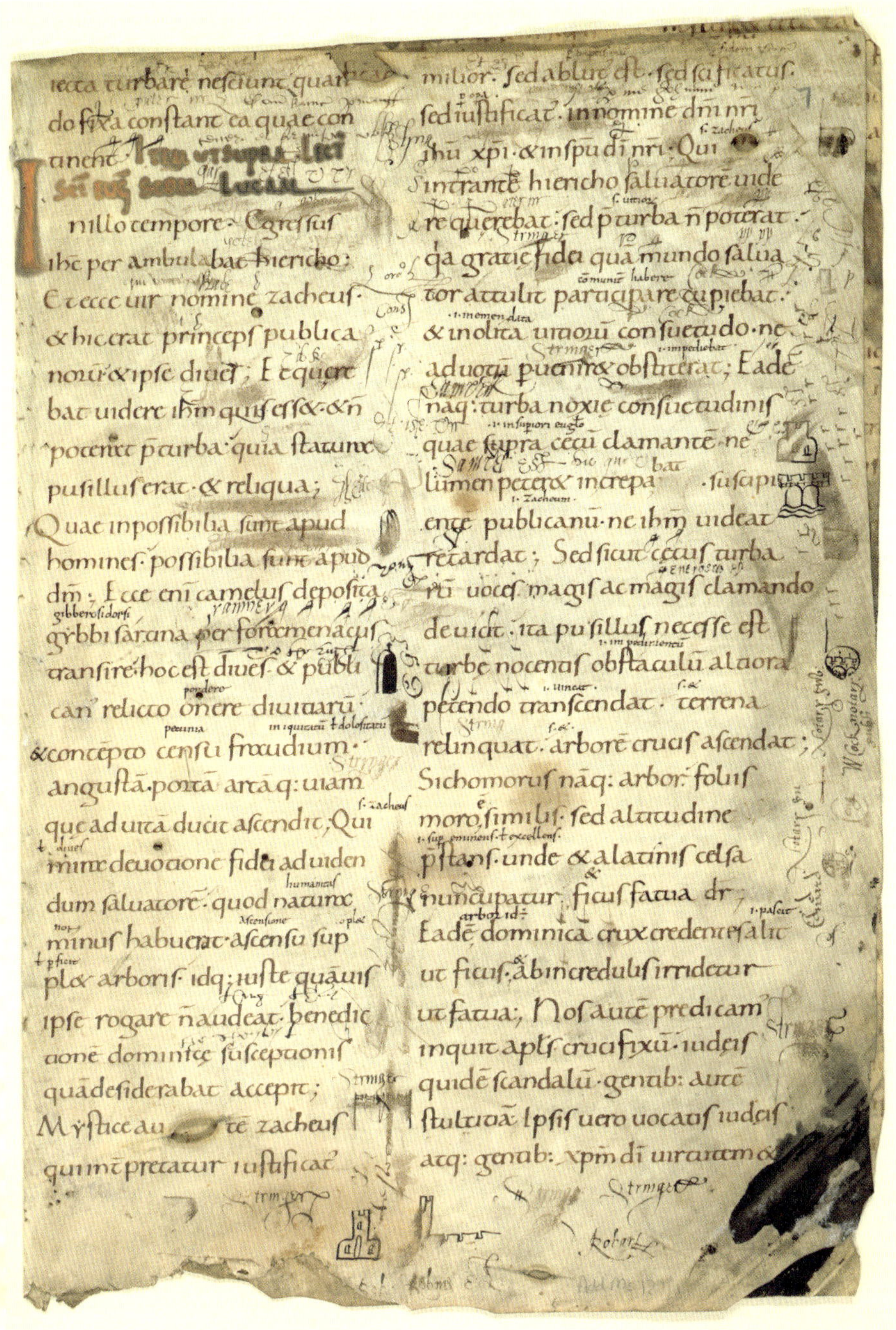

rest of line lost] // [Bede, *In Marci euangelium expositio* on Mk 6.17–29: CCSL 120, 509–10, ll. 803–24 (for Decollation of John the Baptist: 29 August)].

b) **[Fol. 1r, col. 2, line 4**; the second half of each line is lost]. *VI. ID. SEP. NATI*[...] / *INITIUM SANCTI EUA*[*NGELII*] / LIBER GEN[ERATIONIS]dauid filii Abrah[am] ... **[fol. 1v, col. 2]** ... In zara oriens, ad nostram salutem // [fragments of a composite homily, of which a complete version appears in Oxford, Bodleian Library, MS Barlow 4 (Northern France, ix$^{3/4}$; provenance Worcester). The first part is akin to lessons 7–8 of the homily for the third nocturn for the Nativity of the Virgin (8 September) in the Sarum Breviary (Procter and Wordsworth 1886, III, cols. 777–9), the end to Pseudo-Alcuin, *Interpretationes nominum hebraicorum*: PL 100, cols. 723–34, esp. 725.]

c) **[Fol. 2r, col. 1]** // [con]uersationis, sed ad profectum [ma]g[is] uite perfectioris inuitauit. Uocat peccatores, ... **[fol. 2v, col. 1]** ... qui sedens in trono patris cum sancto spiritu uiuit et regn[at Deu]s per omnia secula \seculorum/Amen [Bede, *Homiliarum Euangelii Libri* II, hom. I.21: CCSL 122, 153–5, ll. 202–68 (item II.99, 'In sancti Matthaei apostoli' (21 September) in Paul the Deacon's homiliary)].

d) **[Fol. 2v, col. 1, line 19]** *III KAL. OCT. DEDICATIO BASILICE SANCTI MICHAELIS ARCHANGELI.* Memoriam beati archangeli [michaelis] toto orbe uenerandam [thereafter very damp-damaged, perforated and imperfect]... **[2v, col. 2, bottom]** dei archangelus episcopum ?per? // [BHL 5948; MGH *Script. Rerum Langobardum*, 541–3; PL 110, 60–3; also PL 95, 1522–5].

e) **[Fol. 3r, col. 1]** // paruulos dominus suos uolebat esse discipulos, ... **[fol. 3v, col. 2]** quoniam melius est ut mundi amator in hoc seculo carnaliter uiuens se solum [per]dat // [Haimo of Auxerre, Homilia 7 in festo S. Michaelis archangeli: PL 118, cols. 772C–74A; PL 95, cols. 1526D–28A (Homilia 58 in the augmented version of Paul the Deacon's Homiliary)].

f) **[Fol. 4r, col. 1]** // [recipi]etur sane etiam de continentia coniugali multo maior suauitas ab illis ... **[fol. 4r, col. 1, l. 27]** atque in expectatione patrie celestis omnium pariter electorum sincerissima dilectione fruuntur [Bede, *In Lucae Euangelium Expositio*: CCSL 120, 329–30, ll. 1358–73, within the commentary on Luke 18.29–30].

g) **[Fol. 4r, col. 1, l. 28]** *KL. NOUEMBRIS NATALE OMNIUM SANCTORUM*. LEGIMUS IN ECLEsiasticis hystoriis, quod sanctus **[fol. 4v, col. 2]** [–lines lost–] rome, quod ab antiquis pantheon ... contemplantur. Alia uero ita deo coniuncta sunt angelorum agmina, // [start of a sermon for All Saints (1 Nov.) edited by Cross 1977].

h) **[Fol. 5r, col. 1]** // ordo doctorum est in circumcisionem missorum. ... **[fol. 5v, col. 2, bottom]** ... ut scires me mea diligentius quaesiturum, [Bede, *In Lucae Euangelium Expositio*: CCSL 120, 338–40, ll. 1693–1769 (on Luke 19.16–23), for one martyr].

i) **[Fol. 6r, col. 1, line 1**; only a sliver of the page survives] // Et quamdiu haec u [–rest of line lacking] minimis meis fecist[is – rest of line lacking, and so on] ... **[fol. 6v, col. 2,** top; largely missing] //–it benedictione ... **[fol. 6v, col. 2,** bottom line] suda- [–lost–] fructus [–lost–] -?um [–] -r [unidentified homily including citations of Matthew 25.40, Isaiah 58.7 and Luke 11.41].

j) **[Fol. 7r, col. 1, lines 1–3]** //–iecta turbari nesciunt quando fixa constant ea quae continent [very end of a homily for the dedication of a church].

k) **[Fol. 7r, col. 1, line 4]** *ITEM UT SUPRA LECT. SCI EUG. SCDM LUCAM*. In illo tempore. Egressus ihesus perambulabat hiericho. Et ecce uir nomine zacheus ... et reliqua [Luke 19.1–3]. Quae inpossibilia sunt apud homines, possibilia sunt apud deum, ... **[fol. 7v, col. 2, bottom]** hoc est noue lucis gratia corruscante, in humili credentium // [Bede, *In Lucae Euangelium Expositio*, CCSL 120, 333–5, ll. 1499–1566: beginning of homily on Luke 19.1–10 (II. 129, 'In dedicatione ecclesiae' in Paul the Deacon's Homilary)].

l) **[Fol. 8r, col. 1]** // aedificat supra fundamentum hoc [I Corinthians, 3.12], id est supra fidem christi ... **[fol. 8v, col. 2, bottom]** ... in futurum plenius passuri sunt. Nescitis qu[?omod]o templum dei sunt [corrected to:] estis [cf. I Corinthians 3.16] // [Haimo of Auxerre, *Expositio in Diuini Pauli Epistolas*: PL 117, col. 525C–527A].

Scribes and Script

The surviving main text was the work of four scribes, all writing a fairly neat and regular Anglo-Caroline minuscule:
i) (fols. 1r–4v) a thin, slightly forward-leaning and gently undulating hand, whose 'z's are larger than other letters, and whose 'us' abbreviation is a semi-circle placed well above (not joined to) the end of the relevant word;
ii) (fols. 5r and 6v) a slightly larger and plainer hand which uses a very spiky 'tail' for e-caudata;
iii) (fols. 5v–6r) a more characterful hand with slightly more pronounced serifs, and perhaps a stronger debt to indigenous Anglo-Saxon script than the others;
iv) (fols. 7r–8v) a neat hand, similar in weight and general aspect to scribe i, but clearly distinguished by the treatment of individual letters.

Abbreviation is restrained. Punctuation: point, medial point, and *punctus elevatus* (all for minor pauses), semi-colon (major pause), and *punctus interrogativus*. There are original 'acute' accents. Sentence capitals are a hybrid alphabet in which rustic capital elements predominate. Scriptural quotations are marked by diples.

There are corrections and glosses by several *s.* xi hands. Some of this work (e.g. fol. 1v, col. 2, l. 20, 'omnium'; fol. 3v, col. 2, l. 8, '† ostendit', and possibly also fol. 3r *passim*) was very probably by the scribe of the passage in question, while other interventions were by a different member of the original team (e.g those on fol. 2v, col. 2 were added by main scribe ii). Two further hands are represented. A, who was responsible for numerous interlinear explanatory glosses on fols. 7r–v (e.g. fol. 7r, col. 2, l. 3, 'qui' glossing 'Zacheus'; l. 7, 'participare' glossing 'communiter habere'; l. 9 'obstiterat' glossing, 'id est impediebat'; l. 13, 'publicanum' glossing, 'id est Zacheum'), is broadly contemporary with the original stratum and may be a member of the original team whose principal pages have not come down to us. By contrast, B (who was responsible for adding 'a fidelibus', and possibly also '† in hono[rem] omnium s[anctorum]' to fol. 4r, col. 2, ll. 10 and 13) is manifestly later, writing an elegant and exaggerated Anglo-

Caroline minuscule of a type generally associated with Saint Augustine's Abbey from xi^{2}–xii^{in}.

Decoration

None. Individual homilies are announced by a rubric in red rustic capitals; they are headed by an enlarged red initial (three lines high), followed by one or two lines of display script – rustic capitals (e.g. fol. 1r), uncials (fol. 2r), or hybrid monumental capitals (fol. 4r).

History and Provenance

Written in England in the earlier eleventh century, corrected and glossed very shortly thereafter, the volume was still seeing active use in the second half of the century as the small additions to fol. 4r indicate. The script of this annotation points to a Canterbury (Saint Augustine's) provenance by this time, though the sample is too small for certainty.

The manuscript had been dismembered and was being used for cover sheets by 1580, as numerous additions indicate. Added dates or dated notes include: (on fol. 1r) 1580; (on fol. 2v) 1594 1595, 159–; Annis 1594 1594; (on fol. 3r) 1582 –3 –4 ; (on fol. 4v) capitula / celebrata, 1582–1584; (on fol. 5r) 1580–1582, 1580, 1581, 1582; (on fol. 6v) Uisitationes 1580–82; (on fol. 8v) 1587, 1589. The bifolia 3–4 and 5–6 were probably recovered from the Archdeacon's Court Libri Cleri for 1580 onwards (cf. X.2.3). In contrast to the other sheets, the bifolium 7–8 bears very extensive 'doodling' by divers early modern hands. These include: ink sketches of towered and crenellated structures (at least one probably a church, another possibly a bridge), many names (some repeated) – notably: (fol. 7r) Stringer (many times), Robart, W. Cock notary (cf. fol. 8v), 'notary gwb', Cramner [sic], Strong; (fol. 7v) Iohannes; (fol. 8r) Thomas Cranmer; and (fol. 8v) Stryngham, Royton, Edward, Robartus Royston, and Cock – along with various pen trials, and a couple of apothegms. This bifolium thus shows every sign of having served for some time as a desk-top pen-trial sheet prior to its use as a wrapper.

Commentary

This is the remnant of a once imposing book or set. Judging by the number and quality of the hands represented in the surviving fragments, it was produced in an important and well-run scriptorium. The fragments were initially linked (Ker 1977) to the bifolium PRC 49/2 (**no.** 7), which was subsequently identified as a separate collection – the Homiliary of Haymo of Auxerre (Cross and Hall 1993). Whilst it is just conceivable that these may have been companion volumes, it should be stressed that, contrary to published opinion, there is no scribal connection, and hence no link, between them (see further **no.** 7). Physically and palaeographically closer, in fact, is the enigmatic fragment Add. 122 (**no.** 10), and it is not impossible that it was once part of the present collection; however its exiguous survival and parlous state make certainty on the point elusive (see **no.** 10 for further discussion).

In its complete form, the present volume (or set) was a relative of the homiliary of Paul the Deacon, monk of Monte Cassino († *c.* 797). Compiled at the behest of Charlemagne, this was designed to provide a selection of readings from the Fathers for the (monastic) night office on Sundays and feast days throughout the church year. Paul generally took complete sections – as opposed to extracts – from the works in question, drawing above all on Bede and Gregory the Great. The collection was divided into a *pars hiemalis* (running from the fifth Sunday before Christmas to the Saturday of Holy Week), and a *pars aestivalis* (Easter to Advent), augmented by a *commune sanctorum*. Promoted by Charlemagne as the official homiliary of the Frankish kingdom, it enjoyed fairly wide distribution, and was inevitably subject to alteration and expansion. It was evidently known in England by the late tenth century since Ælfric of Eynsham († *c.* 1010) had access to a version; however the Canterbury fragments are, in fact, the oldest extant English witness. Indeed, they represent the only unequivocally pre-Conquest copy to have come down to us. The next English witness, which is also in Canterbury: U4/20/2 (**no.** 13), dates from around the time of the Conquest. Comparable collections – displaying different degrees of divergence from Paul the Deacon's original compilation – then survive in some number from the end of the eleventh century onwards, showing that several versions of the homiliary circulated in early Norman England. The extant manuscripts of this period can be associated with Bury St Edmunds (a copy imported from France), Canterbury (Saint Augustine's Abbey), Durham, Glastonbury, Lincoln, Norwich, Rochester, Salisbury, and Worcester.

Given that none of the surviving post-Conquest versions belonged to Christ Church, Canterbury, it is tempting to propose the cathedral as a leading candidate for having been the home of one or other, or both, of the earlier copies whose fragmentary remains are there today and which were manifestly re-used locally at the Reformation. If the script of U4/20/2 (**no. 13**) is compatible with a Canterbury origin, the same cannot so easily be said of the present item. The hand-writing of these fragments, although not wholly incompatible with production in Canterbury in the first third of the eleventh century (a period from which the number of identifiable non-deluxe books is small), hardly supports such a proposition since the minuscule forms in question were widely used in southern England at the time, while the display script is not of a distinctively Canterbury form. Thus, although the nature of correcting hand 'B' suggests that the present book was at Canterbury – more probably Saint Augustine's than Christ Church – in the generation after the Conquest, the question of its origin is best left open.

Bibliography

Clayton 1985, p. 218; Cross and Hall 1993.

10 Add. 122

Opus incertum (homiletic fragment)
Southern England; *saec.* XI[1]
Illustration: best-preserved side

Physical Description

A number of small and very decayed fragments, presumably from a single leaf. The most substantial portion is an irregular strip (maximum dimensions *c.* 168 × *c.* 85 mm) that once ran diagonally across the text-area of the page, and which includes parts, all more or less imperfect, of 18 lines of writing. One side of this fragment, though extensively eroded, distorted, stained and mottled (seemingly from damp), remains easily legible; the other side, severely darkened and damaged by an adhesive, is barely so. The smaller fragments, equally irregular, some preserving odd letters, vary in size from *c.* 70 × 75 mm to little more than specs of dust. The largest of them is joined to equally-damaged remnants of a heavy-gauge paper. The parlous state of the item would seem to reflect hard re-use as a cover or board-lining, and severe damp and mould damage. Extremely fragile and highly vulnerable, the item is not currently available for consultation.

The original page was set out in two columns (estimated column width: 85 mm). Space between lines: 10 mm. Height of minims: 3 mm. Ruling: hard point.

Content

Part of a homily which includes a quotation from Psalm 36.25. The following letters or words survive more or less intact on the principal fragment:

[Best-preserved side, column 1] // quar- / -d miser?i / -r, nec ideo / -ceptum est. / integris, / [?mul]tamur. / a et / -demo- / [–?–] /

[Best-preserved side, column 2] //-lum secul[i?] / -abitur in gloria / … -ptura, affliget? / … iusti fame / -quam qui propt- / [?la]rgiretur, teste psal / mista, iunior fui et enim / [sen]ui, et non uidi iustum / derelictum, nec seme[n] / quaerens panem [Ps. 36.25] … / ad iungit. Dispersit / pauperr[?imis] / sed multis … / [–?–] / -imp- / qui[?t].

[Poorly preserved side, column 1] //?ren / -st- / ?creme / ?uestra / ?mosina d? / non solum corpor[aliter] / [?sed] etiam spirit[ual]iter / ?m / corrigimus, / ?inem / [?a]postolus ?si cui offi- / ?est pr ?d /

Scribes and Script

A neat, late standard Anglo-Caroline minuscule with a rectilinear matrix. Minims tends to start with a slight curl to the left and end with a slight curl to the right; ascenders are modestly clubbed. Most 'a's are low-backed but there is one very high-backed example. The horizontal stroke of 't' and the tongue of 'e' are calligraphically extended when they occur at the end of words. Word separation is very generous. Punctuation: 'semi-colon' (usage unclear); *punctus elevatus* (minor pause) and medial point (minor pause). The two surviving sentence capitals seem to be of rustic form.

History

There is no record of the context from which this fragment – doubtless recycled as a wrapper or part of a binding in *s.* xvi – was recovered.

Commentary

The tiny fragments of legible and semi-legible text do not seem to correspond to any of the main published Patristic or Carolingian writings that cite Psalm 36 verse 25, suggesting that they may be part of a less well-known or 'composite' homily.

Handsomely written and spaciously set out in two columns, this must once have been a fairly grand book. It may profitably be compared with the broadly contemporary Add. 127/1 (**no. 9**). Indeed, given that the present item shares with Add. 127/1 the same basic layout, column width, line spacing, and script size, that it shows a similar pattern of damp damage, and that its scribe is closely comparable to the hand responsible for fols. 5r and 6v of that item, it is not impossible that it was once part of the same manuscript. However, as the identification of hands is plausible rather than certain, as the precise text here is currently unidentified, and as the history of the present fragment is a blank, the question must remain open.

Wholly undocumented, exiguous in the extreme, and on the verge of disappearing utterly, this disintegrating fragment provides a vivid and sobering advertisement of the fragility of our knowledge of the literary resources of Anglo-Saxon England – and of the past in general.

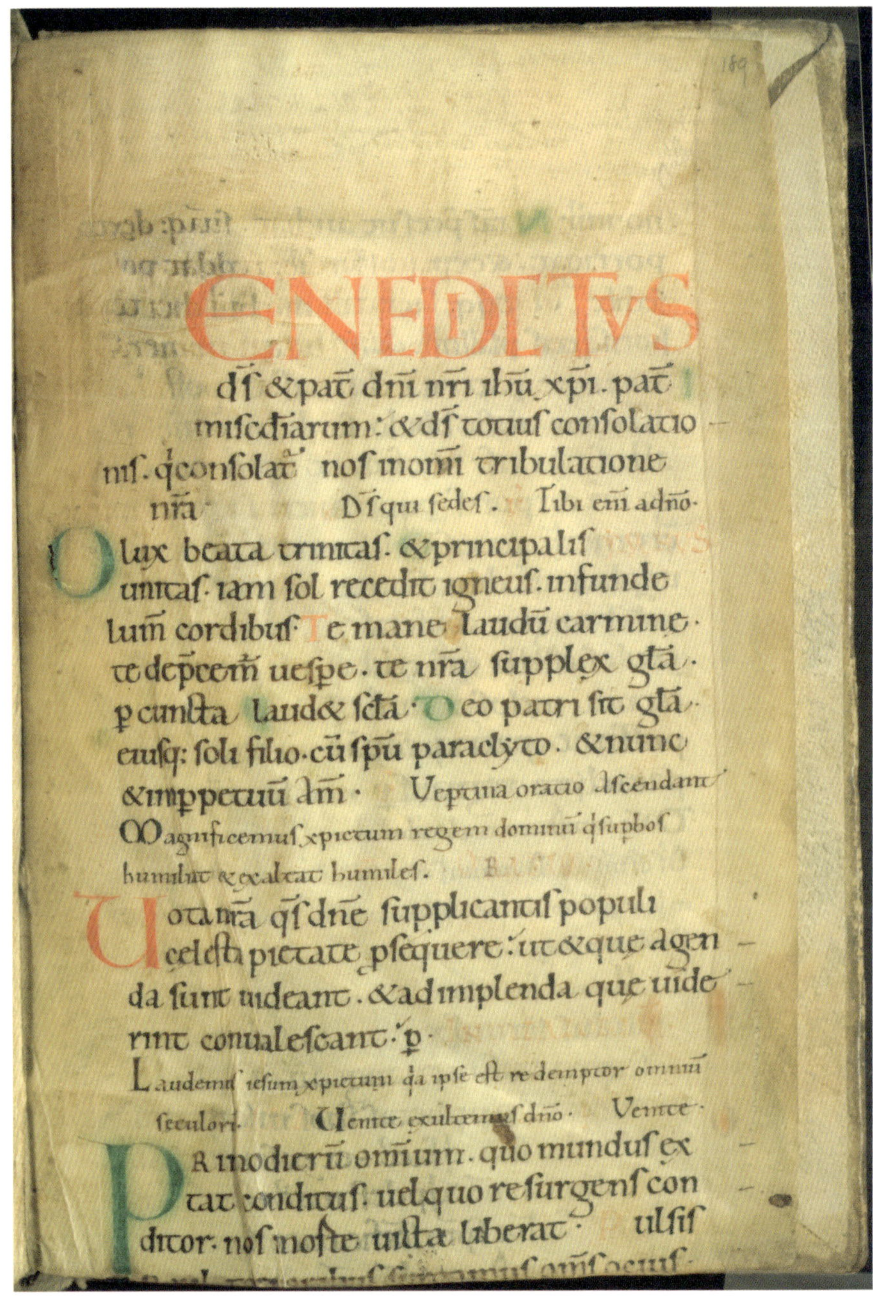

11 Add. 172, endleaf

Collectar
Canterbury; *saec.* XI$^{3/4}$
Illustration: fol. 189r

Physical Description

One bifolium (now fols. 186 and 189) which was cut down and re-used in the s. xi$^{4/4}$ volume, Add. 172 (**no. 15**). The originally blank fol. 186 received the end of the Apocalypse text (gentium in illam (21.26) ... Gratia domini nostri ihesu christi cum omnibus uobis. Amen (22.21)), while the written folio (189) was used as the rear paste-down. The latter has subsequently been 'liberated'. Fol. 189r is mildly stained. Fol. 189v, which was pasted to the back board, is badly damaged: a large quantity of the ink has transferred to the board, and the surface of the parchment is frayed and paste-stained, affecting legibility.

Size: now 190 × 126 mm (the dimensions of the host book); originally probably at least 250 × 150 mm. Written area originally *c.* 172 × 94 mm. Lines: originally 28, of which 26 remain intact (the 27th was truncated, the 28th lost when the leaf was cut down). Space between lines: 7 mm. Height of minims: 3 mm. Ruling: hard point.

Content

Collectar fragment (?reject leaf).
[Fol. 189r] [B]ENEDICTVS deus et pater domini nostri iesu christi, pater misericordiarum et deus totius consolationis, qui consolatur nos in omni tribulatione nostra [Günzel 1993, no. 73.94; Dewick 1914, col. 78].
R. Deus qui sedes [Dewick, col. 53].
V. Tibi enim a domino.
Ymnus. O lux beata trinitas, et principalis unitas, iam sol recedit igneus, infunde lumen cordibus. Te mane laudu[m] [sic] carmine, te deprecemur uespere, te nostra supplex gloria, per cuncta laudet secula. Deo patri sit gloria eiusque soli filio, cum spiritu paraclyto, et nunc et imperpetuum [sic] amen [Dewick, cols. 53, 357; Milfull

1996, no. 1, pp. 109–111].
V. Vespertina oratio ascendant.
Magnificemus christum regem dominum qui superbos humiliat et exaltat humiles [Dewick, col. 71].
ORATIO. Uota nostra quesumus domine supplicantis populi celesti pietate prosequere, ut et que agenda sunt uideant, et ad implenda que uiderint conualescant. Per [Davril 1995, no. 85]
INVITATORIUM. Laudemus iesum christum quia ipse est redemptor omnium seculorum.
[Illegible rubric] Uenite exultemus domino [Psalm 94]
Ps. Venite.
Primo dierum omnium, quo mundus extat conditus, uel quo resurgens conditor, nos morte uicta liberat. Pulsis [in the next line only the tops of the letters survive:] procul torporibus surgamus omnes ocius [(one line wholly lost, doubtless:) et nocte queramus pium sicut prophetam] **[fol. 189v]** nouimus. Nostras preces ut audiat, suamque dextram porrigat, et expiatos sordibus reddat polorum sedibus. Ut quique sacratissimo huius diei tempore horis quietis psallimus, donis beatis muneret. Iam nunc paterna claritas, te postulamus affatim, absit libido sordidans omnisque actus noxius. Ne feda sit uel lubrica conpago nostri corporis, per que [sic] auerni ignibus, ipse crememur acrius. Ob hoc redemptor quesumus, ut proba nostra diluas, uite perhennis commoda nobis benigne conferas. Quo carnis actu exules, effecti ipsi celibes ut prestolamur cernui, melos canamus glorie. Presta pater piissime, patrique compar unice, cum spiritu paraclyto, regnans per omne seculum, amen [Milfull, no. 3, pp. 115–17].
A. Domine in uirtute tua [–obliterated–] rex.
[Obliterated rubric] Ipsum. [Partly obliterated rubric: –?– M N']
Ps. Deus deus meus [Ps. 21]
A. Dominus regit me ... collocauit [very damaged; Dewick, 55, 70 etc.].
[Rubric obliterated] Ipsum.
Domini est terra [Psalm 23].
A. Oculi mei semper ad dominum.
Ps. [Obliterated].
Memor fui nocte [Dewick, 512, 516, 517]

L[obliterated, doubtless *-ectio* ...] Paulus seruus christi ihesu uocatus apostolus segregatus in euangelium ... ex resurrectione [the lower part of this last line has been cut off] mortuorum, Iesu Christi Domini nostri. Per [Romans 1.1–4/5]

Collation of the two hymns with the most recent edition of other early English copies (Milfull 1996) highlights the variants listed below. The reading of the present manuscript is given first, followed by that of Milfull's base text, the mid-eleventh-century Canterbury hymnal in Durham (Cathedral Library, MS B. III. 32).

In *O lux:* Canterbury fragment, laudum [Milfull, l. 5, laudent (our reading is unparalleled in early English copies); carmine [l. 5, carmina (our reading paralleled in CCCC, MS 391 and Bodleian Library, MS Douce 296); uespere [l. 6, uesperi (our reading unparalleled); laudet [l. 8, laudent (our reading paralleled in CCCC, MS 391, BL, Add. MS 37517, MSS Cotton Vesp. D. xii and Harley 2961, and Bodleian Library, MS Douce 296); imperpetuum [l. 12, in perpetuum (our reading unparalleled).

In *Primo dierum:* Canterbury fragment, liberat [Milfull, l. 4, liberet (our reading paralleled in BL, MS Cotton Vesp. D. xii); porrigat et [ll. 10–11, porrigat ut (our reading paralled in BL, MSS Cotton Vesp. D. xii, and Harley 2961); que [l. 23, quam (our reading – assuming that quem was intended – is paralleled in MS Harley 2961); benigne [benignus (our reading paralleled in CCCC, MS 391); regnans per omne seculum [et nunc et in perpetuum (our reading paralleled in BL, Add. MS 37517, MSS Cotton Julius A. vi, Cotton Vespasian D. xii and Harley 2961).

At a later date (s. xii), after the leaf had been incorporated into the host book, a series of informal pencil jottings was added to the top of fol. 189r. Always faint, these are now virtually illegible.

Scribes and Script

The original text is the work of a single scribe writing a neat, tall, rounded, late standard Anglo-Caroline minuscule of the sort pioneered in the second and third decades of the eleventh century by the Christ Church scribe Eadwig Basan, and widely used thereafter (see, e.g., **nos. 12, 13, 15, 17, 18**). Characteristics of the present interpretation of the script include wedge-shaped serifs, gently-rising feet, a generous tilde that ends in a blob, a *punctus elevatus* which is very much a tick and a point, and an 'acute' accent (persèquere, fol. 189r, line 16) which is a long thin line, ending in a small down-stroke; also notable are 'a's whose high back is generally the same height as other minims but which, at the start of a word, may rise to the level of an ascender. A smaller lighter, vertically more compressed version of the script was used for the cues. Punctuation: low point (minor pause), medial point (major and minor pauses), and *punctus elevatus* (major and minor pauses). It is, for a liturgical text, fairly heavily abbreviated.

The hand is very similar to that of the scribe of Add 20 (**no. 12**) and of the more formally written Canterbury pontifical, Cambridge, Corpus Christi College, MS 44, with both of which, moreover, it shares the same highly characteristic accent: it is eminently likely these scribes were one and the same person.

Decoration

The initial B on fol. 189r was not supplied; the space that was reserved implies that a letter at least six lines high was envisaged; a faint lead sketch for the lower bowl remains visible. The remainder of the word (-enedictus) is written in red in two-lines-high monumental display capitals. The principal divisions are headed by large (two-lines-high) coloured capitals, alternately red and green. The green pigment of the 'O' on the recto has attacked the parchment. Individual sentences within *O lux* and *Primo dierum* are headed by small coloured capitals, alternately red and green. The red that was used for the rubrics has – unlike that used for the initials – faded almost to invisibility.

History

The style of the script suggests that the leaf was written in Canterbury (on the question of where exactly in the town the scribe may have been based, see the **Introduction**) during the third quarter of the eleventh century. Re-used shortly thereafter, it had probably in fact been 'rejected' at an early stage of production: the doubtful reading 'laudu[m]' and the erroneous 'imperpetuum' for 'in perpetuum' were not corrected, and whilst the minor initials were supplied, the principal one was not; moreover, it is difficult otherwise to account for the fact that the conjoint half of the bifolium remained blank (being eventually used for the end of the Apocalypse in the 'new' volume). Thereafter the history of the leaf was identical to that of the host book (see further **no. 15**).

⁊ inmon heora penegas to scē
martinus mæssan · iosepes lypas
to eastron · ⁊ heora gescy on þā
monþe nouembre ·

De elemosinis accipiendis
·xl·

Si aliquis uni sacerdoti p missa
uel sua pro confessione aut
clerico pro psalmis & ymnis seu
pro se ipso uel pro quo lib& caro
suo aut uiuente aut mortuo ·
aliquid in elemosinam dare
uoluerit · hoc sacerdos uel clerus
attribuente accipiat · & exinde
quod uoluerit faciat · Si autē
attribuente omnibus sacerdotibus aliquid elemosinam datum fuerit · hanc elemosinam
communem habeant & psalmo-

12 Add. 20

Chrodegang of Metz, *Regula canonicorum* (in Latin and Old English)
Canterbury; *saec.* $XI^{3/4}$
Illustration: fol. 1v

Physical Description

A fragmentary bifolium: the text-area of fol. 1 is substantially complete, but the outer half of that of fol. 2 has been trimmed off, as have all the outer margins. The scar of a later fold runs horizontally across the surviving sheet as a whole (which, when folded, received groups of perforations in two places). Though weathered and stained, the general condition of what remains is remarkably good.

Fragment size: 233 × 274 mm. Sufficient remains to reconstruct the original page size as in the region of *c.* 320 × 200 mm. Written area: 218 × 112 mm. Width of inner margin: 43 mm. Lines: 19. Space between lines: 12 mm. Height of minims: 5 mm. Ruling: hard point (sharp and neat) on what is probably the hair side; the extended horizontal continues right across the leaf (confirming that it was ruled 'open'). The original centre-fold has sewing holes at 3, 40, 70, 90, 125, 165 and 220 mm from the current upper edge (a thread of uncertain date still runs through three of them).

Content

Chrodegang of Metz, *Regula canonicorum* (bilingual version), ch. 39 (Old English), most of ch. 40 (Latin), and parts of ch. 43 (Old English).
[Fol. 1r] // Se healfa dæl þæra preosta … and feower gemacan sceona finde man ælcum. **[fol. 1v]** And nimon heora … on þam monþe nouembre. *DE ELEMOSINIS ACCIPIENDIS. XL.* Si aliquis uni sacerdoti … hanc elemosinam communem habeant et psalmo-// [Langefeld 2003, pp. 249–50 (where this manuscript is siglum 'D'); cf. Napier 1916, p. 48, line 18–p. 49, l. 1].
[Fol. 2r] //þonne hit ger[ist] [–lost–] [myn]stres ealdras, … [æl]þeodigan, mid sw[ylcre] [arwurð]nysse underf[o] … [letters

lost] **[fol. 2v]** [letters lost] and he him heora ... swa [micle ma eo]wer ælc sceal oþres // [Langefeld 2003, p. 255 (where the text surviving in our manuscript is indicated by underlining); cf. Napier p. 51, lines 8–26]. [NB: on the recto only the first half of each line survives, on the verso only the second half.]

Scribes and Script

The fragment is the work of a single scribe, writing an elegant hand to a grand scale; his ink remains a rich, dark black, and the general effect is highly calligraphic. As was customary, different letter-forms were used for the Latin and the Old English texts (high-backed 'a' for Latin, low-backed 'a' for OE; 'd' with a tall straight back in Latin, with a short curving-over one in OE; high-set 'f' in Latin, low-set one in OE; Caroline 'g' – Insular 'g'; Caroline 'r' – Insular 'r'; rising 's' – descending 's', not to mention the OE letters ð, þ and wyn), the scripts being respectively a late, standard Anglo-Caroline minuscule and a late Old English minuscule. The letters of both alphabets are adorned with small feet and wedge-shaped serifs, but while the serifs on Latin letters are purely triangular, those on Old English ones have a slight 'spike' to the left. Notwithstanding the differences in specific letter-forms, the matrix of the Old English alphabet has been fully acculturated to that of the Latin one, and their weight and regularity are identical, creating a single, harmonious aesthetic. There is hardly any abbreviation (merely the use of þ with a tilde for 'þæt', and the suspension of a couple of final 'm's). 'Et' is represented by an ampersand (with a large body and a small head) in the Latin texts and by the Tironian form in the Old English. Punctuation: medial point (used for both major and minor pauses – being slightly bolder when indicating the former as opposed to the latter). In addition, a small 'comma', almost certainly the work of the original scribe, was inserted to indicate word division where this might otherwise have been unclear (fol. 1v, l. 9). Ys are dotted throughout. There are original 'acute' accents (of a distinctive, sharply-angled, thin-tailed form) in the Latin text.

The hand has been plausibly identified as that of the main scribe of the pontifical, Cambridge, Corpus Christi College, MS 44

(Bishop 1960; see also Budny 1997, no. 46), who in addition to using closely similar letter-forms wrote to a stately gauge and practised identical accenting. The same scribe was probably also responsible for the collectar fragment that was re-used as an endleaf in Add. 172 (**no. 11**): though smaller in scale, the writing displays all the same distinctive features. The pontifical, apparently produced for an archbishop of Canterbury – who is more likely to have been Stigand (1052-70) than Lanfranc (see Dumville 1992, pp. 92–3; Budny 1997, I, p. 677; Orchard 2002, I, pp. 76–7) – was doubtless made in Canterbury, though whether at Christ Church or Saint Augustine's Abbey is a matter of debate (see further **Introduction**). Bishop (1960) identified the hand responsible for interlinear Latin glosses in the pontifical as that of the Saint Augustine's Abbey scribe who was responsible for Lit. A. 8 (**no. 17**) and U3/162/28/1 (**no. 18**) along with other items. The late eleventh-century provenance of this manuscript would seem, therefore, to have been Saint Augustine's; however, this is hardly conclusive evidence for the origin of a book that was made at least a generation earlier for the use of an archbishop. The collectar fragment was also at Saint Augustine's Abbey by the end of the eleventh century (see **no. 11**). The medieval provenance of the present item, by contrast, was possibly Christ Church (see **History** below).

Decoration

None, and it is doubtful that there would ever have been more than perhaps an enlarged or embellished first initial. Individual chapters are headed by plain coloured capitals (two lines high), red for the Old English, orange for the Latin – though whether this was a general pattern is now unknowable. The one surviving rubric (for the Latin ch. XL) is written in orange rustic capitals.

History and Provenance

Written in Canterbury (see **Scribes and Script**), this is quite possibly the copy of the text that was recorded among the *libri anglici* in the Christ Church library catalogue from the time of Prior Henry of Eastry (1284–1331): 'Regula canonicorum a.' (James 1903, list II, no. 317, p. 51). The surviving sheet was one of a group of fragments – recovered at unrecorded dates from unidentified contexts – that were (re)discovered in a box in the Cathedral Library in 1946. A shelf-mark was added in pencil to the inner margin by William Urry; a basic identification of the text was pencilled on separately by a similar *s.* xx hand.

Commentary

Chrodegang, bishop of Metz from 742 to 766 and founder of the abbey of Gorze, confident of Charles Martel and of Pepin the Short, was a reformer of canonical life, to which end he wrote his *Rule* (*c.* 755–6), in the first instance for the canons of Metz. In the second quarter of the ninth century a revision of Chrodegang's text was augmented with sections from the *Institutio canonicorum* promulgated by Louis the Pious in 816–17 and with other material to produce a version in eighty-four as opposed to the original thirty-four chapters (the chapters preserved in the present fragment legislate on clothing and on the taking and giving of alms). This fuller edition, the earliest manuscripts of which were written somewhere in western France, was subject to modest revision in its turn. The total number of surviving continental manuscripts of all versions is very modest: a mere nine – to which one further copy, associated with Angers and known in the mid-seventeenth century but subsequently lost from sight, may be added.

The enlarged text had reached England by the earlier tenth century, if not before, and had been translated into Old English before the millennium; a list of names interpolated into chapter two of the only complete copy of the vernacular text links its archetype with the Old Minster, Winchester. Only one pre-Conquest English copy of the Latin text alone survives: Bruxelles, Bibliothèque royale, MS 8558–8563 (part I) of $x^{2/4\text{-med}}$, in which the work is accompanied by Augustine's *Soliloquia* (fols. 38v–77v) and Ps.-Augustine (Caesarius), *De igne purgatorio* (fols. 77v–79v), all written by the same scribe. It would be most interesting to know where this part of this composite volume was produced, but unfortunately there is no evidence to answer the question. There are two other bilingual (Latin-Old English) copies in addition to the present item: one (Cambridge, Corpus Christi

College, MS 191, written at Exeter in s. xi²) is complete; the other (London, BL, Add. MS 34652, fol. 3, of unknown origin and probably of slightly later date, s. xi^{ex}) is even more fragmentary than ours, being a single cut-down leaf. In terms of size and elegance, the copy represented by the Canterbury fragment was originally the most imposing of the three.

The fact that all three bilingual copies date from the second half of the eleventh century is consonant with other evidence for a revival of interest in secular cathedral clergy from the reign of Edward the Confessor (1042–66); indeed we know that the Cambridge manuscript was written and owned by just such a community – the regular canons whom Bishop Leofric established at Exeter on moving his see there in 1050. As noted above, the present fragment is firmly linked to Canterbury by the hand of its scribe. Either Christ Church or Saint Augustine's may have been interested in a 'reference copy' at this time, but such is more intelligible for the former owing to its association with an archbishop, who, moreover, had under his aegis the nearby cathedral of Rochester which was staffed with secular canons until *c.* 1080 (the *Regula canonicorum* defines the role and responsibilities of a bishop in relation to communities of canons). If the circumstance that the same scribe also wrote a pontifical might then raise the possibility that this highly talented calligrapher could have been responsible for a suite of archiepiscopal books, such speculation must immediately be tempered by the fact that the holder of this office for most of the relevant period, the self-serving, secular clerk Stigand (1052–70), is not the most obvious patron for such a venture. The fact that some of this scribe's work was certainly at Saint Augustine's Abbey shortly after the Conquest further complicates the situation. Whether the evidence is best explained in terms of the movement of books, the movement of monastic personnel, or the participation of a non-monastic 'professional' scribe, is an open question.

Bibliography

Ker 1957, no. 97; Bishop 1960, p. 95; Dumville 1992, p. 71; Doane and Pulsiano 1997, no. 109; Gameson 1999, no. 187 with pl. 1 (showing fol. 1r); Langefeld 2003, esp. pp. 46–7.

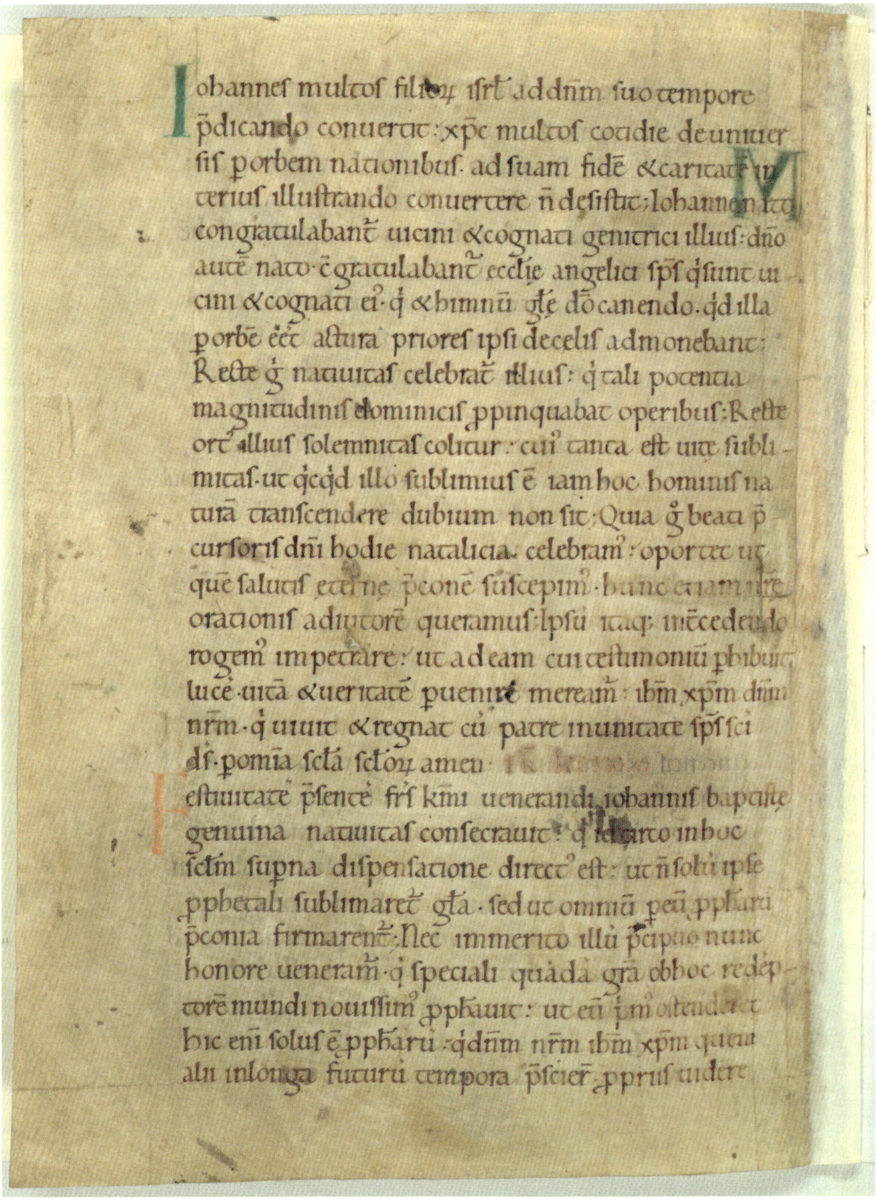

Iohannes multos filiorum isrł ad dnm suo tempore
pdicando conuertit: xpc multos cotidie de uniuer
sis porbem nationibus. ad suam fide & caritate in
terius illustrando conuertere n desistit; Iohannem [illegible]
congratulabant uicini & cognati genitrici illius: dno
aute nato congratulabant ecclie angelica sps q sunt ui
cini & cognati ei. q & hymnu gle do canendo. qd illa
porbe ee actura priores ipsi decelis admonebant:
Recte g natiuitas celebrat illius: q tali potentia
magnitudinis dominicis ppinquabat operibus: Recte
ort illius solemnitas colitur: cui tanta est uite subli-
mitas. ut quicquid illo sublimius e iam hoc hominis na
tura transcendere dubium non sit; Quia g beati p
cursoris dni hodie natalicia celebram: oportet ut
que salutis eterne pcone suscepim. hunc etiam [illegible]
orationis adiutore queramus: Ipsu itaq: intercedendo
rogem impetrare: ut ad eam cui testimoniu phibuit
luce uita & ueritate puenire mereamur: ihm xpm dnm
nrm. q uiuit & regnat cu patre in unitate sps sci
ds. pomia scla sclorum amen. [illegible]
Festiuitate psence frs kmi uenerandi iohannis baptiste
genuina natiuitas consecrauit: q ideirco in hoc
sclm supna dispensatione directus est: ut n solu ipse
pphetali sublimaret gra. sed ut omniu petiu pphtaru
pconia firmaret: Nec inmerito illu pcipuo nunc
honore ueneram. q speciali quada gra ob hoc redemp-
tore mundi nouissim pphauit: ut eu [illegible] ostenderet
hic eni solus e pphtaru. qd dnm nrm ihm xpm quem
alii in longa futura tempora pscier pprius uidere

13 U4/20/2

Homiletic Lectionary
Southern England (?Canterbury); *saec.* XI$^{3/4}$
Illustration: fol. 2v

Physical Description

Two leaves. They are adjacent ones, but it is unclear whether or not they were originally conjugate (and hence the centre of a quire) since their current 'joint' is entirely a modern restoration and there is seemingly no record of their state when recovered from their *s.* xvii host book (for which see **History** below). Both leaves have been cut down, and are moderately stained, but overall their condition is reasonable. They have been artificially joined at their ragged inner margins with modern parchment to form a bifolium and mounted within a stiff folder. They are currently mounted incorrectly: fol. 2 should precede fol. 1.

Size of original parchment: *c.* 299 × 215 mm. The cropped rubrics on fol. 1r reveal that the outer margin was formerly at least 50 mm in width: assuming that the four margins were calibrated according to the 'normal' principles, this would imply a minimum original page size of *c.* 350 × 225 mm. Written area: 253 × 147 mm. Lines: 29. Space between lines: 8–9 mm. Height of minims: 3 or more mm. Ruling: hard point (there are double vertical boundaries, but only the first and last horizontals are extended).

Content

A collection of short homiletic readings in liturgical order. What survives comprises the end of a series for John the Baptist, followed by the start of an item (or set) for SS. Peter and Paul (24 and 29 June respectively). The following account presents the material in its original order. Cross-references are supplied to the corresponding texts in BL, MS Royal 2 C. iii, a *s.* xi^{ex} Rochester manuscript of an expanded version of Paul the Deacon's Homiliary.

[Fol. 2r] // benedicendi restituitur, sed de eo etiam prophetandi gratia uirtus augetur [Bede, *In natiuitate J. Bapt.*: PL 94, col. 210, lines 10–11; Cf. Royal 2 C. iii, fol. 76v, col. 2]. *.X.* Merito ergo per orbem sancta ecclesia que tot beatorum martirum uictorias quibus ingressum regni celestis meruére frequentat, ... Erit enim magnus coram domino [Bede: PL 94, col. 210, ll. 14–27; Royal, fol. 76v, col. 2–77r, col. 1]. *.XI.* Iure igitur tam domini quam precursoris eius natiuitas festiua deuotione celebratur, ... qui dono sui spiritus sedem sibi uteri uirginalis in quo carnem susciperet ipse consecrauit [Bede: PL 94, col. 210, ll. 27–45; as Royal, fol. 77r, col. 1]. **[Fol. 2v]** *.XII.* Iohannes multos filiorum israel ad dominum suo tempore predicando conuertit, ... ut ad eam cui testimonium perhibuit lucem, uitam et ueritatem peruenire mereamur; ihesum christum dominum nostrum, qui uiuit et regnat cum patre in unitate spiritus sancti deus. per omnia secula seculorum amen [cf. Bede: PL 94, col. 210, l. 45–col. 211, l. 15; much fuller version in Royal, fol. 77r, col. 1 ff.]. *Feria lectio .I.* Festiuitatem presentem fratres karissimi uenerandi iohannis baptiste genuína natiuitas consecrauit, ... qui dominum nostrum ihesum christum quem alii in longa futurum tempora prescienter propriis uidere **[fol. 1r]** oculis meruit, et annuntiare presentem [Ps.-Maximus, Hom. 67: PL 57, col. 389, ll. 1–13; fuller version in Royal, fol. 79r, col. 2–79v, col. 1]. *.II.* Veniente enim domino ad baptismum sicut sacratissimum euangelium refert, ... et attestantis uocem patris audiret e celo [Ps.-Maximus: PL 57, col. 389, l. 13–col. 390, l. 4, slightly adapted; cf. Royal, fol. 79v, col. 1]. *.III.* Hic est fratres ille iohannes, quem inspirante domino propheta prenuntiauit esias dicens, Vox clamantis in deserto, parate uiam domini. ... quia ille omnimodis maior erat iohanne qui de uirgine nascebatur [Ps.-Maximus: PL 57, col. 390, ll. 4–16; Royal, fol. 79v, cols. 1–2]. *FERIA LECTIO .I.* [for later rubrics, see **Scribes and Script** below] Precursor redemptoris nostri, iohannes ab angelo uocari iussus est, ... ipso etiam suo **[fol. 1v]** nomine signauit. Meritoque ... per quem suae regenerationis mundo auctor ostenditur. *.II.* Quis fratres huiusmodi prophetam non tota admiratione suscipiat quem tantum recognoscit optinuisse de deo, ... nec pristinum recepisset usum, nisi nomen pueri quo uocandus esset clausi oris eius uincula relaxasset [lines 1–6: Ps.-Maximus, Hom. 67: PL 57, col. 387, l. B21–col. 388, l. B5]. *.III.* Aduertite ergo dilectissimi fratres quantam huic electo domini reuerantiam deuotionis debeamus impendere, ... gaudia stupenti mundo testis fidelissimus reuelauit [Ps.-Maximus: PL 57, col. 390, ll. 19–30; Royal, fol. 79v, col. 2]. *DE SANCTIS APOSTOLIS PETRO ET PAULO .I.* Omnium quidem sanctarum solemnitatum dilectissimi totus mundus est particeps, et unius fidei pietas exigit, ... nostre urbis // [Leo, Sermo 82: PL 54, col. 422, ll. 1–7; Royal, fols. 83v, col. 2–84r, col.1].

Scribes and Script

The extant leaves are written by a single scribe in a neat, upright, late standard Anglo-Caroline minuscule. The hand is elegant, spacious and well-controlled, and there are very generous spaces between words (though the scribe was not particularly concerned to achieve a regular right-hand border). There are regular wedge-shaped serifs and equally regular slightly rising feet, which frequently touch the neighbouring letter. Distinctive forms include a 'g' which often has a very slight gap between the head and the tail, a fairly even-armed 'x', and an ampersand with a small head, a large body and a long upper limb. Abbreviation marks are of generous proportions. The degree of lateral compression, allied to the distinct upward slant of the feet, suggests a date of xi$^{3/4}$. Punctuation: medial point (for minor pause), *punctus elevatus* (minor pause), and 'semi-colon' (major pause). There are occasional 'acute' accents. Sentence capitals are a mixed, though predominantly rustic, alphabet. Rubrics (badly faded) are in red rustic capitals.

Two rubrics were subsequently added in the outer margin of fol. 1r beside 'Feria Lectio I'. The first, 'De sco iohanne & // [the remainder cut off]' is written in a rather retrospective *s.* xi hand. The second, 'R[?equire] retro post na// [the remainder cut away]', probably dates from *s.* xii.

A further addition was made to the outer margin of fol. 1r in an informal cursive hand of late medieval or early modern date; however this was both crossed through and rubbed out and is now difficult to decipher.

Decoration

None survives. Such a volume is unlikely to have had very much, if any. Sections are headed by large plain capitals (two to two-and-a-half lines high), alternately green and red-orange. The green pigment has attacked and eroded the parchment.

History

The manuscript was written around the time of the Norman Conquest. The use of a script type that was widely practised in southern England for much of the eleventh century (see **nos. 11, 12, 15, 17, 18**) impedes localisation on palaeographical grounds alone; however, given that the epicentre of this style of writing was Canterbury, an origin there is not unlikely, a hypothesis to which the early modern provenance of the leaves (see below) lends some support. The second added rubric on fol. 1r indicates that the manuscript continued to be used in the twelfth century. The later annotation on the same page attests to intervention in the late medieval or early modern period which was itself subsequently deemed inappropriate, or conceivably – in a changing religious climate – dangerous, and was vigorously erased. Doubtless a casualty of the Reformation, the leaves were used in the binding of the minutes of Fordwich Borough Court for 1550–1621 (U4/20/1): it seems likely that they have never moved very far from where they were made. The property of Fordwich United Charities/The Archives of the Borough of Fordwich, the minute book and these leaves were deposited in Canterbury Cathedral Library in 1955.

Commentary

The close correspondence between the texts that were drawn upon to create the lections in our fragment and those presented for the same occasions in the expanded homiliary of Paul the Deacon († *c.* 797) – the oldest extant English witness to which is Add. 127/1 (**no. 9**) – shows that the present leaves come from a redaction of that work. On the other hand, comparison with the much fuller texts in the corresponding sections of the Rochester copy, BL, MS Royal 2 C. iii (fols. 76v–84r), which moreover are generally subdivided quite differently, underlines how much variation was possible within this broad tradition. Reflecting in part its more selective content, the present item also stands apart from the other early English witnesses (including Add. 127/1) in terms of presentation: its compact size, long lines, and spacious script are in sharp contrast to their larger, two-column, more densely-written format.

It is greatly to be regretted that so little of this once-handsome manuscript survives, impeding detailed analysis of what is now, for its date, a very rare type of liturgical book. The nature and quality of the script, and the elegant general presentation, allied to its post-medieval provenance, make an origin in one of the Canterbury houses a very appealing hypothesis – though in the absence of any positive evidence it can be no more than that. (See further in general **no. 9**.)

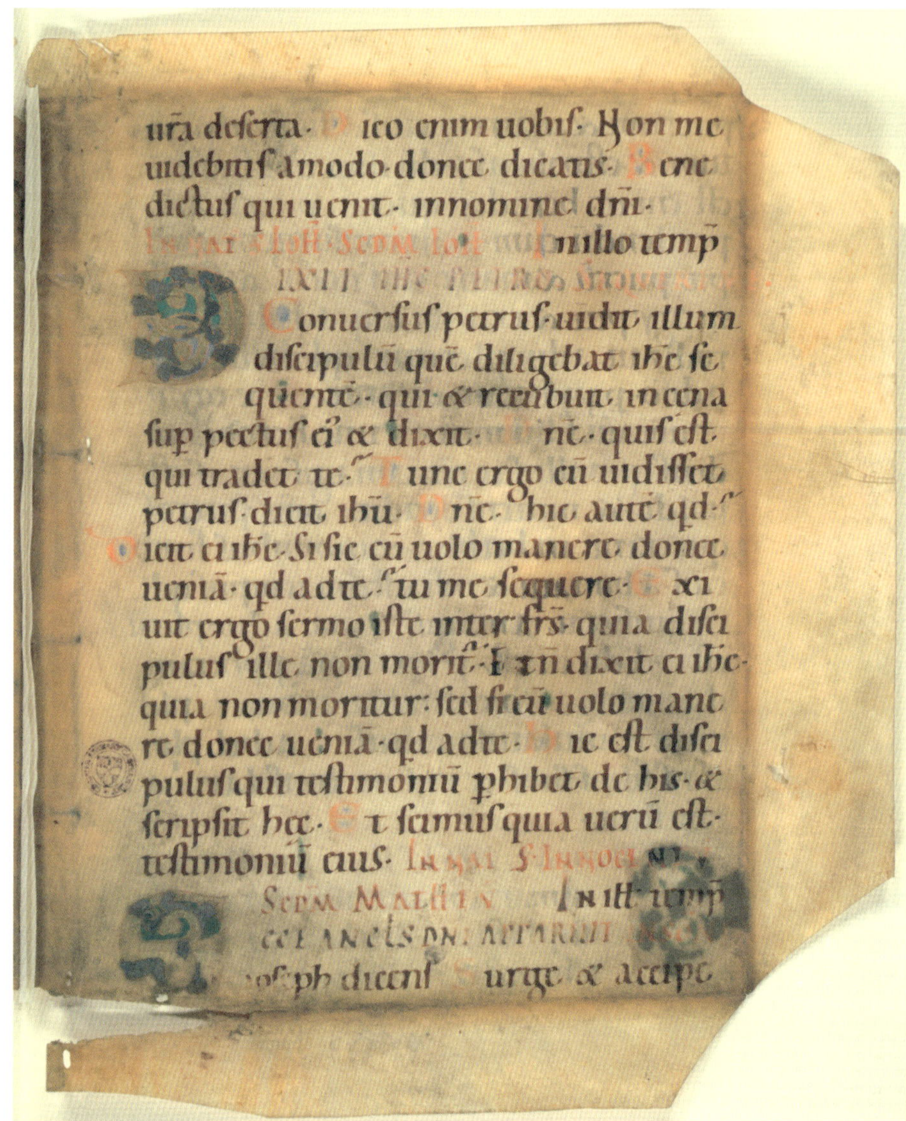

ura deserta. Dico enim uobis. Non me
uidebitis amodo donec dicatis. Bene
dictus qui uenit. in nomine dñi.
In nat s ioh. Secdm ioh. In illo temp
LXII ihc petro ...
Conuersus petrus uidit illum
discipulū quē diligebat ihc se
quentē. qui & recubuit in cena
sup pectus ei & dixit. Dñe. quis est
qui tradet te. Tunc ergo cū uidisset
petrus dicit ihū. Dñe. hic autē qd.
Dicit ei ihc. Si sic eū uolo manere donec
ueniā. qd ad te. tu me sequere. Exi
uit ergo sermo iste inter frs. quia disci
pulus ille non morit. Et n dixit ei ihc.
quia non moritur: sed si eū uolo mane
re donec ueniā. qd ad te. Hic est disci
pulus qui testimoniū phibet de his. &
scripsit hec. Et scimus quia uerū est.
testimoniū eius. In nat s innocent.
Secdm Matth. In ill temp
Angelus dni apparuit ...
Ioseph dicens Surge & accipe

14 Add. 128/12 and Add. 128/72

Gospel lectionary
Southern Germany (Bavaria, Carinthia); *saec.* XI²
Illustration: Add. 128/12, fol. 2r

Physical Description

Two damaged bifolia, showing similar scars of re-use: the outer corners were cut off and strips along all four sides were folded over in order to fit the sheets to the covers of smaller volumes (measuring *c.* 220 × 160 mm), the impressions of whose spines are clearly visible in the inner margins; two pairs of slits for ties perforate the outer margins. One side of Add. 128/72 (fols. 1r and 2v) is mildly discoloured from an adhesive, traces of which also mark Add. 128/12, fol. 1r. Add. 128/12 remains folded; Add. 128/72 has been straightened out. Despite their traumatic history, the written areas of both bifolia are substantially intact.

Page size: 278 × 230 mm (Add. 128/12); 265 × 225 mm (Add. 128/72). Written area: 223 × 152 mm. Lines: 23. Space between lines: 10 mm. Height of minims: 5 mm. Ruling: hard point – on what are now the 'inner faces' of Add. 128/12 (fols. 1v and 2r) and the 'outer ones' of Add. 128/72 (fols. 1v and 2r); these were presumably the hair sides, though it is impossible now to tell.

The text of Add. 128/12 runs continuously from fol. 1v to 2r, indicating that this bifolium stood at the centre of its quire – which was probably the first quire in the book (see **Commentary**). The text missing between the two halves of Add. 128/72 (fols. 1v and 2r) would require one bifolium to accommodate it, suggesting that this sheet was the second from the centre of its quire (i.e. a lost bifolium stood within it (see further **Content** and **Commentary**)).

Content

Gospel lectionary fragments: Add 128/12 has a standard series of readings for Christmas Day, the feasts of St Stephen, of St John, of Holy Innocents, and the first Sunday after Christmas; Add. 128/72 has parts of the readings for Maundy Thursday and Good Friday.

[Add. 128/12, fol. 1r] *INITIUM SANCTI EUANGELII SECUNDUM IOHANNEM.* IN PRINCIPIO ERAT UERBUM Et uerbum ... ex uoluntate **[Fol. 1v]** uiri, ... Plenum gratia et ueritate [John 1.1–14].

IN NATALE SANCTI STEPHANI SECUNDUM MATHEUM. In illo tempore. DICEBAT IHESUS turbis iudeorum et principibus sacerdotum, Ecce ego mitto ad uos prophetas et sapientes ... **[Fol. 2r]** Benedictus qui uenit in nomine domini [Matthew 23.34–9].

IN NATALE SANCTI IOHANNIS SECUNDUM IOHANNEM. In illo tempore. DIXIT IHESUS PETRO, SEQUERE ME. Conuersus petrus uidit illum discipulum ... Et scimus quia uerum est testimonium eius [John 21.19–24].

IN NATALE SANCTORUM INNOCENTIUM SECUNDUM MATHEUM. In illo tempore. ECCE ANGELUS DOMINI APPARUIT IN SOMNO ioseph ... Surge et accipe **[Fol. 2v]** puerum et matrem eius ... Rachel plorans filios suos et noluit consolari quia non sunt [Matthew 2. 13–18].

DOMINICA IN FERIA NATALE DOMINI SECUNDUM LUCAM. In illo tempore. ERAT IOSEPH et Maria ... et benedicit illis Symeon // [Luke 2.33–4; doubtless originally 2.33–40].

[Add. 128/72, fol. 1r] // et plebe dixit ad illos. Obtulistis mihi hunc hominem ... Et pilatus ad iu\di/cauit fieri peticionem eorum **[fol. 1v]** [d]imisit aut[em] illis eum qui propter homicidium et sedicionem missus fuerat in carcerem ... latrones [un]um a dextris, et alium a sinistris // [Luke 23.13–33; doubtless originally 22.1–23.53 for Feria quarta Passio Ihesu Christi].

[Lost bifolium with Luke 23.34–53 and John 13.1–10, the latter presumably introduced by a particularly grand initial, and perhaps other artwork.]

[Fol. 2r] // Dicit ei ihesus, Qui lotus est non indiget nisi ut pedes lauet sed est mundus totus ... ut quemadmodum ego feci uobis, ita et uos faciatis [John 13.10–15; doubtless originally 13.1–15 for Feria V in Caena domini].

FERIA VI, IN PARASCEUE, PASSIO DOMINI SECUNDUM IOHANNEM. In illo [tempore]. EGRESSUS

IHESUS CUM DISCIPUlis suis, trans torrentem cedron, ubi erat hortus ... Iudas ergo cum acc[episset (lost)] cohortem, et a pontificibus [lost: et pharisaeis mi-] **[fol. 2v]** -nistros uenit illuc cum laternis [sic], et facibus et armis ... Cohors ergo et tribunus, et ministri iude[(lost:) -orum conp]rehenderunt ihesum, et ligaue[(lost:)runt eum et addux]erunt ad annam primum // [John 18.1–13; doubtless originally 18.1–19.42].

The scriptural texts depart from a 'normalised' Vulgate (Weber 1983) as follows (the reading in the Canterbury fragments is always presented first).

Mt 2.17: hieremiam [Ieremiam. Mt 23.34: et ex illis [ex illis. Mt 23.34: et crucifigetis – originally omitted, added by a correcting hand. Mt 23.34: sinagogis [synagogis. Mt 23.35: in templum – changed to 'inter templum' by correcting hand. Mt 23.37: Hierusalem x 2 [Ierusalem x 2. Mt 23.37: congare (uncorrected error) [congregare. Mt 23.38: relinquetur [relinquitur.

Lk 23.14: interrogans (a correction *in rasura* by the original scribe, seemingly for 'interrogantem'). Lk 23.18: Exclamauerunt [Exclamauit. Lk 23.18: et dimitte barabban [et dimitte nobis barabban. Lk 23.19 and 23.25: sedicionem [seditionem. Lk 23.21: crucifige crucifige eum [crucifige crucifige illum. Lk 23.22: tercio [tertio. Lk 23.24: peticionem [petitionem. Lk 23.26: apprehenderunt [adprehenderunt. Lk 23.26: symonem [simonem. Lk 23.26: imposuerunt [inposuerunt. Lk 23.27: lamentabantur [lamentabant. Lk 23.33: in locum qui dicitur calvarie [in locum qui uocatur caluariae. Lk 23.33: et alium a sinistris [et alterum a sinistris.

Jn 1.9: uenientem [ueniens. Jn 1.14: gratia et ueritate [gratiae et ueritatis. Jn 13.10: non indiget nisi ut pedes lauet sed [non indiget ut lauet sed. Jn 13.14: laui pedes uestros [laui uestros pedes. Jn 18.1: Egressus ihesus [Iesus egressus est. Jn 18.2: tradebat eum locum [tradebat eum ipsum locum. Jn 18.2: ihesus illuc conuenerat [Iesus conuenerat illuc. Jn 18.3: laternis [lanternis. Jn 18.10: Symon [Simon. Jn 18.10: auriculam eius dextram [eius auriculam dextram. Jn 21.20: tradet te [tradit te. Jn 21.21: Tunc ergo [Hunc ergo. Jn 21.22: Si sic eum [Si eum. Jn 21.23: Sermo iste inter fratres [Sermo iste in fratres. Jn 21.23: Et (over erasure) non dixit ei Ihesus quia non [Non autem dixit ei Ihesus non.

Almost all the divergencies are well-attested variants or – in the cases of Matthew 23.37, John 18.3 and John 21.21 – obvious errors. A notable rare reading is the 'quia' at John 21.23 which ultimately echoes an Old Latin version, being paralleled, for instance, in Brescia, Biblioteca Queriniana, s.n., and BnF, MS lat. 17225, Italian copies dating from *s.* vi and v respectively, whose texts have a strong Old Latin character.

Scribes and Script

The text is elegantly written by a single scribe in a high-grade, late Caroline-early Romanesque minuscule of south German type. The matrix of the alphabet is rectilinear, the strokes are heavy, and the minims fill exactly half of the interval between the ruled lines. The tops of strokes are adorned by wedge-shaped serifs, while most down-strokes end in a curve to the right – the exceptions being 'i' (which has a wedge-shaped foot), and the first strokes of 'h', 'm', and 'n' (which taper to a point). The descender of 'p' also tapers to a point, but that of 'q' is terminated with a horizontal line-serif. Distinctive forms include: the occasional use of curling-backed 'd' alongside the straight-backed form (the latter constructed by drawing a complete oval for the bowl and then running the staff through the side of it); a 'g' whose generous tail forms a complete loop which is bigger than the head; and a striking 'z' which is the size of a majuscule. Punctuation: principally medial points (for both major and minor pauses) along with a rather heavy *punctus interrogativus*; however there is a lone, original 'tick and point' *punctus elevatus* signalling a minor pause on Add. 128/72, fol. 1v. Sentences are headed by bold red capitals with counter-spaces in green or blue. Rubrics are in orangey-red rustic capitals whose form is characteristic of south German manuscripts.

The spaciousness and weight of the script are typical of the formal writing used for gospel books and high-grade liturgica in the major scriptoria of Salian Germany. Both in terms of general aspect and in points of detail the hand belongs to the so-called 'schrägoval' (slanting oval) style, which emerged at the beginning of the eleventh century and continued throughout the twelfth

(Bischoff 1981, pp. 34–8), being widely practised in the duchies of Bavaria and Carinthia (modern Austria). More regularised than early work in the style, yet displaying none of the lateral compression or spikiness that characterises twelfth-century versions of it, the general aspect of our scribe's hand points to a date in the second half of the eleventh century.

Though formally handsome, the initial transcription was not particularly accurate. The original scribe made a modest interlinear insertion on Add. 128/72, fol. 1r, a neat correction *in rasura* on Add. 128/72, fol. 1r and a rather messy one on Add. 128/12, fol. 2r. He also overlooked the '[I]n illo tempore' that should introduce John 18.1 on Add. 128/72, fol. 2r and then had to squeeze it in as best he could (even using a compressed hand, only 'In illo', and not 'In illo tempore' as elsewhere, could be supplied). A different contemporary hand effected two interlinear rectifications on Add. 128/72, fol. 1v. A couple of errors remained uncorrected (see **Content**).

Decoration

Each pericope is introduced by a fine decorated initial ('I' on fol. 1r of Add. 128/12, 'D' on fol. 1v, 'D' and 'E' on fol. 2r, and 'E' on fol. 2v; along with 'E' on fol. 2r of Add. 128/72), accompanied by up to one line of red display script (generally rustic capitals). Their basic letter-shapes adorned with orderly foliate curls, the initials are rendered in gold and silver (now badly oxydised) and set against blue and green grounds with occasional red details; the contours are outlined in orange. Most are three to four lines high. The largest (ten lines high) and most elaborate is the first (I*n principio*), which also includes a blue beast-mask halfway up the stem. The red display capitals that accompany it are bolder than the others and a monumental hybrid alphabet was used (not rustic capitals as elsewhere). It is highly likely that a similarly large initial headed the (lost) incipit of the reading for Good Friday (see **Commentary**). The style of the ornament, like that of the script, points to the southern German territories and to Bavaria and Carinthia in particular, being paralleled in the work of scriptoria in such centres as Regensburg, Salzburg and Tegernsee.

History

The combined witness of the script and decoration indicates that the book was made in Bavaria or Carinthia in the later eleventh century; its subsequent history is undocumented. Notwithstanding their different recent histories, the two bifolia were clearly used in the same post-medieval binding campaign – though where and when is unclear. Faint traces of an informally-written title arranged in two lines can just be discerned at what was then the top of the spine of Add. 128/72: ?'–lus' / '–sias–'. No record was seemingly kept of the context in the cathedral's collection from which Add. 128/12 was recovered, though it has clearly been in Canterbury for some considerable time. Add. 128/72 was purchased in March 2005 from Maggs (their *European Bulletin* 23, Catalogue 1366 (London, 2004), no. 73, with colour illustration on inside front cover) who had obtained it at auction in Munich (Zisska & Kistner, 28 October 2003, lot. 1) – though it is thought to have passed through the London market at an earlier date.

Commentary

This is the remains of a once very fine, south German gospel lectionary. The first bifolium (Add. 128/12) comes from near the beginning of the book: only two or three readings – Matthew 1.18–21, Luke 2.1–14 and Luke 2.15–20 – are likely to have preceded the first surviving lection. In the xi^{med} gospel lectionary from Cologne, Dombibliothek, MS 144, for example, the above-mentioned readings occupy fols. 1r–2r, with John 1.1–14 (the first lection on our bifolium) on fol. 2v. A realistic hypothesis for the start of the present volume – which was slightly more elaborate than Cologne MS 144 – would thus be: a protective blank leaf (fol. 1), a major decorative page for the start of the first text, 'Cum esset desponsata' (fol. 2r), with the remainder of that reading (Matthew 1.18–21) along with Luke 2.1–14 and 15–20 occupying fols. 2v, 3r and 3v. John 1.1–14 (the content of the first surviving recto) would thus have appeared on fol. 4r, the first page of the central bifolium of the quire (which this Canterbury leaf patently was). In the most opulent examples of the genre – ranging from the late tenth-century Codex Egberti (Trier, Stadtbibliothek, MS

24) to the s. xii[1] gospel lectionary perhaps from Prüm (BnF, MS lat. 17325) – the text proper is preceded by full-page images of the four evangelists, and sometimes also by dedicatory images and verses. Whether such was the case in the present, slightly less ambitious manuscript – implying a further preliminary quire before the one just discussed – is now unknowable.

As the second Canterbury bifolium (Add. 128/72) comes from much further into the book, it is impossible to establish its original position in the same way; however, the textual content of the rest of its quire may still be reconstructed with some confidence. The leaves that preceded the first page will have been occupied by part of the long reading Luke 22.1–23.53, a portion of which (23.13–33) appears on fols. 1r and 1v. This reading will have ended on the following leaf, originally the innermost bifolium of the quire, which will also have carried the start of the reading John 13.1–15 – the end of which appears on fol. 2r. It is followed by the start of the long reading John 18.1–19.42, which will have continued over the last leaves of the quire and, perhaps, beyond. The amount of text missing between fols. 1v and 2r would have covered approximately three pages: this indicates that a bifolium and not just a singleton would have been required, and also implies that a particularly large initial, possibly even a miniature, was included (marking the start of the lection for Good Friday), filling the extra space. With this in mind, it is worth considering the circumstance that the hard point rulings on our sheet furrow fols. 1v and 2r when, if it was the second sheet from the centre of a normally-constructed quaternion of the period, one would have expected them to mark the other side (i.e. fols. 1r and 2v). Three explanations present themselves. In the first place, this might merely be the result of an anomaly in assembling the sheets. Secondly, the quire might in fact have been a quinion, with three bifolia 'outside' and one 'inside' the present one. Thirdly, the normal ordering of hair and flesh sides might have been reversed for some or all of this quire, the obvious motive being to ensure that the illuminator could effect the incipit to the Good Friday reading on his preferred side of the parchment.

It is most unfortunate that there is no direct evidence for when and how the manuscript arrived in England, or the state in which it did so. The bifolium that has manifestly been in Canterbury for a long time (Add. 128/12) may have travelled there after the Reformation as a passenger of its unknown host-volume. However, given that the dismembering and recycling of such a manuscript is in line with the treatment meted out to so many unquestionably local items in the sixteenth and seventeenth centuries, and that it clearly predates the secularisation of the monasteries in Germany (1803) – the most obvious occasion for the disposal and dismembering of a fine medieval book in the area in which this one was made – one may reasonably suggest that it reached England and Canterbury at a much earlier date. Christ Church certainly exported high quality books to Germany in the eleventh century – the Arenberg Gospels (New York, Pierpont Morgan Library, MS M 869) went to Cologne or its suburb Deutz, the Eadwig Gospels (Hannover, Kestner-Museum, MS WM XXIa 36) to Hersfeld – and handsome volumes may equally have travelled in the other direction. The betrothal of the young Princess Matilda of England to the Emperor Henry V in 1108x9, her presence in Germany from 1110 (with her marriage to the Emperor in 1114), and her return to England as a widow in 1126, provide the most conspicuous contexts for the transmission of luxury German books to England a generation or so after the present manuscript was made. The illustrated copy of Matilda's life that was made in Germany but had reached England by the later middle ages, ending up in the collection of Matthew Parker (now Cambridge, Corpus Christi College, MS 373), is plausibly suggested to have been brought to England by her in 1126.

15 Add. 172

Cantica Canticorum; *Epistolae Pauli* (glossed); *Apocalypsis Iohannis*
Canterbury, Saint Augustine's Abbey; *saec.* XI$^{4/4}$ (partly datable after 1076)
2° folio: si ignoras te o pulchra
Illustrations: Binding, fols. 1v, 9v, 116r, 147r, 170r

Physical Description

Folios: iv (original parchment leaves, the first the front paste-down) + 189 (fol. 189 was originally the rear paste-down: see **no. 11**). The volume consists of three distinct but broadly contemporary parts which were clearly brought together almost immediately: A) fols. 1–8, quire I; B) fols. 9–162, quires II–XX; and C) fols. 163–89, quires XXI–XXIV.

Structure: the preliminary gathering (front paste-down plus fols. i–iii) consists of two bifolia, the first leaf of the outer one being the paste-down attached to the front board. The main body of the volume comprises 24 quires, whose first rectos are fols. 1, 9, 17, 25, 33, 41, 49, 57, 65, 73, 81, 89, 97, 105, 113, 121, 129, 137, 147, 157, 163, 171, 178, and 186 respectively. Quires I–XI, XIII–XVII and XXII–XXIII are regular quaternions. Quire XII (fols. 89–96) is a quaternion in which leaves 3 and 5 (fols. 91 and 94) are half-sheets; quires XVIII (fols. 137-46) and XIX (fols. 147–56) are quinions; XX (fols. 157–62) a ternion; while the final quire, XXIV (fols. 186–9), comprises two bifolia, the last leaf of which was originally the rear paste-down (fol. 189) – thus matching the structure of the preliminary quire. There are no signatures. The parchment is arranged HF, FH throughout.

Size: 190 × 126 mm. Ruling: hard point throughout (direct impressions on each hair side). **Part A** was ruled (and written) with a narrow column of text (143 × 56 mm, 22 lines) and a wide outer margin, providing space for a gloss that was never supplied. Space between lines: 7 mm. Height of minims: 2 mm. No prickings survive in the margins of this section. **Part B** was likewise prepared for glossing: the main text area measures 136 × 53 mm (17 lines),

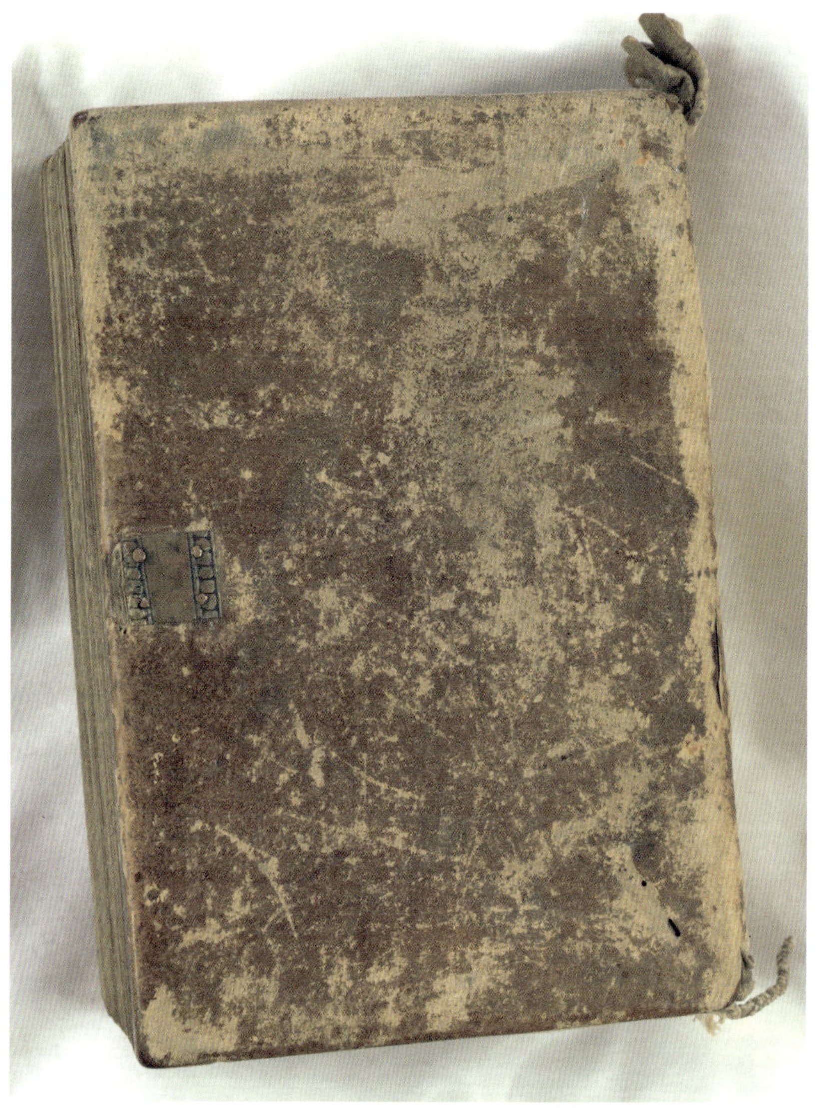

leaving a generous outer margin, with further space for glosses in the upper and lower borders, this all being ruled for a total of up to 54 lines. Space between lines: 9 mm. Height of minims (main text) 1.5 mm. Two sets of prickings run down the outer margin in this section, one set more widely spaced than the other, guiding the horizontals of the main text and those of the glossing space respectively. **Part** C was ruled for a main text of 133 × 68 mm, 21

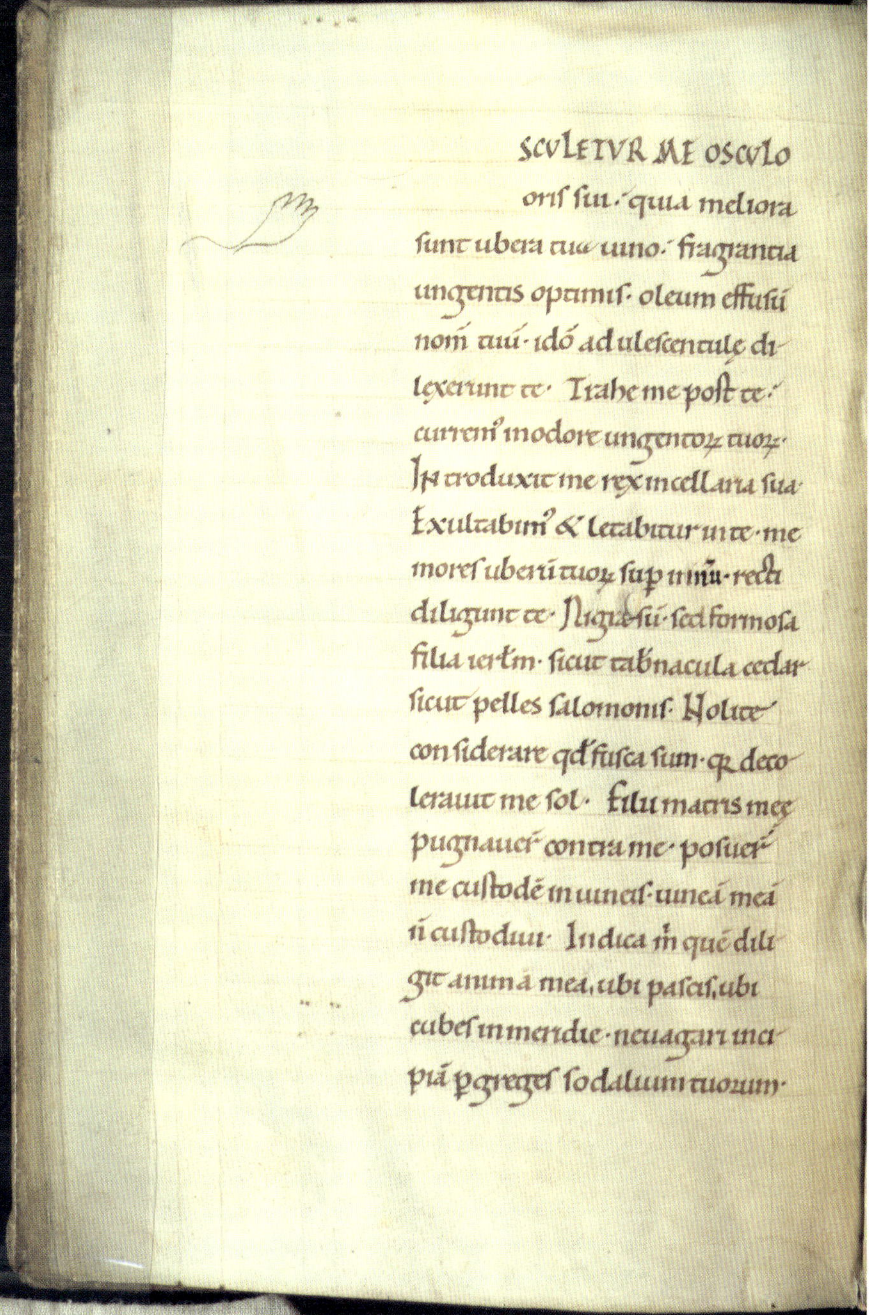
SCULETUR ME OSCULO
oris sui. quia meliora
sunt ubera tua uino. fragrantia
ungentis optimis. oleum effusu
nom tuu. ido adulescentule di
lexerunt te. Trahe me post te.
curremus in odore ungentor tuor.
Introduxit me rex in cellaria sua.
Exultabimus & letabitur in te. me
mores uberu tuor sup uinu. recti
diligunt te. Nigra su. sed formosa
filia ierlm. sicut tabnacula cedar
sicut pelles salomonis. Nolite
considerare qd fusca sum. qr deco
lerauit me sol. Filii matris mee
pugnauer contra me. posuer
me custode in uineis. uinea mea
n custodiui. Indica m que dili
git anima mea. ubi pascas. ubi
cubes in meridie. ne uagari inci
pia p greges sodalium tuorum.

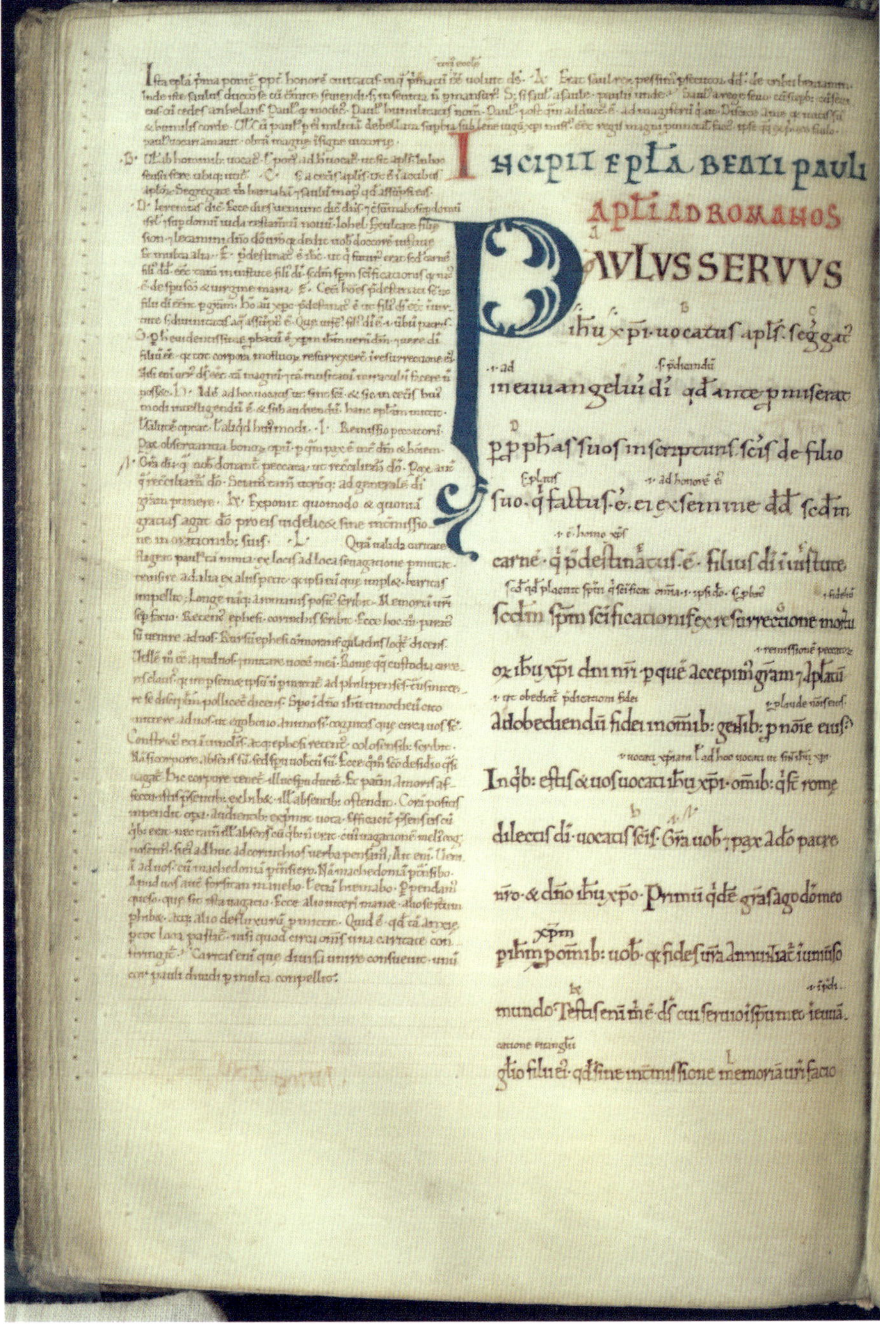

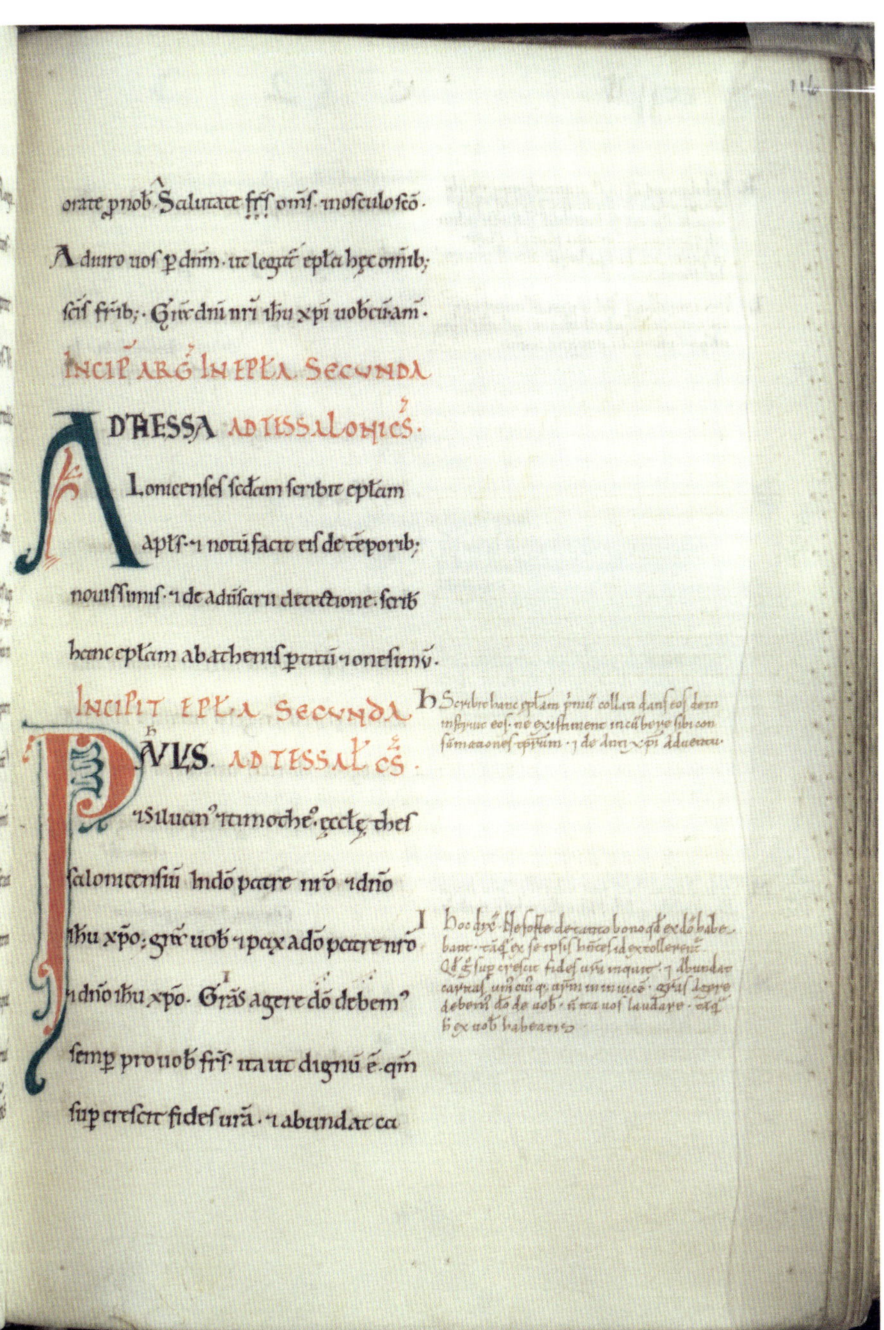

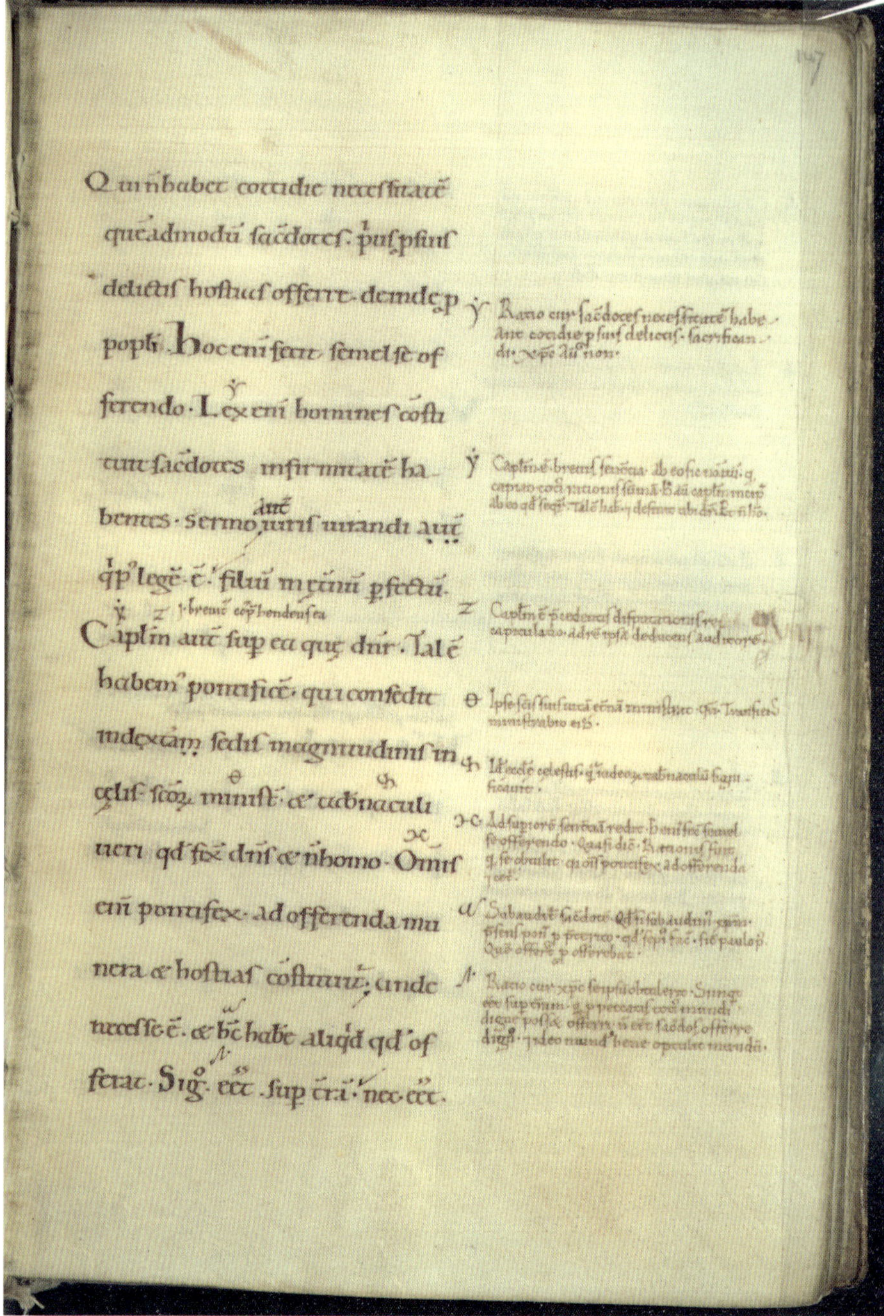

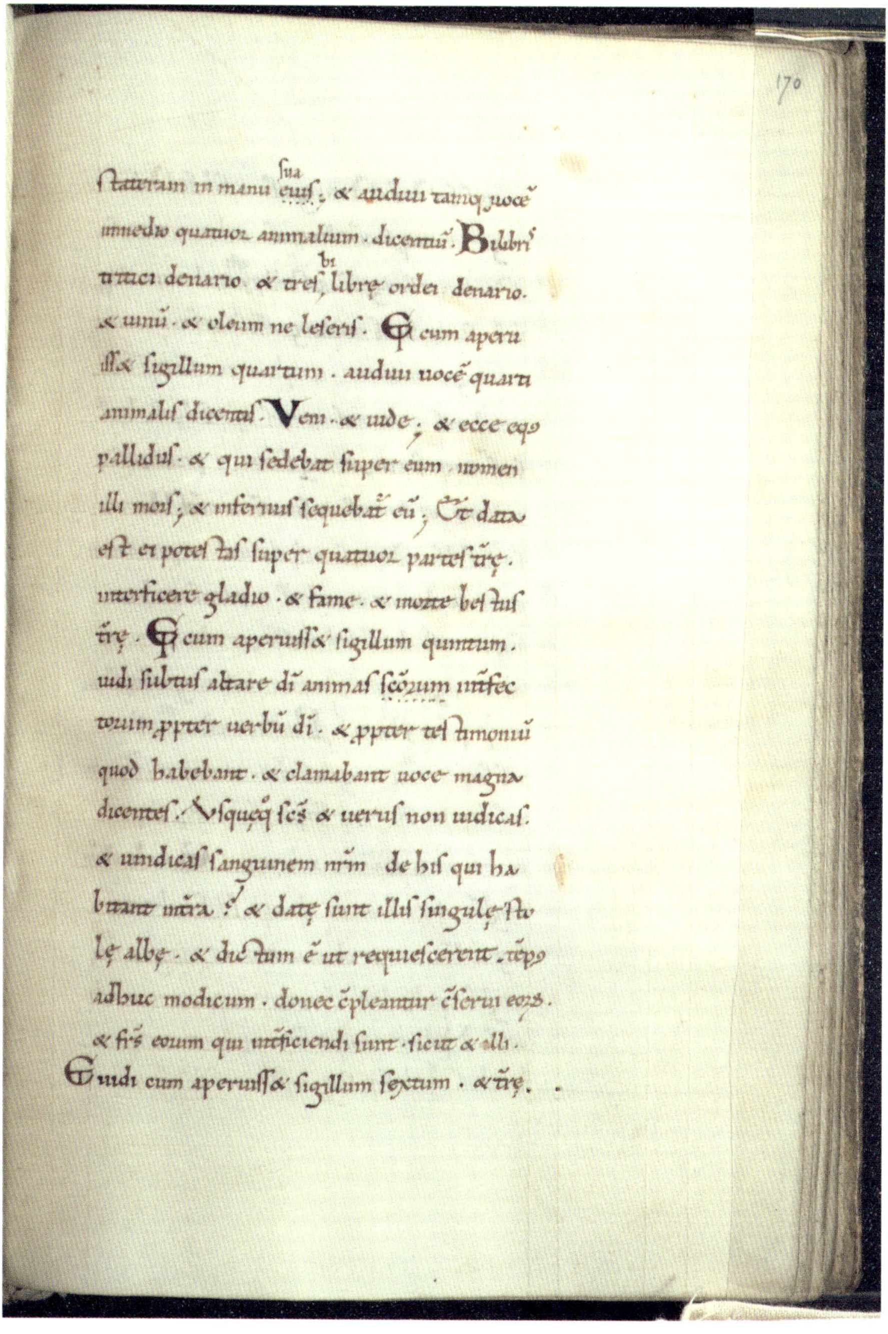
170

stateram in manu sua eius. & audiui tamquam uocem
in medio quatuor animalium . dicentium . Bilibris
tritici denario & tres bilibres ordei denario .
& uinum . & oleum ne leseris . Et cum aperu
isset sigillum quartum . audiui uocem quarti
animalis dicentis . Veni . & uide . & ecce equs
pallidus . & qui sedebat super eum . nomen
illi mors . & infernus sequebatur eum . Et data
est ei potestas super quatuor partes terre .
interficere gladio . & fame . & morte bestiis
terre . Et cum aperuisset sigillum quintum .
uidi subtus altare dei animas sanctorum interfec
torum propter uerbum dei . & propter testimonium
quod habebant . & clamabant uoce magna
dicentes . Usquequo sanctus & uerus non iudicas .
& uindicas sanguinem nostrum de his qui ha
bitant in terra . & datę sunt illis singulę sto
lę albę . & dictum est ut requiescerent tempus
adhuc modicum . donec conpleantur conserui eorum .
& fratres eorum qui interficiendi sunt . sicut & illi .
Et uidi cum aperuisset sigillum sextum . & terre .

lines, with an outer column for glossing, albeit rather narrower than in B or even **A**. Space between lines: 7 mm. Height of minims: 1 mm. No prickings survive in the outer margins of this section.

The contemporary binding is in generally good condition. There are two sewing supports, plus head and tail bands. The spine is flat. The binding originally had tabs at head and tail; only the former survives. Threaded through the head tab are two strips of skin from which once descended bookmarks (one – of uncertain date – survives, though now detached). The wooden boards (*c.* 9 mm thick at the fore-edge and slightly thicker at the spine) have four v-shaped channels on the outside; two vertically aligned channels are visible on the inside of the lower board. Slightly shaped at their exterior edges, the boards are flush with the edges of the leaves. The structure was covered with whittawed skin; the exposed inside lower board reveals irregular turn-ins (that of the long side being about twice the size of those of the two short sides, and extending across half of the board). The front paste-down is still in situ; the rear one – the re-used Anglo-Saxon leaf (see **no. 11**) – has been lifted. A metal plate near the centre fore-edge of the lower cover held in place a 16 mm wide strap (now broken off) which formerly fastened the volume; a couple of holes at a corresponding height but 43 and 35 mm in from the fore-edge on the upper cover received its catch.

Content

Inside paste-down: bookplates and inscriptions (detailed under **History** below).

Preliminaries

[Fol. i recto] [List of content, *ex libris*, shelfmarks]

[*s.* xii] ep[isto]le pauli [–?erasure–] glo. [then added in *s.* xiii] minori · glo. cum [erasure] [then added, ?*s.* xv] 'b'.

[*s.* xii²] hic continent[ur] ista / cantica canticor[um] / ep[isto]le Pauli [later addition: 'glo'] / apocalipsis ioh[ann]is. [*s.* xiv] Dist[inctio] III G[radus] II / [*s.* xiv] Liber s[an]c[t]i Aug[ustini] Cant[uariensis].

[*s.* xvi²] This is Thomas Wyldes booke.

[Fol. i verso–ii verso] [a semi-cursive, *s.* xiv–xv hand] a lection list with a total of 105 entries, comprising a 'temporale' running from 'Dominica prima aduentus' to 'Dominica ante adventus' and 'feria iiii ante aduentus', followed by a short (18 entries) 'sanctorale'/ 'commune sanctorum', which starts with 'In natale Sancti Siluestris' and ends with 'Item plurimorum martyrum'. Most of the entries take the form: occasion, citation, book (mainly the epistles), chapter. The chapter references appear to have been written first in pencil, and subsequently inked; many of the entries on the last page (fol. ii verso) have no chapter reference. (A couple of the book references have been crossed through.)
[Fol. iii] [Originally blank. At an early date (*s.* xii) a series of abbreviated psalm incipits were jotted at the top of the verso, as follows:] deus meus [Ps. 21/62]; judica domine [Ps. 25]; exaudi domine orationem ... [Ps. 63/54]; saluum me fac domine [Ps. 11]; deus laudem meam [Ps. 108]. [Quemadmodum de[siderat] [Ps. 41] and another very faint reference was added lower down on the same page.]

Part A
[Fol. 1r] [Originally blank. A series of abbreviated Psalm incipits was added in pencil at an early date, as follows:] domine quid multiplicati [Ps. 3]; domine deus meus in te [Ps. 7]; conserua me domine [Ps. 15]; ad te domine clamabo [Ps. 136]; deus meus [Ps. 21/62]; exaltabo te domine quoniam [Ps. 29]; Miserere mei deus miserere mei [Ps. 56]; dixit insipiens in corde [Ps. 13/52]; Si uere utique iustitiam [Ps. 57]. [Then added in pencil, possibly by a different hand, is a faint and difficult-to-read abbreviated phrase that includes the words:] 'iudorum', 'zozima', 'cuza', 'bethel', 'ierosalima'. [There follows a final psalm incipit:] Exaudi domine iustitiam [Ps. 16].
[Fol. 1v] [The Song of Songs] [O]SCVLETVR ME OSCVLO oris sui ... [**fol. 8r**, bottom] ceruorum super montes aromatum. [All eight chapter numbers were inserted in pencil in Roman numerals at a later date.]
[Fol. 8v] [Blank apart from some very faint *s.* xii jottings in crayon in the lower margin.]

Part B

[Fol. 9r] Romani sunt in partibus italie ... scribens eis a corintho. Explicit argumentum [Argumentum to Romans: Stegmüller, no. 677]. [The scribe appears to have written the first two lines of the text at the top of the page, erased them and then re-commenced writing the text on the fourth ruled line. Various highly abbreviated notes were added casually, in very faint pencil, in the margins by a s. xii hand (or hands).]

[Fol. 9v] *Incipit epistola beati pauli apostoli ad romanos.* PAVLVS SERVVS ihesu christi, uocatus apostolus segregatus in euuangelium dei ... [This and the other epistles are accompanied by marginal and interlinear glosses. The first interlinear glosses (in vs 1) are: 'id est ad' (above 'in') and 'scilicet praedicandum' (above 'dei'). The marginal gloss begins:] Ista epistola prima ponitur propter honorem ciuitatis, in qua primatum \totius ecclesie/ esse uoluit deus. [Then, keyed to 'Paulus' in the main text:] A. Erat saul rex pessimus persecutor david, de tribu beniamin [Stegmüller, no. 5370; PL 150, col. 105]. [Words in the main text that are the subject of commentary are flagged by series of small superscript capitals (Paulus[A]... uocatus[B]... segregatus[C]... prophetas[D], etc.) which identify the corresponding entries in the marginal gloss. If the Latin alphabet was exhausted, Greek letters and other symbols were used. On most pages the glosses are presented as a series of separate entries; on fol. 9v, by contrast, because of their greater number, they were written as a fairly solid block of text, subdivided only by the appearance of the key-letters.]

[Fol. 36r] *Explicit epistola ad romanos. Incipit argumentum ad chorinthios.* Corinthii sunt achaici, et hi similiter ... **[fol. 36v]** ... discipulum suum. *Explicit argumentum. Incipit epistola eiusdem.* Paulus uocatus apostolus ihesu christi per uoluntatem dei ... [First marginal gloss (for 'sanctificatis', 1.2):] Ideo quia regenerati in christo sanctificati sunt [Stegmüller, no. 5371; PL 150, col. 155]. [Text ends on **fol. 62v**:] ... Karitas mea cum omnibus uobis in christo ihesu. Amen.

[Fol. 62v] [Supplied by the original hand in the margin: *Incipit argumentum in epistola II ad corinthios*, Post actam penitentiam consolatorium ... ostendens.] *Explicit epistola I ad corinthios.*

Incipit II. Pavlvs apostolus ihesu christi per uoluntatem ... [First marginal gloss (on 'Achaia', 1.1):] A. Achaia uocabitur prouincia in qua ciuitas corinthus sita erat. [Second marginal gloss (on 'consolationis', 1.3):] B. A [?for Augustinus] consolatione incepit ... reformare penitentes [Stegmüller, no. 5372; PL 150, col. 215]. [Text ends on **fol. 79r:**] ... et communicatio sancti spiritus cum omnibus uobis. Amen.

[Fol. 79r] *Incipit prologus in epistola ad galathas.* Galathe sunt graeci ... ab Epheso [PL 150, col. 259–60]. *Explicit prologus. Incipit epistola ad galathas.* Pavlvs apostolus non ab hominibus... [First marginal gloss (for 'non', 1.1):] Quidam eum putabant non esse apostolum a christo electum ... praedicabat [Stegmüller, no. 5374; PL 150, col. 259, no. 4]. [Second marginal gloss (for 'hominibus', 1.1):] Qui ab hominibus mittitur mendax est... qui suscitauit illum [Stegmüller no. 5373; PL 150, col. 259, no. 2]. [Third gloss (for 'suscitauit', 1.1):] Nouitatem significat future uite, cuius primi[ti]ue dominica[e] resurrectio [seemingly not in printed editions]. [Text ends on **fol. 87v:**] ... cum spiritu uestro fratres. Amen.

[Fol. 88r] *Incipit argumentum in epistola ad ephesios.* Ephesii sunt asiani ... per tytum diaconum de carcere. *Explicit argumentum. Incipit epistola.* Pavlvs apostolus [ihesu christi – written thus but marked for transposition] per uoluntatem dei ... [First marginal gloss (on 'Paulus', 1.1):] Epistole huius argumentum est. Docet illa bona ... Obsecro uos ego uinctus in domino [Stegmüller, no. 5374; PL 150, col. 287].

[Fol. 97r] *Incipit argumentum in epistola ad philippenses.* Philippenses sunt macedones. ... per epafroditum. *Explicit argumentum. Incipit epistola ad philippenses.* Pavlvs et Timotheus serui ihesu christi ... [First marginal gloss (on 'philippis', 1.1):] Philippenses uiri elegantes erant ... suadebant [Stegmüller, no. 5375; PL 150, col. 307].

[Fol. 103r] *Incipit epistolae argumentum [ad] colossenses.* Colossenses, et hi sunt laodicenses, ... **[fol. 103v]** per tycichum diaconem. *Incipit epistola ad Colossenses.* Pavlvs apostolus christi ihesu per uoluntatem dei ... [First marginal gloss (on 'conseruo uestro', 1.7):] Hunc commendat sciens ... discipulis magister [PL 150, col. 321, no. 5].

[Fol. 109r] *Incipit epistola ad laodicenses.* **[Fol. 109v]** Pavlvs apostolus non ab hominibus ... **[fol. 110r]** et facite legi colosensium uobis. [No glosses.]

[Fol. 110r] *Incipit argumentum in epistola ad thessalonicenses.* Thessalonicenses sunt macedones, ... **[fol. 110v]** scribens eis ab athenis per tithitum et onesimum. *Explicit argumentum. Incipit epistola ad Thessalonicenses.* Pavlvs et siluanus et timotheus ... [First marginal gloss (on 'Pavlvs', 1.1):] Apostolus scripsit ad thessalonicenses hanc epistolam [–erasure–] primam ... cognouerat [Stegmüller, no. 5377; PL 150, col. 331, no. 1].

[Fol. 116r] *Incipit argumentum in epistola secunda ad tessalonicenses.* Ad thessalonicenses secundam scribit epistolam apostolus ... scri[bens] hanc epistolam ab athenis per titum et onesimum [PL 150, 339–40]. *Incipit epistola secunda ad tessalonicenses.* PAVLVS et siluanus et timotheus ecclesie thessalonicensium ... [First marginal gloss (on 'Pavlvs', 1.1):] Scribit hanc epistolam ... et de antichristi aduentu [Stegmüller, no. 5378; PL 150, col. 339]. [NB: in the upper and outer margin of fol. 118v (ch 3, vs 6 ff.) 20 lines of gloss (in two sections) were added in lead by an informal hand at an early date.]

[Fol. 119r] *Incipit argumentum ad timotheum.* Timotheum instruit ... ecclesiastice discipline. *Incipit epistola ad Timotheum.* Pavlvs apostolus christi ihesu secundum imperium dei ... [First marginal gloss (**fol. 119v**, on 'fabulis', 1.4):] Eo quod iudei tantam sollicitudinem expendebant, ... descendisse [Stegmüller, no. 5379; PL 150, col. 345, no. 1].

[Fol. 126v] *Incipit argumentum in epistola II ad timotheum.* Item Timotheo scribit ... ab urbe roma [PL 150, 361–2]. *Explicit argumentum. Incipit epistola.* Pavlvs apostolus christi ihesu per uoluntatem dei ... [First marginal gloss (on 'apostolus', 1.1):] Hoc est apostolus creatus sum ... promissam [Stegmüller, no. 5380; PL 150, col. 361].

[Fol. 131v] *Incipit argumentum in epistola ad titum.* Titum commonefacit et ... qm [changed to 'qui'] script[?ur]is iudaicis credunt. Scrip\ta/ a laodicia [PL 150, 367–8, here copied with an unusually high number of initial errors and corrections]. *Explicit argumentum. Incipit epistola ad titum.* **[fol. 132r]** Paulus seruus dei apostolus ... [First marginal gloss (on 'ueritatis', 1.1):] Ueritas secundum pietatem ... mortuum reuixisse [sic] [Stegmüller, no. 5381; cf. PL 150, cols. 367–8, no. 2].

[Fol. 135r] *Incipit argumentum in epistola ad philemon.* Phylemoni familiares ... ab urbe roma de carcere [PL 150, 371–2]. *Explicit argumentum. Incipit epistola.* Pavlvs uinctus ... [First marginal gloss (on 'Paulus', 1.1):] In presenti negotio ... in uinculis [Stegmüller, no. 5382; PL 150, cols. 371–3].

[Fol. 136r] *Incipit argumentum in epistola ad hebreos.* Hanc epistolam fertur apostolus ad hebreos ... **[fol. 136v]** graeco sermone composuit [PL 150, 376]. *Explicit argumentum. Incipit epistola.* Multifariam ... [First marginal gloss (on 'Multifariam', 1.1):] Id est aliquando prospera ... ostendens [Stegmüller, no. 5383; PL 150, col. 375, no. 3]. [Second marginal gloss (on 'multisque', 1.1):] Amb[rosius], Tota intentio ... discernere uerbis [PL 150, col. 375, no. 4]. [Hebrews ends on fol. **161r**:] salutant uos de itala [fratres – expunctuated]. Gratia [dei – expunctuated] cum omnibus uobis, amen. [Last marginal gloss (on 'perpaucis', 13.22):] Hoc infirmis precipue congruit, ... simul amittunt omnia. [NB: 7 lines of glosses in pencil (s. xii) were added to the upper margin of 160v; these are now so faint as to be illegible.]

[Running headings, identifying the book and giving the chapter number, were added in the later middle ages, around the same time as the lection list on fols. i verso–ii verso.]

[Fols. 161v–162v] Blank apart from a series of faint jottings that were added in pencil to the top of 162v (? s. xii).

Part C

[Fol. 163r] [The Apocalypse. The original scribe began on line 2 with:] quam dedit illi deus palam facere ... [The missing first three words, 'Apocalypsis ihesu christi', were subsequently (s. xii) added informally and to a smaller scale in the upper margin – where there are also two further jottings.] [The text ends on **fol. 186v**:] ... Gratia domini nostri ihesu christi cum omnibus uobis, amen. [Chapter numbers and occasional corrections were added informally in lead or crayon in the margins at an uncertain date.]

[Fols. 187–8] [Originally blank. Numerous faint pencil jottings (s. xii) – seemingly the result of several 'campaigns' (one group being upside down in relation to the main text) – were added to 187v and 188v. A ?*s.* xvi pen-trial, and the *s.* xx accession mark of Major Abbey ('JA 3186/16:9:1946') were added to 188r. At some point fol. 188v also received additions in ink, all of which were then thoroughly erased.]

[Fol. 189] [Freed paste-down: reject leaf from an Anglo-Saxon Collectar (see **no. 11**).]

Scribes and Script

For the preliminary leaves see above.

i) Fols. 1v–8r [Quire I; Song of Songs]. A neat, fairly spacious Norman Caroline minuscule of Mont Saint-Michel type. The work is likely therefore to date from, or shortly after, the abbacy of Scollandus (appointed 1070, consecrated 1072, died 1087), formerly a monk (and scribe) at Mont Saint-Michel (see **Commentary**). Punctuation: medial point (major and minor pauses) and *punctus elevatus* (minor pause).

ii) Fol. 9r [Argumentum to Romans]. A slightly angular Norman or Anglo-Norman hand. Punctuation: medial point (for major and minor pauses).

iii) Fol. 9v, lines 1–4 [start of epistles]. A standard late Anglo-Caroline minuscule of moderate quality. Characteristic features include serifs which almost invariably project only to the right of the upright. This scribe also wrote glosses elsewhere in the text of the epistles. Punctuation: low point.

iv) Fols. 9v, lines 5–24v (main text and gloss) [Quires II–III]. A standard late Anglo-Caroline minuscule with a spacious, rectilinear matrix and with beautifully rounded curvilinear forms; this is typical of the form of the script that was practised at Saint Augustine's Abbey *s.* xi^{2}–xii^{in}, as also found, e.g., in Lit. A. 8 (**no. 17**, where further examples are discussed). This scribe was also responsible for corrections in other stints (e.g. on fol. 34r) and much of the gloss elsewhere. Characteristic forms include a very high backed 'a', a deeply split 'r', heavy wedge-shaped serifs, and generous, slightly rising feet. Punctuation: principally medial point, but also 'semi-colon' and *punctus elevatus* (all used for both major and minor pauses), along with *punctus interrogativus*.

v) Fols. 25r–136v, 157r–161r (main text) [Quires IV–XVII and XX]. A non-standard late Anglo-Caroline minuscule, without the stately calligraphic qualities of scribe iv's hand. Its idiosyncrasies include the use of both a high-backed 'a' and a low-backed one, the latter almost like two **cs** joined together (cc); and a preference for Tironian 'et'. This is conceivably the work of a scribe who had learned to write in the Low Countries or the Sambre-Meuse region but had assimilated his hand to an English style. Note that on fol. 157r he makes an effort to match his hand to that of scribe iv (whose final page this faces), reverting thereafter to his typical form. Punctuation: low point (major and minor pauses), medial point (minor pause), *punctus interrogativus*. This section was glossed by scribes iii and – above all – iv: both appear, e.g., on fol. 29v; scribe iv alone on, e.g., fol. 34r. Scribe v did his own glosses on fol. 136v and then continued as glossator up to fol. 142v (in scribe vi's section).
vi) Fols. 137r–156v [Quires XVIII–XIX – the only two quires in the volume that are quinions]. An Anglo-Norman hand with a square matrix and fairly short, wedge-like ascenders. Characteristic forms include a 'cc' form of 'a', a 'g' with a sharp angle in its tail, and an '&' with a small head, invariably to the right of (as opposed to above) the main body. Punctuation: low and medial point (both used for both major and minor pauses), *punctus elevatus* and 'semi-colon' (both used for minor only). The stint was glossed by scribe v up to fol. 142v; scribe ii takes over as glossator in the last entry on fol. 142v. A different hand supplied or rewrote the final line on fol. 155v and the first line on fol. 156r.
vii) Fols. 163r–186v [Quires. XXI–XXII, plus part of the short XXIV; the Apocalypse]. A compact Norman or Anglo-Norman hand, characterised by extended ascenders with triangular (sometimes split) serifs, and by very generous ct and st ligatures. The ampersand is always placed well above the ruled line, leaning forwards with just the end of its limb reaching down to the line. Sentence capitals are heavy ink letters; when 'Et' starts a sentence, it is regularly written as a digraph with the t within the E. Punctuation: low point (minor and major pauses) and semi-colon (minor pauses). The section was set out for glosses (albeit not as generously as **A** and B), but none was supplied.

Decoration

The initial O for the Song of Songs (fol. 1v) and the **A** for the Apocalypse (fol. 163r), plus the first line of text for the latter ('pocalypsis ihesu christi'), were not supplied. The spaces reserved for the two initials were two and four lines high respectively.

The incipits to the individual Pauline epistles are headed by two-colour (generally red and green, but occasionally blue) embellished initials (up to seven lines high): fols. 9v, 36v, 62v, 79r, 88r, 97r, 103v, 109v, 110v, 116r, 119r, 126v, 132r, 135r, 136v. In colour-scheme and, to a lesser extent, form, they are reminiscent of the secondary initials in many Mont Saint-Michel manuscripts dating from the middle and second half of the eleventh century, as also of those in the late eleventh-century Saint Augustine's manuscripts, Cambridge, Corpus Christi College, MSS 276 and 291. They are generally preceded by rubric in red or green in a hybrid alphabet which mixes square capital, uncial and rustic forms; that on fol. 9v, however, is accompanied by two lines of rubric in coloured rustic capitals of typical Saint Augustine's Abbey form (cf. Lit. A. 8: **no.** 17). They are followed by up to one line of display capitals in colour or ink. Similar but smaller and slightly simpler initials head the prefaces: fols. 36r, 62v (margin), 79r, 88r, 97r, 103r, 110r, 116r 119r, 126v, 131v, 135r, 136r. Generally, if the dominant colour of the epistle initial is green, then that of the preface will be red (and vice versa).

History

All three sections of the volume – an assemblage of the biblical texts that were commonly glossed in the second half of the eleventh century – were probably written fairly shortly after the Norman Conquest. It is possible that part **A** was imported from Mont Saint-Michel, but it is equally likely that it was made at Saint Augustine's Abbey by a Mont Saint-Michel scribe (see **Commentary**); either way, the work or the scribe in question almost certainly arrived in Canterbury after 1070, the date of the appointment as abbot of the Mont Saint-Michel monk, Scollandus. The Lanfranc gloss for the epistles was only available in Canterbury after *c.* 1076 (see **Commentary**). The composite volume was thus probably written, assembled and bound in the last quarter of the eleventh century.

In the twelfth century various notes and jottings were added casually to blank spaces, and a title was written on the first leaf. In the second half of the same century, a fuller list of contents was inscribed on the first leaf, to which a further title was added in the thirteenth century, and a Saint Augustine's Abbey press-mark and *ex libris* in the fourteenth. The book can be identified with item 205 in the late fifteenth-century Saint Augustine's Abbey library catalogue (no. 205: James 1903, p. 209): 'Epistole pauli glo. et in eodem libro Cantica canticorum et Apocalypsis Johannis sine glo. cum B/ 2° fo in canticis, si ignoras. D. 3ª. Ga 2°'. As specified in this entry, a 'b' was added to fol. ir in the fifteenth century. (The library catalogue reveals that shelf two of press three was largely occupied by glossed manuscripts of the epistles.) At some point in the fourteenth or fifteenth century a table of lections was added to the front of the book and running headings with chapter numbers were inserted in the body of the text, attesting to continuing use.

The book evidently passed into private hands at the Dissolution, as is shown by the inscription on fol. i recto in a cursive ?late sixteenth-century hand, 'This is Thomas Wyldes booke'. A subsequent early modern cursive hand wrote on the front paste-down: 'This is my booke / F. [or conceivably 'E'] W.' The second initial raises the possibility – though it can be nothing more than that – that this was a later member of the same family. There are other inscriptions, on the inside paste-down, which might bear on the early modern history of the book; however, these are now so faint and have been so obscured by subsequent bookplates as to be (currently) irrecoverable.

In the nineteenth and twentieth centuries, the volume passed through the hands of some of the greatest English private collectors of manuscripts, as the bookplates on the front paste-down attest. These show that it belonged in turn to Walter Sneyd (1809–88) of Keele Hall, Staffordshire, and George Dunn (1865–1912) of Wooley Hall, Maidenhead – who, as he recorded in a separate pencil inscription, acquired it in December 1903 (when it was auctioned at Sotheby's as lot 274) – then to Charles H. St

John Hornby (1867–1946), and finally to John Roland Abbey (d. 1969). Abbey purchased a large proportion (sixty-eight items) of the Hornby manuscript collection in 1946: the date (16.9.46) and his accession number ('JA 3186') are neatly written in blue ink on fol. 188r. Whilst most of the Abbey manuscripts were dispersed in a series of sales at Sotheby's beginning in 1970, this item was bequeathed to Canterbury Cathedral, to which it was finally delivered in 1979, when presumably '79/41. Add MSS 172' was added in pencil to the very crowded front paste-down. It was omitted from the standard concordance of the Abbey manuscripts: *Illuminated Manuscripts from the Celebrated Library of the Late Major J. R. Abbey: the 11th and Final Part* (London, Sotheby's, Monday 19 June 1989), pp. 208–12.

Commentary

The importance of this volume can hardly be overstated. It includes the oldest copy of Lanfranc's gloss on the Pauline epistles. It retains a binding contemporary with the book: pre-twelfth-century English bindings are extremely rare and this is one of the best-preserved. Moreover, with the juxtaposition of Norman and Anglo-Saxon scribal hands, plus the Lanfrancian commentary, it is a vivid witness to the situation in Canterbury in the generation after the Conquest, as Normans and English were forcibly brought together at Saint Augustine's Abbey – as at Christ Church – under the supervision of William the Conqueror's new archbishop.

The hand that wrote Part A is very close to that of several of the monastic scribes working at Mont Saint-Michel in the mid- and later eleventh century (a few of whom, incidentally, are known by name). The work is reminiscent, for example, of stints in Avranches, Bibliothèque municipale, MSS 59 (scribe ii), 77, 86, 90, 103 and 163, and in London, British Library, MSS Royal 13 A. xxii and 13 A. xxiii. These last two volumes written by Mont Saint-Michel scribes both belonged to Saint Augustine's Abbey in the Middle Ages, and the latter had certainly arrived there by *c.* 1100, as annotations by one or more English hands of a characteristically Saint Augustine's form (akin to that of scribe iv of the present manuscript) show. MS Royal 13 A. xxiii was thus very probably – and MS Royal 13 A. xxii possibly – imported during the abbacy of Scollandus (1070x2–87), former monk – and scribe – of Mont Saint-Michel. It is conceivable that Part A of the present manuscript was also imported at this time; however, it is equally – if not more – likely that it was written in Canterbury by a Mont Saint-Michel scribe. (That a different Norman scribe was active at Saint Augustine's Abbey in this period is apparent from a stint in Cambridge, Corpus Christi College, MS 276, the locally-written copy of Eutropius's *Breviarium*.) Either way (and particularly if the latter were the case), it is conceivable that this is the work of Scollandus himself. Scollandus was named – along with five others – as one of the scribes who participated in Avranches MS 103 (Gregory the Great), one of the stints in which (scribe vi: fols. 193r, line 11–end) closely resembles the work in question.

The scribe responsible for the Preface to Romans on fol. 9r of the present manuscript was also a Norman, and his hand may equally be paralleled in Mont Saint-Michel work, such as Avranches MSS 58 (scribe i) and 103 (scribe iii: fols. 128v–188r, line 4). That the possibly Norman scribe of Part C accomplished his work at Saint Augustine's is demonstrated by the fact that he ended his stint on the blank portion of a reject leaf from an earlier Canterbury manuscript. The scribes of the Pauline epistles have English hands; and if one shows hints of Low Country connections, another is a classic expression of the quintessentially English script that continued to be practised by a few scribes at Saint Augustine's until the beginning of the twelfth century. Collectively, the hands represented in the manuscript indicate that Saint Augustine's was a community of divers nationalities in the late eleventh century.

Lanfranc compiled his notes on the Pauline epistles at Bec in the later 1050s. Within the confines of a series of glosses he offered a synthesis of selected patristic wisdom along with his own teaching. In some copies certain entries are labelled 'Augustinus' or 'Lanfrancus' and, occasionally, 'Ambrosius' (this is very rarely the case in the present manuscript, with the exception of gloss 'B' on fol. 136v which is assigned to Ambrose). It has been shown that Lanfranc took about two-thirds of the content of his gloss from Augustine and from what was then believed to be by Ambrose. His immediate source for the work of the former was a pre-existing collection, the florilegium of Augustine's work that had been compiled by Florus of Lyons († *c.* 860). The 'Ambrose' material for Romans to Galatians was derived from Ambrosiaster's Commentary on the epistles; thereafter Lanfranc relied on Theodore of Mopsuestia and, finally (for Hebrews), on the Latin version of John Chrysostom. While the approach of Augustine tended to be allegorical, that of these other authors was more literal, and the focus of Lanfranc's personal contribution was the elucidation of meaning though grammar, logic and rhetoric.

Eleven manuscripts of Lanfranc's gloss are known to have survived, attesting to circulation in Italy and Germany as well as in France and England during the century after its composition. The present copy is, in fact, the oldest to have come down to us, and some of the circumstances of its descent from the Bec original can be reconstructed. Around 1076 Lanfranc evidently wrote to Anselm (then prior of Bec) asking for the Bec copy of the Pauline Epistles with his gloss. Anselm's extant reply (his ep. 66) reveals that the manuscript was duly sent to Lanfranc, with the hope that a copy would be returned, since it was the only manuscript of the work that they had. This then, was presumably Lanfranc's autograph (or the equivalent), and Add. 172 was presumably copied from it directly – or via a Christ Church intermediary – shortly after it arrived in Canterbury. Certainly, the circumstances provide a *terminus post quem* of 1076 for the writing of this part of the present manuscript. They would also seem to indicate cooperation and the sharing of exemplars between Christ Church and Saint Augustine's – a valuable counterpoint to the picture of rivalry between the two institutions which is highlighted by other sources.

Another slightly later descendant of the Bec copy survives in the form of Manchester, John Rylands University Library, MS lat. 109, fols. 5–126, dating from *c.* 1100 and of Christ Church provenance. A third English copy is British Library, MS Royal 4 B. iv, fols. 1–89, of early twelfth-century date and from Worcester, in which, however, although the Pauline text is complete, only the first three epistles are glossed. In contrast to the Canterbury copies, here many of the marginal glosses – and occasional interlinear ones – are labelled 'Augustinus' or 'Lanfrancus'. Notwithstanding such differences, the Worcester manuscript has a further general affinity to our manuscript, since it also contains the Song of Songs (fols. 89v–95v) and the Apocalypse (fols. 96–119), both glossed, along with the short *Regula Attici*.

'Scholastic' glossed books of the Bible were an emerging phenomenon in the second half of the eleventh century, and comparison of the Canterbury and Worcester versions of Lanfranc's work sheds light on what was, and what was not yet, fixed in their presentation. The two copies have the same basic layout, which was a modest adaptation of that of an ordinary book: the text-block occupied its normal place, with a little extra space allowed for glosses in the three outer margins. Typical of the new genre, Add. 172 is a small book, with the result that the glosses are written to a very small gauge and are, frankly, challenging to read. The dimension of the Worcester copy, consonant with its later date, are more generous (280 × 193 mm), so the glossing script is bigger and more accessible. On the other hand, even making allowance for subsequent trimming, the margins in the Worcester copy were not especially large: the space allowed in the outer margin of Add. 172 was proportionately much greater and to that extent more practical. As noted above, many of the glosses in the Worcester copy are attributed to an authority, which is not the case in Add. 172; the signs used to key the glosses to the text are also quite different in the two manuscripts. The Worcester manuscript advertises the fact that it was produced in stages – which was probably also true of Add. 172, despite its more homogenous appearance. In the Worcester book the scribe of the main text was only responsible for the glosses on the first four pages; thereafter (fols. 8r-43r) they were the work of a different Worcester hand; the spaces for the main text and the gloss were largely ruled with different implements; and the gloss was not supplied after fol. 43r (with the exception of a brief intervention, by another hand, on fols. 45v–6r): these and other features show that the main text was written first and that the glosses were added (or not, as the case may be) subsequently. In sum, all these characteristics reflect the fact that this was a formative and experimental period in the development of glossed books: the optimum format and approach had not yet been realised. There was, it should be said, an element of re-inventing the wheel here, since similar if not better solutions to the problem of integrating text and gloss had been practised in Europe in the ninth century, and the scriptorium of Saint Augustine's Abbey had itself produced superb glossed copies of Boethius and Persius in the second half of the tenth century (Bodleian Library, MS Auct. F. 1. 15, parts 1 and 2).

Alongside its very considerable local significance, Add. 172 is thus also a valuable witness to broader patterns of intellectual, spiritual and bibliographical development. It is, in many ways, typical of what were, in the second half of the eleventh century, the new currents and tools of theological enquiry in Europe as a whole. A (re)birth of teaching through the focused exploration of selected books of the Bible, in which the words of venerable authorities were presented and qualified with new insights, required the production of glossed copies of the texts in question. The most popular subjects for such treatment were, in the first instance, the Psalms, followed by the Pauline epistles, reflecting their primary position as 'set texts' in school curricula; the Song of Songs and the Apocalypse came next. The earliest copies were generally of small size and, in practical terms, poorly planned. Add. 172 epitomises this phase of production. The next stage in the development of glossed books of the Bible is represented by Lit. D. 6 (**no. 25**).

Bibliography

Gibson 1971; Gameson 1995; Gullick forthcoming.

16 Lit. B. 7

Collection of Canons
France; *saec.* XI/XII
2° folio*:* p[re]cedente ex soluendi
Illustration: fol. 48v

Physical Description
Folios: 91 (foliated in modern pencil '1–41', '43–92'), preceded and followed by four unnumbered modern paper endleaves. Size: *c.* 240–248 × *c.* 140–160 mm (the leaves vary appreciably in size; the prickings are well in from the edge). Written area: 182 × 115 mm. 38 long lines. Space between lines: 4 mm. Height of minims: 1.5 mm. Parchment of fairly low quality, with edge-cuts, blemishes, holes, and a very noticeable distinction between hair and flesh sides. Ruling: hard point. Twelve quires (first rectos: fols. 1, 9, 17, 25, 33, 41, 50, 58, 66, 74, 82 and 90), the first eleven being quaternions, the twelfth consisting of a singleton (fol. 90) preceding a bifolium (fols. 91–2). Quires 1–11 are signed in the lower margin of the final verso with a Roman numeral flanked by dots, all within a diamond. Binding: modern (s. xx), quarter leather over partly-bevelled wooden boards. Condition: generally good apart from the discoloration and wear of the first and last leaves.

Content
Versions of the *Collectio IV librorum* and the *Collectio Dacheriana* (Book I), along with other decretals.
[Fol. 1r] *DIUERSORUM PATRUM, SENTENTIE DE PRIMATU ROMANE ecclesie. In libro deuteronomii capitvlo xi°.* Si difficile, et ambiguum apud te iudicium esse perspexeris inter sanguinem, et sanguinem, causam et causam ... ut nullus deinceps intumescat superbia. [Start of the 'Collection in Four Books' (without capitulatio). The material in Books I (fol. 1r), II (14v), and III (29v) is in the standard order; Book IV (fol. 48r), by contrast, has capp. 1–63, followed by cap. 138 plus eight additional caps, then finally capp. 64–72. The individual items are inventoried in Gilchrist 1983, esp. pp. 80–112 (siglum 'C1')

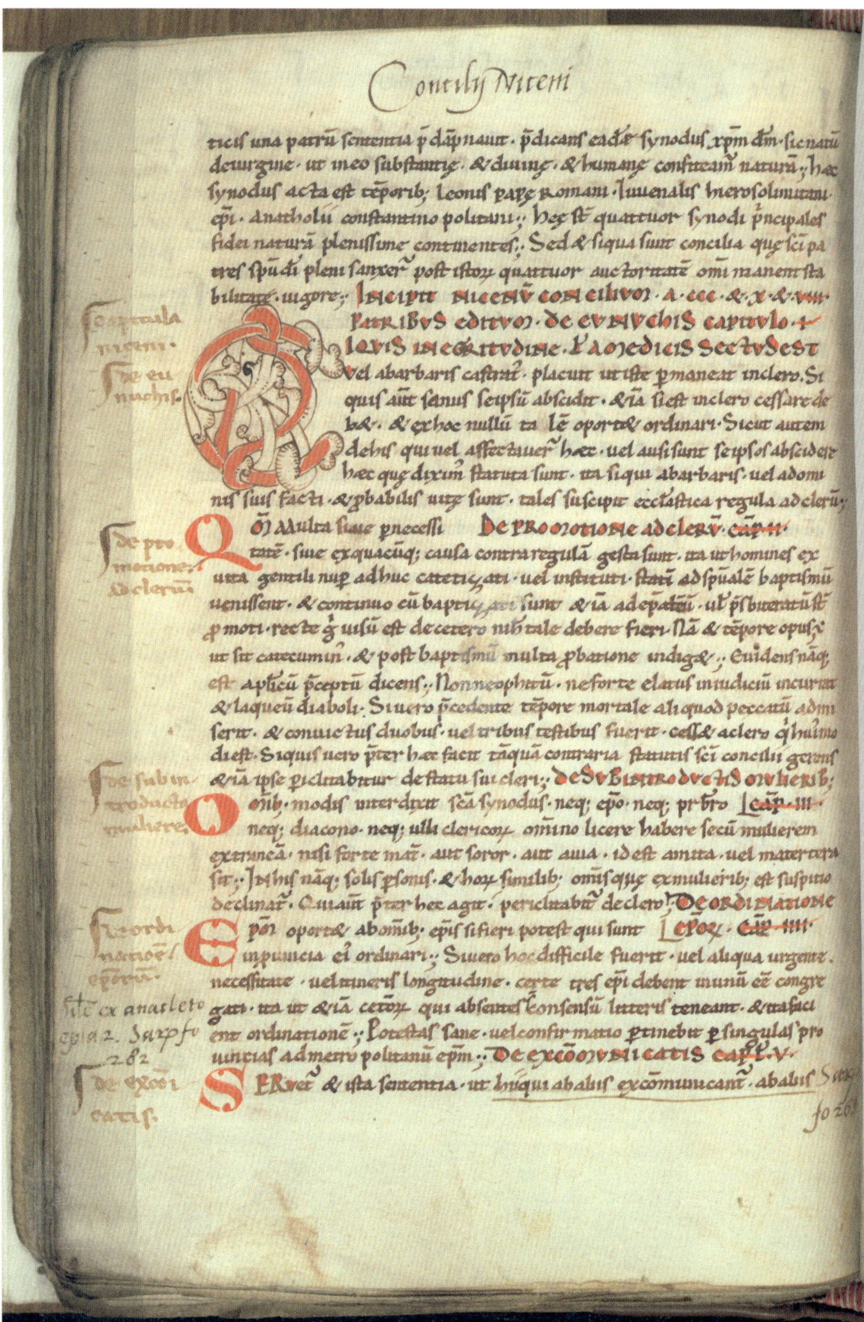

and Fowler-Magerl 2003 (siglum 'VO').] *In decreto Anacleti cap. III.* Anacletus seruus seruorum dei omnibus episcopis et reliquuis christi sacerdotibus salutem. Sacrosancta romana ecclesia non ab apostolis, sed ab ipso domino ... ut apostolico terminentur iudicio. *In decretis Zepherini, Capitvlo I.* Zepherinus romane urbis archiepiscopus omnibus episcopis. Ad romanam ecclesiam ab omnibus ... erunt soluta et in celis. *In decretis Calixta, Capitvlo I.* Calixtus archiepiscopus ecclesie catholice urbis romane omnibus episcopis. Non decet a capite menbra [sic] dissidere ... ratum habere nulla ratio permittit. *In decretis Fabiani Capitvlo II.* **[fol. 1v]** Fabianus episcopus urbis rome omnibus episcopis salutem. Si in rebus secularibus suum cuique ... sed totum aequitati tribuitur. *Item in eisdem capitvlo III.* ... **[fol. 14r]** ... *In decreto Lucii. Capitvlo I.* **[fol. 14v]** Lucius papa romanus episcopis omnibus. Hortamur uos, ut semper testes uobiscum sacerdotes, et diaconos habeatis ... propter testimonium ecclesiasticum.

EXPLICIT LIBER I. INCIPIT LIBER II. De Sacratissimo Pontificatu Romano. Capitvlo I. Simachus papa in generali residens sinodo dixit. Si quis papa superstite ... loci sui ordine priuetur. *Item in eisdem capitvlvm II.* Propter frequentes ambitus quorundam ... uel communione priuetur. *In eisdem item capitvlo tercio* ... **[fol. 29v]** *In decretis Gelasii, capitvlo VII.* Gelasius papa uniuersis episcopis. Quicumque prohibita deprehensi fuerint amisisse, ... periculum subituri proprii sint honoris.

EXPLICIT LIBER II. INCIPIT LIBER III. De pontificali avctoritate, et revali [corrected to *regali*] *potestate. Capitvlo II.* Clemens sancte romane ecclesie episcopus omnibus generaliter fidelibus. Nihil in presenti seculo pontifice clarius ... **[fol. 30r]** ... et suum et singulorum. *In decretis Leonis capitvlo X.* Leo urbis rome episcopus. Pulcherie Auguste. Omnes res aliter, tute esse non possunt, ... et sacerdotalis defendat. *In decretis Gelassii capitvlo tertio* ... **[fol. 47v]** ... *Capitvlo XXII.* Generali decreto constituimus ut execrandum anathema fiat, ... uel permiserit uiolandam. *EXPLICIT LIBER III.*

[fol. 48r] *INCIPIT LIBER IIII. De qvattvor conciliis principalibus in proemio canonvm capitvlo primo.* Canones generalium conciliorum a temporibus constantini imperatoris coeperunt. Inter cetera ... **[Fol. 48v]** ... manent stabilitate uigore. *Incipit Nicenvm concilivm a CCC et X et VIII patribvs editvm. De evnvchis capitvlo I.* Si qvis in egritvdine vel a medicis sectvs est vel a barbaris castratus, placuit ut iste permaneat in clero. Si quis autem sanus se ipsum abscindit, et iam si est in clero cessare debet, ... tales suscipit ecclesiastica regula ad clerum. *De promotione ad clervm. Capitulo II.* Quoniam multa siue per necessitatem, siue ex quacumque causa contra regulam gesta sunt, ... de statu sui cleri. *De svbintrodvctis mvlieribus. Capitulo III* ... **[fol. 54r]** ... *Ne Ivdeis christiana deserviant mancipia. Capitvlo XXVI.* Gregorius papa romanus theoderico et theodeberto francorum regibus. Omnino miramur, quod in regno uestro iudeos christiana mancipia possidere permittitis. Quid ... ab inimicis eius absoluitis. *Ex decreto symachi pape de rebvs ecclesie.* Christiane mentis deuotione sanctimus ... accipienti consentientique anathema. *Cvivs svpra.* Is qui predium rusticum uel urbanum ... qui illud fuerit consecutus. *Capitvlo XL. Ex decretis Gregorii.* Gregorius papa Iohanni defensori. Quod quidam frater de falsis se capitulis accusatum ... **[fol. 54v]** modis omnibus reuocetur. *Ex decretis Gregorii.* Qui nec regiminis in se rationem habuit ... ordinis peccator honoratur. *Ieronimvs dicit.* Non facile est stare in locum petri et pauli ... sed qui exercent opera eorum. *Gregorius.* Nos qui presumus non ex locorum ... sed fidei puritate. *Pelagius* romane ecclesie episcopus universis germaniarum atque galliarum regionum episcopis. Sacrum ordinem romanum ... esse uobis mandamus. *Epistola Gregorii ad sanctvm Iohannem Ravennatem episcopvm.* Quod autem interrogasti de his qui in matrimonio iuncti sunt, ... Si autem ille aliam acceperit seperaetur [sic]. *Incipivnt quedam capitvla ex diversis conciliis svmpta ex concilio anchyritano. De pvellis raptis, capitvlo XI.* Desponsatas puellas, et postea ab aliis corruptas placuit erui, et his reddi quibus fuerant desponsatae, et iam si eis a raptoribus florem pudoris amisisse constiterit. *De esv carnivm capitvlo XIIII.* De his qui in clero sunt presbiteri, uel diaconi, et abstinent se a carnibus ... **[fol. 55r]** ... cessare debet ab ordine suo. *De advlterio. Capitvlo XX.* Si quis adulterium commiserit ... secundum pristinos gradus. *De fornicantibvs feminis. Capitvlo XXI.* De mulieribus que fornicantur ... ut eis X annorum tempus penitentie tribuatur. *De homicidiis.Capitvlo XXII.* Qui uoluntarie homicidium fecerint ... quinquennii tempus tribuit. *Ex concilio Neocesariensi. De presbiteris vxoratis. Capitvlo I.* Presbiter si uxorem duxerit, ab ordine illum deponi debere ... et ad poenitentiam inter laicos redigi oportet. *De secvndis nvptiis. Capitvlo VII.* Presbiterum conubio secundarum nuptiarum interesse non debere ... illis consentiat nuptiis? *De maritis advlterarvm. Capitvlo VIII.* Si cuius uxor adulterium commisisse ... non potest suscepto ministerio perfrui. *Qua aetate presbiter sit ordinandvs. Capitvlo XI.* Presbiter ante XXX annorum aetatem non ordinetur ... Dominus enim tricesimo anno baptisatus est, et tunc predicauit.

Incipit decretale sancti Gelasii pape vrbis Rome. Post proheticas, et euangelicas atque apostolicas scripturas quibus ecclesia catholica per gratiam dei fundata est, ... **[fol. 57r]**... sub anathemate insolubili uinculo in aeternum confitemur esse dampnata *Explicit* [Decretum Gelasianum JK 700; PL 59].

Incipit capitvla sancti Avgvstini Quae debeant pvblica uoce relegere, et manv propria svbscribere, in quibus svspicio est quod manichei sint. [Added marginal rubric (s. xiii):] *Quedam capitula augustini contra manicheum* Qui credit duas esse naturas ingenitas, diuersis principiis existentes, unam bonam quod est deus ... [21 numbered sections, ending on **fol. 57v**:] XXI. Omnibus etiam supradicte peruersitatis auctoribus ... **[fol. 58r]** ... Et me quaecumque ecclesia catholica confitetur, credere, et sequi in omnibus sub testificatione diuina polliceor, atque promitto. ... *consvle finit* [PL 65, cols. 23D–26D].

[Fols. 58r–60r] *Synodvs Aravsica De gratia et libero arbitrio.* Cum ad dedicationem basilice quam in\il/lustrissimus prefectus [maxi – crossed out]et patricius filius noster liberius in a[u – expunctuated]rausica ciuitate fidelissima deuocione contraxit, ... [25 numbered sections, ending on **fol. 60r** with the subscription list:] ... consensi et subscripsi [PL 51, col. 723 ff.].

[Fols. 60r–61r] *Epistola sancti Bonifatii de libero arbitrio.* Dilectissimo fratri cesario Bonefatius. Per filium nostrum armenium presbiterum et abbatem litteras tue fraternitatis accepimus, quas ad nos ut apparet ... **[fol. 61r]** Deu\s/ te incolumem custodiat frater. *Datum VIII KL FBR Lampadio, et horeste voc' consvl'.* **[Fols. 61r–v]** *Epistola Nicholai pape, ad omnes ecclesias.* Nicholas episcopus seruus seruorum dei. Omnibus episcopis catholicis cunctoque clero et populo, salutem catholicam et benedictionem apostolicam. Uigilantiam [sic] universalis regiminis, et assiduam sollicitudinem omnibus debentes ... i. Primo itaque in\s/pectore deo est statutum ut electio Romani pontificis ... [13 numbered sections, ending on **fol. 61v:**] ... XIII. Ut nullus laicus ad quemlibet gradum ecclesiasticum ... et apostolice sedis pace, et communione, atque benedictione gaudere [canons of Synod at Rome, April 1059: JL 4405].

[Fol. 61v] *Regnante domino* nostro iesu christo anno dccclv ab incarnatione eius gloriosissimo Klothario imperatore xv ... apud urbem ualentinam in domo basilice sancti iohannis ... et solli-**[fol. 62r]**-cita pietate adnotare.

Capitvlvm Primvm Concilii Valentini. Quia doctorem gentium in fide, et ueritate fideliter commonentem, obedienterque audimus ... [9 numbered sections, ending on **fol. 64r:**] ... Capitulo nono. Item quia parrochiales presbiteri grauissime, et indigne ... sub pace meliori situm quesituros, ibique pacificam basilicam consecrato\u/s.

[Fol. 64r–v] *Legis Constantiane in canonibus* [written *in rasura* by the same scribe: *recepta dvo*] *capitvla.* Imperator Constantinus augustus ablauio prefecto pretorio. Sanximus namque et edicti nostri forma declarat ... sententia deciderit.

Item Ibi Capitvlo Qvinto. Testimonium etiam ab uno licet episcopo perhibitum, omnes iudices indubitanter accipiant ... **[fol. 64v]** ... hoc perpetua lege firmamus. *Imperator Constantinvs Avgvstvs.* Pro sanctis semper ac uenerabilibus habeatur, quicquid episcoporum fuerit sententia terminatum ... quod episcoporum sententia deciderit.

Cvm promissio nostre paruitatis officii iunctoque obedientie prelationis ministerio causas, et curas, negligentiasque ... **[fol. 65v]** sit anathema maranatha, id est dampnatus, et confusus in aeternum nisi in uita presenti reuertatur per puram emendationem ad deum.

[Fol. 65v] *Sinodvs arverna vt in sinodis prius que ad*

emendationem pertinent dicantvr. Capitvlo Primo. In primis placuit ut quotiens secundum constituta patrum ... [18 numbered sections, but NB: there are two 'XV's, so sections 16–18 are numbered 15–17] ... **[fol. 66v]** ... *De cohabitatione clericorvm cvm extraneis mvlieribus. Capitvlo XVII* [recte 18]. Igitur auctoritate canonica atque mansura ... Quod siquis preceptorum dei inmemor crediderit contempnendum sciat se auctoritate canonica comunionis sine dubio subire iacturum.

[Fol. 66v] *Sinodvs Avrelianensis.* Cvm in dei nomine aurelianense urbe ad sinodale concilium uenissemus, de his que per longum tempus obseruatione cessante fuerant ... et temporum conditione addenda credimus. *De constitvenda sinodo. Capitvlo I.* Primum ut unusquisque metropolitanus in prouincia sua ... [36 numbered and titled sections:] *De constitvenda synodo, capitvlo I.* Primum ut unusquisque metropolitanus ... **[fol. 70r]** ... *De conservando canone, capitvlo XXXVI.* Quo circa haec que inspirante domino communi consensui placuerunt, ... nec dissimulare id est preterire permittitur. [Ends with subscription list:] Lupus in Christi nomine conscripsi ... Vincentius presbiter directus a domno meo sustrisio episcopo subscripsi.

[Fol. 70v] *Ex decretis pape Gregorii VII.* Quicumque militum uel cuiuscumque ordinis uel professionis persona predia ecclesiastica a quocumque rege seu seculari principe, uel ab episcopis inuitis ... excommunicationi subiaceat [c4 CXII, qu 2: col. 687–8. 13 short clauses, each marked by a small red initial; then, emphasised by a much larger initial **[fol. 71v]**:] *De ordinationibus*, Licet noua consuetudo ecclesiae nulla fulta auctoritate ... **[fol. 72r]** ... iiii fluminum, iiii^{or} uirtutum, iiii elementorum, et iiii euangeliorum. *Finivnt decreta Gregorii VII.*

De Loqvela digitorum. De temporum ratione domino uiuante dicturi necessarium duximus utilissimam ... **[fol. 72v]** ... sibi manus insertis inuicem digitis implicabis [Bede, *De temporum ratione*, 1: CCSL 123B, p. 268].

Ex epistola Leonis pape. Hoc quoque obseruandum per omnia decernimus quod a sanctis predecessoribus nostris et a cunctis pene sacrorum canonum conditoribus ... et competentia illis **[fol. 73r]** ecclesiastica sumptis beneficia non negamus. *Ex eadem*, De ordinatis uero a symoniacis nihil aliud quam quod sacra pagina testatur ... **[fol. 73v]** ... potest a pio iudice indulgentiam consequi reconciliationis.

Ex epistola Innocentii Pape. Huiusmodi ergo ordinatus ut putatur id est a symoniaco dampnato id est heretico particeps factus, ... [6 sections, ending:] Ecclesiasticarum institutionum quasdam scripturis ... Que ad orientem uersus nos adorare litterarum forma prestitit.

[Fols. 74r–88v] [*COLLECTIO DACHERIANA*, Book I (form B).] **[Fol. 74r** Capitulatio of 122 chs.:] I. Quod nulli sit ultima penitentia de neganda ... **[fol. 75v]** ... CXXII. Quod usuram non solum clerici exigere debeant sed nec laici nec christiani. *Explicivnt capitvla.* [Then main text:] *Quod nvlli sit vltima penitentia de neganda*, [sic] *Ex epistola Celestini Pape, ad episcopos Galliarum, capitvlo xv.* Agnouimus penitentiam morientibus denegari, nec illorum desideriis annui ... cui occulta omnia nouerit reuelari [c 13, CXXVI, qu. 6: col. 1040. Ends on **fol. 88v.**]

[Fol. 88v] V*rbanus* episcopus seruus seruorum dei dilecto filio .L. praeposito aecclesiae sancti ynantiy [– rubbed and faint but seemingly thus] apud ticinum salutem et apostolicam benedictionem. Saluator predicit in euangelio [c8 CI qu. 3: col. 413] ... **[fol. 90v]** ... ab excommunicatis est omnibus celebrata.

Pelagivs, Iohanni patricio inter cetera. Consecrare enim est simul sacrare ab aecclesiae uisceribus diuisus, et ab apostolica sede seperatus dissecrat potius iste non consecrat. ... **[fol. 91r]** ... etiam conuenerati uideantur. [PL 69, col. 411].

Innocencii Pape, Error cui non resistitur, approbatur et ueritas cum minime defensatur opprimitur. Neglegere ... ut corrigi debeant non occurrit. *Item Avgvstinvs*, Quisquis metu cuiuslibet potestatis ueritatem occultat ... et iste no[n uult – expunctuated]-cere desiderat. *Fabiani Pape*, Qui uero omnipotentem deum metuit nec contra aeuangelium, nec contra apostolos ... ullo modo consentit.

Andreas abbas, Ugoni monacho. Oporteret te dilecte fili, ut dulcem mihi fructum de conuersatione tua quam in operibus manuum et afflictione carnis coram omnibus demonstrabas.

Maxime etiam ... **[fol. 92r]** ... Vere enim non honoras, quem dolore affligis et ad iracundiam prouocas, cui obedire contempnis. [In a different, slightly later hand (scribe iv):] [D]ecreuerunt apostoli et successores apostolorum per omnes ecclesias, VII, diaconos qui sublimiori gradu essent ceteris, circa aram quasi columpne altari assisterent et non sine aliquo septenarii numeri misterio. Hi enim sunt quos in apocalipsi ... **[fol. 92v]** Quales enim diaconi ordinentur apostolus paulus plenissime scribit, et describit ad Timotheum, Ysidorus in libro de genere ecclesiasticorum officiorum ad Fulgentium episcopum [Isidore, *De ecclesiasticis officiis*, VIII, 3–5: PL 83, col. 789B–790A].
[In a different hand again (scribe v):] *De vindicta non proibenda.* De uindicta non proibenda in nouo testamento, Ieronimus di[c]spersionis ['c' expunctuated] dignis ad uindictam ait, Qui percutit malos ... Ananiam et saphiram terrifice multa [sic] [PL 140, col. 775–6; Burchard VI, 43].

Scribes and Script

The book contains the work of five hands, the first certainly, the second and third very probably, French.
i) (fols. 1r–73v and 91r, line 17–92r, line 23) a fairly neat but hurried-looking, functional 'academic' hand, writing a late continental Caroline minuscule which is characterised by sharply-angled serifs and feet, and by much 'biting' of letters. Notable letter-forms include a flamboyant 'z' (whose horizontal strokes are akin to a 'u' and an inverted 'u'), and an ampersand whose 'head' is as big as its 'body' and which has a very heavy 'limb'. From time to time, particularly in later pages of the stint, the pen was either insufficiently or excessively inky – and the writing is, in consequence, faint or blotted respectively. Punctuation: point (for major and minor pause), *punctus elevatus* (minor pause); a triangle of two medial points with a 'comma' below them (major pause); and *punctus interrogativus.* Rubrics and display capitals: a mixed alphabet drawing on uncial, rustic and caroline forms. Many sentence capitals are also stroked in red.
ii) (fols. 74r–77r, line 15). Similar in style to i but with a squarer matrix. Punctuation: point (for major and minor pauses); *punctus*

elevatus (minor pauses); and two points followed by a dash [i.e. :-] (end of section).

iii) (fols. 77r, line 16–91r, line 16). Another, 'younger' interpretation of the same basic script, this hand is more angular than scribe ii but more calligraphic and vigorous than i – from whose work it is further distinguished by the treatment of certain letters. The punctuation marks are the same as in the work of scribe i.

iv) (fols. 92r, line 24–92v, line 7). A more angular, laterally compressed minuscule script of slightly later type (*s.* xii^{1}), practised in France, Normandy and England.

v) (fols. 92v, lines 8–16). A broader less compressed minuscule script which looks typologically slightly earlier than iv but whose position shows that the work here must in fact post-date it. Such a hand is more easily paralleled in France than in England.

In sum: scribe i wrote quires 1–9 (the *Collectio IV librorum*), while scribes ii and iii wrote quires 10, 11 and the start of the short end-quire 12 (the *Collectio Dacheriana*) – to the end of which scribe i then added the letter of Abbot Andrew to Monk Hugo. The reappearance here of scribe i indicates that the work of the three main scribes was broadly contemporaneous, even though the hand of scribe iii is of a slightly younger type. By contrast, scribes iv and v, who made short contributions to formerly blank spaces on the final leaf, probably worked at a slightly later date (xii^{1}); on balance, it is most likely that they, too, made their contributions in France. For the extensive work of later annotators see **History** below.

Decoration

Sections are headed by a bold, occasionally slightly embellished capital (two to four lines high) in red or black/brown, plus rubric in hybrid display script, generally highlighted in red.

Decorated initials, variously constructed from crude interlace, serpentine, and foliate forms with beast heads, appear as follows. Fols. 10v (Ivlivs Romane ecclesie episcopvs omnibvs episcopis. Ivdices alii ... : Gilchrist 1983: I, 99*); 44v (Innocentivs romanvs episcopvs decentio episcopo. Sabbato ieivnandvm esse ratio ... : Gilchrist III, 103); 48r (Canones generalivm conciliorvm a temporibus constantini ... : Gilchrist, IV, 1); 48v (Si qvis in egritvdine vel a medicis sectvs est ... : Gilchrist IV, 2); 55r (Post propheticas et evangelicas ...); 57r (Qui credit dvas esse natvras ingenitas ...); 64r (Imperator constantinvs avgvstvs ...); 65v (In primis placvit vt qvotiens ...); and 66v (Cvm in dei nomine avrelianense vrbe ...). Drawn in the ink of the text, they are generally coloured with the red of the rubric. It will be noted that all appear in the stint of scribe i, and all but one (the most minor) are in quires 6–9. Correspondingly, while a decorated initial heads Book IV (fol. 48r) of the *Collectio IV librorum*, no decorated initials were supplied for the starts of Books I, II and III (fols. 1r, 14v, 29v).

History and Provenance

While the second main component of this volume, the *Collectio Dacheriana*, was drawn up *c.* 800, the first section, the *Collectio IV librorum*, was compiled *c.* 1080x1085: the present copy (which is believed to descend – along with Milan, Biblioteca Ambrosiana, MS C 51 sup. and Paris, BnF, MS lat. 3187 – from Leiden, Bibliotheek der Rijksuniversiteit, MS BPL 111 [1]) was produced within about a generation of this date. Written by French scribes, it is difficult to establish when the manuscript reached England; the hands that made early additions to the final leaf are not diagnostic in this connection.

Extensive annotation demonstrates continuing use throughout the Middle Ages and indeed beyond. There are early 'Nota' marks, perhaps by the original scribe, on fols. 6v and 7r. An informal and untidy hand (probably s. xiii, but still difficult to localise to one side of the Channel as opposed to the other), working in a light brown ink, supplied running headings on every recto, and from fols. 1v–88v added a large number of rubrics in the margins, highlighting the principal sections. The running headings divide the entire volume into five books which start respectively on fols. 1r, 15r (for 14v), 30r (for 29v), 48r and 74r. The scribe prioritised descriptive rubrics (i.e. those characterising the content of the sections) and generally ignored those that identified the authorities whose pronouncements were being quoted. While many of his rubrics could simply have been copied from those in the main text, he also supplied some where there had formerly been none: thus beside the first decretal of Gregory VII on fol. 70v (Quicumque militum uel cuiuscumque ordinis ...) he added, 'De inuadente rem ecclesiasticam per potentem'. Since as a set these rubrics are close to those found in other manuscripts of the collection, it seems likely that this scribe was comparing the present manuscript with another copy of the text (Brett 2004). Many of these marginal rubrics were subsequently retraced; although it is difficult to be certain when this was done, it was quite possibly during *s.* xvi–xvii.

While the date at which the manuscript crossed the Channel is unclear, it was manifestly in England by *s.* xvi, as is abundantly shown by the numerous additions that were made then in Latin and English to the margins of many pages (up to fol. 74r). Several cursive hands – including a neat italic – of *s.* xvi date, flagged points in the margins, often underlining the corresponding passages in the text. References were sometimes supplied (though the nature and identity of the publications in question is not always clear). Thus on fol. 2v, 'Contra pape primatium' is accompanied by, 'Sar fo 239/Sar Eps fo 228', with more of the same on fol. 3r ('Sar fo 229 2[2]8'). Equally, an informal, inky and possibly rather later hand (?*s.* xvii) inserted book and chapter references to the *Registrum Gregorii* on fols. 3v and 4r.

If some of the notes supply the source of a passage, others highlight particular themes. From the issues which inevitably feature prominently in such a collection, those which seem particularly to have interested the annotators include: the nature of papal and episcopal power and the hierarchy of the church in general (e.g. fols. 1v, 2r, 40r, 42r, 43r, 53r–54v, 61r); the sacraments and liturgical practices (e.g. fols. 26r, 37v, 39r, 50r); the laity, their marital customs, and their relationship to the church (e.g. fols. 12v, 40v–41v, 45v–46r). For example, on fols. 1v and 2v, signalled in the neat italic hand, are 'Papa a nemine iudicari deb[et]' and 'Contra Pape primatium' respectively; in the upper margin of fol. 37v the same hand highlighted the question, 'Utrum maius sit sacramentum baptismus aut confirmatio', adding in the side margin beside the appropriate point in the text, 'Resolutio', and promptly summarising it thus: 'Confirmatio maius sacramentum maiorique ueneratione dignus quam baptismo'. To illustrate something of the range of themes that interested this annotator, the following examples of his work, scattered through the book, must suffice: 'Quam ob causam infans in baptismo ter mergendus' (fol. 39r); 'Papa soluendi potestas –?– super terram non in purgatorio' (fol. 43r); 'Stantes ad oracionem Domino uota reddamus' (fol. 50r); 'Episcopal[is] collatio sine inuestitura ad metropolitanos spectabat non ad Rom[ae] pontificem' (fol. 53v); 'De predestinatione et electione' (fol. 62v); and 'Carnes non edenda die sabbati' (fol. 71r). More critically, on fol. 60r (and cf. fol. 58r) is the observation, 'Maledicta glosa que corrumpit textum'; while above fols. 40v–41v (sections concerning, 'Ut singulis ecclesie personis singula ecclesie committantur officia': Gilchrist III, 12) was inscribed the bold running heading, 'Sacrileg[us]'. And in the lower margin of fol. 41r a different and difficult-to-read hand jotted: 'The ponyshment [sic] of Ananias and Saphira was ?in–?– ... by a ?pope'. The italic hand also flagged the list of major church texts and writers, noting, 'Catholica scripta recenset' (fol. 55v), annotating the corresponding list of condemned works: 'Livri damnati'. Amongst vernacular entries one might highlight the splendid observation in this same section (fol. 56r), following a short passage devoted to the judicious memorialisation of martyrs: 'good stuff'! This phrase only reappears on two other occasions, both on fol. 70v, where it was applied to Pope Gregory VII's strictures against those who might fail to respect ecclesiastical jurisdiction in the first place, and freedom of investiture in the second (reproduced: Gameson 2005, ill. 2).

This functional volume thus saw extensive use after, as well as before, the Reformation. Now, as the s. xvi annotating hands can be paralleled in books that are known to have belonged to Matthew Parker (archbishop of Canterbury from 1559 to 1575), it seems reasonable to conclude that this final phase of work happened in his circle; indeed, the hands are probably identifiable as those of Parker himself and his secretary, John Joscelyn. Why this volume remained, or came to rest at, Canterbury when his other manuscripts were deposited in Cambridge is unclear; however, it makes an important contribution to knowledge of Parker's work and outlook, and sheds valuable light, more generally, on attitudes to Canon Law and medieval tradition in the upper echelons of the early Anglican church.

Bibliography

Brooke 1931, esp. pp. 239-41; Gilchrist 1983, esp. pp. 65–6; Kéry 1999, pp. 88, 210, 212; Fowler-Magerl 2003; Brett 2004, esp. pp. 210–11 with pl. 12.1 (showing fol. 3v).

17 Lit. A. 8

Augustine, *Sermones de uerbis Domini et apostoli.*
Canterbury, Saint Augustine's Abbey; *saec.* XI/XII–XII^{in}
2° folio (of text proper, 4r): tuus sermo dei est
Illustrations: fols. 1v, 3r, 3v, 27r, 41v

Physical Description
Folios: i (modern parchment)+152+i (unnumbered, modern parchment). Size: 350 × 260 mm. Written area: 268 × 196 mm. Two columns (column width: 92 mm). Lines: 43 (NB: quire 'Q' was ruled for 45 lines, but only 43 of them were written, the bottom two being left blank.) Space between lines: 6 mm. Height of minims: 2 mm. Ruling: hard point on every hair side. Parchment: robust but variable in tone and texture, with a marked contrast between (yellow) hair sides and (whiter) flesh sides. At some point, small parchment tabs were laced into the lower margins of fols. 128r and 133r.

There is a late medieval foliation in arabic numerals at the centre of the top margin, starting with '.i.' on the first page of the main text (fol. 3v), continuing thereafter on the rectos (thus '.2.' on fol. 4r, '.3.' on fol. 5r, etc.), up to '.150.' on the final recto (fol. 152r). The manuscript was re-foliated in pencil on the lower right hand corner of the leaves by 'JVPH' in 1966, running from '1' on the first medieval parchment leaf to '152' on the last.

The volume is entirely constructed from regular quaternions, the parchment invariably arranged therein: HF, FH. The first rectos of the nineteen quires are: 1, 9, 17, 25, 33, 41, 49, 57, 65, 73, 81, 89, 97, 105, 113, 121, 129, 137, 145. Original signatures (written in stylised capitals by a different hand and in a different ink from the main text) appear at the centre of the lower margin on the final verso of each quire. Although no signature is now visible in quire I, it was clearly included in the counting as 'A'. The extant signatures are: B, 16v; C, 24v; D, 32v; E, 40v; F, 48v; G, 56v; H, 64v; I, 72v; K, 80v, L, 88v; M, 96v; N, 104v; O, 112v; P, 120v; Q, 128v; R, 136v; S, 144v; T, 152v. The binding is modern (?s. xix^{ex}–xx); however, stains from the leather turn-ins

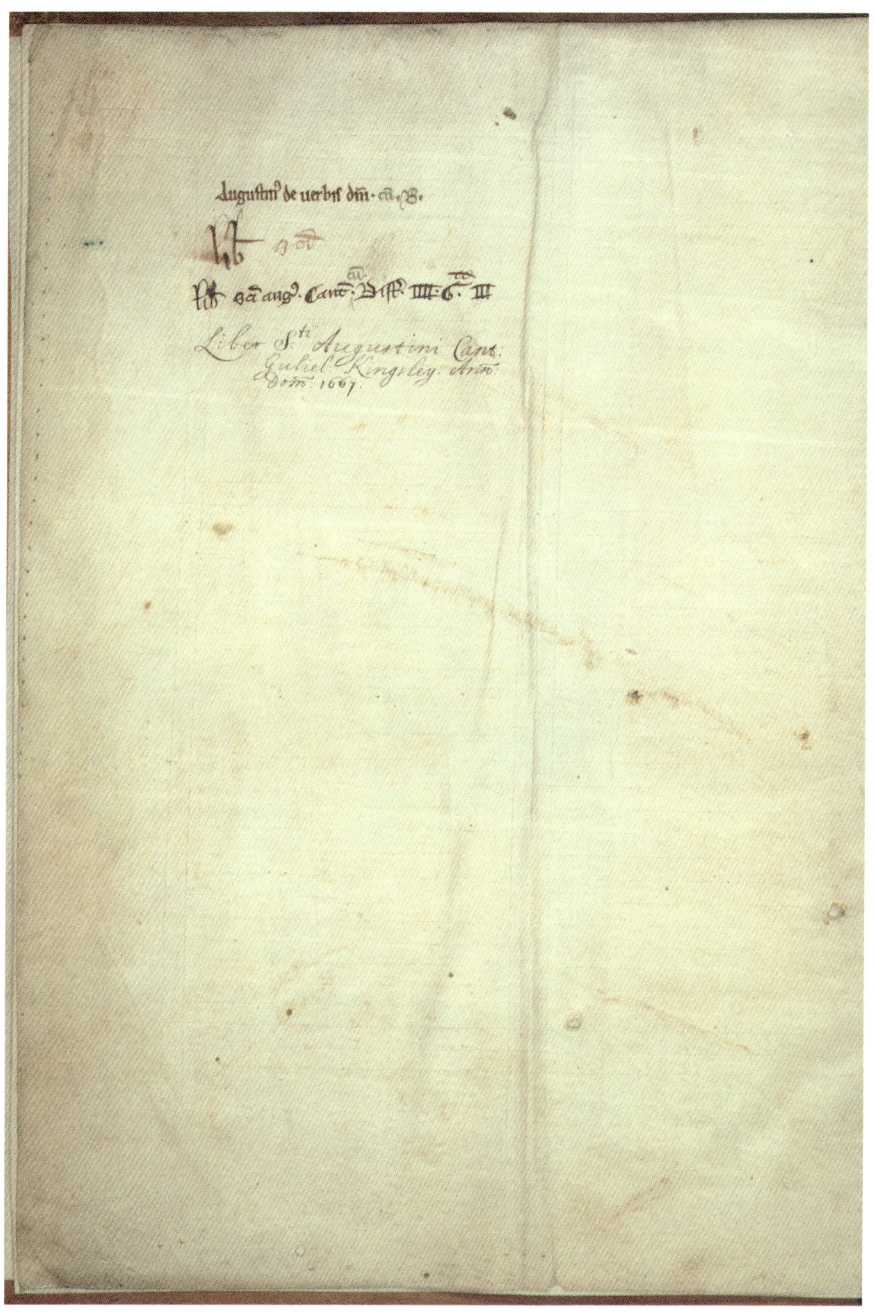
Liber Sti Augustini Cant:
Guliel. Kingsley. Anno
Dom: 1667

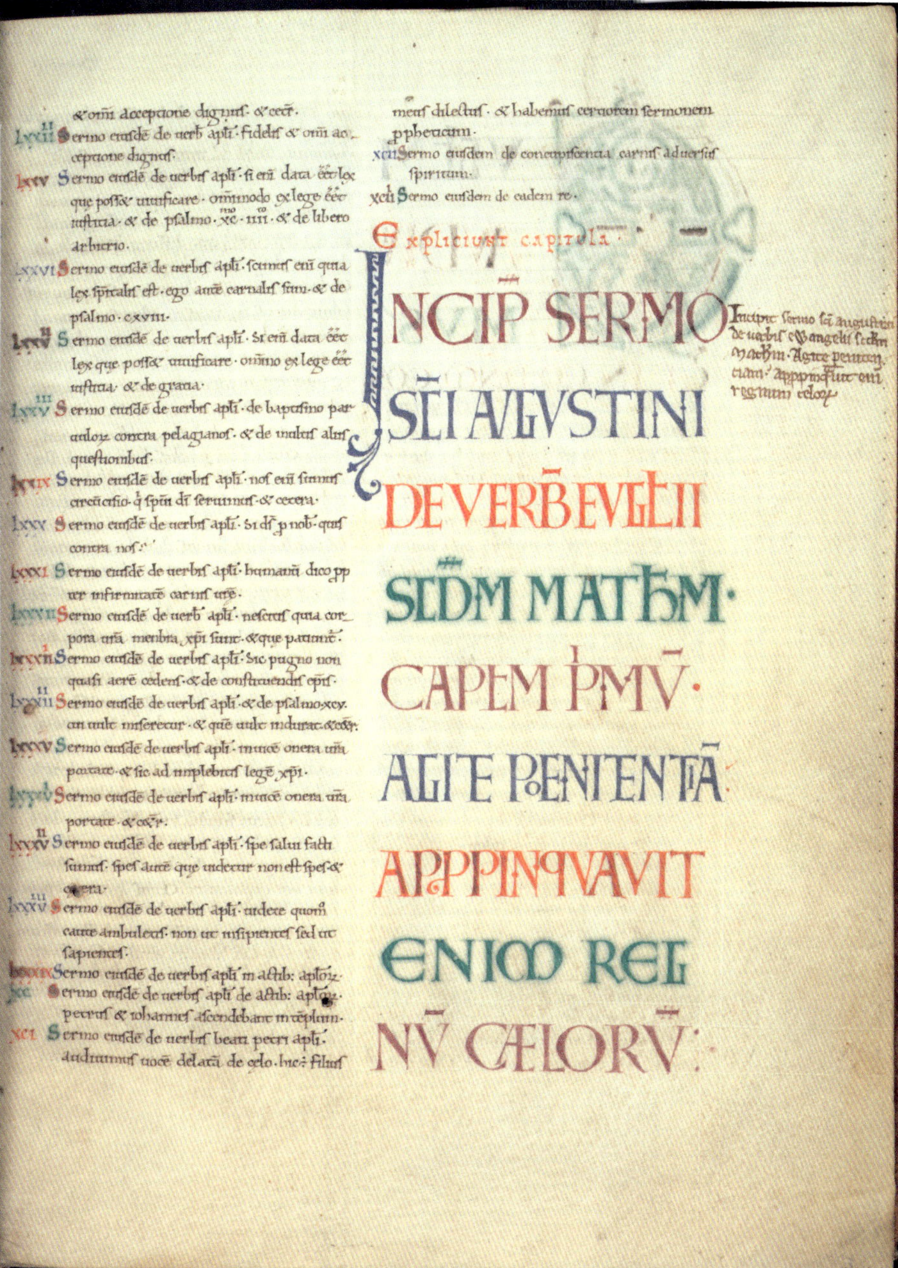

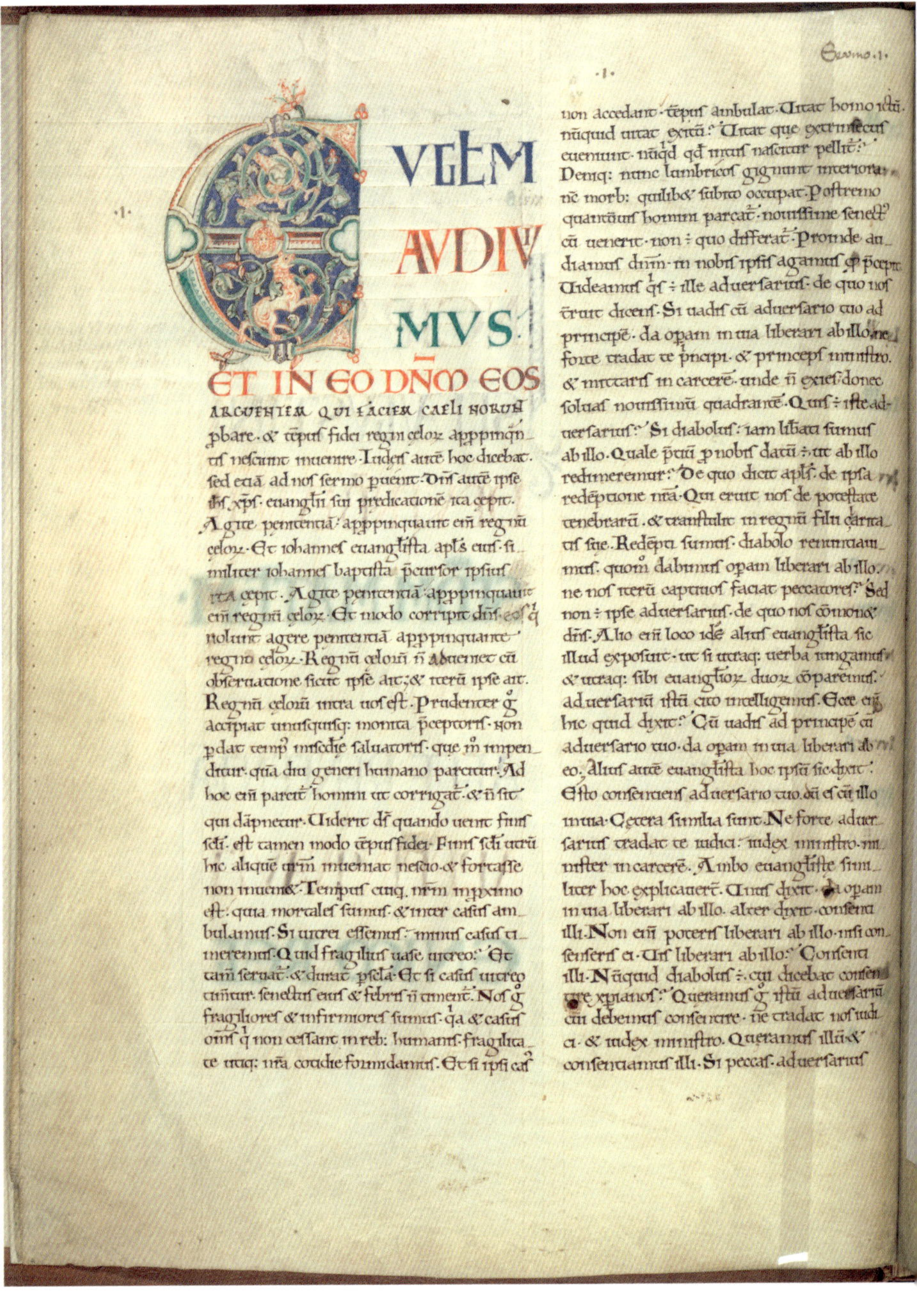

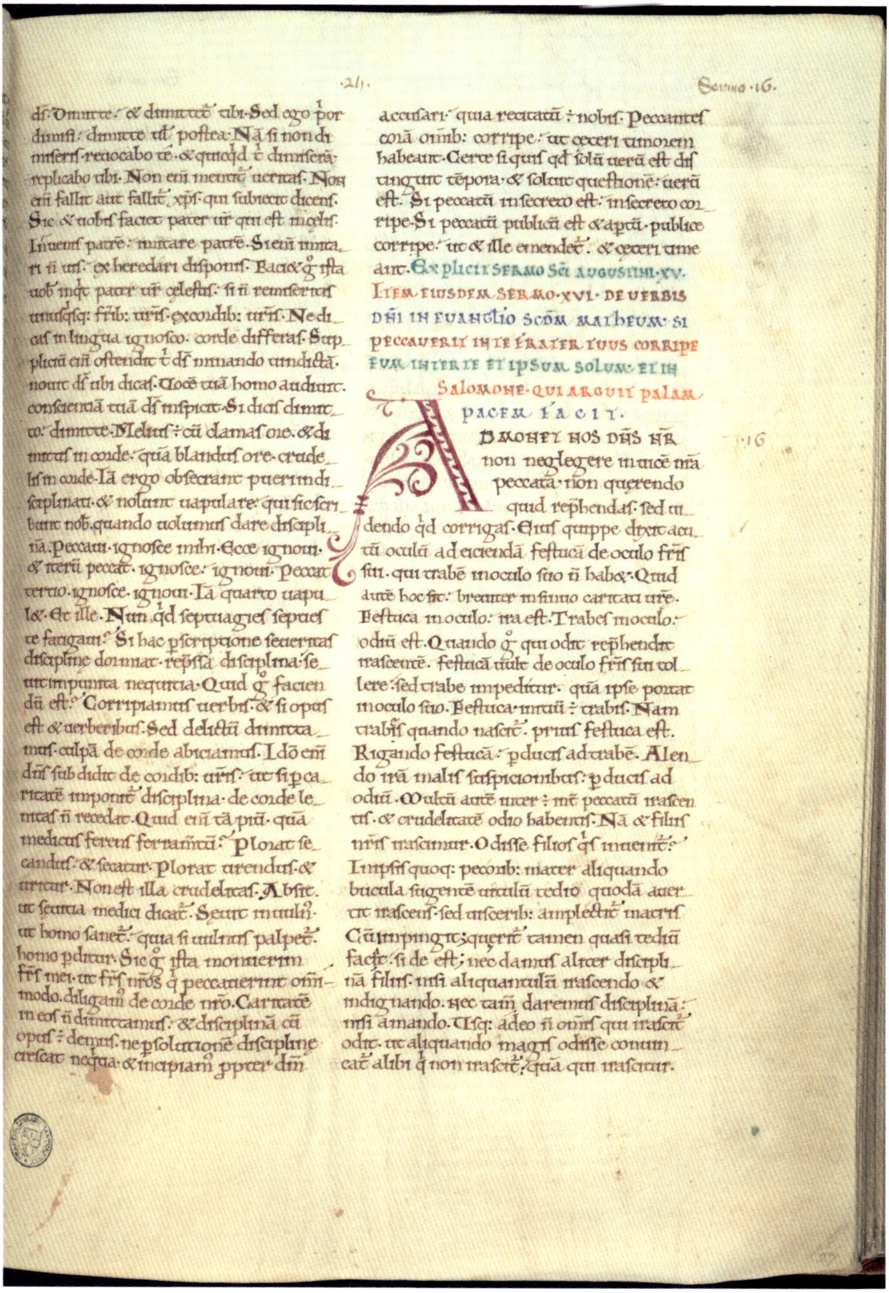
Sermo 16.
Explicit sermo sci augustini xv.
Item eiusdem sermo xvi de uerbis dni in euangelio scdm matheum si peccauerit in te frater tuus corripe eum inter te et ipsum solum et in salomone qui arguit palam pacem facit.

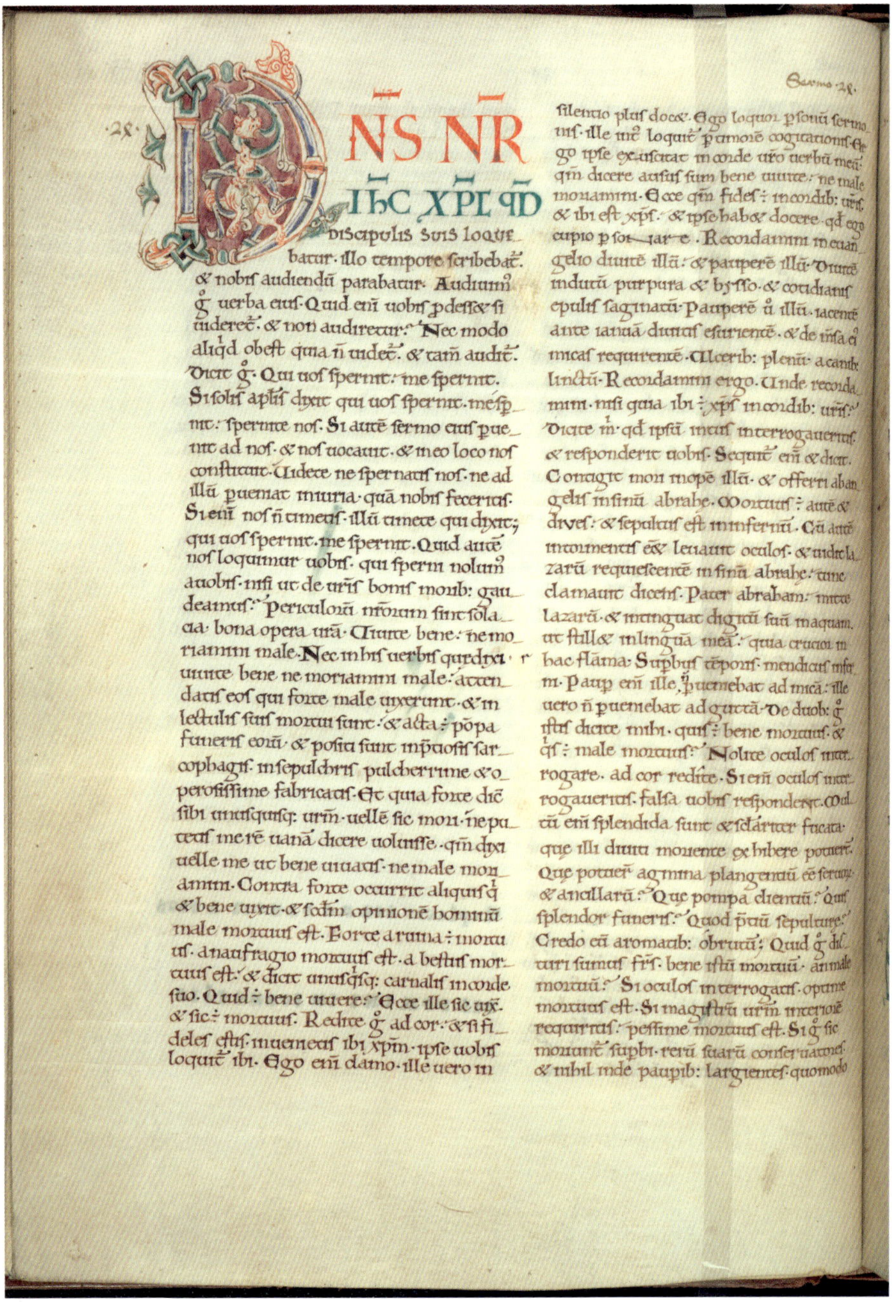

on the inside of the boards of a lost earlier binding can be discerned on the first recto and the last verso; both leaves also bear small green stains, presumably from the metal furniture of a former binding.

Content

A collection of 90 authentic and pseudonymous sermons of Augustine, mainly *De uerbis domini* and *De uerbis apostoli* (essentially the version of the collection classified as type 'B1*' by Verbraken 1976). In the account that follows, the medieval foliation is given in parenthesis after the modern one.
[Fol. 1r (–)**]** Blank
[Fol. 1v (–)**]** A series of title and ex libris inscriptions. a) 'Augustin[us] de uerbis d[omi]ni' [*s.* xii^{2+}], to which 'cu[m] B' was added in the late middle ages [?xv^{2}–xvi^{1}]. b) 'lib[er]' [?*s.* xiii], beside which 'sci' was subsequently scribbled in a poor hand. c) 'lib[er] s[an]c[t]i aug[ustini]. Cant. Dist'. IIII. G^{a}. III' [*s.* xiv]. A late medieval hand subsequently inserted 'cu[m]' plus a now-effaced letter between 'Cant.' and 'Dist'. d) Liber Sti: Augustini Cant: Guliel: Kingsley. Ann[o]: Dom[ino]: 1667 [cf. Lit. D. 6: **no.** 25].
[Fol. 2r (–)**]** [Capitula, headed and subdivided by rubrics in coloured capitals.] *Incipit capitula de uerbis domini secundum Matheum.* .I. Sermo sancti AUGUSTINI de uerbis domini in euangelio secundum Matheum. Agite penitentiam appropinquabit enim regnum celorum. II ... XXIII, Sermo eiusdem de eisdem. *Finiunt capitula secundum Matheum. Incipiunt secundum Lucam.* XXIIII, Sermo eiusdem de uerbis domini in euangelio secundum lucam qui uos spernit, me spernit. ... **[Fol. 2v]** ... XXXVII, Sermo eiusdem de uerbis domini in euangelio secundum lucam, homo quidam descendebat ab hierusalem in hiericho, et incidit in latrones. *Finiunt capitula secundum Lucam. Incipit de Ioh[anne].* XXXVIII, Sermo eiusdem de euangelio secundum iohannem. In principio erat uerbum et cetera. ... LXIIII, Sermo eiusdem de euangelio secundum iohannem. Amen dico uobis, quia uenit hora ... uiuent. *Finiunt capitula secundum iohannem.* LXV, Sermo eiusdem de ueteribus scripturis ac nouis, de trinitate contra arrianos. ... **[Fol. 3r** (–)**]** ... XCI, Sermo eiusdem de uerbis

beati petri apostoli. audiuimus uocem delatam de celo, hic est filius meus dilectus, et habemus certiorem sermonem propheticum. [Then, written to a slightly smaller gauge by the same hand:] XCII, Sermo eiusdem de concupiscentia carnis aduersus spiritum. XCIII Sermo eiusdem de eadem re. *Expliciunt capitula.*
[Fol. 3r (–)**]** [In monumental coloured capitals, the lines purple, blue, red, and green in turn] *Incipit Sermo sci. Avgvstini de verb. Evglii. Scdm. Mthm. Capitulum Primvm. Agite Poenitentiam appropinqvavit enim regnvm Caeolorvm:*
[Fol. 3v (1v)**]** Evangelivm avdivimvs et in eo dominum eos ... [The collection inventoried by Verbraken 1976, items 1–37, 37bis–88, with subdivisions marked by extensive coloured rubrics, decorated initials and coloured display capitals at Dominus noster (fol. 41v, V item 24) and Capitulum euangelii (fol. 56v, V item 38). NB: the incipit of item 14 (fol. 24v) is here, 'Cum sanctum euangelium legeretur ...' ; and there is no extra visual emphasis for 'Sancta et diuina' (fol. 97v, V, item 65), nor 'Audiuimus ueracem' (fol. 98r, V, item 66, the beginning of *De uerbis apostoli.*]

Verbraken item 88, Apostolum eum legeretur **[fol. 147v]** ... ueniet qui exigat. Amen **[fol. 148r]**, is followed immediately by: a) *De concupiscentia carnis adversus spiritum.* Lectio diuina que de pauli apostoli epistola recitata est ... **[fol. 150r, col. 1]** sed non pigeat inde deum precari [Augustine, sermo 151: PL 38, 814]; b) [rubric not supplied] Meminisse debet caritas uestra disputasse me ... **[fol. 152r, col. 1]** lex littere, tollat peccatum lex gratie [Augustine, sermo 152: PL 38, 819]. [Sermones 151–2 are the first of a series discussing Romans 7.5–8.17.]

The numbering of the sermons occasioned difficulties. There are two sets of numbers, one (in Roman numerals) forming part of the original rubric, the other (in Arabic) added by a late medieval hand beside the incipits and in the upper margins. Both systems are basically in step for Verbraken items 1–37 (though the initial rubric for items 25–8 and 34–7 was erroneous and was then changed by the original hand to the correct figure). The pseudonymus sermon, 'Omnium christianorum' [fol. 55v; V item 37bis], was the start of more serious problems. This was

numbered '38' by the late medieval hand – which then continued in unbroken sequence to '91' at the end of the collection. In the original rubric it was initially labelled '38' but then, at a very early date, changed to '37'. The next few items caused considerable confusion: Verbraken 38 (late medieval '39') has no original rubric; at V 39 (40) the original rubric was simply erased and nothing supplied; at V 40 (41) an initial 41 was changed to 40; for V 41 (42) an obliterated original was changed to 40; for V 42 (43) an obliterated original was changed to 41; at V 43 (44) an initial 44 was changed to 43; at V 44 (45) an original 45 was changed to 40; at V 45 (46) an original 46 was changed to 45. Thereafter the initial rubric (generally one higher than Verbraken's item number) was either reduced by one or simply erased. The exceptions are V 58, 61–3 and 78–88 which (through luck or design) were given the 'correct' number initially; V 64 and 68 which have no number; and V 69 where the correction resulted in a different number altogether (60). Finally, Sermo 151 was numbered 89 by the original hand; while sermo 152 was not numbered at all.
[Fol. 152v] Blank, except for two very faint, illegible lead inscriptions (? *s.* xii) towards the bottom of col. 2.

Scribes and Script
The main text is the work of a single hand, writing a moderately calligraphic version of the elegant late standard Anglo-Caroline minuscule that was developed, apparently in Canterbury, in the early eleventh century and continued to be practised at Saint Augustine's Abbey for a couple of generations after the Norman Conquest. The characteristics of this particular version include generous spaces between words but much biting of individual letters within them (in some words, every letter touches its neighbour), gently rising, moderately spiky feet, and slightly angled triangular serifs. Other notable features include: a *punctus interrogativus* with an extended, flowing upper stroke; lengthy tildes which, when they bisect ascenders, curl over and end in a blob; and 'hyphens' marking word-breaks at the ends of lines, which are placed very low – on or below the horizontal ruling. There is moderate use of abbreviations. Punctuation: medial point

(major and minor pauses), *punctus elevatus* (minor pauses) and *punctus interrogativus*. The contrast between the ink tone of some of the punctuation, the accents and the 'tails' of e-caudata on the one hand, and, on the other, that of the text in which they sit suggests that they were added as a different, albeit early, phase of work, possibly by a different hand or hands. (The ink of the main text is sometimes a dark brown, sometimes a much lighter brown (dramatic contrasts occur on, e.g., fols. 121r, 126v–127r, 133v, and 135v).

The same scribe was also responsible for the Augustine fragment, U3/162/28/1 (**no.** 18), and has also been credited with writing Cambridge, Peterhouse College, MS 251, fols. 106–91 (medical texts) (Bishop 1955, p. 189), and doing a sketch inscribed, 'P ego' which was added to the ninth-century 'Royal Bible' (see **no.** 1) (Budny 1997, I, p. 255).

The original scribe did some of his own corrections *in rasura* (e.g. fols. 46v, 85r, 96r (two sections), 118v, 121v and – more extensive – 19v). On other occasions, to make good omissions, he inserted the missing words in the margin, keying them into place with a symbol (often a Φ) (e.g. fols. 7v, 9v, 10v, 13r, 58v, 81r, 93v).

A contemporary hand, writing a slightly less mannered but more laterally compressed version of the same script, added, 'Lectio sancti euangelii secundum Iohannem. In illo tempore dixit Ihesus his discipulis suis Amen amen dico uobis qui non intrat per ostium in ouile ouium sed ascendit aliunde ille fur est et latro, et reliqua' [John 10.1] in the outer margin of fol. 73r (71r) alongside, 'Audistis cum euangelium legeretur qui intrat per ianuam pastor est, qui autem ex alia parte ascendit fur est et latro et dissipare querit, et spargere et tollere' in sermo 49 (Verbraken's numbering).

Further corrections were made in the first half of the twelfth century, some broadly contemporary with the original writing. At least seven hands (which are, in general, more angular than that of the original scribe) may be provisionally distinguished: i) fols. 10v, 15r, 44v, 144v; ii) 21v, 63r; iii) 25v; iv) 35r; v) 35v; vi) 44r; and vii) 83r.

Undatable *nota* signs of various forms were drawn in the outer margins of various pages (including fols. 10r, 51r, 64v, 81r and

84v); 'a's were added beside copious passages throughout the book; there are also a few crudely drawn marker-crosses.

On fol. 104r, three notes, one more distinct than the others, were scrawled in a hasty, ?s. xii–xiii, highly-abbreviated, semi-cursive, beside, 'multo est melior et suauior ueritatis, sed sanis suauis est panis' in Verbraken's sermo 68. On fol. 3r, a ?s. xiii hand copied, in a fairly informal minuscule, the text presented in display capitals.

A late medieval hand added foliation, sermon numbers and running headings ('sermo 1', 'sermo 2', etc.) throughout, and made a couple of short annotations (fols. 11r, 80r); the hand in question also numbered PRC 49/4/1–2 (**no.** 33). A different late medieval hand added (?doodled) a large late medieval capital 'A' in the upper margin of fol. 102r.

The undatable but clearly fairly modern annotation, 'Vide p. 53', was added to the margin of fol. 139v. A note on the modern flyleaf records that the volume was (re)foliated on 31 January 1966.

Decoration

The major artwork appears as follows.

Fol. 3r, A bold display of nine lines of monumental coloured capitals (purple, blue, red, and green), which occupies most of column two, announcing the incipit of Sermo 1.

Fol. 3v, Decorated initial E, accompanied by four lines of coloured capitals (–vangelium / avdivi/mvs / et in eo dominum eos) for Sermo 1, the first of those on Matthew. The initial, 11 lines high, has a bird and a lion within foliage curls in the upper and lower sections of the bowl respectively, a bearded head in the upper terminal, a hooded head in the lower one, and a cross-nimbed, curly haired head within a roundel on the cross-stroke. Initial and display capitals are done in red, blue and green.

Fol. 41v, Decorated initial D, plus two lines of coloured capitals (–ominvs noster / ihesvs christvs qvod) for Sermo 24 on 'Qui uos spernit me spernit' (Luke 10.16), the first of the group on Luke. The initial, eight lines high, and of basic Franco-Saxon form, has simple interlace terminals on the upright; the bowl is occupied by a complete lion, plus a lion's head, amidst foliate curls. The initial is red, blue, green, and purple; the display script red and green. **Fol. 56v,** Decorated initial C, plus two lines of coloured capitals (–apitvlvm / evangelii qvod) for Sermo 38 on 'In principio erat uerbum' (John 1.1), the first of the group on John. The main body of the initial, six lines high, incorporates two open-mouthed beast heads, and terminates in foliate sprigs; further foliage curls, a bird among them, spill thence into the bowl. The colours are the same as those on fol. 41v.

In style, conception and colouring, the initials are typical of those in a group of Saint Augustine's books, which seem to have been decorated by two artists, one more talented than the other. All the initials in Lit. A. 8 are the work of the weaker hand, whose work can also be found in Cambridge, Corpus Christi College, MS 267, and London, British Library, MS Harley 652.

Each sermon is introduced by four or more lines of rubric written in coloured rustic capitals (red, blue, green) (exceptionally these were not supplied on fol. 150r) and by a four-line-high plain or slightly embellished single-colour initial (whose conception reprises forms practised in Canterbury since the tenth century). The remainder of the first line is written in ink rustics. Lead and/or hard point sketches can be seen below some of these initials (e.g. fols. 4r, 5r, 5v (especially), 8r, 11r, 14r, 15r, 35r). Particularly fine specimens appear on fols. 13v, 23v (seemingly re-done *in rasura*), 27r, 44v, 45v, 48v, 76r, 78r, 83v, 113r, 144r and 147v. Subsequent 'artistic' additions include: fol. 53v (outer margin): a faint ink sketch of a standing figure (*s.* xii). In the lower margin of the same page is an undatable, now very faint, sketch of a grotesque (?demonic) head, which was evidently deliberately erased at some point. A decorative motif was added in pencil to the upper margin of fol. 37r.

History and Provenance

Written and corrected at Saint Augustine's Abbey *c.* 1100 or xii^{in}, the volume was read through fairly carefully in the following generation or so (as the multiple corrections attest), and around 1200 a first title was added to fol. 1v. Traces of activity during the thirteenth century are limited to the re-copying of the display text on fol. 3r, and the addition of rough annotations to fol. 104r. In the fourteenth century a Saint Augustine's *ex libris* and shelf-mark were added to fol. 1v, ushering in a new period of activity in the later Middle Ages when the volume was foliated, all the sermons (re-)numbered and running titles supplied in the upper right-hand corner of each page. Given that the titles on the versos are fairly close to the gutter but the writing is controlled and undistorted, it seems probable that the volume was disbound when this was done, indicating a late medieval rebinding. At the end of the Middle Ages, 'Cum B' was added beside the title, and it is in this form that the volume was recorded in the house library catalogue: 'Augustinus de uerbis domini in Euang' cum B. 2° fo. tuus seruia [sic – for 'sermo'] in libro. D'4 G^{a} 3' (Barker-Benfield (ed.) forthcoming, BA1.349, correcting James 1903, list VIII, item 349, p. 222). As the catalogue shows, the works of Augustine essentially occupied *Distinctio* IV, *Gradus* 2–4 of the book collection.

What happened to the book in the aftermath of the Dissolution is undocumented, but its subsequent provenance suggests that it may have been among the many volumes which remained on the abbey site for several generations and that it never moved very far away. In 1667 the book belonged to William Kingsley (inscription on fol. 1v), from whom, presumably, it passed to Canterbury Cathedral (along with four other manuscripts, Lit. C. 15, Lit. D. 6 (**no. 25**), Lit. D. 13 and Lit. D. 17). In the late nineteenth or earlier twentieth century the volume was rebound; it was subsequently re-foliated.

Commentary

The collection *De uerbis Domini et apostoli*, which was certainly in existence by the early eighth century, comprised a series of sermons arranged to form a commentary on the gospels and the Pauline epistles. The fullest such compilation of Augustine's homiletic work, it was also the most popular: there are over 170 manuscripts containing part of the collection (the 'fascicules' devoted to the gospels and the epistles circulated independently of each other), with some seventy manuscripts of the collection as a whole. In its full form, the work consisted of 64 sermons on the gospels, *De uerbis Domini* (items 1–23 on Matthew, 24–37 on Luke, and 38–64 on John); followed by the pseudonymous Sermo 384, 'De scripturis ueteribus ac nouis de Trinitate contra Arrianos'; and then *De uerbis apostoli* (twenty-three items on the Pauline epistles, seven on Acts and the Catholic epistles, and three on the Dead). The witnesses can be classified (Verbraken 1976; Partoens 2003) according to their treatment of the pseudonymous Sermo 384 – which may either begin *De uerbis apostoli* ('Group A'), or be presented as the final item (no. 65) of *De uerbis Domini* ('Group B'). The representatives of Group B may then be further subdivided: the two classes to note in the present context are that whose manuscripts end with the last sermon on the Pauline epistles (known as B1*), and that whose witnesses made sermon 34 the second item in *De uerbis apostoli* (B1**). The former (B1*) is dominated by manuscripts from northern France and England, the latter (B1**) by English witnesses, a couple of which (Cambridge, Trinity College, MS B. 4. 15; BL, MS Royal 5 C. viii) added sermons 151–2 to the end of the collection.

In so far as the evidence of surviving manuscripts is a guide, the collection seems to have reached England after 1066. Oxford, Bodleian Library, MS Bodley 229, a *s.* xi^{1} northern French copy of *De uerbis Domini* alone, had certainly migrated to Exeter by the early twelfth century and may have arrived in the immediate aftermath of the Conquest. Nevertheless, our manuscript is the oldest extant copy of the (full) text actually written in England. Given the connections between Saint Augustine's Abbey and Mont Saint-Michel in the late eleventh century, the fact that the work had been copied at the latter house only a few years previously (Avranches, Bibliothèque municipale, MS 82; *s.* xi^{ex}; now imperfect owing to fire damage), might invite the speculation that it supplied the exemplar for the present manuscript; however, the circumstance that the Montois copy seems to have been a slightly different form of the collection (B1) argues against this. The presence of other versions in Kent after the Conquest is attested by manuscript and documentary evidence. British Library, MS

Royal 5 C. viii from Rochester (xii$^{2/4}$) ends, like our manuscript, with sermons 151–2, yet its item 34 is in a different position from our copy, making it a representative of the B1** type. Nor did the lost Christ Church copy that is described in Henry of Eastry's library catalogue (James 1903, p. 14, no. 16: 'Augustinus de uerbis domini. Sermones lxiv. In hoc uol. cont.: sermo eiusdem de trinitate contra Arrianos de ueteribus et nouis scripturis, De uerbis apostoli. Sermones xxix' – a total of 94 items) correspond exactly to the present collection. If the immediate exemplar of Lit. A. 8 thus remains elusive, this multiplicity of slightly different collections (yet other copies were available in nearby Flanders (e.g. Arras, Médiathèque, MS 60 of s. xi^{1} from Saint-Vaast)) goes some way to explaining the confused numbering and renumbering of the items in the present manuscript.

Lit A. 8 is one of a visually matching set of patristic texts, centring on the works of Augustine of Hippo, that was copied at Saint Augustine's Abbey around 1100. The companion volumes are U3/162/28/1 (**no 18**) and Bruxelles, Bibliothèque royale, MS 444–52 (cat. 1103). Thus the latter, which, being complete, offers fuller scope for comparison, corresponds to the present manuscript in size, layout and visual conception, having the same hierarchy of scripts and allied colour scheme, though no decorated initials. Its physical structure is similarly regular, being composed entirely of quaternions except for the last quire; and it is the work of the same scribe, who used the same devices to effect corrections, including the phi to key insertions into place. It even displays a similar history of additions and re-workings – corrections in the original hand, further corrections in a *s.* xii^{1} spiky hand, *s.* xii copying of rubrics into the margins, plus late medieval running headings. It should be noted, however, that the 'dot and cone' Nota marks that were added to this manuscript in the late Middle Ages are characteristic not of Saint Augustine's but of Christ Church, to which therefore it would seem to have migrated by this time. In view of this fact and given that there is no shelf-mark on the surviving (blank) fol. 1r, it is an open question whether item 373 in the late fifteenth-century St Augustine's Abbey library catalogue (James 1903, pp. 225–6) does in fact describe Bruxelles

MS 444–52 – to which its content exactly corresponds – or another (now lost) copy of the very same collection. The most economical hypothesis is that the extant manuscript, unquestionably of Saint Augustine's origin, had an extended sojourn at Christ Church in the later Middle Ages but had either been returned to the abbey by the time its library catalogue was drawn up in the 1490s or, if not, was recorded there anyway as a known possession. Be all that as it may, the writings of Augustine of Hippo were collected fairly steadily at Saint Augustine's Abbey – as elsewhere in England – from the later eleventh century. Other copies of his works that were made there during this period were less homogenous in appearance than these.

Bibliography

Römer 1972, p. 100; Verbraken 1976, p. 221; Gameson 1995, pp. 126 and 144, with pl. 8b (showing fol. 41v, detail); Partoens 2003, p. 34.

18 U3/162/28/1

Augustine, *Enarrationes in Psalmos*.
Canterbury, Saint Augustine's Abbey; *saec*. XI/XII or XII^{in}
Illustration: fol. 1r

Physical Description

One bifolium (probably the outer sheet of a quire), mounted in a guard book. Three of the four corners of each page have been cut off (to facilitate the turning-in of the edges). Now straightened out again, the individual pages bear multiple folding scars, and all their surfaces are damaged, above all the final verso (which is partly illegible in consequence). Page size: 363 × 260 mm. Written area: 261 × 198 mm. Two columns (column width: 102 mm). Lines: 42. Space between lines: 6–7 mm. Height of minims: 2 mm. Ruling: hard point, on hair sides (fols. 1r and 2v). The line of prickings to guide the horizontal rulings is distinctly wobbly, and the ruling itself was hastily done (irregular overruns are common). Pairs of holes (for sewing) survive in the gutter at [–lost–] and 48 mm, 114 and 120, 184 and 190, 257 and 262, and 324 and 330 mm from the upper edge of the leaf.

Content

Augustine, *Enarrationes in Psalmos* (CPL, 283): portions from the commentaries on Psalms 40 and 42.
[Fol. 1r] // quia sine peccato, q[uonia]m omnis qui facit peccatum seruus est. Nunquid ... [PL 36, col. 459/6] ... **[fol. 1v** ends:] Plantata est ibi ecclesia Christi, unde// [PL 36, col. 462/9].
[Fol. 2r] // mortales sumus, ex eo quod prime nostre cause ... [PL 36, col. 479] ... **[fol. 2v** (very damaged) ends:] pro nobis mortem. [PL 36, col. 482] *EXPLICIT TRAC [TATUS DE PSALMO XL DUO] INCIPIT TRACTATUS DE PSALMO XL TERTIO.*

The amount of text that is missing between the end of fol. 1v and the beginning of fol. 2r would fill six folios: thus assuming that the volume was predominantly composed of regular quaternia, the present bifolium was presumably the outer sheet of a quire.

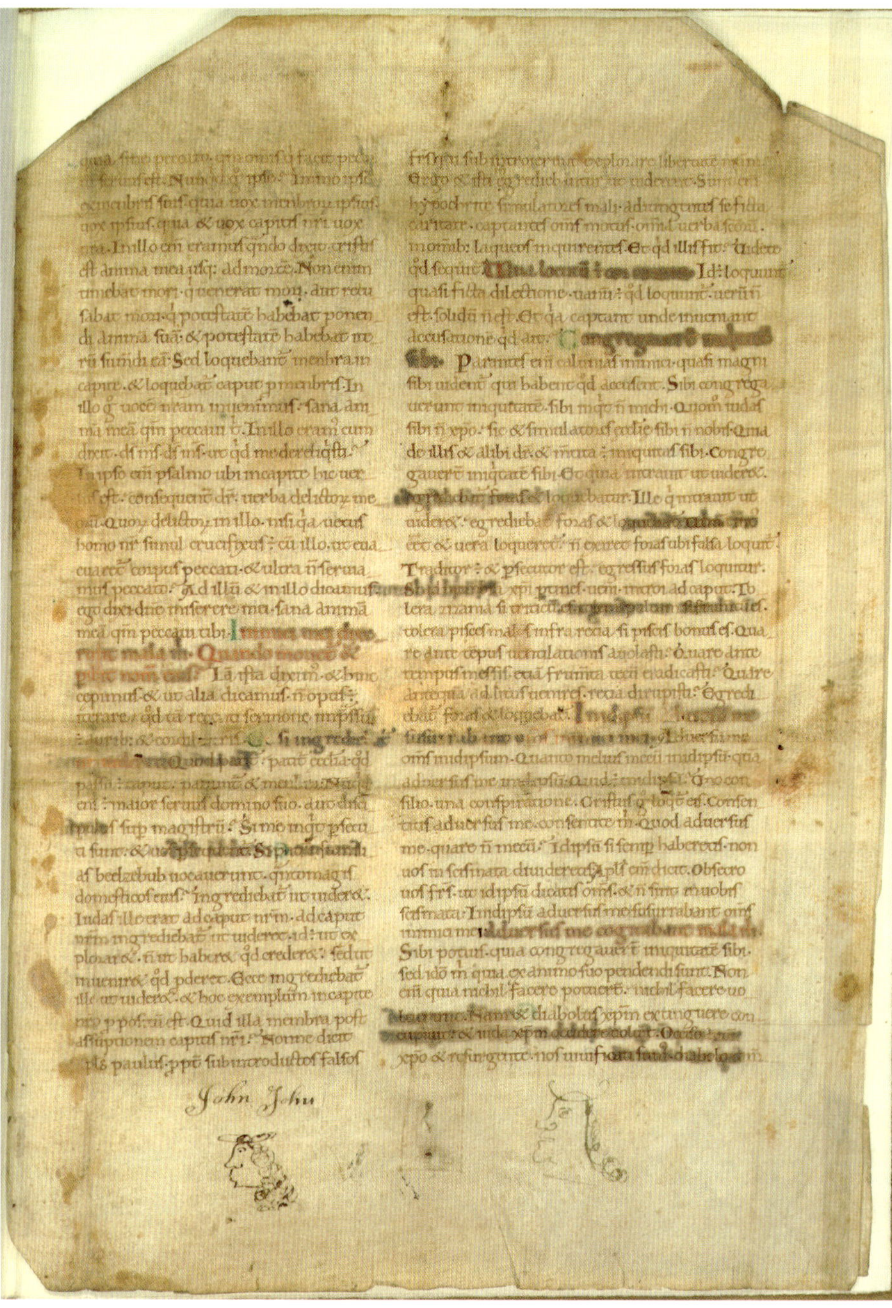

Augustine's *Enarrationes* was normally presented in three volumes: the Canterbury leaf would come from vol. I of such a set (see further **Commentary**).

Collation of the legible portion (fols. 1r–2r) against CCSL 38, pp. 454 ff. highlights the following variants; the readings of the *s.* xii[1] Rochester and Exeter copies (BL, MS Royal 5 D. iii, fol. 184r ff. and Oxford, Bodleian Library, MS Bodley 289, fol. 125r ff.) are also recorded for Psalm 40. The reading in the printed edition is given first; Canterbury, Exeter and Rochester are identified by the sigla C, E and R respectively.

Page 454/33, seruus est peccati [C **fol. 1r**, E, R: peccatum seruus est. Page 454/35, animam suam ponendi [C, E, R: ponendi animam suam. Page 454/42, ?E: In illo enim eramus [C, R: In illo eramus. Page 454/8, Et ingrediebantur [C, E, R: Et si ingrediebantur. Page 454/8/1, Quod passus est Christus patitur et ecclesia [C, E, R: Quod patitur, patitur ecclesia. Page 454/8/2, Numquid enim seruus est maior [C: Numquid enim est maior seruus. [E, R: Nunquid enim seruus maior est. Page 454/8/5, Iudas ille ad caput nostrum erat [C, E, R: Iudas ille erat ad caput nostrum. Page 454/8/10, subintroierunt proscultare libertatem nostram? [C, E, R: subintroierunt explorare libertatem nostram. C: Ergo et isti egrediebantur [E, R: Ergo et isti ingrediebantur. C, R: ficta caritate [E: facta karitate. Page 454/8/15, Uidete quid sequitur [C, R: Uidete quod sequitur (E ambiguous – 'qd'). Page 455/23, quia habent quod accusent [C, E, R: qui habent quod accusent. Page 455/32, ueni intro, haere capiti [C, E: ueni introi ad caput (R: ueni, introi ad caput). Page 455/33, intra retia [C, E, R: infra retia. Page 455/9/3, Quid est: aduersum [C, E, R: quam aduersus me inidipsum. Quid est in idipsum? Page 455/9/5, Consentitis aduersum me, consentite mihi [C, E, R: Consentitis aduersus me, consentite mihi. Quod aduersus me. Page 455/9/20, maledicos appellatos [C fol. 1v, E, R: maledicus appellatur. Page 456/9/23, Numquid et uos discipuli eius uultis esse? [C, E, R: Numquid et uos uultis discipuli ipsius esse? Page 456/9/26, maleuolo [C, E, R: maliuolo. Page 456/9/27, non ex aliquo malo uerborum [C, E, R: non ex aliquo malo uerbo. Page 456/9/27, non quid [C: non quod (E, R ambiguous – 'qd'). Page 456/10/6, quando uos exsultastis occidisse eum [C, E, R: *om*. eum. Page 456/10/7, Illi saeuierunt [C, E, R: Illi sepelierunt. Page 456/10/15, Quia Adam forma erat futuri [C, E, R: Quia adam erat forma futuri. Page 456/11/2, congregauit [C, E, R: congregaret. Page 457/11/17, Proinde si sic illi dicamus [C, R: Proinde sic hic illi dicamus [E: Proinde sic\hic/illi dicamus. Page 457/11/19, Quomodo nobis [C, E, R: Quodmodo uobis. Page 457/12/3, intellegit [C, E, R: intelligit. Page 457/12/5–6, E, R: ne perderent locum [C: ut (corrected by the original hand to 'ne') perderent locum. Page 457/12/6, eradicati a regno [C, E, R: Eradicato regno. Page 457/12/7, Suscitatis reddidat illis tribulationem, reddidit [C, E, R: suscitatus reddidit illis. Reddidit. Page 457/12/8, Ciuitas enim illa [C, E, R: *om*. enim.

(Psalm 42) Page 478/5/52, et gratias gestiebat agere Deo [C **fol. 2r**: et gestiebat agere gratias deo. Page 478/6/2, tristis es, inquit, anima [C, *om*. inquit. Page 478/6/4, in languoribus [C, ?in angoribus. Page 478/6/5, Animae dicit [C, Anime dici. Page 478/6/11, Quare tristis es, caro mea sed [C, *om*. mea. Page 478/6/13, Quare doles [C, quare dolens. Page 478/6/18, Non ergo anima alloquitur carnem [C, Non alloquitur anima carnem. Page 479/6/22, imago dei est [C, imago est dei. Page 479/6/27, neglegit [C, negligit. Page 479/7/9, Ille enim nouerat [C, Ille enim non nouerat (possibly originally 'mouerat'). Page 479/7/12, nemo tollit illam [C, nemo tollit eam. Page 479/7/13, et iterum sumo eam? [C, +ad me? Page 479/7/15, bene credit [C, bene credidit. Page 479/7/16, Abrahae [C, habrahe.

Limited though the sample is, the near-universal agreement of the three copies of English origin or provenance is striking: with a couple of very minor exceptions, their texts for the commentary on Psalm 40 are identical, sharing virtually every departure, great and small, from the printed 'Ur'-text. While further work would be needed to establish how localised this tradition was, the evidence would seem to indicate a relationship between these particular witnesses, inviting the hypothesis of ultimate descent from a single exemplar.

Scribes and Script

The work of two scribes is preserved: one wrote everything except the last two and a half lines of fol. 2r, column 2 ('membra sua' … 'habrahe'), which were done by the second hand.

Scribe 1 wrote a late standard Anglo-Caroline minuscule (cf. **nos.** 8, 11–13) in a form characteristic of the scriptorium of Saint Augustine's Abbey, Canterbury, in the generation after the Norman Conquest (see **nos.** 15, 17). The present specimen is a hurried-seeming and fairly densely-applied yet still competent essay in this potentially very elegant script; its peculiar forms include an 'x' with a very long left 'leg', and a *punctus interrogativus* whose main body is fairly long and horizontally aligned. The same scribe was also responsible for the small number of – invariably interlinear – corrections. Punctuation: low point (major and minor pauses), medial point (major and minor pauses), *punctus elevatus* (minor pause), and *punctus interrogativus*. Sentence capitals are a stylised uncial-based alphabet, typical of Saint Augustine's Abbey in this period. In the commentary on Psalm 40 (though not that on 42), key lemmata are presented in red in ordinary minuscules, sometimes headed by a green initial; some, though not all, of the other scriptural citations are similarly distinguished. (Quotations are signalled throughout MSS Bodley 289 and Royal 5 D. iii, being fully 'highlighted' in the former, and marked by a coloured initial and marginal 'quotation marks' in the latter.)

A number of scribes at Saint Augustine's Abbey in the late eleventh century and the early twelfth practised this type of script, which appears in some twenty books (partial lists in Gameson 1995, pp. 102–3 with n. 28, and Budny 1997, p. 689). Given the homogeneity of the basic style, the different grades of book for which it was used, and the undoubted chronological spread of the work of the individual practitioners, it is difficult to be certain how many scribes were involved, and isolating the oeuvre of particular hands is a treacherous business. That said, scribe 1 of the present item almost certainly also wrote Lit. A. 8 (**no.** 17) and Bruxelles, Bibliothèque royale, MS 444–52; he may also have been responsible for Cambridge, Peterhouse College, MS 251, fols. 106–91, and might have contributed to Cambridge, Corpus Christi College, MS 291 and Oxford, Bodleian Library, MS Bodley 391.

Scribe 2 used the same basic script but is quite distinct since his interpretation of the forms was appreciably plainer and more rectilinear: serifs and feet are altogether less pronounced, while curving forms tend to be 'squared off'.

Decoration

None in the surviving fragment. The initial 'B' (for Psalm 1) at the start of the volume is likely to have been decorated – as is the case in the broadly contemporary copies of the same work from Christ Church and Rochester (respectively, Cambridge, Trinity College, MS B. 5. 26 and BL, MS Royal 5 D. iii). The fact that the secundo folio reference for our volume in the late medieval library catalogue is 'de domino', the very first words of the commentary on Psalm 1.1 after the lemma (PL 36, col. 67), implying that the latter occupied a whole page by itself (presumably fol. 1 v), lends strong support to the hypothesis of a major decorated incipit. We may note that, while one of the two comparable volumes containing the work of Augustine of Hippo that were written by the same scribe is articulated by enlarged coloured penwork capitals alone (Bruxelles, Bibliothèque royale, MS 444–52), the other does have decorated initials (Lit. A. 8: **no.** 17). The only surviving rubrics in the present fragment – the explicit to the commentary on Psalm 42 and the incipit to that on 43 (at the end of the very damaged fol. 2v) – are presented respectively in red (now oxydised) and green, written in a form of rustic capitals typical of Saint Augustine's Abbey work of this date (cf., e.g., Add. 172 and Lit. A. 8: **nos.** 15 and 17).

History

Written at Saint Augustine's Abbey, Canterbury, *c.* 1100, by a known scribe of that community, the fragment is almost certainly the remains of the 'Prima pars Augustini super psalterium, 2° fo. *de domino*. D.4. G.2' listed in the house's late medieval library catalogue (James 1903, list VIII, no. 336, p. 221). The

'Approbatus' that was added in a s. xvi² Italic type hand to the lower margin of fol. 2v (at right angles to the original text) suggests that the volume had been broken up and was being quarried for wrappers within a couple of generations of the Dissolution. At a later date (s. xvii–xviii) the name 'John' was written twice in the lower margin of fol. 1r. In the same margin are two rather crude sketches – in different ink and probably by different hands – of a long-haired male head in profile. The bifolium is said to have been recycled – perhaps in a second phase of re-use – as the wrapper of a parish register from Elmstone, Kent; the volume in question was doubtless that parish's composite Register of Baptisms, Marriages and Burials for the period 1551–1730, now U3/162/1/A1. Casual treatment during this stage of its history is reflected in a circular stain on fol. 2v, seemingly from a mug or other such vessel. An inscription on the modern cover records the provenance ('... Parish of Elmstone, Kent') and notes that the bifolium was 'Restored and bound at Cath. Lib. Canterbury by P. Maple, June 1951'. Lost from sight for an extended period in s. xx² (see Watson 1987, p. 13), it had been rediscovered and deposited in the Cathedral Archive by *c.* 1990.

Commentary

The *Enarrationes in Psalmos,* a massive collection of commentaries on the psalms, originated as a series of independent compositions which Augustine then put into order to form this more comprehensive work. If his responses to individual psalms tended to be coloured by their opening words or titulus, overarching themes are nevertheless articulated, most notably the prophetic insight of the texts into the life of Christ and his church. The commentary on Psalm 40, for instance, turns on Christ's passion.

The extant manuscripts as a whole (Wilmart 1931, pp. 257–315 with CCSL 38, p. vi) attest to a strong and fairly continuous tradition. Starting with a handful of witnesses in late Antiquity, the numbers rise modestly but steadily in the eighth, ninth and tenth centuries, mushrooming dramatically in the eleventh, to well over the combined total of the ninth- and tenth-century witnesses, and then more than doubling again in the twelfth century, before tailing off thereafter. As the impressive number of manuscripts copied in the eleventh and, above all, the twelfth century underlines, this was a Romanesque text par excellence, possessed by every religious foundation worthy of the name. Those in England were no exception.

Although known to Aldhelm and Bede, the text was clearly a rarity in late Anglo-Saxon England – from which only one part-copy is extant (Oxford, Trinity College, MS 54; $x^{3/4}$). This changed with the Norman Conquest, whereafter the work was perceived as a core text for any respectable library, and copies were energetically transcribed. The work was generally presented in three volumes, and all the surviving early English copies are (or were) parts of such sets. The same was doubtless true of the Saint Augustine's Abbey copy represented by the present fragment – which may plausibly be matched with the *prima pars* of the sole three-volume set recorded in the late medieval library catalogue (James 1903, p. 221, nos. 336–8) (the house had two extra copies of part III: nos. 339–40). Such sets, produced in the couple of generations after the Conquest, survive – at least in part – from Durham, Christ Church, Canterbury, Rochester, Bury St Edmunds, Exeter, and Salisbury, as well as from Saint Augustine's. The Durham and Christ Church copies are probably older than the present fragment; the Bury, Exeter, Rochester and Salisbury ones younger. The other complete English copies of volume I range in 'page count' from around 170 folios (Oxford, Bodleian Library, MS Bodley 289) up to 250 (BL, MS Royal 5 D. iii) depending on their *mise-en-page*; the original manuscript from which the present fragment comes is likely to have been close to the lower figure.

U3/162/28/1 shows striking physical similarities in size, layout, and articulation to two other contemporary manuscripts from Saint Augustine's Abbey: Bruxelles, Bibliothèque royale, MS 444–52, and Lit. A. 8 (**no. 17**). Wholly written in the same script type, and very probably by the same scribe as the present fragment, these too contain works by Augustine of Hippo. Moreover, it is a reasonable hypothesis that the lost parts II and III of the three-volume *Enarrationes* also matched the present manuscript – their part I. The abbey scriptorium evidently produced at least some of the great Father's works as a matching set.

Bibliography

Ker 1960, p. 30; Gameson 1995, esp. p. 102 with n. 28, and p. 144.

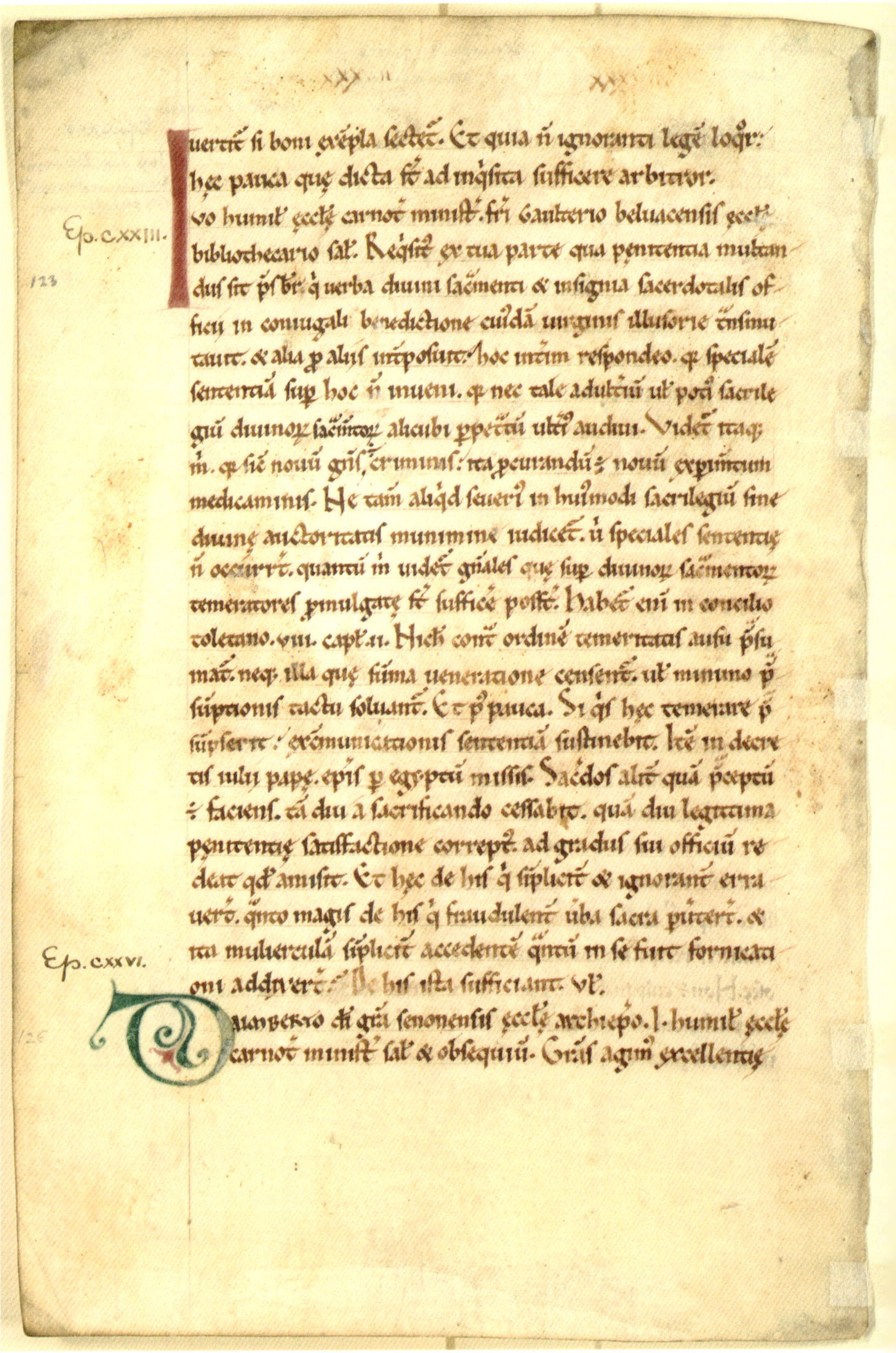

19 Add. 127/15

Ivo of Chartres, *Epistolae*.
Canterbury, Christ Church; *saec*. XII[in]
Illustration: fol. 2v

Physical Description

Three folios, mounted separately; apart from modest rubbing of the surfaces, which has affected the occasional word, they are in generally good condition with fairly full margins. Page size: 280 × 182 mm. Written area: 198 × 127 mm. Lines: 27. Space between lines: 8 mm. Height of minims: 3 mm. Ruling: ink.

Content

[As currently ordered (for the probable original order, see **Commentary** below).]
[Fol. 1r] // et uo [sic] habere studeatis. Eadem ... tam pro eorum excellentia, quam pro eorum munificentia. Valete [end of Ivo Carnotensis, Ep. 106 to Henry I of England: PL 162, col. 125]. Reverende anglorum regine matildi, Iuo ... Quoniam unam te esse ... et episcopum in celebratione diuinorum sacramentorum induere. Valete [Ep. 107]. Pascali summo pontifici, Ivo ... Quanta caritate ... et testifican- **[fol. 1v]**tium ... in oculis dei me presente conscind-// [Ep. 108, breaking off at PL 162, col. 127A].
[Fol. 2r] //[concupiscen]tia. Usque adeo manent inter uiuentes ... **[fol. 2v]** ... haec pauca que dicta sunt ad inquisita sufficere arbitror. [Ep. 125, starting imperfectly: PL 162, col. 137–8]. Ivo humilis ecclesie carnotensis minister, fratri Gaulterio baluacensis ecclesie bibliothecario salutem. Requisitus ex tua parte ... De his ista sufficiant. Vale [Ep. 123; PL 162, cols. 153–4]. Daimberto dei gratia senonensis ecclesie archiepiscopo, Ivo ... Gratias agimus excellentie // [start of Ep. 126; PL 162, col. 138].
[Fol. 3r] // genitos quorum conuersatio in monasteriis uel religiosis ecclesiis probata fuerit, ... Hierophilus de trapezoboli **[fol. 3v]** frisie, transmutatus est ... Scripsistis nobis dilectissimi filii, ut apostolica [–erasure–] et compassionis uiscera aperi[entes]// [part of the Prologue to Ivo Carnotensis, *Decretum*: PL 161, col. 55B–col. 56C; Brasington (ed.) 2004, pp. 132–6].

In the upper margin of fol. 1r an early hand has written, 'XX' and 'XXVI'. In the upper margin of fol. 2v are two partly obliterated numbers by the same hand: 'XXX?I' and 'XXX?II'.

Scribes and Script

The extant leaves are written by a single scribe in a version of the so-called 'prickly' script, the angular, post-Conquest Christ Church hand, characterised by sharp 'breaks' within forms that were normally curvilinear, and by split, wedge-shaped serifs. This particular hand looks like a slightly later and less well controlled version of that of the scribe of Cambridge, Trinity College, MS B.3.9 (Ambrose; Christ Church; *s.* xi/xii). The writing is sometimes placed on the ruled lines, sometimes just above them. The ink is brown. Corrections are done in the same script-type and ink (except that at fol. 2v, line 9, which is in a darker ink). Fairly extensive use is made of abbreviation; the tildes invariably rise sharply from the left to the right. Punctuation is by low and medial points (both used for major and minor pauses), *punctus elevatus* (for minor pauses) and *punctus interrogativus*. The points themselves are generally diamond-shaped. Sentences are headed by stylised rustic capitals.

Decoration

No major decoration survives. The initials heading the epistolae are elegant coloured capitals with undulating contours and hairline serifs, whose form and colour (red, green or purple) is typical of Christ Church work of this period. One (fol. 2v: the D to ep. 126) is in two colours: green embellished with a purple flourish.

History and Provenance

Written at Christ Church, Canterbury (*teste* script and capitals), this was presumably the copy of Ivo's letters that is listed in Henry of Eastry's catalogue ('Epistole Yuonis Carnotensis Episcopi': James 1903, list II, no. 126, p. 31). Casual use in *s.* xvi–xvii is revealed by the post-medieval doodles on fol. 3v, which include pointing hands, the word or name, 'Stranger', and a date which has been re-worked to read '1699' (the second digit may originally have been '5'). A note kept with the fragments records that they were 'Removed from the binding of a XVI book by J. B. Sheppard c. 1880'; the title of the book in question is, unfortunately, not stated. Identifications of the author and the letters were ostentatiously written in the margins in ink in a flowing *s.* xix–xx hand, the numerals being repeated in pencil by a different hand; on fol. 2r the same annotator supplied the incipit of the acephalus letter. Collectively these notes show both the commendable scholarship and the very different conservation standards of a century ago.

Commentary

Ivo of Chartres (*c.* 1040–1116), who had probably been a student of Lanfranc at Bec in the later 1050s, was abbot of Saint-Quentin (a community of regular canons) at Beauvais from 1078, then bishop of Chartres from 1090 to 1116. He is known above all for his legal collections, the *Decretum* (*c.* 1094) and the *Panormia* (*c.* 1095); a third compilation, the *Tripartita*, is also – though less securely – attributed to him. The *Decretum*, a sprawling collection of 3760 canons loosely organised in seventeen books, was less popular than its more concise and orderly successor, the *Panormia*, which comprised just over 1000 canons arranged in eight books. The manuscript evidence shows that, whilst in the first generation after the Norman Conquest Lanfranc's collection (the so-called *Collectio Lanfranci*) was the dominant canon law text in England, Ivo's works were being acquired in the early twelfth century, fairly shortly after their 'publication'. A Christ Church copy of the *Decretum*, datable to before *c.* 1127, survives as Cambridge, Corpus Christi College, MS 19, fols. 1–333. Rochester had a manuscript of the *Panormia* by *c.* 1125, while a *s.* xii^{1} Saint Augustine's Abbey copy is extant in the form of Cambridge, Corpus Christi College, MS 94. It should be noted that the Prologue which was originally composed for the *Decretum* (the text on fol. 3 of the present item), also circulated as a preface to the *Panormia*, as part of Ivo's letter collection, and independently.

Ivo was the author of some 300 letters, which enjoyed a respectable circulation in the twelfth century, above all in France, but also in Germany and England. There are four surviving English copies of some part of the collection that date from before *c.* 1130: Cambridge, Jesus College, MS Q. G 5 (Durham; xii^{1}); London, British Library, MS Royal 6 B. vi (Rochester; xii^{1}); Worcester Cathedral Library, MS Q. 1 (Worcester; xii^{1}); and the present fragment, which is probably the earliest of the four. Though of modest dimensions, it was clearly an elegant book: produced at Christ Church in the early twelfth century, it shows the hallmarks of its fully-fledged Romanesque 'house style'.

It is highly likely that the Canterbury fragments come from a copy of Ivo's *Epistolae* which incorporated his Prologue to the *Decretum*. Such an arrangement is well attested in French copies from an early date, wherein the Prologue generally appears in the vicinity of ep. 100, most frequently between epp. 103 and 104 (cf. e.g. Paris, BnF, MSS lat. 2481, 2483, 2485; Vatican City, Biblioteca Apostolica Vaticana, MS Reg. lat. 60, etc., all later than the present item). The only early English manuscript with a comparable arrangement is the Rochester copy, London, British Library, MS Royal 6 B. vi. This probably dates from the time of Bishop Ernulf (1115–24) – who, incidentally, had studied under Ivo at Beauvais before becoming a protégé of Lanfranc and then Anselm at Canterbury – and is approximately contemporary with the Canterbury fragments. Just enough survives of the Canterbury manuscript to suggest that the order of its letter collection was similar but not identical to that of the Rochester copy. The texts of the Prologue tell a similar story. Once allowance has been made for the different habits of the two copyists with respect to abbreviation and certain spellings, we are left with one short phrase where the texts seem to display different readings (Canterbury, fol. 3v, 8 lines up: 'Rothadu[m] u[er]o ep[iscopu]m s[an]c[ta]e suessionis eccl[esia]e synodus cui karolus int[er]fuit rex conde[m]nauit…' : MS Royal 6 B. vi, fol. 96r, line 8, 'Rothadu[m] u[er]o s[an]c[ta]e suesionis eccl[es]i[a]e ep[iscopu]m a synodo cui Karolus int[er]fuit rex condemnatu[m]'), and one passage that implies some affiliation between the two copies. On Canterbury fol. 3r, line 21 the equivalent of one line, 'mutatus est in asponam. Alexander ab alia helinopoli', was omitted (through eye-skip – be it of our scribe or that of his exemplar), and then supplied by the original scribe in the upper margin. In MS Royal 6 B. vi (fol. 95v) this very same line plus the one before and the one after it were rewritten *in rasura* by the original scribe: the fact that the replacement writing is to a smaller scale and the lines are slightly longer than usual leaves no doubt that this was done in order to fit extra words into the middle of the passage – indicating that in the original transcription, exactly the same phrase had been omitted. The loss of the rest of the Canterbury book impedes further comparison of the two manuscripts. What can, however, be said with confidence is that, although not copied one from the other, they show a family relationship, and they were certainly closer to each other than to any of the other extant early English copies.

Whatever the exact nature of the connection, the Rochester manuscript certainly helps in the task of ordering the Canterbury leaves, indicating that, far from being scattered folios, they probably come from one small section of the book – possibly even a single quire – and that leaf 3 very probably preceded the others. The content of Canterbury fols. 3, 1 and 2 corresponds to that of MS Royal 6 B. vi, fols. 95r–96r, 98r and 101r, and 103r–v respectively.

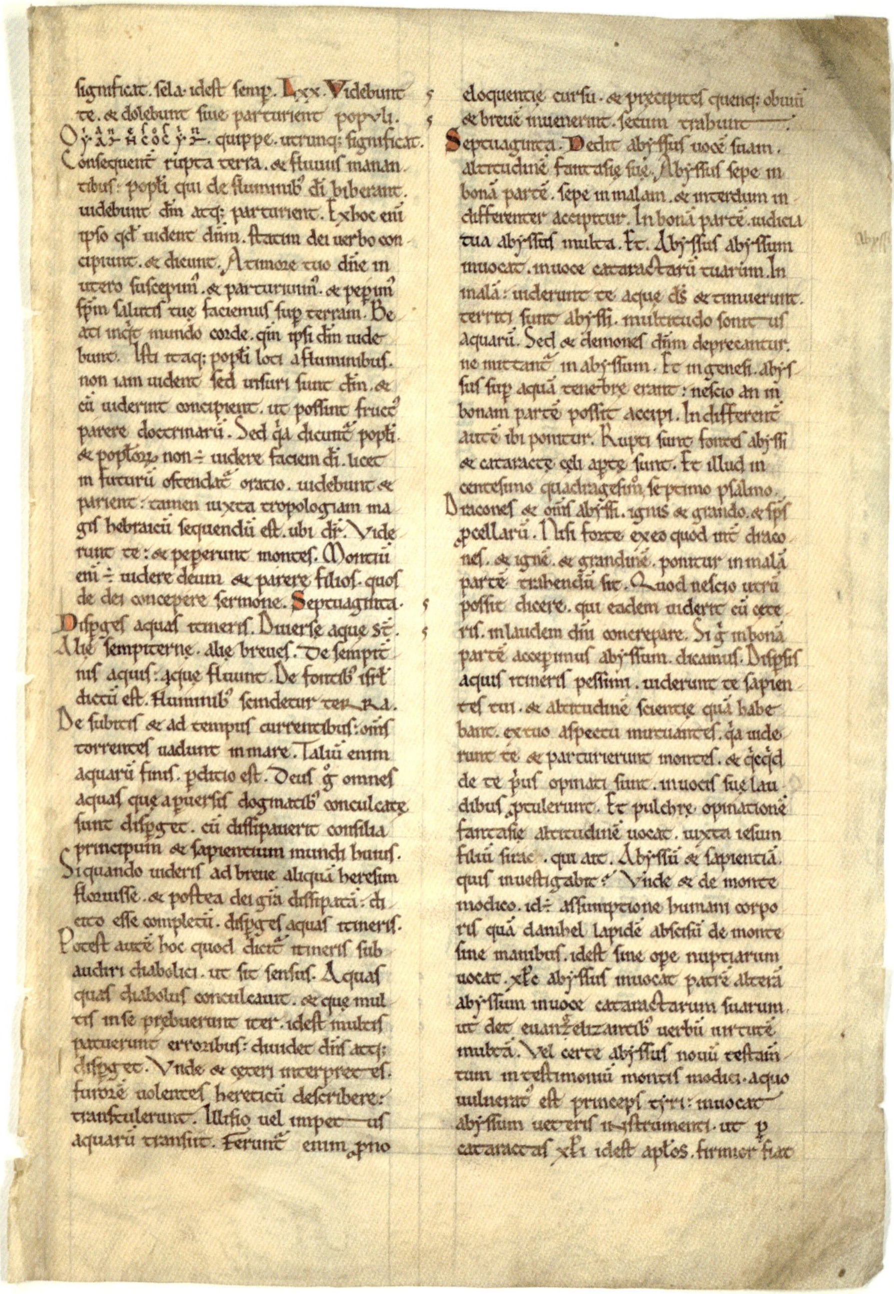
significat. sela idest semp. LXX. Videbunt
te. et dolebunt siue parturient populi.
[illegible] quippe. utrunq; significat.
Consequent rupta terra. et fluuius manan
tibus: popli qui de fluminib; di biberant.
uidebunt dnm atq; parturient. Ex hoc eni
ipso qd uident dnm. statim dei uerbo con
cipiunt. et dicunt. A timore tuo dne in
utero suscepim. et parturiuim. et pepim
spm salutis tue facienus sup terram. Be
ati mudo corde. qm ipsi dm uide
bunt. Isti itaq; popli loci a fluminibus.
non iam uident sed uisuri sunt dnm. et
cu uiderint concipient. ut possint fruct
parere doctrinaru. Sed qa dicunt popli
et poplor non e uidere faciem di. licet
in futuru ostendat oratio. uidebunt et
parient: tamen iuxta tropologiam ma
gis hebraicu sequendu est. ubi dr. Vide
runt te: et pepererunt montes. Montiu
eni e uidere deum et parere filios. quos
de dei concepere sermone. Septuaginta.
Dispges aquas itineris. Diuerse aque st.
Alie sempiterne. alie breues. De sempit
nis aquis: aque fluunt. De fontib; ist
dictu est. Fluminib; scindetur terra.
De subitis et ad tempus currentibus: omis
torrentes uadunt in mare. Taliu enim
aquaru finis. pditio est. Deus g omnes
aquas que a puersis dogmatib; conculcate
sunt dispget. cu dissipauerit consilia
principum et sapientium mundi huius.
Siquando uideris ad breue aliqua heresim
floruisse. et postea dei gra dissipata: di
cito esse completu. dispges aquas itineris.
Potest aute hoc quod dicit itineris sub
audiri diabolici. ut sit sensus. Aquas
quas diabolus conculcauit. et que mul
tis in se prebuerunt iter. idest multis
patuerunt erroribus: diuidet dns atq;
dispget. Unde et ceteri interpretes.
furore uolentes hereticu describere:
transtulerunt. Illisio uel impetus
aquaru transiit. Ferunt enim pro
eloquentie cursu. et precipites quenq; obuiu
et breue inuenerint. secum trahunt.
Septuaginta. Dedit abyssus uoce suam.
altitudine fantasie sue. Abyssus sepe in
bona parte. sepe in malam. et interdum in
differenter accipitur. In bona parte. iudicia
tua abyssus multa. Et. Abyssus abyssum
inuocat. in uoce cataractaru tuarum. In
mala: uiderunt te aque ds et timuerunt.
territi sunt abyssi. multitudo sonitus
aquaru. Sed et demones dnm deprecantur.
ne mittant in abyssum. Et in genesi. abys
sus sup aqua tenebre erant: nescio an in
bonam parte possit accipi. In different
aute ibi ponitur. Rupti sunt fontes abyssi
et cataracte celi aperte sunt. Et illud in
centesimo quadragesimo septimo psalmo.
Dracones et omis abyssi. ignis et grando. et sps
pcellaru. Nisi forte ex eo quod int draco
nes. et igne. et grandine. ponitur in mala
parte trahendu sit. Quod nescio utru
possit dicere. qui eadem uiderit cu cete
ris. in laudem dni concrepare. Si g in bona
parte accepimus abyssum. dicamus. Dispsis
aquis itineris pessimi. uiderunt te sapien
tes tui. et altitudine scientie qua habe
bant. ex tuo aspectu mutuantes. qa uide
runt te et parturierunt montes. et qcqd
de te pius opinati sunt. in uoces sue lau
dibus ptulerunt. Et pulchre opinatione
fantasie altitudine uocat. iuxta iesum
filiu sirac. qui ait. Abyssu et sapientia
quis inuestigabit? Vide et de monte
modico. id e assumptione humanam corpo
ris qua danihel lapide abscisu de monte
sine manibus. idest sine ope nuptiarum
uocat. xpc abyssus inuocat patre alteria
abyssum in uoce cataractarum suarum.
ut det euangelizantib; uerbu uirtute
multa. Vel certe abyssus nouu testam
tum in testimoniu montis modici. a quo
uulneratus est princeps tyri: inuocat
abyssum ueteris instrumenti. ut p
cataractas xpi idest aplos. firmiter fiat

20 X.1.11 flyleaves

Jerome, *In Prophetas minores*
Canterbury, Saint Augustine's Abbey; *saec.* XII^{in}
Illustration: fol. 2r

Physical Description

Two consecutive leaves. They were re-used – along with a leaf from a large-format late medieval antiphonal – to cover 'Comperta et Detecta, liber 12' of 1571–2: one of the Jerome leaves (numbered '1') is still bound at the end of this volume; the other (numbered '2') is now physically separate from the host book but is boxed with it. Fols. 1r and 2v bear multiple, distinct offsets (running vertically) from the late medieval antiphonal leaf, which would seem to have been Add. 128/46, fol. 1 (the verso of which bears the corresponding rubric, 'Ex officio comperta lib. 12, 1571, 1572'); the recto of the present fol. 1r appears to have abutted the lower half of its 1r. Add. 128/46 includes a further three leaves from the same late medieval service book; and another leaf from the same volume was used for the cover of X. 1. 10. The other sides of the present leaves (i.e. fols. 1v and 2r) are in fairly good condition, though the date '1571' was written repeatedly in the inter-columnar space of fol. 1v.

Size (cut down on all sides): 301 × 210 mm. Written area: 252 × 165–70 mm. Two columns (column width: 77 mm). Lines: 44. Space between lines: 5.5 mm. Height of minims: 2–2.5 mm. Ruling: pencil. The current binding of the host volume (replacing the antiphonal leaf) presumably dates from *s.* xix^{ex} or xx^{I}. The original two-volume set from which our leaves come is likely to have had a total of about 280 folios.

Content

Jerome, *In Habbakuk*, II, iii, 8.9–10/13 (from Jerome, *In Prophetas minores* (CPL, 589)).
[Fol. 1r] // Et de quibus dicitur. Equum et ascensorem deiecit in mare, [PL 25, col. 1319, line 12; CCSL 76, p. 632, l. 511] ... Illo autem mortuo et putens obrutis [PL 25, 1320, l. 25; CCSL, p.

633, l. 575, continuing directly on **fol. 1v:**] si serui fodiant contradicunt phylistum et iurgium est. Si uero ... Id est abscondita eius aperta fecisti, non ad breve tempus, sed in perpetuum. Hoc enim [PL25, 1321, l. 45; CCSL, p. 635, l. 643, continuing directly on **fol. 2r:**] significat, sela, id est semper. Lxx. Videbunt te et dolebunt siue parturient popvli. ... cataractas christi id est apostolos, firmior fiat [**fol. 2v**] predicatio. Si quis autem uoluerit hoc quod dr [sic; *recte*: 'deus'] dedit abyssus uocem suam ... sed gentes et ethnici permanserunt, in furore domini deducuntur ad tartarum, // [PL25, 1324, l. 43; CCSL, p. 638, l. 770].

Collation of the text from 'Videbunt te' against CCSL 76, p. 634, l. 603–p. 637, l. 703 highlights the following variants. (The reading in the Canterbury fragment, siglum 'C', is always presented first.)

C: tenentes [CCSL, p. 634, l. 613, texentes; C: comatice [l. 614, commatice; C: sullimes [l. 615, sublimes; C: potentes [l. 616, potestates; C: hec [l. 617, hae; C: laudauerunt, et tunc [ll. 620–1, laudauerunt te, tunc; C: superbi [l. 621, superi; C: in plusu [l. 621 in plausum; C: et uictorem [l. 622, ut uictorem; C: leuatarum [l. 624, eleuatarum; C: demonstrarunt [l. 624, demonstrarent; C: errore [ll. 625–6, horrore; C: eruditio, lumen [l. 628, eruditio tua, lumen; C: uident [l. 651, uiderunt; C: ostendatur [l. 654, extendatur; C: aquis, aque [l. 660, aquis et quae; C: sapientium [l. 666, sapientiam; C: precipites quenque [l. 674, praecipites ut quemcumque; C: breuem [l. 675, leuem; C: Et Abyssus abyssum inuocat, in uoce cataractarum tuarum. [l. 679, Et: Abyssus abyssum inuocat et reliqua; C: Uiderunt te aque deus et timuerunt, territi sunt abyssi, multitudo sonitus aquarum [l. 680, Viderunt te aquae deus et reliqua; C: Sed et demones dominum deprecantur [l. 680, Sed et daemones deprecantur; C: quadragesimo septimo psalmo [l. 685, quadragesimo octauo psalmo; C: qui eadem [l. 688, qui eam; C: parturierunt [l. 693, paturierunt; C: et quicquid [l. 693, quicquid; C: opere nuptiarum [l. 699, opere nuptiali; C: uerbum uirtutem multam [l. 701, uerbum uertute multa.

Orthographical divergences apart (e.g. ll. 614 and 615), the present copy is notable for the relatively high number of variants (e.g. ll. 679 and 680), rare readings (e.g. l. 701) and errors (e.g. ll. 621, 624).

Scribes and Script

The surviving text was the work of a single scribe, writing a neat, regular, not especially spiky version of the prickly script that was characteristic of groups of Canterbury scribes in the late eleventh and earlier twelfth centuries (cf. **nos. 19** and **22**). There are angled wedge-shaped serifs and sharply rising feet, while steeply-angled fine lines terminate the cross strokes of 'e' and 't' and the tails of 'g'. Other characteristic forms include an 'ur' abbreviation which looks like an 'a', an ampersand with a very long leg, and the frequent, though not invariable, use of capital rho within the *nomina sacra* for Christ (χPς, etc.). The scribe uses a mixed (primarily rustic) alphabet for sentence capitals which is equally characteristic of Canterbury; if a sentence capital happened to coincide with a margin, it was sometimes calligraphically extended. There is generous word separation, but much biting of letters within words. The scribe was skilful at using spacing and variations in letter-forms to justify his right-hand margin without having to break words. Punctuation: low points (for major and minor pauses), *punctus elevatus* (for minor pauses), and *punctus interrogativus*. Double 'i's are invariably dashed. Quotations are signalled by diples in the margins.

The scribe may also have written Oxford, Bodleian Library, MS Fell 2, the last volume of a multi-volume passional from Saint Augustine's Abbey (see Ker 1979).

A late medieval hand (or hands) added small cues – echoing key words in the adjacent text – in some of the margins: fol. 1r, top margin, 'bonis'(?); fol. 2r, outer margin, 'abyss[us]'; fol. 2v, '6ag[–]nte' (for 'sexaginta'?).

There is a difficult to decipher, ?s. xvi^2 notary scrawl on fol. 1v (upside down in relation to the original text).

Decoration

Sections are headed by two- to four-lines-high plain coloured capitals (red or green), the rest of the word in question being written in small rustic capitals in ordinary ink.

History

Written at Saint Augustine's Abbey, Canterbury, in the early twelfth century, this is presumably the copy of the work that is recorded in the house's late medieval library catalogue: 'Secunda pars ieronimi super minores prophetas, 2° fo., omnem hominem' (James 1903, p. 220, no. 327). The previous entry records the *Prima pars* of the same work. The manuscript was clearly broken up by 1571 at the latest, whereupon the present folios were re-deployed as the endleaves of Visitation reports. The responsibility of the diocesan registrar, such records were first stored in the office-holder's home, then in a variety of repositories around the town. By 1870 they were kept in the upper floors of the Christ Church gateway, and were then gradually transferred to the cathedral archive, a process completed by 1993. Our host volume (X.1.11) would seem to have been (re)bound at some point between s. xix^{ex}–xx^{in}, when the antiphonal leaf that formed its wrapper was separated from it.

Commentary

Poorly represented prior to the ninth century, Jerome's *In Prophetas minores* has thereafter a common pattern of transmission and survival: a comparatively large number of ninth-century copies gives way to significantly fewer from the tenth and earlier eleventh centuries, followed in turn by a very dramatic increase in the late eleventh and twelfth centuries. The earliest known manuscripts of English origin or provenance all date from this last period: Durham had received an imported Norman copy of the whole work by 1096 (Durham Cathedral Library, MS B. II. 9), while at least one part of it was transcribed at Christ Church in the 1080s (Cambridge, Trinity College, MS B.3.5); over the next generation Bury St Edmunds, Battle, Saint Augustine's Abbey, and then Worcester all acquired at least part of the work (respectively, Bodleian Library, MS e Mus. 26; British Library, MS Royal 4 C. xi; the present fragment; and British Library, MS Royal 4 C. ii; there is in addition Cambridge University Library, MS Gg. 4. 28 of unknown provenance).

It has reasonably been suggested (Ker 1979) that the present fragments – and hence the Saint Augustine's Abbey book they represent – were copied from the slightly earlier Christ Church manuscript, Cambridge, Trinity College, MS B.3.5. The latter was written entirely by the Christ Church monk Eadmer, the biographer of St Anselm, and the most recent analysis of his scribal development would place this work in the 1080s (Gullick 1998, esp. pp. 179–80); his exemplar would seem to have been rife with errors. The scribe of the present leaves made no attempt to imitate the format of Eadmer's copy (41 long lines with a written space of 230 × 153 mm): rather he used the two-column layout that was more fashionable by his day. He likewise followed his own preferences in relation to abbreviations and certain orthographical practices, and inserted additional accents. He also made nine errors of his own (four of which he subsequently corrected).

One may usefully compare the present fragments with the slightly later copy of Jerome, *In psalmos* from Saint Augustine's Abbey, Oxford, Bodleian Library, MS Laud Misc. 300. Written in a bolder version of the prickly script, with a written area only slightly larger than that of our manuscript and, like it, set out in two columns (width 72 mm, 40 lines), the dimensions of this manuscript are 400 × 270 mm. It has a single decorated initial (for the Preface), a couple of fine arabesques (for *Beatus uir* and *Domine exaudi*), and some more modest ones (for *Quid gloriaris* and *Dixit domino*). Though bigger and bolder than the present leaves, MS Laud misc. 300 probably gives a reasonable general impression of the book from which they came.

Bibliography

Ker 1979 (reproducing most of fols. 1v and 2r as pls. 31 and 33).

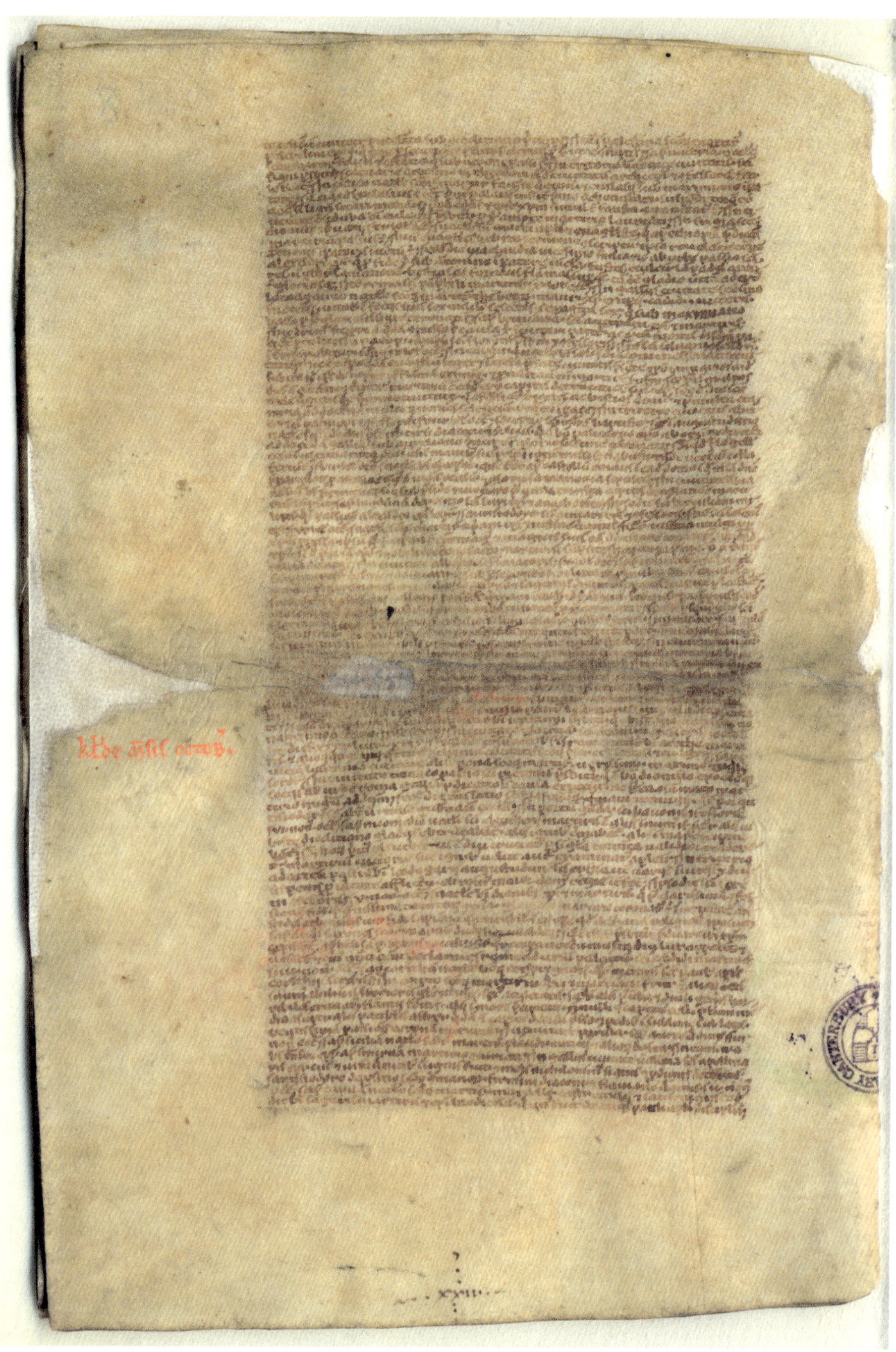

21 Add. 127/20

Usuardus, *Martyrologium*
France, England or Normandy; *saec.* XII[1]
Illustration: fol. 8v

Physical Description

A single quire of four bifolia, now contained within a modern parchment wrapper. The parchment (arranged HF, FH) is of low quality, with a very noticeable distinction between hair and flesh sides. A major fold-scar runs horizontally across the middle of all the leaves, damaging the text and causing ragged splits, which have been repaired.

Size: 170 × 114 mm. Written area: 127–30 × 66 mm. Lines per page: 86–7. Space between lines: 1.5 mm. Height of minims: 0.5 mm. Prickings to guide the horizontal rulings survive at the outer edge of some leaves; notwithstanding the high number of written lines, there are only 25 prickings. No ruling is now visible. A contemporary signature (XXII – flanked on all four sides by a flourish consisting of two dots and a diple) appears in the centre of the lower margin of the final verso. On fol. 2r (showing through to 2v) is a green offset stain either from a 'Lombardic' 'E' on its side or from an upright 'M'. There are red pigment stains on fol. 8v.

The quire signature indicates that this was but part of a much larger volume: there must have been at least one more quire after the present one, bringing the total to a minimum of twenty-three (implying a book of over 180 folios).

Content

Usuardus, *Martyrologium*, from the start of 1 January to the end of item two for 6 October.

[Fol. 1r] *Incipit martirologium.* ¶ Ianuarius habet dies XXXI et luna XXX. ¶ kalende mensis ianuarii. ¶ circumcisio [written next within the text area is: 'incipit martyrologium' – presumably the cue for the marginal rubric – whereafter the main text resumes:] domini nostri Iesu Christi. ¶ Rome natal[?e] sancti almachii martyris, qui iubente urbis prefecto cum diceret, hodie octaue dominice diei sunt, cessate a superstitionibus idolorum ... [PL 123, col. 602; Dubois 1965, p. 152]. [The incipits of subsequent months appear as follows: February on fol. 1v; March, 2v; April, 3r; May, 4r; June, 5r; July, 5v; August, 6v; September, 7v; and October on 8v. At the bottom of **fol. 8v** the text breaks off incomplete:] ... II [pridie] nonas octobres. ¶ Apud capuam natalis sanctorum martirum marcelli, casti, emilii et saturnini. ¶ Eodem die beati sagaris martiris et episcopi lao?dicensis qui unus fuit de antiquis pauli apostoli discipulis. // [PL 124, cols. 543–4; Dubois 1965, p. 315].

Usuardus introduced his text with a preface from Augustine's *Contra Faustum* (Festiuitates sanctorum apostolorum seu martyrum antiqui patres in uenerationis mysterio celebrari sanxerunt ... [Bk 20, ch. 21: PL 42, cols. 384–5]) and began the text proper with *Vigilia natalis Domini* on VIIII kal. Ian. (24 December) [see Dubois 1965, pp. 146–51]. Whilst it is not impossible that this material appeared at the end of the now lost previous quire of the present manuscript, it is altogether more probable that – in common with other later copies, such as BL, MS Royal 7 E. vi from Christ Church, Canterbury – it started (as it does now) with Kalende mensis ianuarii (1 January); the presence of the rubric, 'incipit martyrologium' both beside and within the start of this version of the text, supports this. The text evidently finished in the following quire (Q. 23). The content of the previous twenty-one quires is, unless more of the volume be discovered, uncertain (see further **Commentary**).

Scribes and Script

The text is written in a microscopic hand – so small, indeed, as to be on the verge of illegibility for anyone who is not both myopic and familiar with its idiosyncrasies – whose minute scale makes palaeographical analysis difficult. Squat, crowded and unattractive, the writing is seemingly the work of a single French or Anglo-Norman scribe; the ink is (now) brown. Distinctive features – possibly as much a product of the size as of the hand per se – are a rather square general matrix yet quite a sharp 'attack', the regular truncation of ascenders and descenders, and a lack of feet and serifs except on some of the more generous ascenders. Punctuation: point (for minor pauses – it is impossible to make a meaningful distinction between low and medial positions at this scale), and 'semi-colon' (major pauses). Tironian 'et' is regularly used. A simple 'paraph' mark frequently indicates the start of each new item on a particular date.

Very densely written (the letters are heavy and inky for their size, and some have 'blotted') and heavily abbreviated, the written area is a solid, uninviting mass – yet it is set within margins that are still wide and virtually empty. Moreover, there is minimal visual articulation within the text: while marginal rubrics signal the start of each month, there is no use of paragraphs, nor any variation of script or spacing, to mark even these divisions. At least one person read the text with care, for corrections were entered in the margin in darker ink by a broadly contemporary hand; however, in so far as one can judge, this would seem to be the work of the original scribe himself. Whether all of the previous twenty-one quires were written in an equally compressed manner is an open question.

Decoration

None. Rubrics, entered in the margins (no space was left in the written area), are written in bright red ink. The first (fol. 1r, signalling the text as a whole) was done entirely in minuscules; the second (fol. 1v) entirely in capitals; the rest are generally in a mixture of minuscules and (predominantly rustic) capitals. The formula varies: February (1v), March (2v), April (3r), July (5v), September (7v) and October (8v) have the full phrase, 'K[a]l[en]de m[en]sis Februar[ii]' etc., while for May (4r), June (5r) and August (6v), just the name of the month ('Maius', etc.) is given.

History and Provenance

There is seemingly no direct evidence for the history and provenance of this item, even its country of origin being open to debate. All that is clear is that at some point the volume was broken up, this portion being recycled as endleaves or wrappers. The fact that one leaf bears the offset from a late medieval capital might suggest that this happened during, rather than after, the late Middle Ages. The context from which the fragments were salvaged does not appear to be recorded.

Commentary

Usuardus († *c.* 877), a monk of Saint-Germain-des-Prés in Paris, worked at the compilation of his martyrology over an extended period in the third quarter of the ninth century. Distinguished from other early martyrologies by its orderliness and concision – having brief notices of martyrs and their localities for each day of the year – the text was enduringly popular throughout the Middle Ages, being customised as appropriate. Thus the basic text of the *s.* xi^{ex} Saint Augustine's Abbey copy (BL, MS Cotton Vitellius C. xii, fols. 114–56) incorporates many locally-significant figures and occasions, such as Hadrian (fol. 115r, 9 Jan.), Laurentius (fol. 118r, 2 Feb.); Ælphege (fol. 125v, 19 April), translation of Mildred (fol. 129v, 18 May), deposition of Dunstan (fol. 130r, 19 May), Augustine (fols. 130v–1r, 26 May), Mildred (fol. 131v, 5 July), deposition of Eanswith (fol. 139r, 31 Aug.), deposition of Theodore (fol. 142r, 29 Sept.) deposition of Honorius (fol. 143v, 30 Sept.), Liuinus (fol. 149r, 11 Nov.), and the ordination of Augustine (fol. 149v, 16 Nov.). The use of such a martyrology was part of the daily life of regular communities: the fourteenth-century Custumal of Saint Augustine's Abbey specified that the relevant section should be read each day in chapter (Thompson 1902-4, I, p. 223; II, p. 182). Accordingly, copies attracted – indeed might be designed to receive – obits. Such was the case, for instance, for the two surviving English versions that are broadly contemporary with the present item, the aforementioned example from Saint Augustine's and the so-called 'Durham Cantor's Book' (Durham Cathedral Library, MS B. IV.24), as also for the mid-twelfth-century Christ Church copy (BL, MS Royal 7 E. vi plus MS Cotton Claudius C. vi, fols. 168–9). In point of fact, the Custumal of Saint Augustine's specified that the names of the dead should be inscribed in the martyrology (Thompson 1902-4, I, pp. 296, 352, 364). There are – seemingly – no such additions in the present item.

The scribe of the present manuscript exerted himself to compress the maximum amount of text into as small a space as possible, with no regard for the convenience of the reader: his eight folios correspond to thirty of the Saint Augustine's Abbey copy (fols. 114r–144v) and fifty-six of the Christ Church one (fols. 2r–57r). Indeed, the cramped aspect of his work is in striking contrast to the spacious and elegant appearance of these latter books, wherein each entry, clearly separated from the next, is headed by a coloured initial and rubric, with the start of each month distinguished by an elaborate K L monogram (decorated in MS Cotton Vitellius C. xii, arabesque in MS Royal 7 E. vi) plus display script.

Martyrologies (generally with obituaries) were not infrequently associated with the *Regula S. Benedicti* and/or other texts of key importance for the day-to-day running of Regular or communal life. An example of the first 'formula' which is broadly contemporary with the present item is the Corbie Martyrology-Obituary-*Regula*, BnF, MS lat. 17767. The aforementioned Durham Cantor's book and the mid-twelfth-century Christ Church Martyrology include Lanfranc's *Constitutiones* alongside the *Regula S. Benedicti*, the Usuardus and other material; and it is clear from an entry in their earliest library catalogue, that Rochester had a similar compilation by 1125 ('A martyrology concerning the birthdays of the saints, the rule of St Benedict and the Customs of Archbishop Lanfranc in one volume': *Textus Roffensis*, fol. 229r). It is not unlikely that the larger collection to which the present quire once belonged was something similar; however, its microscopic and informal script makes it poorly suited to important day-to-day public use. In so far as appearance is a guide to function, this quire looks like the product of an individual cleric who transcribed the text (and others) either for personal use or – just conceivably – as an interim stage on the way to a more accessible presentation. In comparison with the altogether more legible copies mentioned above which show many indications of long service, the present item, perhaps unsurprisingly, bears no obvious indications of use.

22 Lit. E. 42 and Lit. E. 42A, part 1

Multi-volume passional
Canterbury, Christ Church; *saec.* XII¹ (one part datable after *c.* 1123; one part before 1128x37), with later additions.
Illustrations: fols. 9r, 16v, 29v, 35v, 50r, 69r, 76r

Physical Description

Folios: 81. Brutally re-used as wrappers and binding material in s. xvi, the leaves have been reclaimed, straightened, and consolidated. Most have been bound – slightly disordered – as a single volume (Lit. E. 42), foliated (with re-numberings) '1'–'75'. Subsequently acquired pages, which remain as individual leaves or bifolia, are shelved as Lit. E. 42A; though physically separate, these have nevertheless been foliated '76'–'81' as a continuation of the main volume. A further bifolium survives in Maidstone, Kent County Archives Office (S/Rm Fae. 2), and three substantial portions are in the British Library (MSS Cotton Nero C. vii, fols. 29–78; Harley 315, fols. 1–39; and Harley 624, fols. 84–143).

In its original form, the work comprised seven volumes. Fols. 1–30 of Lit. E. 42 (plus the late medieval supplement fols. 69–72) come from vol. I; fols. 31–42 plus the Maidstone leaves from vol. II; the portions in the British Library from vol. III; Lit. E. 42, fols. 73–4 are a late medieval supplement to vol. IV; Lit. E. 42, fols. 43–57, 62–3, 75–8 come from from vol. V; and fols. 58–61, 64–8, and 80–1 from vol. VI. The probable position of the Canterbury leaves within their original quires is reconstructed by Ker 1977, pp. 289–94. No quire signatures survive on the Canterbury leaves (most of which have lost their lower margins); three original signatures do, however, appear in MS Harley 624: fols. 91v, 'II'; 99v, 'III'; and 124v, 'XXI'.

The leaves at Canterbury vary considerably in size and condition. All are more or less weathered, worn, discoloured, cut down, stained, scarred by folding and perforated by slits for lacing, sometimes with extensive damage to the text and decoration. A few are highly fragmentary. Most are supplemented by modern parchment repairs and surrounds. Many bear titles showing that

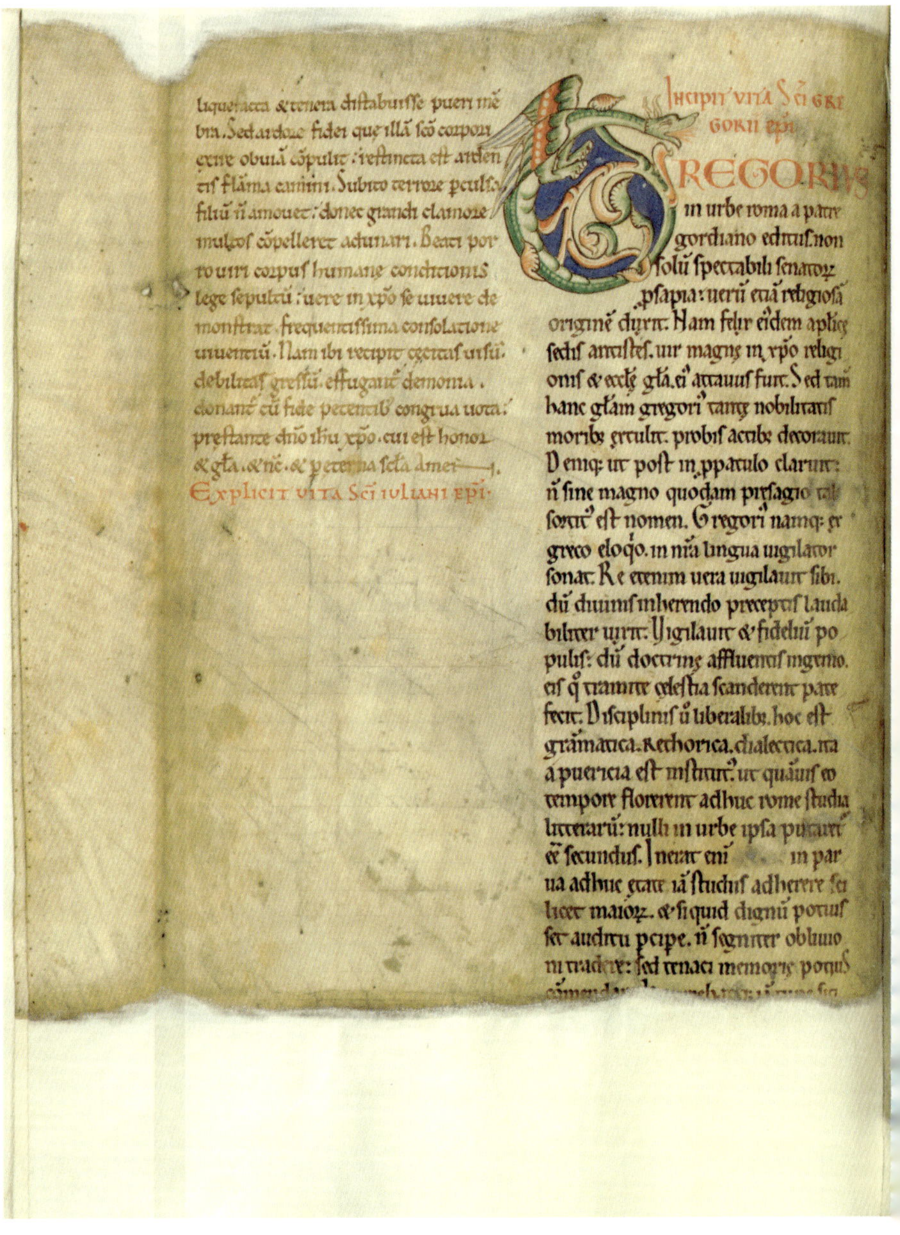

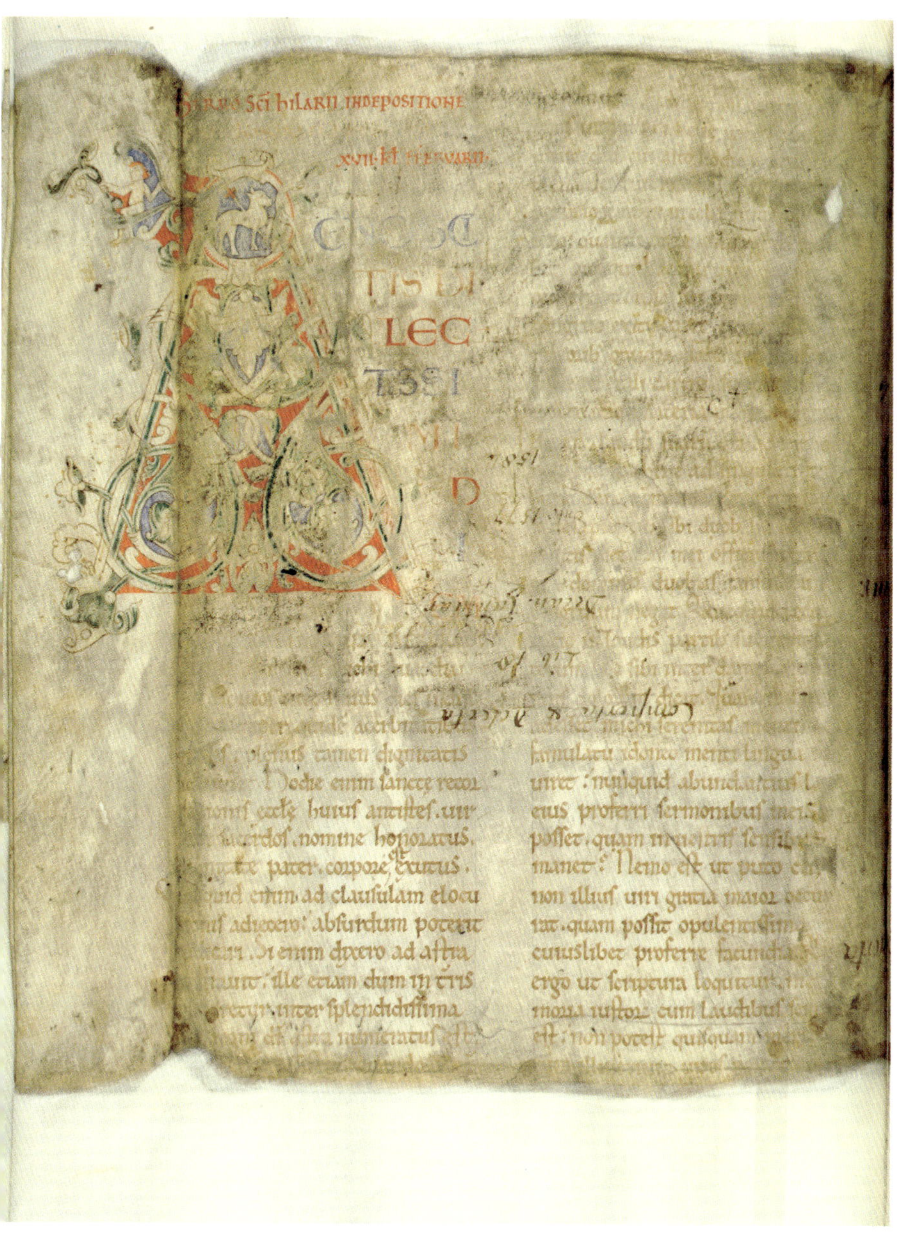

INCIPIT PASSIO SCI MAXIMILIANI
MARTIRIS IIII IDUS MARTII
VS CO
ETANO
LINO
CON
SVLIBUS QVAR
TO IDUS

Incipit passio Sci ypoliti martyris
R
EGRES
SUS
BEA
TUS
YPO
LITUS

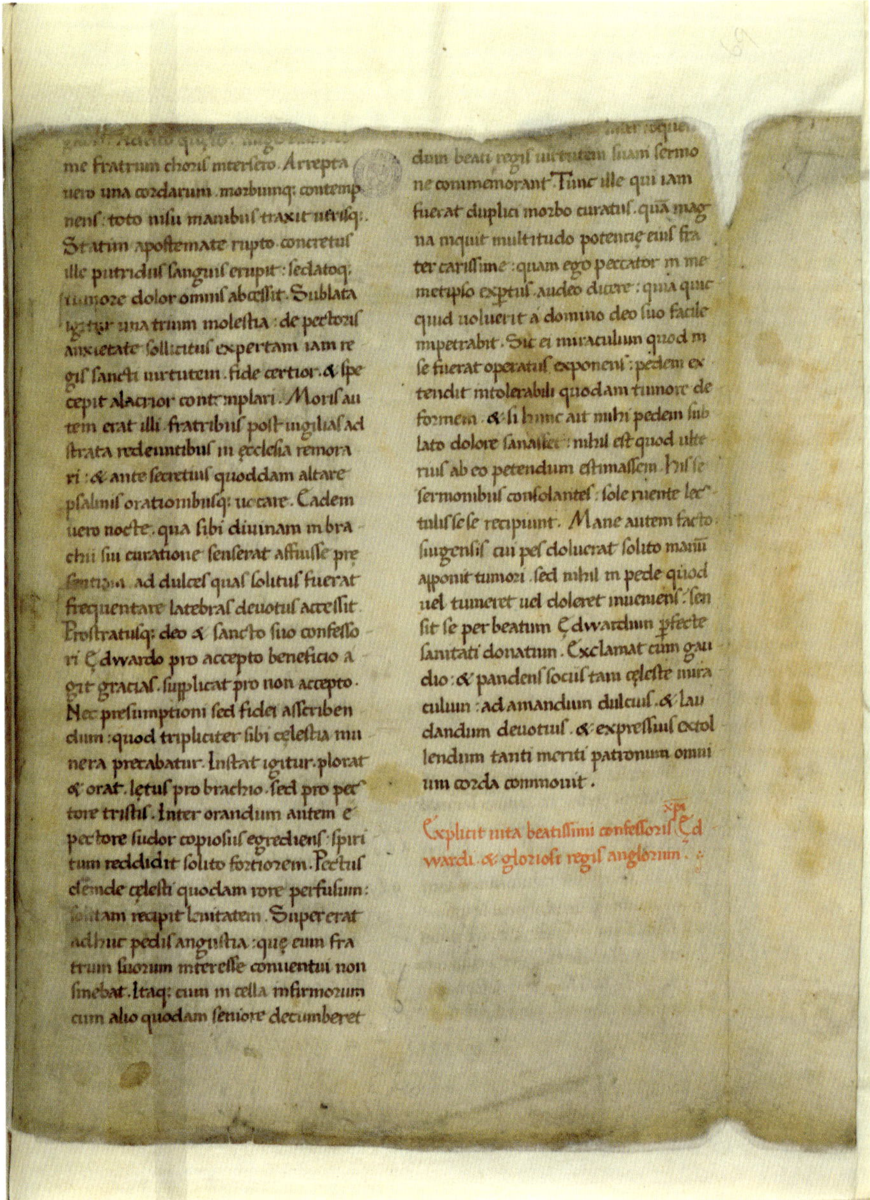

me fratrum choris interesse. Arrepta
uero una cordarum . morbumq; contemp
nens: toto nisu manibus traxit utrisq; .
Statim apostemate rupto concretus
ille putridus sanguis erupit: sedatoq;
tumore dolor omnis abscessit. Sublata
igitur una trium molestia: de pectoris
anxietate sollicitus expertam iam re
gis sancti uirtutem . fide certior & spe
cepit alacrior contemplari. Moris au
tem erat illi fratribus post uigilias ad
strata redeuntibus in ecclesia remora
ri: & ante secretius quoddam altare
psalmis orationibusq; uacare. Eadem
uero nocte. qua sibi diuinam in bra
chii sui curatione senserat affuisse pre
sentiam . ad dulces quas solitus fuerat
frequentare latebras deuotus accessit.
Prostratusq; deo & sancto suo confesso
ri Edwardo pro accepto beneficio a
git gratias. supplicat pro non accepto.
Nec presumptioni sed fidei asscriben
dum: quod tripliciter sibi celestia mu
nera precabatur. Instat igitur. plorat
& orat. letus pro brachio. sed pro pec
tore tristis. Inter orandum autem e
pectore sudor copiosus egrediens: spiri
tum reddidit solito fortiorem. Pectus
deinde celesti quodam rore perfusum:
solitam recepit leuitatem. Supererat
adhuc pedis angustia: que eum fra
trum suorum interesse conuentui non
sinebat. Itaq; cum in cella infirmorum
cum alio quodam seniore decumberet

dum beati regis uirtutem suam sermo
ne commemorant. Tunc ille qui iam
fuerat duplici morbo curatus. quam mag
na inquit multitudo potentie eius fra
ter carissime: quam ego peccator in me
metipso expertus audeo dicere: quia quic
quid uoluerit a domino deo suo facile
impetrabit. Sic ei miraculum quod in
se fuerat operatus exponens: pedem ex
tendit intolerabili quodam tumore de
formem. & si hunc ait mihi pedem sub
lato dolore sanauerit: nihil est quod ulte
rius ab eo petendum estimassem. His se
sermonibus consolantes: sole ruente lec
tulis sese recipiunt. Mane autem facto
surgens is cui pes doluerat solito manu
apponit tumori. sed nihil in pede quod
uel tumeret uel doleret inueniens: sen
sit se per beatum Edwardum perfecte
sanitati donatum. Exclamat cum gau
dio: & pandens sociis tam celeste mira
culum: ad amandum dulcius & lau
dandum deuotius. & expressius extol
lendum tanti meriti patronum omni
um corda commouit.

Explicit uita beatissimi confessoris Ed
wardi. & gloriosi regis anglorum.

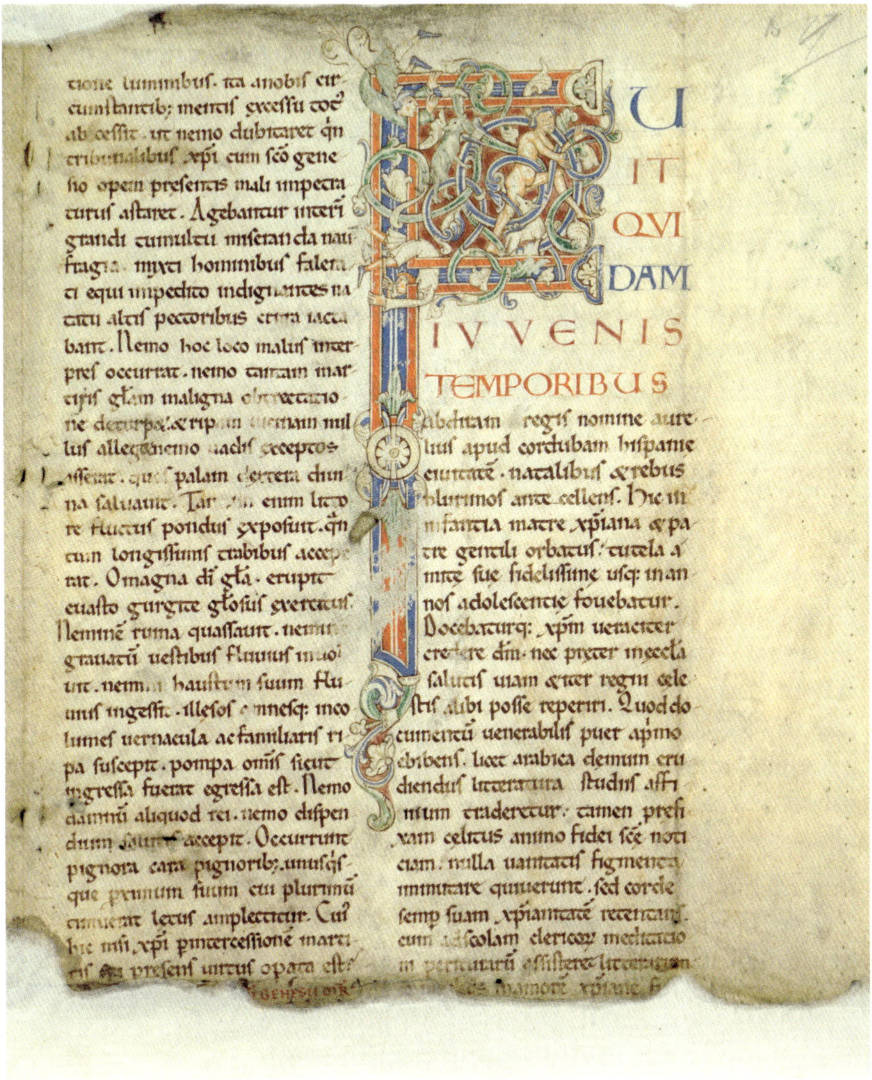

they were recycled as covers for material from the archdeaconry court in the 1570s and 80s; the sides that were then the 'outsides' are particularly discoloured, stained, and abraded, with considerable loss and effacement of text; virtually no legible text remains on fols. 38v–39r, to take an extreme case.

The dimensions of the largest folio (75) are: *c.* 388 × 275 mm. [The dimensions of the three British Library portions are within the range: 375–82 × 242–70 mm.] The written area varies slightly from volume to volume: vols I and II, 277 × 190 mm; [vol. III, 304–7 × 191–5 mm]; vols. V–VI, 305 × 190 mm. All the volumes were laid out in two columns (column width: *c.* 86 mm [British Library portion: *c.* 88–9 mm]). Lines: vol. I, 35; vol. II, ?36 [none of the surviving pages from this portion has a complete text-page]; vol. III, 39; vols. V–VI, 39. Space between lines: *c.* 8 mm. Height of minims: *c.* 3 mm. Ruling: ink and lead.

Content

The individual items are here calendared in their original order. Further details of how much of each entry survives, with references to printed editions, are provided by Ker 1977 – though note that a significant amount of the text in question may be more or less illegible.

Volume I. [Fol. 1r–v] Genovefa [BHL, no. 3336] // exiguitate census, uirtus deerat construendi. Ad cuius cum officium presbiteri solito conuenissent ... ; **[fol. 2r]** Theogenes [BHL, no. 8107]); **[fol. 2r–v]** Lucianus [BHL, no. 5010]; **[fols. 3–4v]** Julianus [BHL, no. 4529]; **[fols. 5r–6v]** Furseus [BHL, no. 3210]; **[fols. 7r–8v]** [though the relevant part of fol. 8v is missing], Marius, Martha, Audifax, Abacuc [BHL, no. 5543]; **[fol. 8v]** Agnes [BHL, no. 156]; **[fol. 9r]** Patroclus [BHL, no. ?6520]; **[fols. 9r–12v]** Vincent [BHL, no. 8628]; **[fol. 13r–v]** Asclas [BHL, no. 722]; **[fols. 13v–14v]** Babillas [BHL, no. 890]; **[fols. 15r–16v]** Julianus [BHL, no. 4544]; **[fol. 16v;** s. xii^{2} addition**]** Gregory [BHL, no. 3639]; **[fols. 17r–19r]** Polycarp [BHL, no. 6870]; **[fols. 19r–25v]** Leucius, Tyrsus, Galenicus [BHL, no. 8280]; **[fol. 26r]** Sabinianus [BHL, no. 7438]; **[fols. 26r–8r]** Aldegundis [BHL, no. 245]; **[fols. 28r–9r]** Balthildis [BHL, no. ?906]; **[fols. 29v–30v]** Honoratus [BHL, no. 3975]. [Plus late medieval supplement, **fols. 69–72:** Edward the Confessor (by Ailred of Rievaulx, BHL, no. 2423); Wulfstan of Worcester, abbreviated version (cf. Darlington (ed.) 1928, pp. xx–xxii, 68–108).]

Volume II. Maidstone, Kent County Archives, S/RM. Fae. 2: Amandus [BHL, no. 332]; Dorothea and Theophilus [cf. BHL, no. 2323]. **Lit. E. 42 [fol. 31r]** Perpetua and Felicitas [BHL, no. 6633]: // prior reddendo spiritum perpetuam expectabat. Perpetua autem ... ; **[fols. 31r–4r]** Quadraginta milites [BHL, no. 7539]; **[fols. 34r–v, 36r–v, 35r–v]** Gregory [BHL, no. 3641]; **[fol. 35v]** Maximilian [BHL, no. 5813]; **[fols. 37r–38v]** Longinus [BHL, no. 4965]; **[fols. 38v–39r]** Gertrude [BHL, no. 3490]; **[fols. 39r–40v]** Miracula eiusdem uirginis [BHL, no. 3495]; **[fols. 41r–42v]** Cuthbert [by Bede]: ... Uolens autem latius monstrare diuina dispensatio quanta //.

[**Volume III:** British Library portions.]

Volume IV [Late medieval supplement: **Lit. E. 42, fols.** 73r–4v: a version of the Seven Sleepers] // in usum sed iussit incidi baltheos sanctorum septem et dixit eis. Pro eo ... egressus est malchus, et uidens lapides foris speluncam miratus est, et non ascendit in cor//.

Volume V. Lit. E. 42, [fols. 43r–6v, 49r–v] Stephen [BHL, no. 7861]: // adiuuante ihesu continuata oratione pugnabat. Parum ... ; **[fol. 47r–v]** Walburga [BHL, no. 8766]; **[fol. 48r–v]** Oswald [Bede, *Historia ecclesiastica*, pp. 250–4]; **[fol. 48v]** Cassian [BHL, no. 1632]; **[fol. 50r]** Taurinus [BHL, no. 7990]; **[fol. 50r–v]** Hippolytus [BHL, no. 3961]; **[fol. 51r–v]** Assumption BVM; **[fol. 52r]** Philibert [BHL, no. 6805]; **[fol. 52r–v]** Symphorianus [BHL, no. 7967]; **[fol. 53r–v]** Bartholomew [BHL, no. 1002]; **[fols. 75r–v, 62r–63r;** addition s. xii^{med} (post 1128x37)] Miracles of Audoenus at Canterbury [printed: Wilmart 1933; Ker 1946] **[fol. 63v,** blank]; **[Lit. E. 42A, fol. 76r]** Genesius [BHL, no. 3307]; **[fols. 76r–77v]** Georgius, Aurelius, Felix et socii [BHL, no. 3408]; **[Lit. E. 42, fol. 54r–v]** Adrian [BHL, no. 3744b]; **[fol. 54v]** Audomarus [BHL, no. 767]; **[fols. 55r–56v]** Protus and Hyacinthus [BHL, no. 6975]; **[fol. 56v]** Felix and Regula [BHL, no. 2888]; **[fol. 57r–v]** Exaltation of Holy Cross; **[fol. 57v]** Cornelius [BHL,

no. 1958]; **[Lit. E. 42A, fol. 78r–v]** Lucia and Geminianus [BHL, no. 4985]; **[fol. 79r–v]** Euphemia [BHL, no. 2708].
Volume VI. [Lit. E. 42A, fol. 80r] Maurice [BHL, no. 5737]; **[fol. 80r–v]** Miracula eorundem martyrum [PL 71, 771–3]; **[fol. 81r–v]** Emmeram [BHL, no. 2539a]; **[Lit. E. 42, fol. 58r–v]** Firminus [BHL, no. 3003]; **[fol. 59r–v]** Cosmas and Damianus [BHL, no. 1970]; **[fol. 60r–v]** Pelagia [BHL, no. 6605]; **[fol. 61r–v]** Denis [BHL, no. 2175]; **[fol. 66r–v]** Demetrius [BHL ?]; **[fols. 66v–68v]** Miracles of Demetrius [BHL ?]; **[fol. 64r–v]** Eustace [BHL, no. 2760]; **[fol. 65r]** Rumwold [BHL, no. 7385; printed: Love 1996]; **[fol. 65r–v]** Hubert [BHL, no. 3994]: ... Tribulationem patientibus strenuus consolator aderat, et carcere preclusis nec non diu ali//.

Scribes and Script

The poor condition of many of the leaves makes identifications difficult, however the principal divisions between hands (or types of hand) are indicated below, numbered according to the order of their appearance in the leaves as currently bound. All the writing is careful and even. In general, abbreviation is restrained and word separation generous. All the early scribes (1–6) punctuate with low point (for major and minor pauses), *punctus elevatus* (for minor pauses) and *punctus interrogativus*; and they mark the start of sentences (and sometimes also holy names) with a mixed alphabet of stylised rustic and uncial forms. Running headings in the upper margins, where preserved, are in rustic capitals in ordinary ink.

1 Fols. 1r–16v, col. i; 17r–42v [vols. I and II]. A modest version of the Christ Church prickly hand, characterised by liberal use of angled, triangular serifs.

2 Fol. 16v, col. ii [*Vita Gregorii*], a s. XII$^{3/4}$ addition. A neat, laterally compressed proto-Gothic hand with residual Romanesque elements. The scribe seems to have been acculturating his hand to the aesthetic of the original stratum, whose punctuation and sentence capitals he matches. His ink remains much darker than that of the original stratum.

3 Fols. 43r–57v [vol. V], 76r–81v [vol. VI]. A Christ Church prickly hand similar to that of scribe 1 but with consistent

differences in the treatment of certain letters – the bowl of 'a' and the tail of 'g', for instance, are more rounded, while the backs of 'c' and 'e' are more angular.

4 Fols. 58r–61v; ?64r–65v [vol. V]. A taller, slightly thinner and less spiky version of the Canterbury prickly hand.

5 Fols. 62r–63r [63v is blank] [vol. V]; 75r–v [Miracles of Audoenus at Canterbury: vol. V] s. ?xii^{med} or possibly even later. A heavy, very spiky hand with pronounced serifs and much 'biting'.

6 Fols. 66r–68v [vol. VI]. A slightly less mannered Canterbury Romanesque hand of xii^{1} (possibly slightly later than scribes 1, 3 and 4).

7 Fols. 69r–74v. An elegant humanistic minuscule, modestly customised to the appearance of the original stratum. The hand is that of the itinerant Dutch scribe, Theodoric Werken (on whom see Mynors 1950; de la Mare 1976; Parkes 1997). After plying his trade in Cologne and Italy during the 1440s, Werken seems to have come to England by the end of that decade. In the 1470s he was working for Christ Church, Canterbury, for whom in 1474 he produced a two-volume copy (Cambridge, Trinity College, MS B.3.21 and Cambridge University Library, MS Ff. 3.10) of John Chrysostom's Homilies on John in the Latin translation of Franceso Aretino, transcribed from the printed edition of 1470; and then in 1477–8 a two-volume copy of the letters of Jerome (Cambridge, Trinity College, MSS R. 17. 4 and R. 17. 5) taken from the Roman edition of 1468. His work in the present manuscript probably dates from around the same time.

8 A poor and difficult to date but presumably s. xv–xvi hand retraced damaged passages on, e.g., fols. 1r, 9r, 32r.

The British Library portions (vol. III) preserve the work of at least three original scribes. 1) MS Harley 624, fols. 100r–114v. This hand is very similar to, though slightly more spacious than, that of scribe 1 in the Canterbury leaves; it is difficult to decide whether or not they are indeed one and the same. 2) MS Harley 315, fols. 1r–15v, col. 2, line 4; MS Harley 624, fols. 84r–99v; and ?MS Cotton Nero C. vii, fols. 29r–59v. A neat and unexaggerated prickly hand, broadly similar to that of the previous scribe.

3) MSS Harley 315, fol. 15v, col. 2, line 4– fol. 39; Cotton Nero, fols. 60r–78r; Harley 624, fols. 115r–143v; plus corrections throughout all three British Library portions. A bold spiky hand whose ink was – or at least remains – darker than that of the other scribes.

Decoration

Rubrics are in red and green. Most are written in hybrid capitals of a form typical of Christ Church, Canterbury; however, a few (fols. 48v, 50r, 52r, 57v), all from the original vol. V, are in a rounded minuscule of late standard Anglo-Caroline form. Texts are subdivided by three-line-high plain initials in blue, red or purple.

The individual *passiones* are headed by an elaborate decorated initial – generally constructed from panels and interlace-adorned terminals in the Anglo-Norman version of the Franco-Saxon style, and coloured in red, green, blue and purple (plus an orangey-pink for some of the human flesh) – accompanied by lines of capitals of Canterbury form in the same colours. The first line of text thereafter is normally written in rustic capitals in ordinary ink. The surviving decorated initials are as follows:

Fol. 2r, B: constructed from Franco-Saxon style terminals and panels, with foliage curling into the bowls. The foliage in the upper bowl transforms into a monster; a man clambers through that in the lower bowl. There is a beast mask at the join between the bowls.

Fol. 8v, S (only a fragment, amounting to about a third of the letter, remains): includes a quadruped in foliage, and a human head.

Fol. 9r, P: historiated with St Vincent who is attached by his wrists, ankles and neck to a frame; he is being tortured by two men, one wielding a pair of flails, the other a pike (or grappling iron). The stem of the letter includes a roundel containing the Agnus Dei, complete with cross, book and one pulled-back curtain. The outline of the bowl includes a foliate boss of Anglo-Saxon ancestry.

Fol. 13v, N: constructed from three dragons whose tails turn into foliage, all set against a purple ground.

Fol. 16v [addition of s. xii$^{3/4}$], G: formed from a curling dragon whose tail turns into foliage. The work is crisp with effective colour shading. The leaf-forms, which herald the so-called 'Channel Style', are akin to those in the Lambeth Bible (Lambeth Palace Library, MS 3 and Maidstone Museum, s.n.).
Fol. 19r, E: including two tulip-like foliate sprigs and an acanthus roundel of late Anglo-Saxon form.
Fol. 26r, P (very damaged): with a beast amidst ebullient foliage in the bowl, and a foliate roundel of Anglo-Saxon form on the stem.
Fol. 28r, B (very damaged): the two bowls, which are joined by a lion mask, contain a ?quadruped and a dragon amidst foliage curls. The lower section of the upright includes a human figure in a striding or climbing posture, who is looking upwards; the content of the upper section and of the roundel in-between is difficult to make out.
Fol. 29v, A (very damaged): filled with elaborate curls of foliage. Within a foliate roundel at the apex appears the Agnus Dei (with cross and book), facing right. Beside it, facing left, a human figure sits astride foliage that flows out of the letter. When in pristine condition, this initial will have been reminiscent of, though of a lesser quality than, some of the letters in the Lambeth Bible.
Fol. 31r, I: the top of the stem is filled with a man carrying a small, thin monster; he stands on a roundel containing a bust portrait of an animal (possibly a calf); the upright includes a quadruped with a fish in its mouth.
Fol. 34r, B (very damaged): the upright includes two human figures; the upper one fights with a spear against the dragon head that forms the terminal of the upper bowl; the lower one is upholding a roundel with a bust of an angel. A second such roundel (complete with angelic bust) links the contours of the bowls. Within the bowls, four beasts stride through foliage. A hybrid (with human torso and dragonesque lower body) squats at the bottom of the letter.
Fol. 35v, T (well preserved): its arms are formed from two loops of foliage, that on the left containing an animal playing a harp, that on the right has an animal bowing a stringed instrument. A man wearing a knee-length tunic and holding a roughly-hewn

stick occupies the upright; a quadruped with long ears bites its fore-leg in the field at the bottom of the stem.

Fol. 38v, C (very damaged): historiated with a male figure standing beside a building, holding a flaming horn in his right hand and a small ?urn in his left; he turns his head up to a hand of God above. The two ends and the mid-point of the letter-form are decorated with roundels within which are spiral forms.

Fol. 39r, E (very damaged): the upper and lower terminals are dragon heads, from whose mouths spew foliage that curls back into the space within the letter; the cross-stroke is adorned with a quadruped.

Fol. 48v, S (very damaged – only top half survives): the letter-shape is formed from vegetal tubes which turn into ebulliant foliate curls, through which a naked man is clambering.

Fol. 50r, R (well preserved): the terminals of the upright are formed from particularly heavy interlace; the bowl and leg are composed of a mass of monsters, human figures and heads. A beast mask is half way up the stem.

Fol. 52r, C (well preserved): two rather portly bear-like beasts terminate the arms (which they are in the act of chewing); a third lion-like quadruped, eating its right fore-leg, is in a panel mid-way up the back. The main field is filled with a standing haloed figure (doubtless St Simphorianus), holding a book in his right hand and a palm-branch in his left; the figure type is closely similar to that used for Christ in the Sherborne Pontifical (BnF, MS lat. 943), a manuscript written at Christ Church in the late tenth century: as this volume reached Sherborne soon after it was made, the model for this figure type – or another copy of it – must have remained at Christ Church.

Fol. 54v, D: historiated with an enthroned, haloed ecclesiastic (doubtless St Audomarus/Ouen) who wears elaborate robes (including a chasuble and pallium) and a mitre with a red cross on the front. He holds a crosier in his left hand; his right hand is uplifted, palm towards the beholder. A beast mask appears at the bottom of the letter, beneath his feet. Notwithstanding the damaged surface and loss of pigment, it is clear that this figure was more fully and richly painted than most motifs in the book.

Fol. 56v, T (very damaged): it had circles for arms and simple, rectilinear knot-work at the top and bottom of the stem, and a twist in the middle, but otherwise none of the detail remains legible.
Fol. 57v, T: modestly conceived with an upright formed of plait-like interlace, and foliage tendrils for arms.
Fol. 65r, P (damaged): the bowl contains a quadruped within foliage tendrils; the upright is adorned at the top with a sprig ending in a dragon head, and at the bottom with a flourish of foliate tendrils.
Fol. 66v, M: a simple but bold red arabesque initial.
Fol. 75v, Q [xii^{med+}]: a simple arabesque initial in green and ochre.
[**Lit. E. 42A**] fol. 76r, F: decorated with foliage tendrils and a foliage boss. In the space between the horizontal cross-strokes, a naked man, his leg being bitten by a quadruped, clambers through the foliage, alongside another quadruped. Where the horizontals meet the verticals, two clothed men (one with an axe) clutch the main lines of the letter; both are in head-over-heels contortions, one the mirror image of the other.
Fol. 80r, M (the entire surface is very damaged with considerable loss of colour and detail): smaller than most, the letter is formed from two foliate-tailed dragons which project from the open mouth of a small rampant lion shown in profile.
Fol. 81r, P (a substantial portion of the top of the letter has been lost owing to the trimming of the leaf): what remains shows that the bowl was adorned with foliate curls, while the descender comprised two fairly plain, coloured panels with a foliate sprig at the bottom.

With the possible exception of fol. 57v, all the original decorated initials seem to be the work of one artist. The decorated initials in volume III (the British Library portion) are the work of a different hand whose style is tighter and neater and whose repertoire, though broadly similar, is distinguished by a lesser debt to Anglo-Saxon foliate forms and by more fish. One initial in vol. III (MS Harley 624, fol. 115r, for Germanus) is distinct from the rest and was painted, if not necessarily designed, by a third hand.

History

The series of monumental volumes represented by this collection of fragments was written at Christ Church, Canterbury, doubtless over an extended period of time, in and around the 1120s (see further **Commentary**). Close attention to the palaeography and content might permit further unravelling of the 'internal history' of the compilation – the contributions of British Library scribe 3 to volume III, for instance, and of Canterbury scribe 6 to vol. VI might represent the latest stage of the initial phase of work on the portions in question – however such a study would be out of place here.

Volume I (represented by Canterbury fragments) received an additional text, plus decorated initial in the second half (probably third quarter) of the twelfth century. John of Salisbury may have used the set, referring to it as the *grandia uolumina*, to make his abbreviation of the *Vita Anselmi* for the canonisation process of 1163 (Southern 1990, p. 420; cf. PL 190, col. 1038). At the end of the century, volume III (MS Cotton Nero C. vii, fols. 78v–79v) received a verse epitome of the Life of St Anselm – a text which was probably composed after 1163 and possibly before 1170 (Sheerin 1974). There was some modest re-writing in the thirteenth century (MS Harley 624, fol. 96r).

The set features in the early fourteenth-century Christ Church library catalogue as items 359, and 361–6 (James 1903, p. 52) – the first being described as: *Vita Sancti Silvestri, continet uitas et passiones sanctorum quorum festa celebrantur a die Sancti Siluestri usque ad festum Sancti Ignacii* – and subsequent annotations and additions indicate that it continued in use up to the Reformation. In the Canterbury portions notable late medieval annotations survive on fols. 57v ('lectio prima', 'secunda' etc.), and 62v (a pointing hand in ink, highlighting the reference in the text to Prior Elmer), along with characteristic Christ Church marks on, e.g., fols. 60r and 65v. Lectio/capitula divisions, rubrics, glosses and pointing hands were added to the British Library portions, and the original (red) lection numbers in the *Vita et passio Ælphegi* (MS Cotton Nero C. vii, esp. fols. 48r–49r) and the *Vita Dunstani* (MS Cotton Nero C. vii, fols. 73v–78v) were emended and supplemented. Major late medieval supplements in Canterbury (fols. 69–74) were written by Theoderic Werken, probably in the 1470s (see **Scribes and Script**); that in MS Cotton Nero C. vii, fols. 10–28 (a *Vita Augustini*) was added a generation or so later. In addition, a very poor and difficult to date but most probably sixteenth-century hand made a series of corrections in the Canterbury portion (fols. 1r (*in rasura*), 9r, 32r, 34v, and 54v), and also flagged certain sentences with a discreet line.

The history of the set in the immediate aftermath of the dissolution of the cathedral priory (1540) and the establishment of the New Foundation (1541) is elusive, notwithstanding a couple of tantalising references. In 1560 John Bayle informed Matthew Parker that he had borrowed, 'Fyve great legends of maistre Mylles [monk of Christ Church, then prebendary of the cathedral 1541–65]', taking a sixth 'out of our lybrarye' (Luard 1865, p. 163). It is not impossible that this refers to the present manuscripts, implying that much of the set had been temporarily 'salvaged' by a former monk turned prebend. However, the volumes in question may equally, if not more probably, have been Christ Church's six-volume set of *lectionalia* (James 1903, p. 52, nos. 371–6; cf. Ramsay 1995, p. 375). Equally, in the third quarter of the sixteenth century a 'Liber uocatur passionale S. Ignatii' from Canterbury was in the hands of William Bowyer, keeper of records in the Tower of London († by 1576), since a Parkerian transcript with that title was recorded to have been taken 'ex quodam vetusto libro quondam eccl. Cantuar. iam in manibus m^ri^ Bower' (CCCC, MS 298, fol. 54v: James 1912, II, p. 84). The early fourteenth-century library catalogue lists both a 'Passionale sancti Ignacii, primum' (no. 360) and a 'Passionale sancti Ignacii, secundum' (no. 361), one of which was a portion of the present item. Correspondingly, it is just possible that Bowyer owned this part of our manuscript which, based on the dates added to its extant portions, was not scrapped until 1574. It is altogether more likely, however, that the book in question was the second slightly later Canterbury copy of much the same collection which survives as London, British Library, MS Cotton Otho D. viii, fols. 8–173.

Be all that as it may, one volume of the passional described here certainly passed relatively intact (albeit subdivided) into private hands – both Harleian portions had belonged to, and were annotated by, John Dee (1527–1608), and then Simonds D'Ewes (1602–50), whose library was sold by his grandson to Robert Harley in 1705 – while the others were manifestly being dismembered locally throughout the last third of the sixteenth century. Recycled as covers for the proceedings of the archideaconal, consistory and probate courts, and in one case (the Maidstone bifolium) for the Common Expenditors' Accounts of the Commissioner of Sewers for the Level of Romney Marsh, the leaves bear dates that indicate a period of re-use that extended from at least 1572 (fols. 58–59) to 1596 (fols. 80–81).

Thus they remained until the late nineteenth century. Then in 1888 sixty-one of the leaves in Canterbury were extracted from their early modern contexts and regrouped by Dr Joseph Brigstocke Sheppard, librarian to the Dean and Chapter (the text added in ink to the upper margin of fol. 27r presumably dates from this period). Correspondence kept in the Cathedral Archive reveals that various attempts were made during the 1930s and 40s to reclaim additional leaves from the probate records which, prior to the Second World War, were kept in a Public Record Office repository in Canterbury, and these presumably came to comprise the remaining fourteen folios in Lit. E. 42; certainly, relevant leaves are recorded as being returned to Canterbury from the Kent County Archives Office at Maidstone in 1951. Fols. 76–79, formerly at Lambeth Palace as the covers of Visitation records for the Canterbury Diocese for 1580–5 and 1586–92, were transferred to Canterbury in 1955; fols. 80–81, formerly wrapping Eastry Rentals of Quitrents, 1512 and 1596, were deposited by the Church Council in 1966: collectively these sheets now comprise Lit. E. 42A, part I.

Commentary

These volumes represent the culmination of the continuous phase of book production at Christ Church, Canterbury, that started in the aftermath of the Norman Conquest. Their realisation has been associated with the interests and influence of Eadmer; whatever the truth of the point, they certainly include some of his most recent work – his *Vita Anselmi* (in the British Library portion) and his writing on the miracles associated with the relics of St Ouen (Canterbury portion). Both texts provide indirect evidence for the date of the undertaking. The former cannot have been composed much after 1123 (Southern 1963, p. 238; though this is possibly a very early insertion, the circumstance that it includes work by the artist who decorated the rest of vol. III implies that it was part of the same phase of work). To the latter, a different hand has added a supplement which includes a miracle said to have been witnessed by Elmer, prior of Christ Church from 1128 to 1137 (Wilmart 1933; Ker 1946), and the fact that this was not included in the original phase implies that that was copied before the event in question.

Produced over a fairly long period of time, the set shows an evolution of format (with vols. III–VI being larger than I–II) and preserves contributions from at least six main scribes and two principal artists, as outlined below.

Vol. I	Format I	Scribe 1[1]	Artist A
Vol. II	Format I	Scribe 1	Artist A
Vol. III	Format II	?Scribe 1 (or 7)[2]	Artist B (and C)
		Scribe 2[3]	
		Scribe 3[4]	
Vol. V	Format II	Scribe 4[5] [Rubric style 2]	Artist A
Vol. VI	Format II	Scribe 5[6]	Artist A
		Scribe 6[7]	

Notes: 1 This is Canterbury scribe 1 as described in **Scribes and Script** above. 2 British Library scribe 1 as described above. 3 British Library scribe 2. 4 British Library scribe 3. 5 Canterbury scribe 5. 6 Canterbury scribe 3. 7 Canterbury scribe 6.

As noted above, all the original decorated initials in the Canterbury leaves seem to be the work of one artist, with the possible exception of that on fol. 57v. His talent as a draughtsman was comparatively modest – the designs are characterised by rather angular, sometimes poorly controlled outlines – and he was weak at doing heads, human and animal alike; however, the bright palette and striking colour juxtapositions animate the designs. Particularly notable is the way pink shading is used to suggest and model form for the naked figure on fol. 76r, as also for the flesh on fol. 9r, which, unfortunately, is now rather rubbed. The visual repertoire, broadly paralleled in many Christ Church manuscripts of the late eleventh and early twelfth centuries, includes a couple of elements of Anglo-Saxon ancestry (such as the foliate bosses on fols. 9r, 17r, 26r and 76r, and the figure type reproduced for Simphorianus on fol. 52r), numerous motifs characteristic of early Romanesque art (various animals along with numerous foliate curls and blossoms), plus occasional exercises (notably the once-magnificent initial on fol. 29v) that herald the great work of the mid-twelfth century, as embodied in the Lambeth Bible. Considered as a whole, the work is perhaps most closely akin to that in Cambridge, Trinity College, MS R. 15. 22 (Boethius, etc.) and one of the hands in Cambridge, St John's College, MS A. 8 (Josephus). The artwork of the British Library portion is more closely comparable to the work of another of the artists represented in St John's, MS A. 8 (e.g. fol. 219r) and to that in the legal collection, British Library, MS Cotton Claudius E. v.

There is no obvious logic as to why some *passiones* are headed with historiated initials, others with decorated ones. Equally, iconographic elements are interwoven with purely or seemingly decorative ones: the Agnus Dei on fol. 29v and the Angel on fol. 34r, for example, appear alongside a naked man and beasts in foliage, and a man fighting a dragon (?St Michael); while on fol. 52r Simphorianus is 'framed' by three drôle beasts who are doing their best to ignore him. Both points are, of course, wholly typical of the genre in the Romanesque period, as comparison with similar collections underlines: in the broadly contemporary *Vitae et passiones sanctorum* from Anchin Abbey (Douai, Bibliothèque municipale, MS 837), for instance, many entries are headed with more or less elaborate arabesque initials, some (e.g. for Augustine of Hippo, Cassian, Ciriacus *et al.*, and Sixtus) have decorated ones, while a couple of initials (for Germanus of Auxerre and Hippolitus) are historiated with an image of the saint in question.

The historiations in the present manuscript do, however, include the earliest surviving English illuminations of certain subjects, most notably the martyrdom of Vincent of Saragossa. As in the contemporary passional of Zwiefalten (Stuttgart, Württemburgische Landesbibliothek, MS bibl. 2°. 57), it is the episode of the flaying that was selected for inclusion. These two portrayals are broadly similar. However, the Zwiefalten Vincent, naked and suspended from both hands tied together over the top of a rough-hewn frame, is a more passive and obviously suffering figure than the Canterbury saint who, clad in a loin cloth and tied separately by wrist, ankles and neck to three of the four bars, appears still vigorous in the face of extreme suffering. Moreover, whereas the Zwiefalten version includes an additional seated figure (?Decius), urging the tormentors on and underlining the state's victimisation of the saint, Canterbury has instead an Agnus Dei, underscoring how in his suffering and death, Vincent echoes the sacrifice of Christ.

Bibliography

Wilmart 1933; Ker 1946; Dodwell 1954, pp. 66, 70, 70, 78 with pl. 42d (fol. 36v); Ker 1977, pp. 289–97; Southern 1990, pp. 418–21; Gameson 1995, pp. 105, 119, 136, 140, 143 and 157 with pls. 4a (fol. 19r), 5b (fol. 9r) and 6a (fol. 52r); Love 1996, esp. pp. xxiv, clxxvi; Parkes 1997 with pl. 8 (fol. 74v); Gullick and Pfaff (2001), p. 291, n. 17. (For MS Harley 315: Watson 1963; Sheerin 1974.)

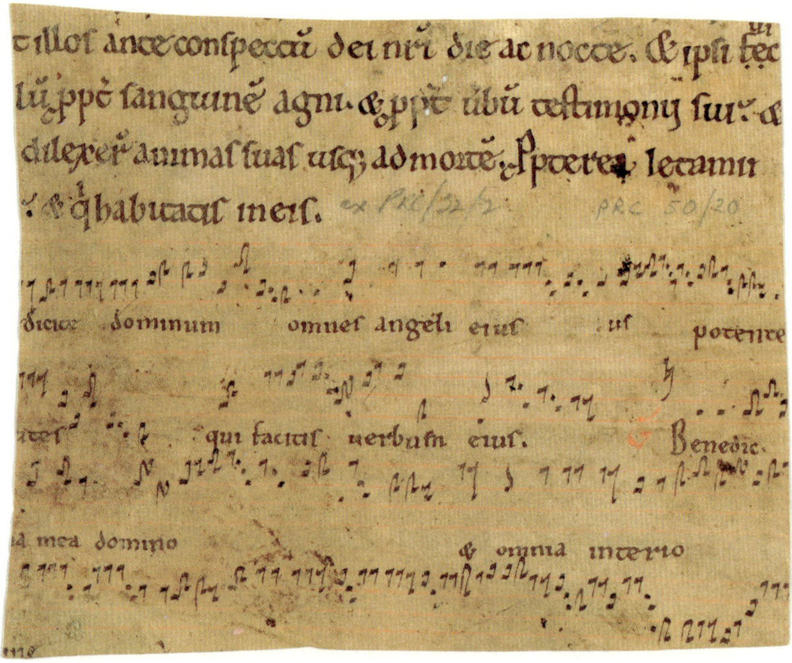

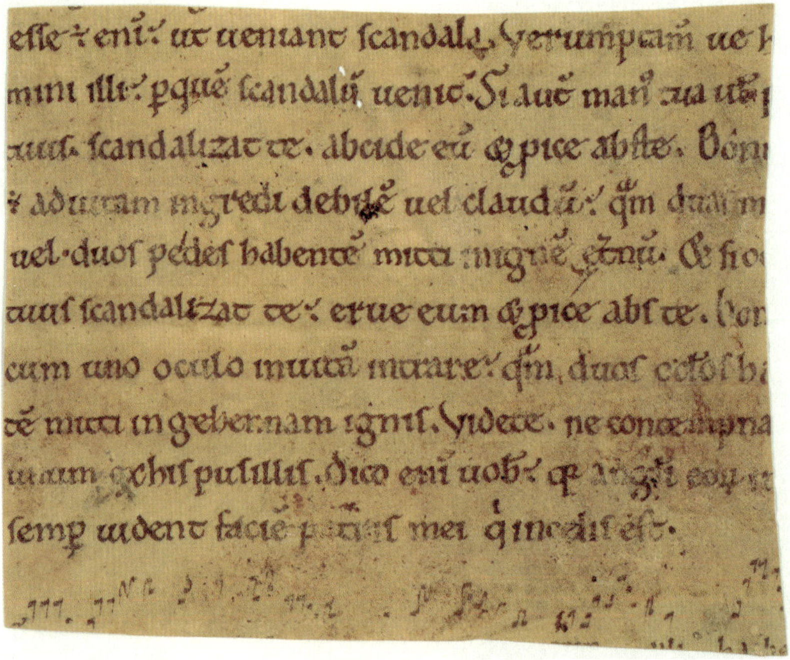

23 PRC 50/20

Liturgica (with notation)
England; *saec.* $XII^{1-2/4}$.
Illustration: recto and verso

Physical Description
One small fragment, drastically cut down on all sides, now measuring *c.* 83 × 103 mm. Both faces are browned and rubbed. The fragment preserves the equivalent of eleven incomplete lines of text: the greater part of four lines of ordinary text followed by four lines of musical notation plus text on one side; ten lines of ordinary text and one line of musical notation plus text on the other. Space between ordinary lines: 7 mm. Height of ordinary minims: 2 mm. Ruling: hard point.

Content
Fragments from a Mass for St Michael (29 September), probably from a missal.
[Recto] //[accusaba]t illos ante conspectum dei nostri die ac nocte. ... Propterea letami[ni caeli], et qui habitatis in eis. [Apocalypsis Iohannis 12.10–12; the reading was doubtless originally 12.7–12]. [Then, accompanied by four-line staff notation:] [Bene]dicite dominum omnes angeli eius us [sic] potente[s uirt]utes qui facitis uerbum eius. *V.* Benedic [anim]a mea domino et omnia interio[ra].//
[Verso] //[ne]cesse est enim, ut ueniant scandala ... semper uident faciem patris mei qui in caelis est [Matthew 18.7–10; the reading was doubtless originally 18.1–10]. [Only the staff with notation and the tops of a couple of ascenders survive from the next line.]

Scribes and Script
The fragment is the work of a single hand, writing a characterful Anglo-Norman Romanesque script; while the general matrix is square, strokes tend to be topped with angled triangular serifs and finished with rising feet, adding a measure of angularity. Punctuation: low point (for major and minor pauses) and *punctus*

elevatus (for minor pauses). Sentence capitals are a mixed alphabet. The same scribe wrote the chant sections. The notation (on a red four-line staff) is of 'Norman' form.

Decoration

None preserved.

History

A note pencilled on the fragment itself records that it comes from PRC 32/2, the Register of Wills of the Consistory Court for 1459–84. It may thus provide an example of the recycling of liturgical books before the Reformation.

24 Add. 128/58

Augustine, *In euangelium Iohannis*
England; *saec.* XII$^{2/4}$
Illustration: fol. 1r

Physical Description
One incomplete and very battered bifolium (originally the central sheet of a quire). It was re-used as a wrapper s. xvi, and hence was cut down, its corners sliced off, and its edges folded over. The face that was then the outside (fols. 1v–2r) is very darkened, stained and weathered; in addition, large strips of paper were stuck to it as reinforcement, one of which bears isolated and incomplete lines of writing in a s. xv–xvi hand; further paper fragments adhere to the turn-ins. Stains on the better-preserved outer – then inner – face (fols. 1r–2v) suggest that it, too, had several substantial paper attachments, which have been removed; one reinforcement strip remains. There is a series of pairs of holes along the gutter through which thongs were laced. The sheet is now mounted in a card folder.

Maximum dimensions: 398 × 275 mm. Written area: 280 × 198 mm. Two columns (column width: 88 mm). Lines: 40. Space between lines: 7 mm. Height of minims: 2.5 mm. No rulings are now perceptible, suggesting that it was done in hard point. If the volume contained *In euangelium Iohannis* alone, it will originally have comprised about 200 folios. If, as is quite likely, Augustine's work was prefaced by the text of St John's Gospel itself (as is the case, for instance, in the earlier Christ Church copy, Cambridge, Trinity College, MS B. 4. 2, and in the Rochester one, BL, MS Royal 3 C. x, which is broadly contemporary with the present item), an additional ten or so folios would have been required.

Content
Augustine, *In euangelium Iohannis* (CPL, 278), end of Tractatus CI – end of Tractatus CIII:
[Fol. 1r] // peruolat saeculum. Vnde dicit idem ipse euangelista in epistola sua. Nouissima hora est. Ideo ... [PL 35, col. 1895, l.32;

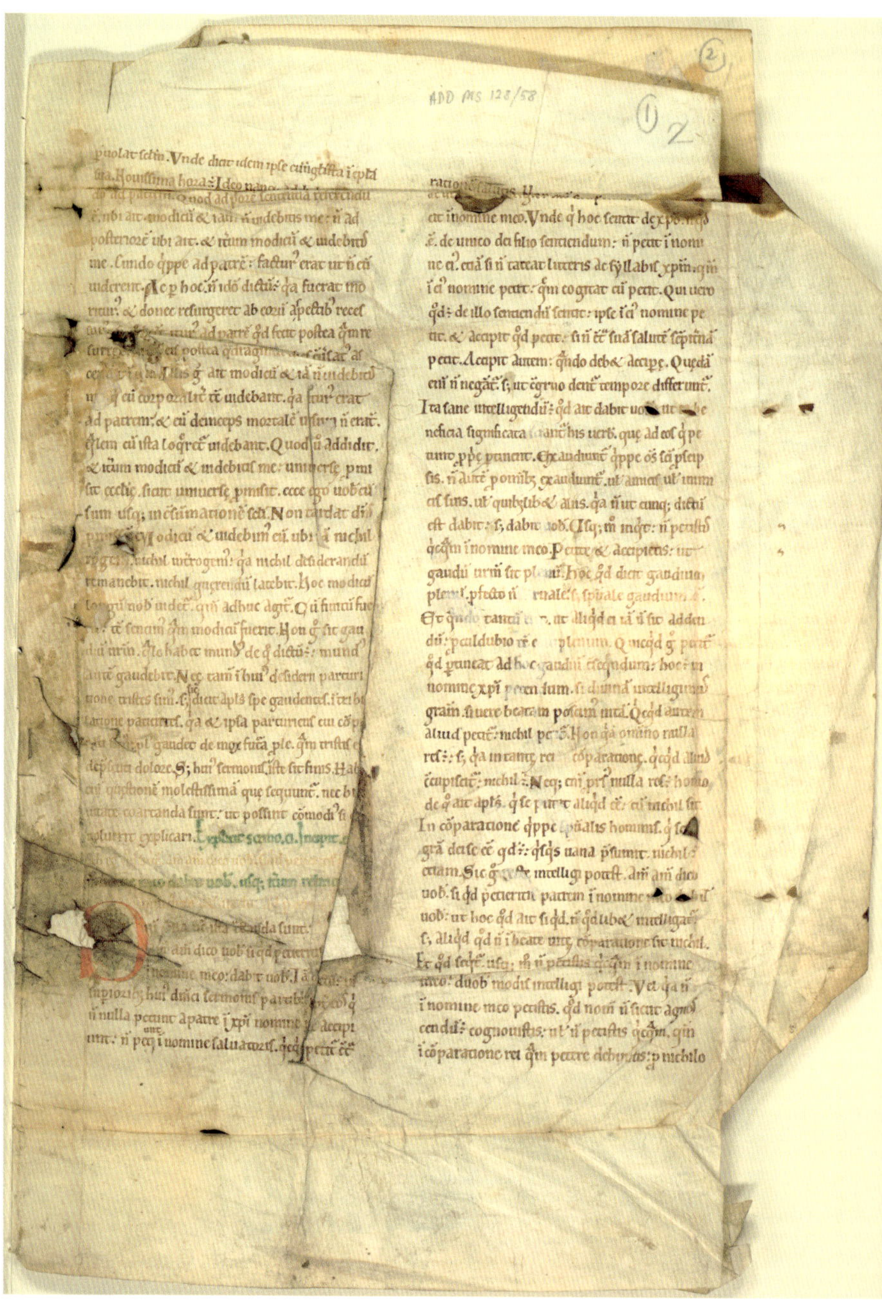

CCSL 36, p. 593, l. 4] … uoluerit explicari. *Explicit sermo ci. Incipit cl//* [lost, then very faded but seemingly] *ab eo quod dominus ait. Amen dico uobis si quid petieritis* [–lost–] *meo dabit uobis, usque Iterum relinquo* [–lost–]*et* [?]*uado ad patrem*. Domini uerba nunc ista tractanda sunt, Amen amen dico uobis … uel non petistis quicquam, quoniam in comparatione rei quam petere debuistis pro nichilo [PL 35, col. 1897, l. 6; CCSL 36, p. 595, l. 23].
[Fols. 1v–2r] [largely obliterated owing to wear and tear, discoloration, and the attachment of two large paper strips. Tractatus CII finishes, and CIII starts, on fol. 2r, col. 1.]
[Fol. 2v] Ex hoc alimento est quod sciebant eum nosse omnia [NB: the tilde is misplaced, so it in fact reads: 'omiam'], nec opus ei esse ut eum quis interroget. Quod [PL 35, col. 1900, l. 8; CCSL 36, p. 599, l. 12] … Confiderunt, et uicerunt. In quo, nisi in illo? Non enim uicisset ille mundum, // [PL 35, col. 1901, l. 34; CCSL 36, p. 600, ll. 33–4].

In so far as it remains legible, the text seems to have been fairly accurately transcribed and is close both to the printed editions and to the Rochester copy, BL, MS Royal 3 C. x. Collation of the best-preserved section (fol. 1r, start of Tractatus CII) against CCSL, pp. 594–5 merely reveals the following very modest variants; the reading in our manuscript (siglum C) is presented first.

C: in nomine eius etiam [CCSL 36, p. 594, l. 11, in eius nomine, etiam. C: Non quia omnino nulla [p. 595, l. 9, non quia nulla omnino. C: agnoscendum est [p. 595, l. 22, cognoscendum est.

The only notable 'correction' is to 'non peti in nomine' (exactly as PL col. 1896, l. 19 and in Rochester) which was changed to 'non petiunt …'.

Scribes and Script

The surviving text is the work of a single scribe writing a fairly handsome, upright, book hand which, notwithstanding a rectilinear matrix and much biting of letters, is still wholly Romanesque. Characteristic features are the curl to the left at the bottom of descenders (especially 'q'), and the very high-backed 'a'. The ink is (now) brown. Punctuation: low point (principally for major pauses but also for some minor ones), *punctus elevatus* (for minor pauses) and *punctus interrogativus*. The text is moderately abbreviated. Sentence capitals are a mixed alphabet in which different forms (uncial-based and rustic-based) of the same letter are employed. A few of the many scriptural citations that pepper the work are signalled by diples in the margins.

Decoration

None survives. The one visible sermo incipit (fol. 1r, for CII) is headed by a large (over three-lines-high), plain, red capital ('D'), followed by a couple of letters in ink capitals. The accompanying rubric is presented in alternate lines of green and (now very faded) red minuscules. The Rochester copy, MS Royal 3 C. x, which gives a similar emphasis to the individual sermons, has a decorated initial (including the Agnus Dei) at the beginning of Augustine's work (fol. 14v), and another (with the eagle of St John) at the start of the text of St John's Gospel which precedes it (fol. 3r).

History

Of undocumented origin and early provenance, the volume was presumably in Kent by the end of the Middle Ages (if not before), given its re-use in the area. The manuscript was evidently dismembered and this sheet was used as a wrapper in the later sixteenth century: written in ink on the 'spine' of the bifolium (as it was re-used) is '6, Comperta'; at the top of fol. 2r, written in a bold, inky hand, is: 'Ex Officio / Comperta & Detecta / 1582, 1583, 1584, 1585 / Lib. 6'. It was formerly the cover of X.8.12.

Commentary

In euangelium Iohannis, a series of 124 sermons which collectively represent a systematic commentary on the whole of St John's Gospel, was composed in at least two sections. Its exact dates are debated but the probable outer limits for the collection as a whole are *c.* 408x20. The three homilies that feature in the present fragment treat chapter 16, verses 16–23, 23–28, and 29–33 respectively.

Some 200 manuscripts of the work are currently known (Wright 1972 and 1981). An exiguous late Antique witness gives way to a strong survival from the Carolingian period; more modest numbers in the tenth century are followed by a steep climb, first in the eleventh century and then again in the twelfth; the numbers fall sharply in the thirteenth and fourteenth centuries, rising again in the fifteenth. If this diachronistic distribution conforms to a common pattern for such a text, the number of copies made between *c.* 1050 and 1150 (approximately half of the surviving total) remains striking, attesting to a peak of popularity in the Romanesque period.

Though clearly known in England both before and after the Viking age, as is attested by the writings of Bede and Ælfric respectively, no pre-Conquest manuscripts of the work survive and it is debatable whether many ever existed. Be that as it may, the situation changed dramatically with the Norman Conquest, whereafter – judging by the number of extant copies – it became one of the most popular texts of all. Its re-importation to England thus coincided exactly with its period of greatest universal popularity. An identifiable example of an imported copy is Oxford, Bodleian Library, MS Bodley 301, made in Normandy *c.* 1100 and brought to Exeter.

Most English Romanesque manuscripts of the work – including the Kentish ones, Cambridge, Trinity College, MS B. 4. 2, British Library, MS Royal 3 C. x, and Durham Cathedral Library, MS B. II. 16 – share a number of features which distance them from many continental copies and give them a certain group identity (see Wright 1972, pp. 64–6 and 71). Most include the text of St John's Gospel at the beginning, have an extended title (which a few also repeat at the end), and include all 124 items in a single volume, rather than dividing the collection into two volumes at nos. 54/55. Many of the extant copies from areas which might reasonably be suspected to have supplied exemplars in the later eleventh century – Flanders, for instance – are thus ruled out as probable archetypes, and this is also the case for the Norman copy that came to Exeter (MS Bodley 301). Such a presentation is, however, paralleled in the late eleventh-century Rouen, Bibliothèque municipale, MS A. 85 (of Saint Ouen, Rouen, provenance and possibly origin), suggesting that a manuscript like this stands behind many of the English Romanesque copies. Owing to the highly fragmentary condition of the present manuscript, it is sadly impossible to know whether it, too, shared the features of this group.

Copies dating from the late eleventh or early twelfth century can be associated, with greater or lesser certainty, with Bury St Edmunds, Canterbury (Christ Church), Durham, Exeter, Glastonbury, Lincoln, Rochester, Salisbury, Winchester and Winchcombe. The work was certainly transcribed at Saint Augustine's Abbey in the late eleventh century, but the volume in question (Durham Cathedral Library, MS B. II. 16) migrated to Durham. As no other manuscript of the text can be associated with Saint Augustine's, though it certainly had two copies by the time of its late medieval library catalogue (James 1903, List VIII, pp. 221–2, nos. 341–2), it is a leading contender for having been the home – if not necessarily the origin – of the present item. The work, it may be noted, does not feature in the library lists of two other potential local 'contenders', Dover Priory and St Radegund's, Bradsole. Unfortunately, the 'colourless' nature of the text, script and articulation of the surviving fragment has not, to date, permitted a telling relationship to be established with other copies of the work – or indeed with any other manuscript.

25 Lit. D. 6

Glossed Gospel of St Matthew
England or Northern France; *saec.* XII$^{2/4}$
2° folio: (fol. 5r) nationem cristi nuntiat; (fol. 7r, main text) [C]um multi scripsisse manassen manasses
Illustrations: fols. 1v, 2r, 6r, 41r

Physical Description

Folios: 122 original parchment leaves, of which fol. 1 was originally the front paste-down and fol. 122 the rear paste-down. These are now preceded and followed by modern parchment endleaves. The parchment is of modest but serviceable quality: the hair sides are much yellower than the flesh sides and the follicle marks are readily perceptible; some sheets are patently edge-cuts; flaws are common; some large slits and holes were sewn up; there is a large 'untreated' hole in the middle of the text area on fol. 41. The entire lower border of fol. 28 was cut away at an uncertain date. The general state of preservation is, however, very good.

Page size: 260 × 182 mm (except quire V [fols. 38–45] the pages of which measure 256 × 172 mm). Written area (gospel text): 188 × 56 mm. Lines (gospel text): 17. Space between lines (gospel text): 12 mm. Height of minims (gospel text): over 2 mm at the start, diminishes slightly thereafter. Space between lines (gloss): 4–5 mm. Height of minims (gloss): over 1 mm. Although prickings often survive in all three outer margins (there was no pricking in the inner margin), the marginal gloss has occasionally been cropped, attesting to trimming. The ruling was done in lead or ink. Whilst the spacing of the ruling for the gospel text was fairly consistent, the number – and hence the spacing – of the horizontals for the marginal gloss could vary (with either two or three lines for each main ruling)

Collation: fol. 1, originally a paste-down; I^{4} (fols. 2–5); II–XI^{8} (first folios on 6, 14, 22, 30, 38, 46, 54, 62, 70, and 78); XII^{9} (fols. 86–94: a quaternion with an extra singleton (fol. 92)); XIII–XV^{8} (first folios on 95, 103, and 111); XVI (fols. 119–122, structure uncertain).

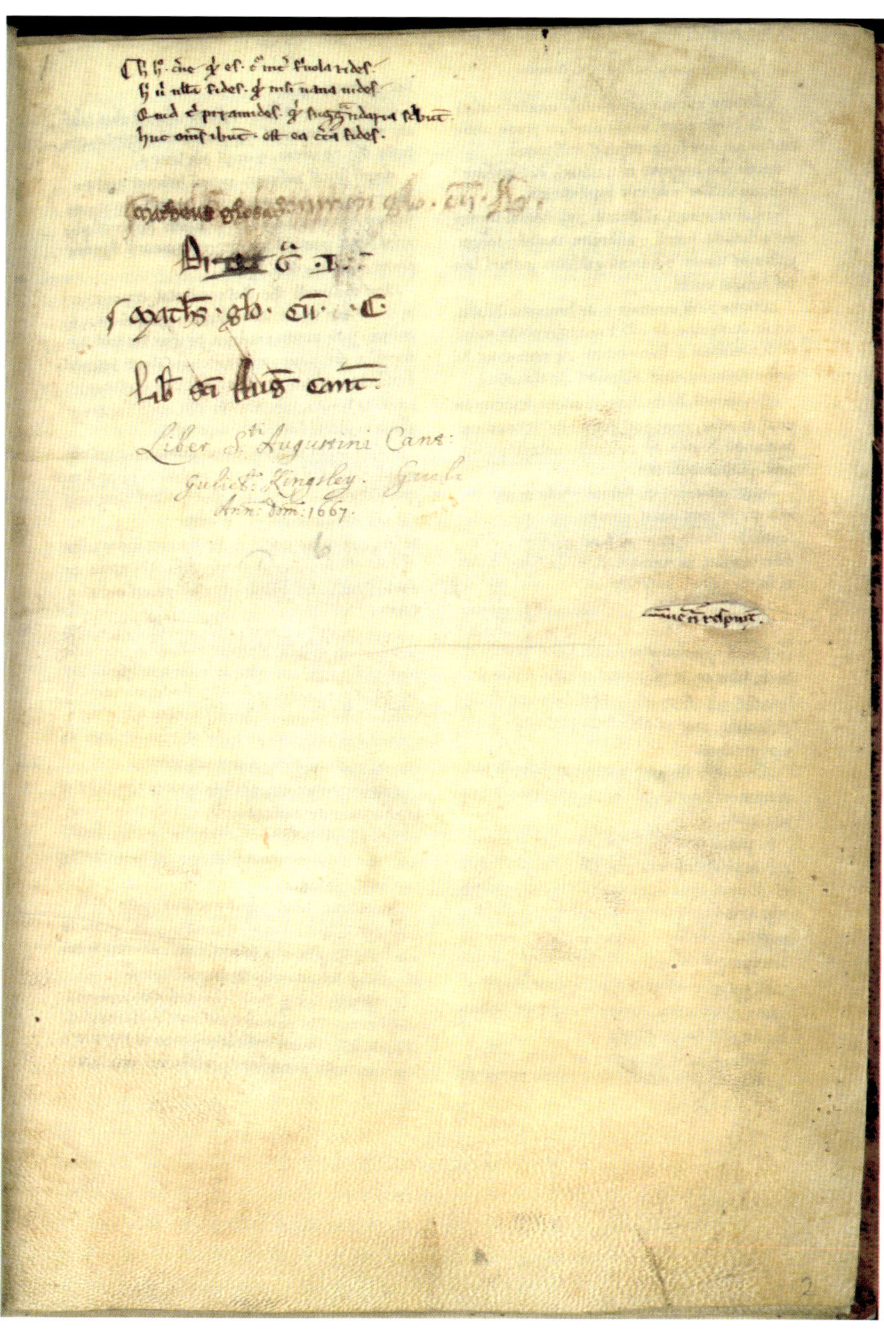

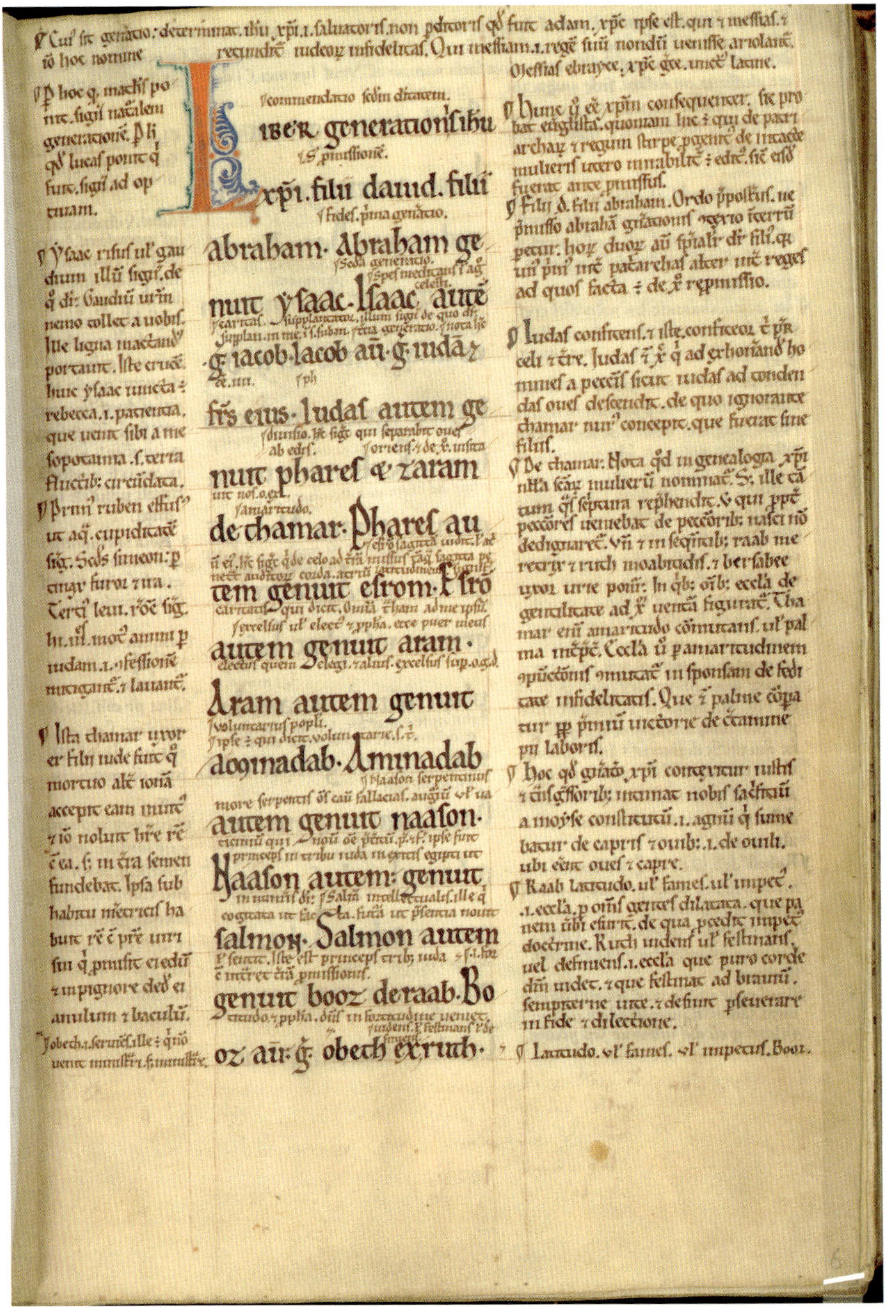

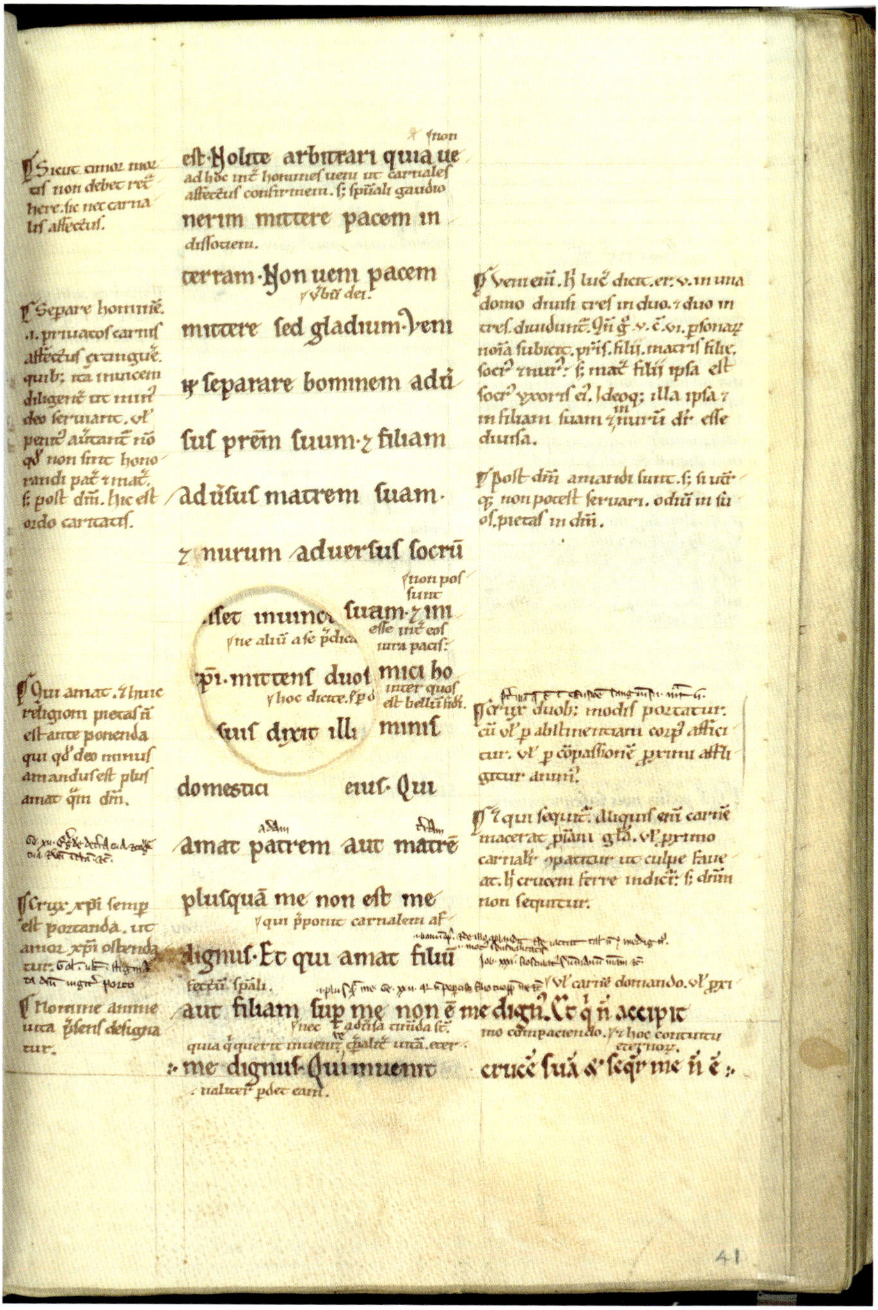
est. Nolite arbitrari quia ue
nerim mittere pacem in
terram. Non ueni pacem
mittere sed gladium. Veni
enim separare hominem adu
sus patrem suum et filiam
aduersus matrem suam.
et nurum aduersus socrum
suam. et ini
mici ho
minis
domestici eius. Qui
amat patrem aut matrem
plusquam me non est me
dignus. Et qui amat filium
aut filiam super me non est me dignus. Et qui non accipit
me dignus. Qui inuenit
crucem suam et sequitur me non est
41

The current binding (brown ?calf over pasteboard, the spine covering gone) is modern (Riviere, *s.* xix). Nevertheless, plentiful traces of a former structure survive. Folio 1 (formerly the front paste-down) preserves very clearly the contours of two lacing-in channels in the shape of 'V's on their sides (cf. Szirmai 1999, fig. 8.18 (b)) from a lost medieval wooden board, plus the outline of the turn-ins of the leather cover; certainly one and probably both of the corner turn-ins was of overlapping form. The offsets from the lost lower board on to fol. 122 are fainter; nevertheless, two similar V-shaped channel scars and one leather turn-in mark can be discerned. There are, in addition, scars from a metal clasp fixture in the form of a pair of adjacent rust-stained holes in the parchment, one larger than the other. The principal hole continues through the next three leaves, the stain being transmitted through a further three. The form of the channels points to a 'Gothic' as opposed to 'Romanesque' form of board attachment: we can be reasonably confident, therefore, that the structure which left these impressions post-dated the written volume, and was presumably not the original binding.

Content

[Fol. 1r] Originally pasted to front board.

[Fol. 1v] Three lines of Hebrew (aligned vertically), the first two crossed through. A further Hebrew jotting (closer to the gutter and seemingly aligned horizontally) has been thoroughly erased. The legible texts are reproduced and discussed by Roth 1964, where the script is described as 'a typical medieval Anglo-Jewish hand or hands of "Ashkenazi" type, dating probably from the mid-thirteenth century', and the following provisional translations are offered. Line 1: '4 dinars on this and on \2/ rings and Holy [?] to Adam of Sangis [probably for Sandwich] or Hugh of Monighan ... [unintelligible] who admits.' Line 2: 'Hugh [?] of Canterbury on this and Marcus [?]'. Line 3: 'Half a mark on this and Epistles and Mark. Second [day of the scriptural portion] After the death [of the two sons of Aaron: Leviticus 16] ... Adam of Sangits [Sandwich]'.

[Fol. 2r] A series of discrete additions, one below another, by

different hands at different dates.
i) At the top are four lines of verse (*s.* xiii), 'Hic homo cerne quid es, ... est ea certa fides'.
ii) a *s.* xiii[1] title, 'Matheus glosatus' (written over a partially-erased earlier and lengthier title: '–?– glo. cum. –?–').
iii) a ?*s.* xiv shelfmark, title, and *ex libris*. Both parts of the shelfmark have been changed – the first number rewritten very heavily (presumably to cover an earlier version), the second erased. It now says 'Di. III. Ga. I'. (The former *distinctio* number is difficult to discern; the previous *gradus* number would seem to have been 'III'.) The title now says: 'Math[eu]s. glo[satus]. cu[m]. .C.' (the 'C' may be a very early replacement for a different letter which has been erased). The final line, 'Lib[er] S[an]c[t]i Aug[ustini] Cant[uariensis].', has not been tampered with.
iv) Written in a flowing *s.* xvii[2] hand: 'Liber Sti: Augustini Cant: / Guiliel': Kingsley. Guili / Ann': dom': 1667.' [cf. Lit. A. 8 (**no. 17**)].
v) Pencilled in a modern hand: 'D6'.
[Fol. 2v] [Written in very small script in the upper margin, seemingly the guide words for a more formal rubric that was never supplied:] Incipiunt capitula super Math[eu]m. [Then, in the main hand but lacking the initial:] [N]atiuitas cristi magi cum muneribus ... [28 sections: 'A' family]. [None of the initials was supplied but many of the guide letters for them remain visible in the margins. The series ends on **fol. 3r/col. 1**:] ... [P]assio ihesu et sepultura, et resurrectio eius, itemque mandata, et doctrina eius, et de bapthismo.
[Fol. 3r, col. 2] [A series of short notes added in ink by several (?five) *s.* xii–xiii hands of varying degrees of formality, including] 'Iero[ni]m[us]. Oculus meus depredatus ...' ; 'Cum Moyses esset princeps in populo dei consilium iethro gratanter admisit'; 'Petrus apostolorum princeps pauli correctionem non respuit. Balaam uocibus asine ... sapientia fabrum et feminam' [ex Peter of Blois, *Compendium in Iob*: PL 207, col. 797A].
[Fol. 3v] A series of now very faint jottings in crayon.
[Fol. 4r–4v, col. 1] [C]um multi scripsisse euangelia legantur soli iiii euangeliste, matheus, Marcus, lucas, iohannis ... si non

recusemus conpassionem [an abridgement of the Gloss on the prologue, 'Matheus cum primo ... sacramentum' : Stegmüller, 10451, and see 11827].

[Fol. 4v, col. 1– fol. 4v col. 2] [M]attheus in hac uita que .iiii. temporum cursu labitur, ... fuit enim homo natura, sed in figura uitulus leo et aquila [Stegmüller, 11827; glossa ordinaria].

[Fol. 4v, col. 2– fol. 5r, col. 2] [N]omen libri euangelium graece, bonum nuntium latine, quod etsi sit commune; proprium hoc nomen habet annuntiatio saluatoris in carne, ... a longe dispensationem christi reuelandam preuiderint [Stegmüller, 9947].

[Fol. 5r, col. 2] In sapientia dei patris discimus mundum calcare cum sua sapientia ... timore ac tremore nostram salutem operamur [Stegmüller, 7496].

[Fol. 5v] Matheus cum primum praedicasset euangelium in iudea, ... unde et aliorum euangelia deciderunt, nec recepta sunt [Stegmüller, no. 589; PL 114, cols. 63–4]. [Remainder of page blank.]

[Fol. 6r] Liber generation\i/s ihesu christi filii dauid ... **[fol. 118v]** ad consummationem seculi. Explicit euangelium ?s[icut]. [The apparatus begins (in the upper margin):] 'Cuius sit generatio; determinat, ihesu christi, id est saluatoris, non perditoris quod fuit adam, christus ipse est, qui et messias ... Messias ebrayce, christus grece, unctus latine'. [Stegmüller, 11827 (18)]. [The first interlinear gloss (over 'Liber generationis') is:] 'Commendatio secundum diuinitatem'.

[Marginal and interlinear glosses continue, albeit with varying intensity, throughout the text. The final interlinear gloss (to 'ad consummationem seculi') is:] 'Cum finitis laboribus, mecum regnabitis'. [The final marginal gloss (to the same) is:] 'Nota quod usque in finem seculi non sunt desituri, qui diuina mansione sunt digni'.

[Fol. 119r–20v] [Three paragraphs in the glossing hand.] 1) **[fol. 119r]** Prima sabbati diluculo sicut omnes consentiunt, ... Venit ergo maria magdalene annuntians discipulis, et alie que cum ea erant quas Lucas commemorat [*Enarrationes in Matthaeum*: PL 162, col. 1498D–1500A (where attributed erroneously to Anselm of Laon; for an association with Geoffrey Babion see Stegmüller

2604; and cf. Augustine, *De consensu Euangelistarum*: PL 34, col. 1201)]. 2) **[fol. 119r]** Plures quidem fuerunt apparitiones quod innuit Paulus dicens, Uisus est iacobo … sic ueniet quemadmodum uidistis eum euntem in celum [*Enarrationes in Matthaeum*: PL 162, col. 1500A–B]. 3) **[fols. 119r–120v]** Homo id est deus habuit duos filios, duos populos, iudeos et gentes. Portionem substantie. Substantia est omne quod uiuimus, sapimus, cogitamus, loquimur … [The text is itself subdivided, generally by paraphs, into a series of short subsections, the last being:] [I]N ecclesiasticis non queruntur uerba sed sensus, id est panibus uita sustentanda est, non siliquis. **[Fol. 120v** also bears a series of very faint pencil jottings.]

[Fol. 121r–v] [A series of short paragraphs (lacking their initials) (*s.* xii–xiii). The first is:] [T]anta dignitas humane conditionis esse cognoscitur … ad ymaginem et similitudinem nostram. [The last, which begins on **fol. 121r** and ends on **fol. 121v**, is:] Vbi celum in die lucis splendore uestitur … Denique quisque talis est qui in hoc contemptu ne puniat sententia uidicantis [cf. Augustine, *De spiritu et anima*, c. 35: PL 40, col. 805]. [Above the end of this was added informally:] 'Deus est homo et homo est deus'. [The remainder of **fol. 121v** is covered with very faint pencil jottings.]

[Fol. 122r] [A series of jottings in several *s.* xiii hands (one of which is very similar to the hand that contributed the verses to fol. 2r), some working in ink, others in pencil. The first ink one is:] 'fuit homo missus a deo' [John 1.6]; [the last ink one is] 'Vbi habundauit delictum superhabundauit / et gratia'. [One note in the middle concerns excommunication:] 'Excommunicatio non t[ra]n[sact]a(?) sit in tertiam personam …'.

Scribes and Script

[For the endleaf additions see **Content** above.]

i) Fols. 2v–3r, col. i [the capitula] a compressed and fairly informal transitional script, which looks slightly later than the main body of the book (?xii$^{\text{med}-2}$). [Fol. 3r, col. ii: a series of *s.* xiii hands.]

ii) Fols. 4r–5v; a neat, compressed transitional Romanesque-early Gothic book script (*s.* xii$^{2/4}$), characterised by a square matrix, by split, club terminals, and by a 'g' whose bowl and tail are both multangular; the writing tends to lean forwards slightly. Punctuation: low point (major and minor pauses). The same hand probably also wrote the marginal glosses in the main body of the book, plus the texts on fols. 119r–120v. Whether by accident or design, while the main text is generally black, the gloss is brown (cf. e.g. the slightly later glossed Matthew, Durham Cathedral Library, MS A. IV. 10, whose gospel text is very black, the apparatus very brown).

iii) Fols. 6r–118v (main text). An elegant and regular, neat, upright, transitional Romanesque-early Gothic script; the ink is a rich black. Notwithstanding lateral compression, the rounded forms remain curvilinear. There are wedge-shaped serifs and curling feet. The back of 'a' rises high and then curls right over to drop down in front of the letter. The hand becomes slightly smaller as it progresses. Sentence capitals are stylised rustics; small ink rustics are also used for Maria (fol. 10v). Punctuation: medial point (for major and minor pauses); *punctus elevatus* (minor pause); *punctus interrogativus*. Minimal use of abbreviation. Corrections *in rasura* by the original scribe (fols. 52v, 71v) and by crossing through (fols. 13r–v, 20v, 50v, 64r). Very occasional accents. Both the ampersand and the Tironian 'et' are used, the latter (the more common) being almost z-shaped. Double 'i's are dashed.

iv) Corrections on fols. 39r (the bottom three lines re-written *in rasura*) and 41r (an insertion beside the penultimate and final lines) were done by a prickly Romanesque hand, seemingly of Kentish type, that one would most naturally date to *s.* xii$^{2/4}$.

v) *Saec.* ?xii^{2}, capitula identifications in crayon in a slightly loose hand. Some of the glosses were lightly crossed out at an uncertain but probably early date (fols. 107v, 108r).

vi) Fol. 121r–v, *s.* xii–xiii compressed and inky, semi-cursive hand.

vii) Fol. 77r, additional marginal gloss, *s.* xii–xiii.

Further marginal and interlinear glosses were added in ink in various informal *s.* xii–xiii hands, e.g. fols. 8v, 9r, 25r, 41r, 66v. Other glosses and jottings were added in faint ink, crayon or lead in informal hands, e.g. fols. 40v, 63v, 64v, 77r and 99r. Chapter numbers were added informally in pencil at an uncertain but probably quite early date.

Decoration

There are three modest but elegant arabesque initials. Fol. 6r (Liber: 1.1), a four-line-high L in red, embellished with flourishes in green and blue; the IB and R (but not the e) that follow are written in small capitals in the ink of the text. Fol. 98r (Vigilate ergo quia: 24.42), a blue and red 'V' with most of the rest of the line written in ink capitals. Fol. 116v (Vespere autem sabbati: 28.1), an elaborate red and blue 'V' plus one line of ink capitals.

Chapters are headed by plain coloured capitals (red, blue or green), occasionally of slightly elaborated form, generally accompanied by one or two words in ink capitals. *Altera autem die que est* [*post parascheuen conuenerunt principes sacerdotum et pharisei*] (27.62; fol. 116r) is highlighted by an elaborate ink 'A' and a line of capitals. *Christ autem generatio sic erat* (1.18; fol. 7v) is not emphasised at all (it is simply written as the last line of its section), whereas *Cum esset*, immediately afterwards, is signalled, by a green initial, as the start of the new section.

History

Wherever the volume was written, corrections in a *s.* xii$^{2/4}$ prickly script appear to indicate that it was in Kent at a very early date. Annotations suggest that it was much used in the twelfth and early thirteenth centuries; but then around the middle of the thirteenth century, as the Hebrew inscriptions reveal, it was repeatedly pawned by Kentish men presumably associated with Saint Augustine's Abbey. That it was ultimately redeemed is shown by the late medieval shelf-marks and *ex libris*, and it can be identified with item 157 in the late fifteenth-century library catalogue of Saint Augustine's Abbey (James 1903, p. 206): 'Matheus glo. cum C'.

The history of the volume between the Dissolution and the second half of the seventeenth century is obscure, but by 1667 it was in the hands of William Kingsley – presumptively Canon William Kingsley, grandson of the archdeacon of Canterbury of the same name – who presumably donated it to Canterbury Cathedral along with Lit. A. 8 (**no. 17**), Lit. C. 15 (Cicero, *s.* xv²), Lit. D. 13 (Prick of Conscience, *s.* xiv^med^), and Lit. D. 17 (*Noua Statuta*, *s.* xiv–xv).

Commentary

If the earliest glossed texts were the Psalter and the Pauline epistles (see **no. 15**), in the twelfth century the gospels – and primarily that of St Matthew – began to move to centre stage; the early apparatuses, produced at a time when gospel commentaries *per se* were rare, seem to echo the teaching of the schools of northern France. What is believed to have been one of the first 'commentaries' from this period, *Nomen libri* (Stegmüller, no. 9947), an abbreviation of Paschasius Radbertus's *Expositio in euangelium Matthei* (PL 120, cols. 31–994), was known to the compiler(s) of the present manuscript (cf. fols. 4v–5r). However, if the three paragraphs on fols. 119–20 are genuinely from the *Enarrationes in Mattheum* that is sometimes ascribed to Geoffrey Babion (Stegmüller 2604), and not from its source (Augustine), they are unlikely to have been copied before the second quarter of the twelfth century, when that text is thought to have been composed. In terms of the content of the apparatus accompanying the gospel text itself, the present manuscript has more in common with a representative of an earlier generation, Oxford, Trinity College, MS 20 (?northern France, *s.* xi/xii or xii^in^), than with those of later ones such as Durham Cathedral Library, MS A. IV. 10 (made in northern France, reaching Durham through the agency of Hugh Puiset, bishop 1153–95) or Oxford, Bodleian Library, MS E.D. Clarke 35 (from Trois-Fontaines). Indeed, in the parts that were sampled (principally the beginning and end of the text) the content of both marginal and interlinear glosses was much the same in Lit. D. 6 and Trinity MS 20, bar minor changes in word order. The presentation, on the other hand, is quite different. Trinity MS 20 is a smaller, more cramped, and altogether less formal book; and whereas in the present manuscript the marginal apparatus is divided into convenient short paragraphs, there it is presented as a continuous block.

Although more sophisticated than that of Trinity MS 20, the layout of the present volume – like the content of its apparatus – belongs to a phase when the gloss was still fluid. Following the conventions of the 'second stage' of Romanesque glossed book design (for the previous stage, see Add. 172 (**no. 15**)), the biblical text occupies the central column throughout, and was written – either in whole or sequentially – before the gloss was added; positioning the commentary was seemingly to some extent an ad hoc procedure. Though still practised in the middle of the twelfth century, such an approach had by then been superseded. Equally, the 'pre-standardised' type of gloss that was used here was overtaken in the middle years of the twelfth century when, at Paris under Peter Lombard, the first steps towards formalising its content seem to have been taken. All these facts, along with the intervention of what is probably a Kentish prickly hand making corrections, indicate a date for the present book in the second quarter of the twelfth century.

A hundred or so years later, the volume was apparently pledged at least three times. Though just conceivably done at Oxford or Cambridge, the Kentish names of the individuals involved, the repetition of the act, and the small sums thereby raised, strongly favour Canterbury, which was the known provenance of the manuscript subsequently, which had an important Jewish community whose banking activities, great and small, are fairly well documented, and where the premium on a book is likely to have been lower than in a university town. The modest sums in question suggest that this was most probably done to raise petty cash to meet needs which, if pressing, were fairly minor. In the mid-thirteenth century, long after the appearance of the *glossa ordinaria*, a manuscript with a 'primitive' apparatus may have seemed expendable in such circumstances; one might hypothesise that the same was true of the copies of Mark's Gospel and of the Epistles which, one of the pledge-notes reveals, were also 'sacrificed' in this way.

Bibliography

Roth 1964.

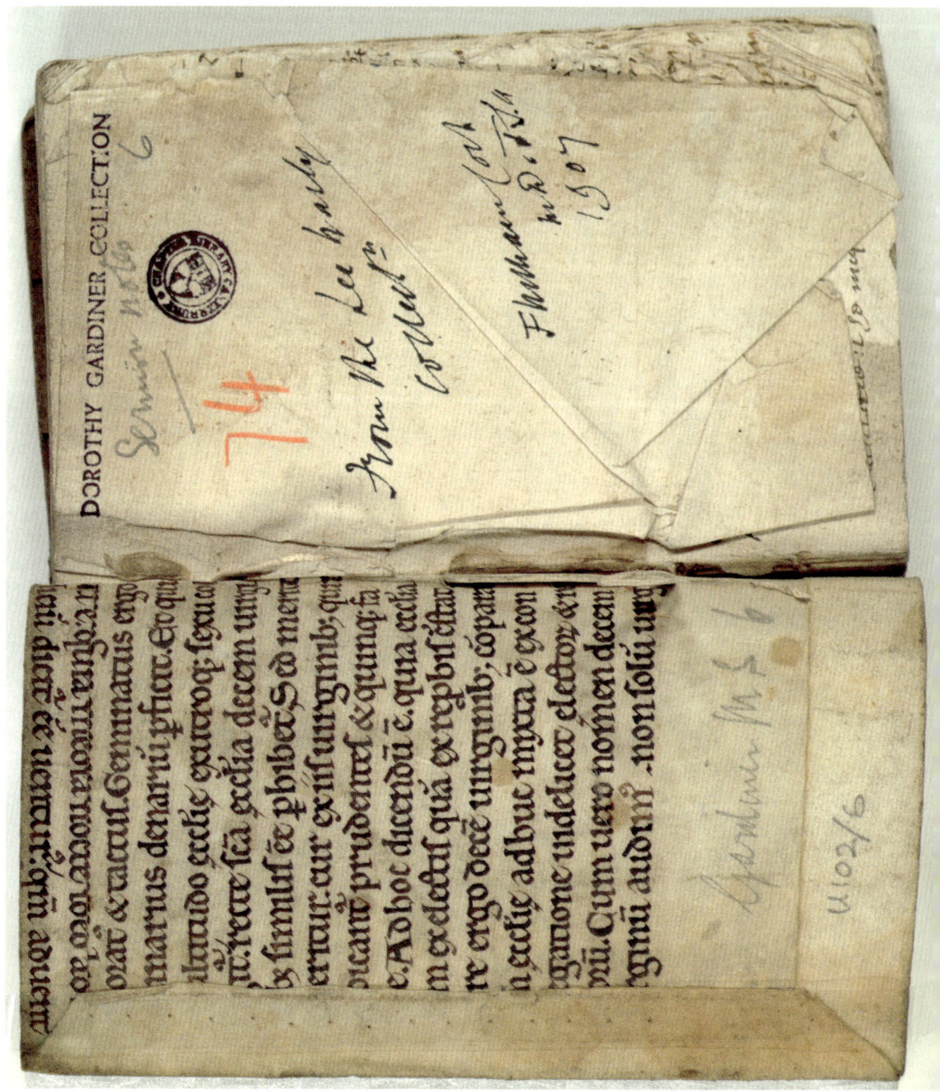
DOROTHY GARDINER COLLECTION
74

26 U102/6, Cover

Opus incertum (homiletic fragment)
England; *saec.* XII$^{2/4\text{-med}}$
Illustration: inside front cover (plus note-book)

Physical Description
This item comprises the lower portion of a single folio which was re-used as the cover of a *s.* xvii paper manuscript, where it remains. Strips along all four of its 'new' outer sides were turned in and glued down to form stronger edges for the cover. The early modern paper gatherings were sewn onto three leather thongs, which were then laced into the present fragment. The new outer side of the fragment is very grubby, and letters have been lost through abrasion. The inside, by contrast, is relatively fresh – though parts of the text are here hidden by the turn-ins and by the body of the paper manuscript it covers.

Lower margin, as preserved: 65 mm. Outer margin (and prickings survive along its turned-in outer edges): 52 mm. Two columns. Column width: 75 mm. Lines: a maximum of 18 preserved. Space between lines: 7 mm. Height of minims: 3.5 mm. Ruling: crayon.

Content
Unidentified homiletic text, with an exposition of the parable of the wise and foolish virgins (Matthew 25.1–13). The readily legible portions are as follows.
[Outside, column 1] [Turned-over:] // enim oleu[?m] leticia ?significet ... Psalmista qui dicit [–lost–] deus deus / [outside lower cover:] ... oleo ? [–?–] magna et enim letit- [–?–] non habere peccati. Fatue ergo uirgines oleum non sumpserunt in uasis, quia uidelicet leticiam de bono opere non posuerunt in corde suo ut de bono opere deo placerent, sed solum modo hominibus. Prudentes uero acceperunt oleum in uasis suis cum lampadibus, hoc est interne leticie gaudium [–?–] bonis operibus posuerunt; dicentes cum paulo apostolo, Gloria nostra hec est testimonium conscientie nostre [II Corinthians 1.12]. Moram autem faciente sponso, dormitauerunt omnes et dormierunt. Dormitare enim e[st] ante somnum languescere, do[?rmi]re uero //

[Outside column 2] [Turned-over:] //[?iu]dicium dicitur esse uenturus, quoniam aduentus illius subit et ?reperit. Unde et ipse dicit: Dies domini sicut fur in nocte, ita [outside proper:] ueniet. Et alibi. Si sciret pater familias qua hora fur ueniret, uigilaret utique, et non sineret perfodi domum suam [Matt. 24.43]. Clamor factus est. Iste clamor uocem angelorum sign[ifi]cat uocantium? uniuersum genus humanum de sepulchris. Exite obuiam ei. Ista erit uox angelorum dicentium: surgite de sepulchris uestris, et occurrite regi uestro ad iudicium preparati. Tunc surrexerunt omnes uirgines ille, et ornauerunt lampades suas. Verbo preteriti perfecti, rationem futuri temporis exponit dicens, Surrexerunt pro eo //

[Inside, column 1] [NB: the start of each line is concealed by the turn-in; however the reading is rarely in doubt and has, in general, been silently restored here:] //odoratus et tactus. Geminatus ergo quinarius denarium perficit [cf. Matt. 25.14 ff.]. Et quia multitudo ecclesie ex utroque sexu colligitur, recte sancta ecclesia decem uirginibus similis esse perhibetur. Sed merito queritur, Cur ex iis uirginibus quinque dicantur prudentes et quinque fatue. Ad hoc dicendum est, quia ecclesia tam ex electis quam ex reprobis constat. Iure ergo decem uirginibus compar[?atur] ?quoniam ecclesia adhuc mixta est ex congregatione uidelicet electorum et reproborum. Cum uero nomen decem uirginum audimus, non solum uirgi//

[Inside, column 2] [NB: a significant part of the start of each line is concealed by the paper book and the thongs; what can be seen is as follows:] // qui iam in animabus cum christo regnant. / … –rs ecclesie que adhuc peregri- / –r in corpore, illi scilicet occur- / … ?cum suis corporibus domino adiu- / … uenienti, et illi parti que / … –um eo uentura est, et ita implebitur / … –d dicitur. Exierunt obuiam sponso / … Potest et aliter intelligi. / … scriptum in euangelio secundum / … –eum quod passo domino in cruce / –sisset spiritum terra mota est, pe- / … –sse sunt, monumenta aperta sunt. / … –ta corpora sanctorum qui dormie- / … –rrexerunt de quibus auctori //

Scribes and Script

A single scribe, writing a neat, compact transitional Romanesque to proto-Gothic book hand, in which the treatment of 'rounded' forms is on the cusp between curvilinear and multangular. There are heavy, slanted triangular serifs, flat or upward-curving feet, and much 'biting' of letters. The ink remains a rich, dark black. Characteristic forms include an 'a' whose elongated back curls right over the main body of the letter, both straight-backed and curving backed 'd' (the latter resembling a back-to-front '6'), and a dramatic lightening-bolt-shaped 'tail' for e-caudata. Punctuation: low point (for major and minor pauses) and a *punctus elevatus* that is very much a 'tick and point' (for minor pauses).

History

The manuscript was written in England, probably late in the second quarter of the twelfth century. There is no direct evidence for its origin or medieval provenance. Its early modern provenance, however, would tend to suggest that it was in Kent by the end of the Middle Ages.

The fragment was re-used in s. xvii to form the cover of a paper book (containing notes written in various hands of that date) which is associated with Henry Oxinden/Oxenden of Barham in Kent (1609–70). In common with Oxinden's other books and papers, this note-book descended through his family to his great grandson, Lee Warly (1714–1807). Warly's library was bequeathed to the parish of Elham, Kent, but the present volume would seem subsequently to have passed to F. William Cock (jotted on the first paper leaf in an inky cursive are: 'From the Lee Warly collection' and 'F William Cock MD & FSA, 1907'), and then to the local historian and editor of Oxinden's works, Dorothy Gardiner (1874–1957), with whose collection it finally came to Canterbury Cathedral ('DOROTHY GARDINER COLLECTION' is stamped in ink on the first paper page). Other jottings on the first page, seemingly in three different hands, are: 'Sermon notes' (in pencil), '6' (in pencil), and '74' (in red crayon).

27 SB B 232, final page

Membrum disjectum from manuscript with *passiones Katerinae et Ælphegi*, etc.
Main manuscript: Saint-Albans; *saec.* XII^{med}
Illustration: exposed face

Physical Description
A single leaf, now glued to the final page of 'Scrapbook' B 232. It measures *c.* 202 × 137 mm. There is no ruling. The exposed face is stained, weathered and creased (though no more so than many other flyleaves). The edge that was formerly the inner margin is warped and torn, but sewing holes remain distinguishable at *c.* 14, 50, 147 and 175 mm from the top of the page.

Content
The exposed side bears the title, 'Passio. S[anctae]. katerine. et. s[ancti] elphegi'. Above this was added, 'D[istinctio]. VII^{a}. g[radus]. VIII'. Scrape marks around the first two numbers of the gradus reference may indicate that these were re-written *in rasura*, or might simply be the result of subsequent localised damage to the surface. The page is otherwise blank. The verso is presumably also blank, but as it has been firmly glued to the leaf of the scrapbook, certainty on this point is currently impossible.

Scribes and Script
The title was boldly but a little carelessly written in a characterful minuscule, in which rounded forms (e.g. the 'a's, 'g's, and 's's) are at least as prominent as compressed and angular ones. If this would seem to favour a fairly early date, the fact that such a 'title' script may have been deliberately 'artificial' and archaising means that it is prudent to ascribe the work to the broadest time-frame feasible, namely xii^{2}–xiii^{in}.

The shelf-mark is clearly a later addition; judging from this very small sample of forms, it could date from almost any point during *s.* xiii–xiv.

History

Certainly part of the main volume (for which see **Commentary**) by *c.* 1200 and probably *ab initio,* the present leaf was still joined to it in the late Middle Ages, but had evidently come adrift before the volume was acquired by Matthew Parker († 1575). The scrapbook in which the leaf is currently mounted was assembled in 1872; the location from which it had been recovered is seemingly unrecorded.

Commentary

Item 281 in Prior Eastry's catalogue of Christ Church's library reads: 'Passio sancta Katerine Virginis u[ersifice] / In hoc uol. cont.: Passio Sancti Elphegi, uersifice' (James 1903, p. 49). The main body of the volume in question is very probably Cambridge, Corpus Christi College, MS 375 which contains, *Passio Katerinae metrice*; an extract from Vital de Blois, *Geta*; *Passio Ælphegi metrice*; two hymns for Ælphege; two hymns for St Alban; a Hymn for Peter and Paul; and the hymn, *Salue festa dies celebri* (see further James 1912, II, pp. 219–21; Page and Bushnell 1975, pl. 19; Thomson 1982, I, p. 120). The dimensions of Corpus Christi MS 375 (*c.* 210 × 140 mm) correspond fairly closely – making allowance for their different histories and states of preservation – to those of the present leaf which, it therefore seems safe to say, was once the front flyleaf. The main manuscript was written at Saint Albans in the mid-twelfth century, presumably (in view of its content) for presentation to Christ Church.

28 PRC 50/17/1–3

Lectionary
England; *saec*. XII^{med}
Illustration: PRC 50/17/2, pages 4, 1

Physical Description
Parts of three bifolia. PRC 50/17/1 is a substantial horizontal strip (165 × 415 mm) cut from a bifolium; it preserves 17 complete lines from three columns of text, plus a sliver from the edge of the fourth column. The leaf originally stood at the centre of a quire. PRC 50/17/2 is a relatively complete bifolium. Its corners have been cut off, its (cropped) outer margins were formerly folded over, and the inner margins (now strengthened with a modern repair) were pierced with three pairs of slits (for laces); nevertheless, the text of both sides is wholly intact. Sheet size: 335–40 × 490 mm. Page size: 340 × 244 mm. The disjunction in the text from the first folio to the second shows that the leaf was not the centre of a quire. The bifolium PRC 50/17/3 similarly had its corners cut off, its edges (formerly) folded over, and its gutter pierced for laces. Its general condition is worse than 50/17/2: the areas around the fold and part of the upper margin are very damaged (with significant loss of text) and have been repaired with modern parchment; however, the surviving margins are fuller. Page size: 365 × 265 mm.

Collectively, these leaves allow us to reconstruct a book of *c*. 380 × 275 mm with a written area of 292 × 185 mm, set out in two columns, 80 mm wide. Lines: 32. Space between lines: 10 mm. Height of minims: 5 mm. Pricked in both margins. Ruling: lead or crayon (largely worn away, giving an illusion of hard-point).

The bifolia are currently preserved unfolded, within transparent sleeves, and bear no foliation or numbering. In the following account, sections are identified by: shelf-mark of item, side of leaf, page (numbered according to the order in which one would have encountered them in the original book), and column, as appropriate.

sibunt gentes multe per ciuita
tem hanc: & dicent. Quare fecit
dominus sic ciuitati huic grandi?
Et respondebunt. Eo quod de
reliquerint pactum dei sui. &
adorauerint deos alienos. Ue
qui edificat domum suam in in
iusticia. & amicum suum oppri
met frustra: & mercedem eius
non reddit ei. Tui oculi &
cor ad auariciam & ad sangui
nem innocentem fundendum.
& ad calumniam & ad cursum
mali operis. Ue pastoribus qui
disperdunt & dilacerant gre
gem pascue mee. Uos disper
sistis gregem meum. eiecistis
eos & non uisitastis. Ecce ego
uisitabo super uos maliciam
studiorum uestrorum. Ad prophetas.
Contritum est cor meum in medio
mei. & contremuerunt omnia
ossa mea. Factus sum sicut uir
ebrius uino a facie domini & a
facie uerborum sanctorum eius. quia
adulteris repleta est terra.
quia a facie maledictionis lu
xit terra. Propheta namque & sa
cerdos polluti sunt: & in do
mo mea inueni malum eorum
dicit dominus. Confortauerunt
manus pessimorum. ut non con

uerterentur a malicia sua. Ec
ce ego cibabo eos absinthio.
& potabo eos felle. A prophetis
enim ierusalem egressa est pol
lutio super omnem terram. Ecce
turbo dominice indignationis
egredietur. & tempestas erum
pens super caput impiorum
ueniet. Putas ne deus e uici
no ego sum dicit dominus. & non
deus de longe? Si occultabi
tur uir in absconditis. & ego
non uidebo eum? Numquid
non celum & terram ego im
pleo? Audiui que dixerunt
prophete prophetantes in nomine
meo mendacium. atque dicentes.
Somniaui. somniaui. Usque
quo istud in corde est propheta
rum uaticinantium seductionem
cordis sui? Propheta qui ha
bet sermonem meum. loqua
tur sermonem meum uere. Quid
paleis ad triticum? Numquid
non uerba mea sunt quasi
ignis. & quasi malleus conte
rens petram?
Hoc uerbum quod factum
est ad ieremiam a domino
dicens. Uocem terroris audiui
mus. formido. & non est
pax. Ue quia magna dies

lege dedit: quã ego ostendi
uobis. Et ait dñs michi. Pro
phã suscitabo uobis de me
dio fratrũ u̅roꝝ similẽ tui.
& ponã uerba mea in ore ei⁹.
Loquet(ur)q; ad eos omĩa que p̃
cepero illi. Qui autẽ uerba
eius audire noluerit: ego
ultor existam. Benedixitq;
moyses filiis isr̃l ante mortẽ
suam. & ait. Dñs de syna ue
nit. & de seir ortus est nobis.
Apparuit de pharan: & cũ eo
scõꝝ milia. In dextera eius
ignea lex: dilexit populos.
Om̃s sc̃i in manu illius sunt.
Beatus es tu isr̃l. Quis similis
tui pop̃le qui saluaris: In
dño scutũ auxilii tui. & gla
dius glẽ tue. Negabunt te
inimici tui. & tu eoꝝ colla
calcabis. Ascendit ergo moy
ses sup montẽ nebo in uerti
cẽ phasge: ostenditq; ei dñs
terrã promissionis. Dixitq;.
Hec est terra, p qua iuraui a
braham. & ysaac. & iacob.
Mortuusq; est ibi moyses: &
sepeliuit eũ dñs in ualle ter
re moab. & non cognouit
homo sepulchrũ eius usq;
in presentẽ diẽ. Centũ & ui

ginti annoꝝ erat. Non cali
gauit oculus eius. nec den
tes illius moti sunt. Fleuer(unt)
q; eũ filii isr̃l triginta dieb;.
Iosue uero repletus est spũ
sapientie. & obedierunt ei
filii isr̃l. Non surrexit ult(ra)
pph̃a in isr̃l sicut moyses:
quẽ nosset dñs facie ad faciẽ
in omnib; signis atq; porten
tis. que misit p eum ut face
ret.
Eremias pph̃a fuit sacerdos
ex sacerdotib; & a matris ute
ro sc̃ificatus. uirginitatẽ sua
euangelicũ uirum: xp̃i ecclie
dedicans. Hic uaticinari ex
orsus est puer. & captiuita
tẽ urbis atq; iudee ñ solum
spũ: sed & oculis carnis intu
itus est. Incip̃ ex libro ieremie pph̃e.
Verba ieremie filii
helchie de sacerdoti
bus qui fuerunt in
anathot in terra beniamin:
quod factũ est uerbũ dñi
ad eũ in dieb; iosie filii a
mon regis iuda. in tercio de
cimo anno regni ei⁹. usq; ad
consummationem undecimi
anni sedechie filii iosie re
gis iuda: usq; ad transmi

Content

Lections based on Old Testament and Patristic texts (excerpts from Exodus, Numbers, Deuteronomy and Jeremiah, along with Augustine, are preserved).

[PRC 50/17/1] Augustine, *In euangelium Iohannis*, tractatus 42 and 43; Augustine, *Speculum* (extract) with Jeremiah 6.8, often more or less edited and synopsised; all now imperfect.

[Side one, page one, column 1 (only a sliver remains)**]** //inquit … que … [selections from the end of Augustine, *In euangelium Iohannis*, tractatus 42, then an extract from the start of 43: includes PL 35, col. 1706 bottom line – 1707, line 6]. **[Page one, column 2]** // Ego facio quod debeo, uos non facitis quod debetis. … attendite. Secundum alterum iudicium … et iudicet. Ibi iudicium secundum afflictionem hic iudi- // [abridged PL 35, col. 1707, ll. 37–47; col. 1708, ll. 53–6; col. 1709, ll. 7–8]. **[Page two, column 1]** //–uerit mortem non uidebit in eternum, nisi quia uidebat … euaditur, infeliciter non time- // [PL 35, col. 1710, ll. 17–37 abridged]. **[Page two, column 2]** // Hoc ait propter illud quod dixerunt, … Est ergo inquit Pater meus qui glorificat me, quem uos dicitis quia deus // [PL 35, col. 1711, ll. 33–43 (NB perniciem for PL peruicaciam at l. 40)].

[Side two, page one, column 1] // ut uideret diem meum, et uidit et gauisus est. Magnum testimonium … et gauisus est. Quis explicat [PL 35, col. 1712, ll. 9–19]. **[Page one, column 2]** //[quinqua]ginta annos nondum habes, et abraham uidisti. Et dominus … semen abrahe factus erat. Et ut abraham f[ieret]// [PL 35, col. 1713, ll. 4–18 with differences of order]. **[Page two, column 1]** //–por et mirabilia facta sunt in terra, … auaritie student, [Augustine, *Speculum*: PL 34, col. 938, ll. 22–31, with Jeremiah 6.8]. **[Page two, column 2]** [only a sliver remains, but it clearly included the start of a new section (two initial Is survive, one for the biblical reading, 'IN ILL[o tempore] etc.', the other for the homily, 'IN ista –'). The preserved word-fragments (from the start of each line) are:] unig- … ama- … in po- … scies … Argen- … quia … *Lectio* … IN ILL- … iudeo … –dotum … et m- … *Ome-* … IN ista … apot … –entiam … argu … mod//

[PRC 50/17/2. Page one] // legem dedit, quam ego ostendi uobis. Et ait dominus michi, … que misit per eum ut faceret. [Deuteronomy

18.17–19; 33.1–3; 33.29; 34.1; 34.4–5; 34.8–11, more or less edited or condensed]. [Rubric:] *D*[remainder faded to illegibility]. [Marginal rubric (cropped):] *Sent[?entiae] sancti ier[?onimi] de excel[?entie] Ieremi[e]*. IERemias propheta fuit sacerdos ex sacerdotibus, et a matris utero sanctificatus, ... carnis intuitus est. *Incipit ex libro ieremie prophete.* UERBA ieremie filii ... [Jeremiah 1.1; 1.3–continuing on page two (the verso)–1.10:] et edifices et plantes. [Marginal rubric cropped.][*Lectio*] *II*, Et factum est uerbum domini ad me dicens. Quid tu uides ieremia? Et dixi, Uirgam uigilantem ... ut liberem te. [Jeremiah 1.11–19, fairly complete]. [Marginal rubric obliterated.] *Lectio III*. Et factum est uerbum domini ad me dicens // [end of page; probably Jeremiah 2.1].
[Lacuna]
[PRC 50/17/2. Page three] Ideo in gladio et fame ... non sunt reuersi [Jeremiah 14.14–22; 15.1–7]. [Marginal rubric rubbed.] *Lectio II*. Audite uerbum domini domus David. Iudicate ... [Jeremiah 21.11–12; 22.2–3; 22.5; 22.8, continuing on **page four** (the verso): 22.8–9; 22.13; 22.17; 23.1–2; 23.9–11; 23.14–15; 23.19; 23.23–6; 23.28–9:] ... Nunquid non uerba mea sunt quasi ignis, et quasi malleus conterens petram. [Marginal rubric rubbed.] *Lectio III*. Hoc uerbum quod factum est ad ieremiam a domino dicens, Uocem terroris audiuimus, formido et non est pax. Ue quia magna dies // [Jeremiah 30.5; 30.7, where it breaks off].
[PRC/50/17/3. Page one] [column 1 is imperfect, text being lost from the outer edge and the upper corner; the reading of the damaged first line is uncertain; then:] // erit ipse [lost] maledixerit tibi in maledictionem reputabitur ... priuauit te honore disposito [Numbers 24, 9–11, lightly edited]. *SABBATO. Lectio I*. [F]ornicatus est populus cum filiabus moab, ... eorum qui ante numerati sunt [Numbers 25, 1–15; 26, 1–2; 26, 63–4, edited]. **[Page two]** *Lectio II*. Dixit quoque dominus ad moysen, Ascende in montem istum abarim, et contemplare terram ... [cog]nouerant uiros, trigin[ta] duo milia [Numbers 27.12–13; 27.15–16; 27.18; 27.20–22; then (marked by a rubbed marginal rubric) 31.1–2; 31.5–10; 31.14–18; and 31.32, all more or less heavily edited]. *Lectio I* [? – a hole]. Quadragesimo igitur ... locutus est moyses ... Uos uidistis uniuersa ... [Deuteronomy 29.2; 29. 5] ... nec calciamenta, manna de celo pluit uobis, et aquam de petra produxit, ac // **[Page**

three; top of both columns lost] //moysen. Ecce ... [lost] panes de celo. Dixeruntque moyses et aaron ad omnes filios israel. Uespere scietis quod dominus eduxerit uos de egypto ... et exibit ex ea aqua ut bibat populus. Fecit moyses ita coram senioribus Israel [Exodus 16.4; 16.6–7; 16.10; 16.13–20 [lost lines] 16.31; 16.35; 17.1–2; 17.4–6, all edited]. [Marginal rubric: *Victoria de amalechitis*] *Lectio II.* Venit autem Amalech, et pugnabat ... Et fecit sic, Moyses autem [Exodus 17, 8, doubtless continued on **page four,** where the top of both columns are lacking and which now starts:] // igitur lapidem posuerunt ... Fecit Moyses que ille suggesserat. Dimisitque cognatum, qui reuersus abiit in terram suam [Exodus 17.12–14; 18.1–5; 18.9; 18.11–13; 18.18–24; 18.27, edited]. *Lectio III* ?[numeral partly lost]. Mense tercio egressionis Israel de egypto ... descendet dominus coram // [Exodus 19.1–3; 19. 10–11; breaks off at end of page].

Scribes and Script

All the fragments are the work of a single scribe, writing a transitional Romanesque-Gothic book hand. The basic matrix is rectilinear, but the script is stately and spaciously set out; although some rounded forms (such as the tops of 'e', 'n', and 'm', and the back of 'a') are broken, others (such as most of the bowls) remain more curvilinear; and while down-strokes tend to finish with penturn serifs, there is very little 'biting' of the letters. Characteristic forms include an 'ur' abbreviation which is like a low-backed 'a', and diamond-shaped points. Despite the maltreatment of the leaves, the ink remains a rich black. Sentence capitals – a mixed alphabet in which rustic forms predominate – have their counterspaces stroked in red. Punctuation: low point (for major and minor pauses); *punctus elevatus* (for minor pauses), and *punctus interrogativus.* A few passages on 50/17/1 (all including references to 'The Lord' or 'Christ') are flagged in the margin by a circle or a triangle of dots plus a long descending line, all done in red, blue or green, and clearly contemporary with the original work.

Decoration

Each reading is flagged by a monumental coloured LC [lectio] digraph with a florid tilde, plus the relevant numeral. The start of the lection proper is marked by a two- to five-lines-high coloured initial, either embellished or arabesque. The arabesques are decorated with small, simple, symmetrical, rather formal motifs, and are rendered in red, blue, ochre and green (the last has attacked the parchment). Rubric titles are written in red, green or blue rustic capitals, with an initial in one of the other colours.

History

There is no evidence bearing on the early history of this book. The re-use of the leaves in the late sixteenth century is attested by annotations: in one of the intercolumnar spaces on PRC 50/17/2 is written '1585'; in one on 50/17/3 is written, 'Curatores / Lib. 1 / 1584–1606 / Curationes'. The gutter of 50/17/3, though largely restored, still preserves a couple of original portions which show that, when it formed the spine of the wrapper, it too bore a title – from which 'Curatores' and '1584–1606' survive. A pencil note records that this sheet was recovered from PRC 8/1, the register of the archdeaconry court for the years in question. In the margins on one side of 50/17/1, at right-angles to the main text, are a series of jottings (now partly obliterated) by *s.* xvi^{2}–xvii^{1} hands. Legible portions include: 'SF', 'Si tibi nulla Sy', 'Copia [–?–] narrare', 'Originalis', 'Facta collatione', and 'doctrina'.

Commentary

In general conception, presentation and decoration, the present manuscript closely resembles Add. 128/54 (**no. 29**). The two items have different line-counts, however, and were written by different scribes. Whilst using a broadly similar type of script, the two hands consistently differ in the formation of certain letters – the scribe of 28 uses an open-tailed 'g', for example, whereas that of 29 loops its tail round to join the main body of the letter, making a form akin to an '8' – and, equally telling, in their abbreviation marks, punctuation, and ampersands – which in 28 are invariably 'upright', but in 29 always lean forwards. It is more likely, therefore, that the two manuscripts were companion volumes rather than part of the same book; the discovery of further, better-preserved leaves would help to clarify the issue.

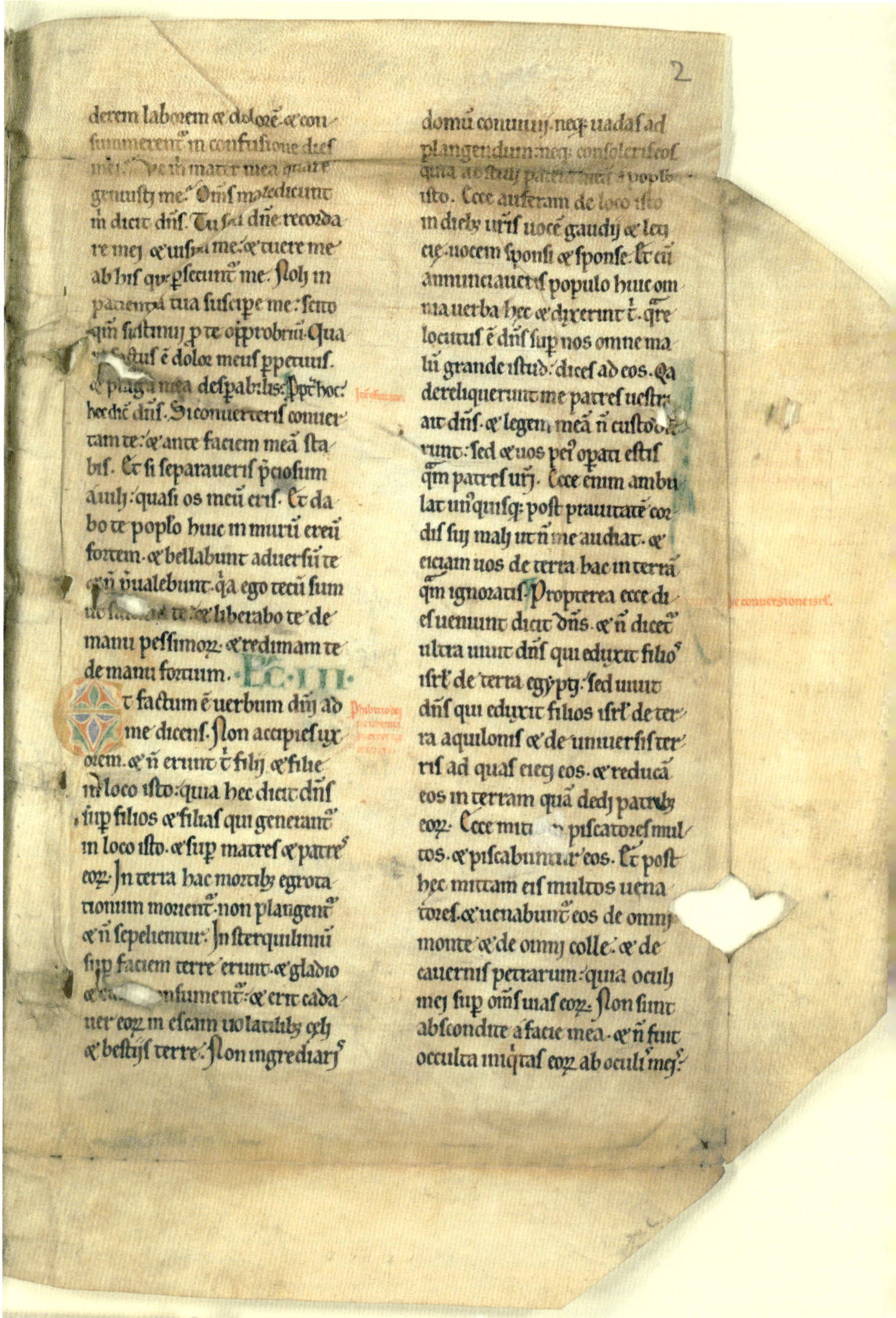

29 Add. 128/54

Lectionary
England; *saec.* XII$^{3/4}$
Illustration: fol. 2r

Physical Description
One damaged bifolium. It was subsequently re-used (upside down and back-to-front) as a wrapper: consequently, its corners were cut off, its edges folded over, it was perforated for the insertion of four thongs, and what was then its 'outer' side (fols. 1r and 2v) has been exposed to considerable wear and tear. Accordingly, the surface of fols. 1r and 2r is rubbed and darkened, and much of the text more or less obliterated. The bifolium, its leaves straightened out again, is now mounted in a guard folder. Notwithstanding subsequent maltreatment, the distinction between the white and veiny flesh side (fols. 1r and 2v) and the yellow, follicle-marked hair side (fols. 1v and 2r) remains pronounced. As the text does not continue from one folio to the next, this bifolium was not the centre of a quire. Maximum dimensions: 385 × 280 mm (prickings survive at the outer edge). Written area: 286 × 182 mm (written above top line). Two columns (76 mm). Lines: 34. Space between lines: 9 mm. Height of minims: 4 mm. Prickings in both margins. Ruled in lead and crayon. Sewing holes appear at *c.* 35, 90, 135, 192, 248, 300 and 350 mm from the top of the leaf.

Content
A series of lessons based on Jeremiah: the scriptural texts have been heavily edited and abbreviated, and discrete passages are combined. The summary below follows the current order of the leaves. For the well-preserved inside faces, the scriptural texts that were drawn upon are fully inventoried; for the badly damaged and difficult-to-read outer ones, only the beginnings and ends of the lections (as currently preserved) have generally been identified. **[Fol. 1r]** [*Lectio II*, starts imperfect] // domini ad ieremiam dicens, Vade [then largely obliterated] ... Hec dicit dominus [?Jeremiah

28.12 adapted; then 28.15; 18, 16; ending with ? 52.5 adapted:] fuit obsessa usque ad [und]ecimum annum regis sedechie.

Lectio III [accompanying rubric virtually obliterated]. V[erbum quod factu]m est ad [ie]remiam a domino quando misit ad eum rex sedechias [21.1] ... [34.6:] locutus est ieremias ad regem un- **[fol. 1v]** -iuersa uerba haec. [Marginal rubric (very worn):] // *per ieremiam ad regem sedechiam.*

Lectio IIII. Et misit rex sedechias ad ieremiam dicens, Ora pro nobis dominum ... [37.3–7; then 34.8–9; 34.10–13; 34.17; finally 34.21:] exercituum regis babylonis qui recesserunt a uobis. [Marginal rubric:] *Comminatio dei, quia pactam seruis libertatem rex et populus dissoluit.*

Lectio V. [Marginal rubric:] *Vir ieremias capitur et ceditur et ?incarceretur.* Ergo cum recessisset exercitus caldeorum ... et daretur ei torta panis cotidie excepto // [37.10–20, abbreviated]. [Marginal rubric:] *Vir ieremias a rege relevatur.*

[Fol. 2r] [starts imperfect:] //[ui]derem laborem et dolorem et consummerentur [20.18; then 15.10–11; 15.15; 15.18–21:] ... et redimam te de manu fortium. [Marginal rubric:] *Item confortatio.*

Lectio III. Et factum est uerbum domini ad me dicens, Non accipies uxorem ... [16.1–5; 16.9–19:] ...[ends on **fol. 2v**:] Vere mendacium possederunt patres nostri uanitatem quae eis non profuit. [Marginal rubric:] *Prohibitio dei ne ieremias duceret? ut* [then faint and rubbed] *de conuersione israhel.*

Feria Sexta Lectio I. [Marginal rubric, damaged and imperfect:] *Vbi ?in initio* [?r]*egni ioachim sacerdotes et falsi prophetae...* [–?–] *ieremiam capiunt* ... [–?–] *et principes eum liberant.* In principio regis Ioachim, factum est uerbum istud a domino dicens [26.1] ... ut non traderetur in manu populi et interficeret [eum] [26.24].

[Rubric obliterated, *Lectio II*] Uerbum domini q[uod factum est] ad ieremiam [25.1–2; then 25. 8–9, breaking off at:] et adducam eos su[per t]err[am] istam et //

Scribes and Script

The surviving text is the work of a single scribe writing a calligraphic late Romanesque book hand, in which some early Gothic features are readily apparent. The rounded letter-forms are still curvilinear, feet are curling extensions of down-strokes, and the writing is spaciously set out on the page; however, the individual letters have been subject to modest lateral compression, and the overall aesthetic is rectilinear. When they occur at the ends of words, certain letters were invariably given a more calligraphic treatment: the cross-stroke of 'e' was extended, the body of 'i' was lengthened – like a 'j'. The writing is placed significantly above the ruled lines. The ink remains dark. Abbreviation was modestly used. Double 'i's are dashed. Punctuation: low to medial point (for major pauses), *punctus elevatus* (for minor pauses) and *punctus interrogativus*. Occasional 'acute' accents. Sentence capitals are a mixed alphabet, calligraphically treated and brushed in red. Major subsections within the lections are flagged by a green paraph and are accompanied by a marginal rubric written in red in minuscules (the work of the same scribe).

Decoration

The lections are introduced by a bold title ('LC III' etc.) done in red, green or blue in monumental capitals with a flamboyant tilde. They are headed by a compact (three- to six-lines- high) arabesque initial, very formally-patterned, coloured in red, yellow-ochre, blue and green.

History

There is no evidence concerning the early history of what was originally a large and handsome book. The volume was evidently dismembered and this sheet was used as a wrapper in the later sixteenth century: written in ink on the 'spine' of the bifolium is 'Acta Curia 29, 1581, 1583'; and there are two sets of inscriptions on fol. 2v (both upside down in relation to the original text). At what was then the top, written in ink that is now yellow and very faint is 'Liber instantiam et partiam 1581', '1581–83' and 'Liber 29', along with other notes that are now partly obliterated and very difficult to decipher. Lower down, in much darker ink, is repeated: 'Ad instantiam Partiam, 29, 1581–1583': the sheet was formerly the cover of Y.4.23. A note kept with the sheet records that it was at one stage: 'Box ABC in XYZ, Bundle Q'.

Commentary
See **no. 28.**

30 Add. 127/24

Missal
Canterbury; *saec.* XII^{med}
Illustration: Unit C, face 1

Physical Description

Parts of 26 folios, all damaged, many terribly so. One is so burned and discoloured that no trace of writing remains discernible; most others have suffered charring, shrivelling, and extreme wear and tear; while two pairs of bifolia were, at some stage straightened out, then folded in half vertically, and used to secure six pairs of cords – which are still in place with the remnants of twine wrapped around them (see Gameson 2005, ill. 1) – into a binding structure (perhaps as pads). In addition, individual faces bear the stains of turn-ins and/or adhesive. The condition of the fragments – some fixed together inside out and non-sequentially – means that it is neither possible nor desirable to mount them in their original order. The separate units (which range in extent from fragments of a single page to a near-complete quire) are currently preserved within separate folders, identified by the letters, 'A' to 'L', mainly arranged – in so far as is feasible – according to their original order.

Size of best-preserved leaf: *c.* 228 × 158 mm. Written area: 168 × 110 mm. Lines: 21. Space: 8 mm. Height of minims: 4–5 mm. Ruling: lead. On the best-preserved bifolium (Unit C), sewing holes appear at [?], 48, 76, 105, [?], 165, 195 and 215 mm from the upper edge [the two areas represented by '?' are too damaged and repaired to evaluate].

Content

A 'select' missal. The extant fragments include text from the following sections (in varying degrees of preservation and legibility): Dominica infra octauam epiphanie; Dominica in Septuagesima; Dominica in Sexagesima; Dominica in Quinquagesima; Feria Quarta cinerum; Dominica I in quadragesima; Dominica II in quadragesima. Then: In natale unius uirginis et confessoris; In

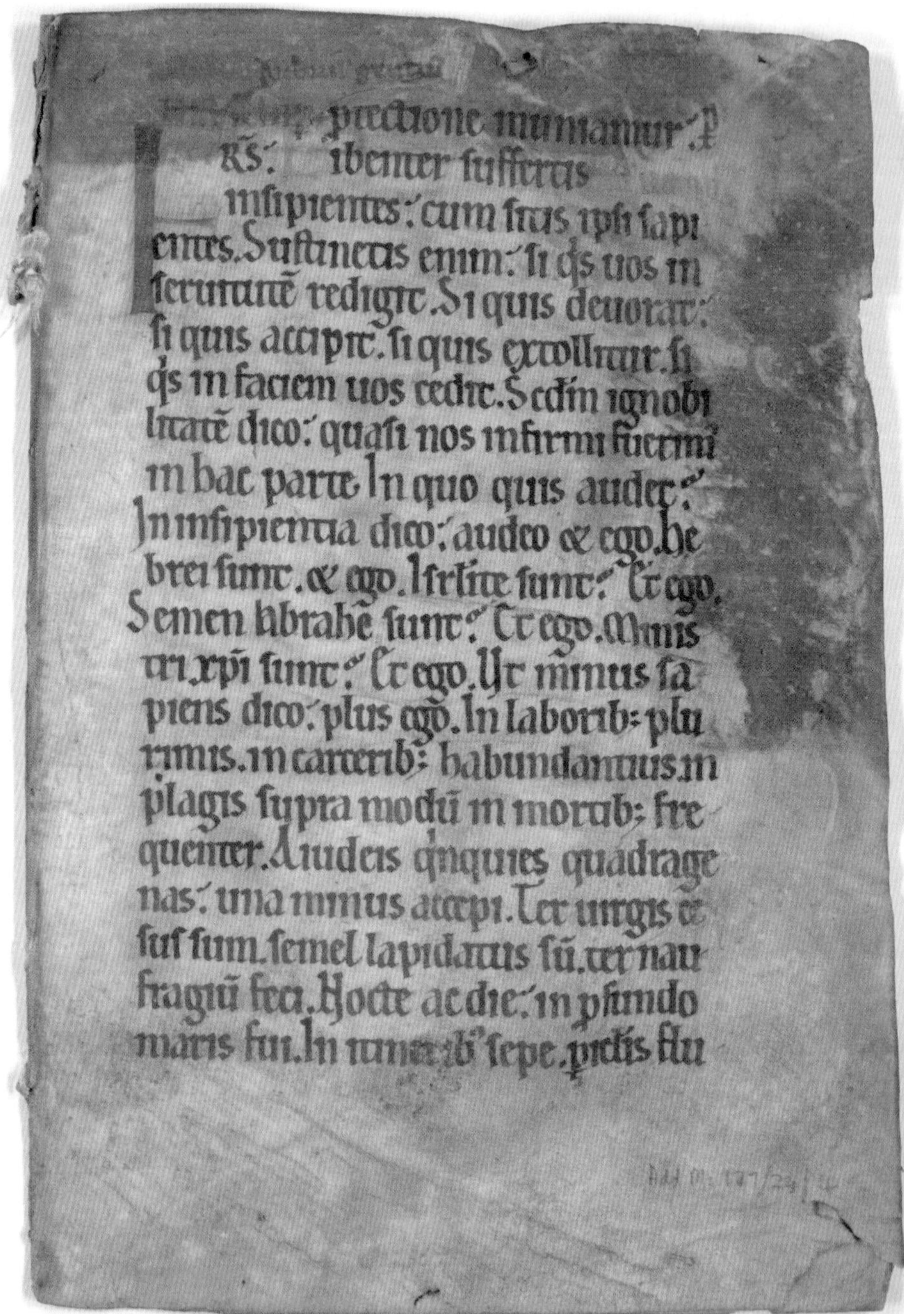

[illegible] perceptione muniantur. P
RS. Libenter suffertis
insipientes: cum sitis ipsi sapi
entes. Sustinetis enim: si quis vos in
servitutem redigit. Si quis devorat:
si quis accipit. si quis extollitur. si
quis in faciem vos cedit. Secundum ignobi
litatem dico: quasi nos infirmi fuerimus
in hac parte. In quo quis audet:
In insipientia dico: audeo et ego. He
brei sunt. et ego. Israhelite sunt: Et ego.
Semen Abrahe sunt: Et ego. Minis
tri Christi sunt: Et ego. Ut minus sa
piens dico: plus ego. In laboribus plu
rimis. in carceribus habundantius. in
plagis supra modum in mortibus fre
quenter. A iudeis quinquies quadrage
nas: una minus accepi. Ter virgis ce
sus sum. semel lapidatus sum. ter nau
fragium feci. Nocte ac die: in profundo
maris fui. In itineribus sepe. periculis flu

honore sanctorum quorum corpora habentur; De sancta trinitate; In honore sanctae crucis; In commemoratione BVM; Pro pace; Pro seipso sacerdote; Pro amico familiaris; Pro infirmis; Pro iter agentibus; Ad pluuiam postulandam; Pro uiuis et defunctis; In agenda mortuorum; Pro una defuncta; Pro defunctis fratribus et benefactoribus.

The following calendar of content presents the surviving text in its original order. Owing to the way several of the leaves were subsequently re-used – turned inside out, fixed together in pairs, then folded in half horizontally – and to the lack of any consistent numbering on the various portions therein, the identifications of the individual folios are inevitably rather cumbersome, and the terminology inevitably varies according to their current state. The first and last (legible) words of each separate portion (folded quadrants, etc.) of every page have been given in order to facilitate identification of the relevant section within this three-dimensional jig-saw puzzle. Wherever possible, reference is made to the printed edition of the Missale Romanum [MR – vol. I, unless otherwise indicated], but sometimes also to those of Bec [B], Robert of Jumieges [RJ], and Westminster [WM].

[**Unit A** (two bifolia which were opened, pierced with thongs, then folded together horizontally), inner bifolium, first half, face a] //[agno]uimus intus reformari mereamur. Qui te[cum] [MR I, 34; WM I, 68].

Lectio ysaie propheti. Domine deus meus honorificabo te, laudem tribuam nomini tuo ... sempiterna ... nomen eius. Notas **[A, inner bifolium, face b]** facite in populis uirtutes eius ... Annunciate hoc in uniuersa terra. Dicit dominus omnipotens [WM I, 68–9, for Dominica infra octauam epiphanie]. *G*[*raduale*] Omnes de Saba [MR 34]. *V*[*ersus*] Vidimus stellam [MR 34].

Secundum Iohannem. In illo tempore. Uidit iohannes Ihesum uenientem ... quia hic est filius dei [John 1, 29–34; MR 34]. *Of*[*fertorium*] Reges tharsis [MR 34]. *Sec*[*reta*] Hostias tibi ... tui ap// [MR 35; end of leaf].

[A, inner bifolium, second half, face a] // horam et fecit similiter. Circa undecimam ... Tolle quod tuum est et uade. Volo autem et

[A, inner bifolium, second half, face b] huic nouissimo dare ... pauci uero electi [Mt 20, 1–6; MR 41–2]. *Of*[*fertorium*]. Bonum est confiteri ... altissime [MR 42]. *Sec*[*reta*] Muneribus nostris quesumus domine precibusque susceptis ... exaudi [MR 42]. *Com*[*munio*] Illumina faciem tuam [MR 42]. [*Postcommunio*] ... requirant [et] querendo ... percipiant [MR 42].

[*Dominica in Sexagesima.*] Exurge quare ... et libera nos [MR 42]. [*Psalmus*] Deus auribus [MR 42]. *Or*[*atio*]. Deus qui conspicis quia ex nulla ... aduersa omnia [MR 42; end of leaf; continues directly on **Unit** C (a reasonably well preserved bifolium)**, face 1]** \doctoris gentium/ [the original reading here is lost or was erased; these relevant words were supplied in the upper margin by a *s.* xiii hand] protectione muniamur. Per [MR 42].

Ad Romanos [sic: recte II Cor. 11, 19 ff.; MR 43, abbreviated] Fratres. Libenter suffertis insipientes ... periculis flu- **[Unit C, face 2]** -minum periculis latronum ... Deus et pater domini nostri ihesu Christi scit qui est benedictus in secula, quod non mentior.

G. Sciant gentes ... terram [MR 43–4]. *V*. Deus meus pone ... uenti [MR 44]. *T*[*ractus*]. Commouisti domine terram et conturbasti eam [MR 44]. *V*. Sana contriciones [MR 44]. *V*. Ut fugiant [MR 44].

Secundum Lucam. In illo. Cum turba plurima conueniret et de ciuitatibus [end of leaf; continues directly on **Unit** B (a pair of bifolia folded together lengthways), **inside bifolium, face 1]** [tatibus – cancelled] properarent ad ihesum; dixit per similitudinem .... Credentes salui fiant **[Unit B, face 2 of same folio]** Nam qui supra petram ... in patientia [Lk 8, 4–15; MR 44]. *Of*. Perfice gressus meos ... sperantes in te domine [MR 44]. *Sec*. Oblatum tibi domine sacrificium uiuificet ... muniat [MR 44]. *Com*. Introibo ad altare dei ... meam [MR 44]. *Postcom*. Supplices te rogamus ... deseruire concedas. Per [MR 44].

Dominica in quinquagesima [end of leaf].

[Unit A, outer bifolium, right-hand leaf, face 1] [E]sto michi ... eris et enutries me [end barely visible; MR 45]. [Followed by one or two words in a different *s.* xii hand, of which only '–ug–' remains legible.]

Or. Preces nostras quesumus domine ... custodi [MR 45].

Ad Corinthios. Fratres, Si linguis hominum ... non querit que sua sunt. Non **[Unit A, outer bifolium, left-hand page inside (i.e. face 2 of same folio)]** irritatur, non cogitat ... Maior autem horum, est caritas [I Cor. 13, 1–13; MR 45]. *Gr.* Tu es deus ... tuam [MR 45]. *V.* Liberasti ... ioseph [MR 45]. *Tractus.* Iubilate domino omnis terra [MR 45] **[continues on Unit B, outer bifolium, right-hand page:]** seruite domino in letitia [MR 45]. *V.* Intrate ... ipse est deus [cf. MR 45]. *V.* Ipse fecit ... pascue eius [cf. MR 45]. *Lucam.* In illo tempore. Assumpsit dominus [crossed through] Ihesus duodecim discipulos suos ... ut taceret. Ipse **[Unit B, outer bifolium, inside left-hand page (i.e. face two of the same folio)]** uero multo ... dedit laudem deo. [Lk 18, 31–43; MR 46]. *Of.* [Benedictus] es domine doce ... oris tui [MR 46]. *Sec.* Hec hostia quesumus ... sanctificet [MR 46]. *Com.* Manducauerunt et saturati ... a desiderio suo [MR 46]. *Postcom.* Quesumus omnipotens deus et qui celestia ... muniamur. Per [MR 46].
In capite ieiunii m[issa] [end of page].
[Unit B, outer bifolium, inside, right-hand page] //[dis]simulans peccata hominum ... quia tu es dominus deus noster [MR 48, acephalus]. *Ps.* Miserere mei [deus, miserere mei] [MR 48]. [*Oratio* – Rubric lost] Concede nobis domine pres[idia] ... continentie mu[niamur] auxiliis. Per [MR 48].
Lectio Iohelis Prophete. Hec dicit dominus deus, Conuer[timini] ad me in toto corde ... Egrediatur sponsus de cubili [suo et] **[Unit B, outer bifolium, other face of same folio]** [spon]sa de thalamo suo ... in gentibus. Ait dominus omnipotens [Joel 2, 12–19; MR 49]. *G.* Miserere mei deus Miserere mei ... anima mea [MR 49]. *V.* Misit de cello ... conculcantes me [MR 49]. *Lc.* Domine non secundum peccata nostra ... nobis [MR 49]. *V.* Domine ne memineris ... nimis [MR 49]. *V.* Adiuua nos deus salutaris ... nomen tuum [MR 49].
Secundum Mattheum **[end of page; Unit A, outer bifolium, inside face, right-hand side]** In illo [tempore]. Dixit dominus ihesus discipulis suis, Cum ieiunatis, nolite fieri ... ibi est et cor tuum [Mt 6, 16–21; MR 49–50]. *Of.* Exaltabo te domine ... sanasti me [MR 50]. *Sec.* Fac quesumus domine his nos muneribus offerendis conue- **[Unit A, outer bifolium, outside face, left-hand**

side] [-nienter] ... aptari ... celebramus exordium [cf. MR 50]. *P*[*re*]*f*[*atio*] [VD – very damaged] Qui corporali ieiunio uitia comprimis ... per christum dominum nostrum [cf. MR 50]. *Com.* Qui meditatur [sic] in lege ... tempore suo [cf. MR 50]. *Postcom.* Percepta nobis domine prebeant ... medelam. Per [MR 50]. *Super populum.* [Inclinantes se domine] maiestati ... nutritiantur auxiliis. Per. [MR 50].

D[*ominica prima in*] *quadragesima.*

Inuocauit me ... adimplebo eum [MR 55]. *Ps.* Qui habitat [MR 55]. *Or.* Deus qui ecclesiam tuam annua ... operibus exequatur. Per [MR 56].

[Unit B, inner bifolium, inside face, right-hand side] *Ad Corinthios.* Fratres. Hortamur uos ne in uacuum gratiam dei recipiatis ... Ut castigati et non mortifica- **[Unit B, inner bifolium outside face, left-hand side]** -ti. Quasi tristes ... et omnia possidentes [ex II Cor. 6, 1–10; MR 56]. *G.* Angelis suis mandauit ... uiis tuis [MR 56]. *V.* In manibus portabunt te ... pedem tuum [MR 56].

Secundum Mattheum. In illo [tempore]. Ductus est dominus ihesus in desertum ... manibus tollent te, ne forte offendas **[Unit C, face 3]** ad lapidem pedem tuum ... et ministrabant ei [Mt 4, 1–11; MR 57].

Of. Scapulis suis ... ueritas eius [MR 57]. *Sec.* Sacrificium quadragesimalis ... uoluptatibus temperemus. Per. [cf MR 57]. *Com.* Scapulis suis ... ueritas eius [MR 57]. *Postcom.* Tui nos quesumus domine sacramenti libatio ... purgatos **[Unit C, face 4]** in mysterii ... consortium. Per. [MR 57].

D II [*Dominica secunda in quadragesima*]. Reminiscere miserationum ... ex omnibus angustiis nostris [MR 70]. *Ps.* Ad te domine leuaui [MR 70]. *Or.* Deus qui conspicis omni nos uirtute ... in mente. Per. [MR 71].

Thessalonicenses. Fratres. Rogamus uos et obsecramus ... Non in passione de // [end of page; ex I Thess. 4, 1–7].

[In *s.* xiii, a phrase was written down the inner margin of this page, at right angles to the main text, by an informal hand. The first few words have been erased (or lost through wear). The end reads: confido e[st] erubescaui.]

[Unit D (an incomplete bifolium), face 1] [badly damaged, outer

and lower edges lost; bears pencil number '11'] //-pientium mori illi autem sunt in pace.
In natale uni[us uirginis et confessoris] //
Loquebar de testimoniis tuis ... dilexi ni[mis] [MR 441]. *Ps.* Beati i// [?immaculati in uia qui ambulant in lege domini: Ps. 118]. *Coll[ectio]* Deus qui inter cetera potentie ... gradiamur. Per. [MR 441].
Lectio libri sap[*ientie*]. Confitebor tibi domine rex ... De altitudine [a couple of lines lost; **Unit D, face 2**] [in]usta liberasti me ... domine deus noster [Eccl. 51, 1–8, 12; MR 444].
Lectio libri sapientie. [D]omine deus meus exaltasti super terram ... dicam nomini tuo [domine] deus meus [Eccl. 51, 13–17; MR 443]. *G.* Dilexisti iusticiam et odisti ... oleo leticie. Alleluia [MR 441].
[Rubric and start of text lost or damaged] //?-sa christi accipe palmam preparatam a domino.
S. Mattheum. [very damaged] //?Dixit ihesus discipulis suis parabolam [han]c, simile est regnum [damaged, lost; presumably Mt 13, 44–52: MR 445].
[Unit D, face 3 (numbered '12')] [very damaged conjoint leaf fragment]. Hec nos domine quesumus gratia semper exercea// [lost] ... et sancta, N, uirginis tue ... letificet. Per.
De sancta trinitat[*e*].
Benedicta sit sancta trinitas ... misericordiam suam [MR 450]. *Ps.* Benedicamus [MR 450]. [Rubric lost] Omnipotens sempiterne deus qui dedisti ... aduersis [MR 450].
[Rubric lost, text very damaged] Fratres. Gratia domini nostri ihesu christi [lost/damaged] ... omnibus nobis. *G.* Benedictus es domine ... sedes super cherubin [MR 450]. *V.* Benedicite deum caeli ... [damaged/lost].
[Unit D, face 4] [very shrivelled and charred] ... Et uos testimonium per[hibebitis quia] ab inicio mecum estis ... quia ego dixi uobis [ex Jn 15, 26–16,4; MR 450].
[*Of.* – very charred] ... unigenitusque dei filius sanctus quoque spiritus quia fecit nobiscum misericordiam suam [MR 450]. [*Sec.* – very burnt] ... inuocationem huius oblati[onis] ... [MR 451].
[Unit E (a single folio, shrivelled and damaged), **face 1 (numbered '13')]**

[*Missa in honore sanctorum quorum corpora habentur*] –uenite benedicti patris mei percipite regnum cum gaudio magno. *Ev[angelium]* Leuatis ihesus oculis. *Of.* Mirabilis deus in sanctis suis ... benedictus deus [WM II, 1073–4; B 235]. *Sec.* Suscipiat clementia tua domine quesumus de manibus nostris munus oblatum quod per sanctorum tuorum GREGORII, AUGUSTINI, ÆDBURGIS atque MILDRITHE necnon et eorum quorum reliquie in ista continentur ecclesia sacras orationes ab omnibus nos emundet peccatis. Per [cf. MR 449]. *Com.* Ego uos elegi de mundo ut eatis et fructum ... maneat [B 229; cf, e.g. MR 410]. *Postcom.* Diuina libantes misteria que pro sanctorum tuorum GREGORII, AUGUSTINI, ÆDBURGIS atque MILDRITHE necnon et eorum quorum reliquie in ista continentur ecclesia ueneratione tue obtulimus maiestati, presta quesumus domine ut per ea ueniam mereamur peccatorum et celestis gratie donis reficiamur. Per. [cf. MR 449].

De sancta cruce.

[*Introitus*] Nos autem gloriari ... ihesu christi [rest of line damaged] **[Unit E, face 2]** uita et resurrectio ... liberati sumus [MR 453]. *Ps.* Deus m[isereatur] [MR 453]. *Coll.* Deus qui unigeniti filii tui domini ... ubique protectione gaudere. Per eundem [MR 453].

Ad Philipenses. Fratres. Christus factus est ... dei patris [Phil. 2, 8–11; MR 453]. *Gr.* Christus factus est ... crucis [MR 453]. *V.* Propter quod ... omne nomen. Alleluia [MR 453]. *V.* Dulce lignum ... celorum et dominum [MR 453].

Secundum Matheum. In illo tempore. Ascendens ihesus ierosolimam assumpsit duodecim **[Unit F (three bifolia), first recto (numbered '14')]** discipulos suos secreto ... Et tertia die resurget [MR 454].

Of. Protege ... sacrificium nostrum. Alleluia [MR 454]. *Sec.* Hec oblatio ... offensam. Per [MR 454].

Praefatio. VD Æterne Deus. Qui salutem humani generis in ligno crucis constituisti, ut unde mors oriebatur, inde uita resurgeret. Et qui in ligno uicerat; p[?er] lignum quoque // [lost; cf. RJ 244–5]. **[Unit F, first verso]** [Postcom. – acephalus] // crucis letari facis honore, eius quoque perpetuis defende subsidiis. Per [MR 454].

[Supplementary cues written in the upper margin in an informal s. xiv hand, including the Marian prayer, Deus qui salutis; cf. WM II, 620.]
De sancta Maria. Salue sancta pariens ... seculorum [MR 456]. *Ps.* Et gaudium matris habens ... [??]. *Coll.* Concede nos famulos tuos ... leticia. Per [MR 456].
Lectio libri sapientie [Eccl. 24, 14–16]. Ab initio ... in partes dei mei // [lost] [plenitu]dine sanctorum // [lost] [MR 456].
[Unit F, second recto (numbered '15')] // in tua se clausit uiscera factus homo [MR 456].
V. Post partum uirgo inuiolata permansisti. Dei genitrix intercede pro nobis [MR 457].
Ev. In illo. Factum est cum loqueretur Ihesus ad turbas extollens uocem quedam mulier de turba dixit illi, Beatus uenter qui te portauit ... custodiunt illud [Lk 11, 27, 28; MR 457].
Of. Felix namque ... christus [then illegible] [B 249; cf. MR 457].
Sec. Tua domine ... prosperitatem [MR 457].
Praefatio. VD. Æterne Deus [continuing in a later hand, s. xii/xiii–xiii[1]:] Et te in ueneratione sancta dei genitricis uirginis marie [thereafter increasingly shrivelled and damaged].
[Unit F, second verso ('15')] // una precamur supplices ut tuis precibus adiuti laudemus trinitatem. *Postcom.* Sumptis domine salutis ... maiestati. Per [MR 457].
De S. Maria in aduentu d[omini]. Omnipotens sempiterne deus, qui terrenis corporibus uerbi ... consequi mereamur. Per eundem [RJ 201]. *Secr.* Intercessio quesumus domine beate marie semper uirginis ... acceptos. Per [B 250; RJ 245]. *Postcom.* Celesti munere saciati, quesumus omnipotens deus, tua nos protectione custodi ... intercedente sancta MARIA propiciatus **[Unit F, third recto (numbered '16')]** indulge, ut ueniente sponso filio tuo unigenito accensis lampadibus eius digni prestolemur occursum. Qui tecum [B 250].
[Rubric rubbed to illegibility.] Concede quesumus omnipotens deus, ut intercessio nos sancte dei genitricis MARIE sanctarumque omnium ... patrocinia sentiamus [B 255; cf. MR 459].
Sec. Oblatis quesumus domine placare muneribus ... periculis. Per eundem [B 255; MR 459]. *Postcom.* Sumpsimus ... consequamur. Per [B 255; MR 459].

[Rubric damaged: ? *missa pro congregatione*]. Omnipotens sempiterne deus **[Unit F, third verso]** qui facis mirabilia magna solus ... benedictionis infunde [B 255 (where *pro prelatis*); MR 465]. [Singular forms added between the lines by a contemporary hand.]
Secretum. Hostias ... sentiant ad medelam. Per [B 256; cf. MR 465]. [Singular forms added.] *Postcom*. Quos celesti ... concede. Per [B 256; MR 465].
Pro pace missa. Deus a quo sancta desideria recta ... tranquilla. Per [MR 460–1].
Sec. Deus qui credentes in te populos **[Unit F, fourth recto (numbered '17')]** nullis sinis concuti terroribus ... faciat esse securos [MR 461].
Postcom. Deus auctor pacis ... timeamus. Per [MR 461].
[*Missa pro ?sacerdote ipso*] Suppliciter te deus pater omnipotens ... absoluere. Per [B 257; MR 463].
Sec. Deus misericordie deus pietatis ... queso miserere **[Unit F, fourth verso]** mei serui tui et sacrificium ... accipere delictorum. Per [B 257; cf. MR 463]. *Postcom*. Deus qui uiuorum es saluator ... sanctitatis suscipiat. Per [B 257; cf. MR 463–4].
Missa familiaris pro amico.
Or. Omnipotens sempiterne deus miserere famulo tuo N ... perficiat. Per. [MR 470]. [A slightly later hand has added feminine plural forms between the lines.]
[Unit F, fifth recto ('numbered 18')] *Sec*. Proficiat quesumus domine ... dirigatur. Per [MR 470]. [Masculine plural forms added.] *Postcom*. Sumentes domine ... protegas. Per [MR 470]. [Masc. pl. forms added.]
Missa pro familiaribus. Familiam huius cenobii quesumus domine ... fortitudo. Per eundem [B 255; RJ 250]. *Sec*. Respice quesumus domine ad hostiam ... te gubernante custodiamus. Per [cf. B 255]. [*Postcom*.] Suscipe domine preces nostras et immo custodie tue hoc sanctum ouile circun- **[Unit F, fifth verso]** -da incolumitatis et pacis. Per [cf. B 255 and MR 479].
Pro familiaribus. Deus qui caritatis dona ... perficiant. Per [MR 471]. *Secr*. Miserere quesumus domine famulis et famulabus ...

felicitates acquirant [MR 471]. *Postcom.* Diuina libantes ... maiestati. Per [MR 471]. [Stained and damaged.]
[Largely obliterated: *missa pro infirmis*] Omnipotens sempiterne Deus salus ... [MR 462] ... **[Unit F, sixth recto (numbered '19')]** .N. pro quo misericordie ... actionem. Per [MR 462]. [Pl. forms added.]
Sec. Deus cuius nutibus uite ... salute letemur. Per [MR 462]. [Pl. forms added.] *Postcom.* Deus infirmitatis humane singulare ... mereantur. Per [MR 462–3]. [Pl. forms added.]
Pro iter agentibus. Coll. Adesto domine supplicationibus ... [pro]tegantur auxil[io] [remainder lost] [MR 461]. [Pl. forms added.] *Sec.* [Start lost] **[Unit F, sixth verso]** [assu]me ut uiam ... gaudemus. Per [MR 461–2]. [Pl. forms added.] *Postcom.* Deus infinite misericordie et maiestatis immense ... comes esse dignare. Per [cf. MR II, 283–4]. [Pl forms added.]
Ad pluuiam postulandam. Deus in quo uiuimus mouemur ... appetamus. Per [B 265; MR 471].
Sec. [O]blatis domine placare muneribus... tribue pluuie ... [remainder of page lost except the rubric *Postcom.*] [Ends on **Unit J** (a single leaf, weathered and shrivelled) (**numbered '13/2'**), **recto:]** //tis dignanter infunde. Per [B 265; cf. MR 471].
Pro serenitate aeris postulanda. Ad te nos domine clamantes exaudi, et aeris serenitatem ... sentiamus. Per [B 265; WM II, 1159]. *Secr.* Preueniat nos domine quesumus gratia tua semper ... per/pro-ficient ad salutem. Per [B 265; MR, 471]. *Postcom.* Plebs tua domine capiat sacre benedictionis augmentum ... deprecationibus adiuuatur. Per [B 265].
Pro defuncto a primo... Quesumus domine ut anime famuli tui N cui primum ii, iii, iiii obitum diem commemoramus ... **[Unit J, verso]** perenne\m/ ei infundas. Per [B 268; MR 486]. [Masculine pl. forms added.] *Secr.* Adesto domine supplicationibus nostris et hanc oblationem ... pro anima famuli tui N placidus ac benignus assume. Per [B 268; MR 487].
Prefatio. VD per christum dominum nostrum per quem salus mundi per quem uita hominum, per quem resurrectio mortuorum ... in eterne saluationis partem restituas. Per quem.

Postcom. Omnipotens sempiterne deus colocare digneris animam et spiritum famuli tui N cuius diem depositionis iii ... inter sanctos et electos // [breaks off; B 268; MR 487].
[Unit I, side 3] // beatorum. Per [?B 270].
[*Or*]. Quesumus domine pro tua pietate ... partem restitue [B 271; MR 489].
[*Sec.*] His sacrificiis quesumus domine anima ... misericordiam consequatur [B 271; MR 489].
[*Missa pro defunctis fratribus et benefactoribus*] *Or.* Deus uenie largitor et humane salutis [MR 489].
[Unit I, side 4] [*Sec.*]... propicius preces humilitatis ... tribue peccatorum [MR 489].
[*Postcom.*] ... quesumus misericors deus, ut ... hoc sacrificium ... beatitudinem. Per [MR 490].
[*Missa in anniuersario*]
... indulgentiarum domine da anime ... luminis [MR 490]. [Plurals added.]
[*Secr.*; mainly lost.]//domine supplicationibus nostris pro- [MR 490].
[Unit H, side 3] // [very damaged]... purgata ... indulgentiam -riter et requiem ... sempiternam.
[Rubric lost.] Deus cuius miseratione animae fidelium ... sine fine letentur. Per [B 272; MR 490].
Sec. Pro animabus famulorum ... mereamur eternam. Per [B 272; MR 490]. *Postcom.* Deus fidelium lumen ... [damaged; B 272].
[Unit H, side 4] [*Pro fidelibus defunctis.*] Fidelium deus omnium conditor ... supplicationibus consequantur. Per [MR 492; B 272]. *Secr.* [Ho]stias quesumus domine quas tibi pro animabus famulorum ... dones et premium. Per [B 272; MR 492]. *Postcom.* [A]nimabus quesumus domine famulorum ... redemptionis facias esse participes [B 272; MR 492].
Missa Generalis [*pro uiuis et defunctis*] Omnipotens sempiterne deus qui uiuorum dominaris ... [shrivelled; B 272; MR 472]. [Continues on **Unit G** (a very shrivelled, still-folded bifolium)**, first recto (numbered '25'):]** // in carne retinet, uel futurum iam ... delictorum suorum omnium u[eniam?] et gaudia consequi mereantur [eterna. Per] [B 273; cf. MR 472]. [*Saec.* xiii addition

in upper margin: decreuimus quosque uel presens adhuc [then illegible]: part of the previous phrase of the same prayer]. [Rubric lost, text damaged] Deus cui soli cognitus est ... beate predestinationis liber ... [B 274; cf. MR 472]. *Postcom.* Purificent nos quesumus omnipotens et misericors deus ... [B 274; MR 473]. [Most of the rest burnt and shrivelled.]

[Unit G, first verso] // nostrorum solue uincula omnium delictorum ... intercedente beata et gloriosa sempiterne uirgine dei genitrice Maria cum omnibus ... domnum papam, pontifices et ... abbates nostros ... omnis congregatio ... reges et principes ... omnem populum christianum et nos famulos tuos atque locum istum cum omni[bus] habitantibus in eo ... consanguinitate ... [cf. 'Pietate tua', B 274; MR 473].

[Unit G, second recto (numbered '26')] // hostia totius mundi ... [pre]mia eterne concede, qui uiuis [MR 473]. Sumpta quesumus domine celestia sac[ramenta] [MR 473] [damaged].

[Unit G, second verso] // opera enim illorum, sequuntur illos [Apoc. 14, 13; MR 485].

[Requ]iem eternam dona eis domine et lux perpetua luceat eis ... [Whole line replaced *in rasura* by a s. xii^2–xii/xiii entry:] [Absol]ue, domine, animas eorum ab omni uinculo delictorum.

De profundis clamaui ad te domine ... *V.* Quia [apud] te propitiatio ... te domine.

Lectio liber Machabeorum. In diebus illis. Vir fortissimos ... [II Macc. 12, 42–6; MR 484; very damaged].

[Unit H (an imperfect, very shrivelled, folded bifolium, numbered '24/21'), first recto] [Burnt, start lost, then barely legible.] ... Hoc enim uobis ... et in tuba dei descendet ... Itaque consolamini inuicem in uerbis [lost] [I Thess. 4, 12–17; MR 484].

[Rubric largely lost.] In illo. Dixit Ihesus discipulis suis et turbis iudeorum. Omne q– [lost] mihi pater ad me ueniet. Et eum ad me non eiciam ... **[Unit H, first verso]** ...Et ego resuscitabo eum in nouissimo die [Jn 6, 37–40; MR 485]. [*Off.*] Domine Ihesu Christe, rex glorie libera animas omnium fidelium ... de morte transire ad uitam [B 277; MR 486]. *V.* Quam olim.

Secundum Iohannem. Dixit Ihesus discipulis suis et turbis Iudeorum, Ego sum panis uiuus, qui de celo descendi ... manducauerit [Jn 5, 51–5; MR 486].

[Unit I (incomplete, open bifolium), side 1] //– dare nobis ad manducandum ... eis Ihesus. Amen amen dico uobis nisi ... carnem filii hominis ... qui manducat meam carn[em et bibit] meum sanguinem habet uitam [eternam] Et ego resuscitabo eum in nou[issimo die][Jn 6, 51–5; MR 486].
S[ecundum Iohannem.] In illo. Dixit martha ad Ihesum, Domine si fuisses hic frater meus non fuisset mortuus. Sed et nunc scio ... [Jn 11, 21–7; B 277; MR 485]
[Unit I, first verso] [Rubric very rubbed.] Deus qui nos patrem et matrem honorare precipisti ... fac uidere. Per [MR 491]. [With interlinear additions.]
Secr. [Sus]cipe sacrificium ... coniunge. Per [MR 491]. *Postcom.* Celestis participatione sacramenti quesumus domini ... coronet eterna. Per [cf. MR 491].
Pro animabus [illegible]. Miserere quesumus domine animabus omnium benefactorum nostrorum defunctorum et pro beneficiis ... in celis [burnt; B 269].
[**Unit K:** a single burnt leaf, on which no text remains visible; **Unit L:** two shards of parchment without any writing.]

Scribes and Script

All the original, main text that remains easily visible appears to be the work of a single scribe, who wrote a neat, fairly handsome, transitional late Romanesque – early Gothic book hand. Individual strokes are thick (*c.* 1 mm) and regular. The general matrix of the script is rectilinear, and 'c', 'e', and 'o' along with the bowls of 'd' and 'g', in particular, are distinctly so; however, round elements – even of the letters just cited – remain curvilinear. The tops of minims are articulated with wedge-shaped serifs; the tail of 'g' and the lower terminal of 's' are decorated with a long line-serif; and the tilde often has oblique serifs at both ends. As a whole, the writing is fairly densely applied to the page, with the principal texts filling over half of the space between rulings. The cue texts – which are written by the same hand in a smaller, less elongated version of the same script – occupy approximately a third of the space. The red rubrics are also the work of the main hand. Sentence capitals are a mixed alphabet in which rustics predominate. The lower portion of the 'us' abbreviation (akin to a ';') has a long, straight, sharply angled tail. Double 'ii's are regularly 'dashed'; there are occasional 'acute' accents. Punctuation: *punctus elevatus* (for minor pauses) and points (for major ones), along with the *punctus interrogativus*. The points are generally diamond-shaped.

A contemporary hand (or hands) inserted alternative singular, plural or feminine forms, as appropriate, between the lines (e.g. on many folios in Units F, I and J).

One section is by a slightly later hand (*s.* xii/xiii): it is impossible now to tell whether this was added *in rasura*.

There are additions, annotations and re-workings on various pages (e.g. Units C, first recto; F, first verso; G, first recto and final verso, J) by several *s.* xiii and xiv hands.

Decoration

Main sections are headed by three- to five-lines-high initials in red, blue, yellow or green; most are fairly plain, but one (Unit C, face 3) is slightly patterned. Cues are headed by one to one-and-a-half-line-high plain coloured capitals

History

The prominent presence of 'Gregorii, Augustini, Ædburgis atque Mildrithe' (all written in capitals) in the secret and postcommunion prayers within the votive mass in commemoration of the relics held in the church in question, implies that the book was written for use in Canterbury (see further **Commentary** below). The various annotations indicate that the volume was still in active use in the thirteenth and fourteenth centuries. The number of sewing holes might indicate several (re-)bindings. The date at which the volume was broken up, and these parts recycled as binding material, is unclear. There are seemingly no records relating to the recovery of the fragments, nor even a note of the source(s) from which they came.

Commentary

These pitiful fragments provide a particularly vivid witness to the dismembering, recycling and destruction of medieval books –

though the date(s) of the damage and re-use in question (whether the late Middle Ages, the Reformation, or indeed both) is unclear.

Particularly notable portions of the surviving text include the prayer in the *Missa pro familiaribus* (Unit F, fifth recto), *Pietate tua* in *Pro uiuis et defunctis* (Unit G, first verso), and above all the *Secreta* and *Postcommunio* in the *Missa in honore sanctorum quorum corpora habentur* (Unit E, face 1). The first seeks God's guidance for the 'familiam huius cenobii' which, *prima facie*, implies use in the context of a regular community; while the circumstance that the second specifies 'domnum papam, pontifices et abbates nostros ... reges et principes' in addition to 'omnem populum christianum' among those to be safeguarded, seemingly betokens one with a particular interest in the ecclesiastical hierarchy.

Crucial to the localisation of the manuscript thereafter are the *Secreta* and *Postcommunio* within the 'Mass in honour of the saints whose bodies are held'. These read as follows: 'May your clemency accept, O Lord, we beseech you, from our hands the offered gift which, through the sacred prayers of your saints Gregory, Augustine, Eadburh and Mildred and also of those whose relics are held in that church, may cleanse us from all sins'; 'Pouring out the divine mysteries – which for the veneration of your saints Gregory, Augustine, Eadburh and Mildred, as also of those whose relics are contained in that church, we offer to your majesty – we beseech you to hurry, O Lord, so that through them [the mysteries] we may merit the forgiveness of sins and may be refreshed by the gifts of heavenly grace'.

The collocation of Gregory (pope and instigator of the Roman mission, † 604), Augustine (Roman missionary to Kent, † 604x9), Eadburh (abbess of Minster in Thanet from 716, † 751) and Mildred (a previous abbess of Minster, † ?700x716) points unmistakably to use in East Kent and, in particular, Canterbury – but by which foundation therein is a moot point. Gregory was widely revered. Augustine's cult was largely restricted to the abbey that bore his name; moreover, the relics of St Mildred, initially at Minster, were translated to Saint Augustine's Abbey in 1035.

Eadburh had most probably also been buried at Minster, though a counter-tradition would locate her at Lyminge. According to the traditions of Lanfranc's foundation of Saint Gregory's (established 1084/5, probably as canons regular), the archbishop had translated thereto from Lyminge in 1085 relics of SS. Mildred and Eadburh. It is clear, incidentally, that there was already confusion over the identity of the 'Eadburh' in question – whether the abbess of Minster or the earlier foundress of Lyminge, Æthelburh. Saint Gregory's (specious) claim to Mildred was vigorously contested by Saint Augustine's Abbey.

In favour of Saint Gregory's as the home of the present manuscript is the fact that pride of place is given to the name of that pope, while the two female saints whose relics were claimed to be there both appear; the manifest weakness of the case is the presence in second place of Augustine, whom they are not known to have claimed and whose house was the outspoken rival to their pretensions. The fact that their church burned down in 1145 – around the time the present manuscript was produced – could be interpreted either as a potential incentive for, or as a major distraction from, investing in such a book. Equally, if the presence of both male and female forms in some of the services is readily intelligible in relation to a foundation of regular canons which was certainly by this date 'Augustinian', the circumstance that 'Pietate tua' singles out 'abbates nostros', but not any grade of 'canones', is not.

In favour of Saint Augustine's Abbey, which did, of course, have an 'abba', is the prominent presence of Augustine (naturally following his master Gregory, important secondary relics of whom the foundation proudly held) as well as Mildred, ownership of whose relics they staunchly defended; the obvious weaknesses are the presence of Eadburh whose cult was not prominent there, along with the added female forms. A third possibility is Saint Mildred's, a Canterbury church affiliated to Saint Augustine's, whom many of the features, including the slightly distant nature of the references in the texts to all the saints and relics, might suit best of all; what is debatable in this case, however, is whether the foundation would be described as a 'cenobium'. The script and decoration of the manuscript are of little help in resolving the matter since they are rather nondescript, and in any case there is a dearth of material from Saint Gregory's and Saint Mildred's with which to make comparison. In sum, the question of the specific home of this book is best left open.

Bibliography

Orchard 1995, p. 92; Brooke 2002, pp. xlii–xliii; Gameson 2005, ill. 1.

31 Add. 127/22

Breviary
England; *saec.* XII[med]
Illustration: fol. 3v

Physical Description

Three bifolia mounted in a modern guard-book: two sheets remain together (foliated 1–4), one is now separate (foliated 5–6). The six leaves are in fact consecutive, their correct order being 6, 1–4, 5 (the bifolium 5–6 is folded inside out, and has evidently been thus for a long time), and they were evidently the three inner bifolia of their quire. Their general condition is good, although fol. 1r is more weathered than the rest, fol. 4 has had a single slit cut into it for a lace, and fol. 6r had been damaged by liquid (despite a major stain, it remains fully legible). Size: 193 × 145 mm. Written area: 143 × 92 mm. Lines: 34. Space between lines: 5 mm. Height of minims: 2 or 3 mm. Ruling: hard point (now virtually invisible). Though worn and damaged, the gutters preserve clear evidence of twelve sewing holes (at *c.* 13, 30, 50, 55, 70, 95, 115, 130, 145, 165, 175 and 180 mm from the top of the leaf).

Content

Part of the temporale of a monastic Breviary: eleventh to twentieth Sundays after Pentecost, corresponding broadly to *The Monastic Breviary of Hyde Abbey* (Tolhurst (ed.) 1930–9), II, 159v–164v: parallels are noted below. In the following calendar, the leaves are treated in their original order.

[Fol. 6r] [acephalus] // omnipotens. *Ad horam*, *Or.*, Familiam tuam domine dextera tua perpetuo circundet auxilio ... persequatur. Per. *Alia.* Conuersa quesumus domine familiam tuam, ... multiplicetur et donis. Per. *In euangelio. A.*, Omnis qui se exaltat ... dominus [T, 159v]. *Or.* Deus qui omnipo[tentiam]
Dominica I mensis Septembris. Or., Omnipotens sempiterne deus qui abundantia pietatis tue ... oratio non presumit. Per.
Sec. Marcum. In illo. Exiens ihesus ... decapoleos, et reliqua [Mark 7, 31]. Surdus ille ... gratia liberari [T, 159v (Bede)]. *X.* Obsurduit

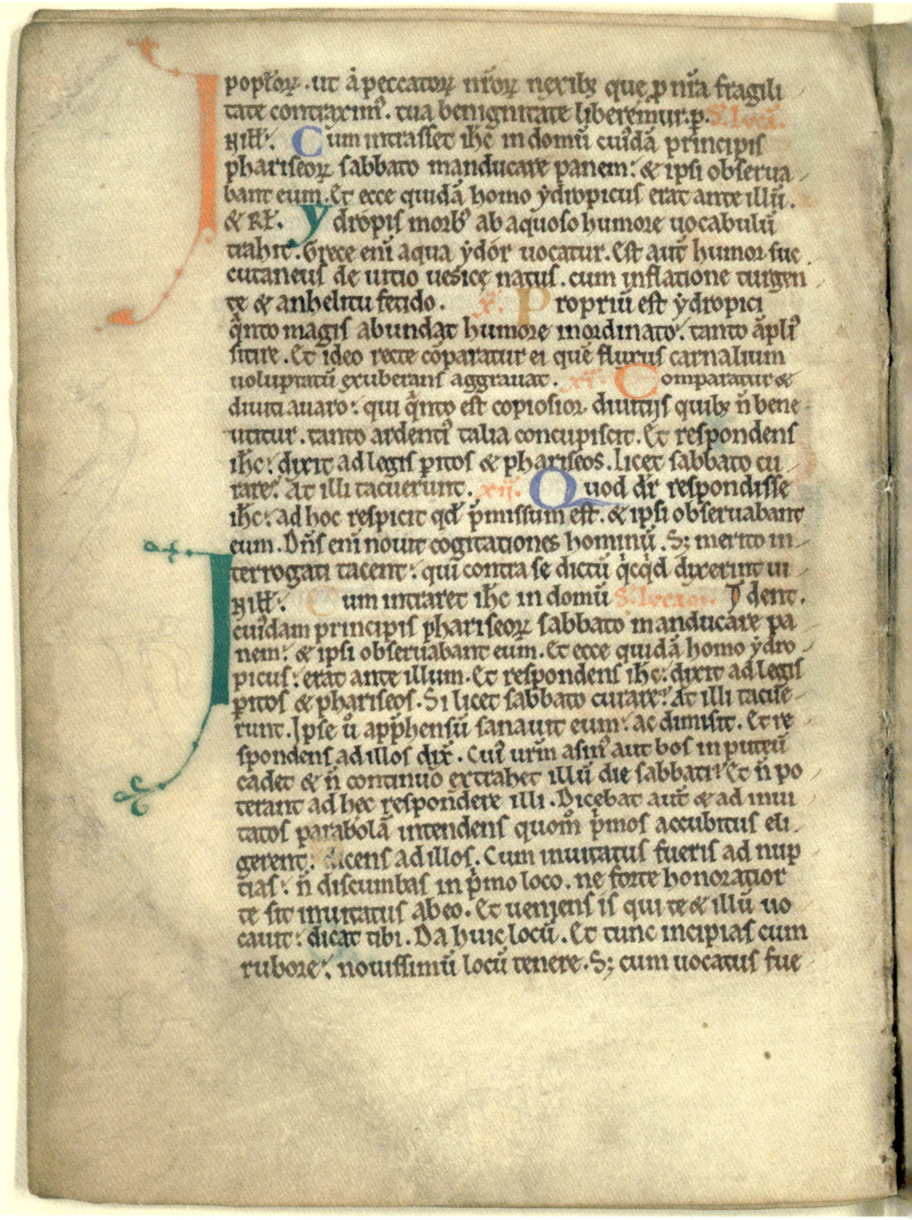

... presumpsit [T, 160r] *XI*. Et merito clausit aures ... aperuit [T, 160r]. *XII*. Merito clausit os ... impleuit. Et heu miser generis humani defectus [T 160r, extended].
Sec. Marcum. In illo. Exiens ihesus ... **[Fol. 6v]** et mutos loqui [Mark 7, 31–7]. *Or*. Omnipotens sempiterne [T, 160r]. *In euang. A*., Quanto ... loqui [T, 160r]. *Or*., Omnipotens. *Or*., Praesta quesumus omnipotens deus ut inter innumeros uite presentis errores, tuo semper moderamine dirigamur. Per. *Alia*. Tuere domine populum tuum ... et mentis et corporis. Per. *In euang. A*., Bene omnia ... [T, 160r]. Omnipotens.
Dominica XIII. *Or*., Omnipotens et misericors deus de cuius munere ... curramus. Per [T, 160v].
Sec. Lucam. In illo. Dixit ihesus discipulis suis, beati oculi [Luke 10, 23]. Non oculi scribarum ... ea paruulis [T, 160v]. *X*. Beati oculi ... audierunt [T, 160v]. *XI*. Abraham exultauit ... appellati [T, 160v]. *XII*. Sed hi omnes ... uiderunt. Apostoli autem in presentiarum habentes dominum ... nequaquam per angelos aut uarias uisionum species opus habebant doceri [T, 160v, extended].
Sec. Lucam. In illo. Dixit ihesus ... [continuing on **Fol. 1r**] que auditis, ... Uade et tu fac similiter [Luke 10, 23–37]. *Or*. Omnipotens et misericors [T, 160v]. *In euang. A*., Homo quidam ... relicto [T, 160v]. *Or*. Omnipotens et misericors. *Alia*. Omnipotens sempiterne deus per quem cepit esse quod non erat, ... pura mente seruire. Per. *Alia*. Porrige dexteram tuam quesumus domine plebi ... et sempiterna gaudia comprehendat. *In euang. Ant*., Quis tibi uidetur proximus fuisse ... et tu fac si- **[Fol. 1v]** -militer. Alleluia [T, 160v]. *Or*. Omnipotens et mi[sericors].
Dominica XIIII. *Or*., Omnipotens sempiterne deus, da nobis fidei spei et caritatis augmentum, ... fac nos amare quod precipis. Per.
Sec. Lucam. In illo. Dum iret ihesus [Luke 17, 11–12; T, 160v]. Leprosi non absurde ... erroris [T, fol. 160v]. *X*. Non enim uel abscondunt imperitiam suam ... intermisceat [T, 160v]. *XI*. Vera ergo falsis inordinate permixta, ... maculantem [T, 160v]. *XII*. Hi autem tam uitandi sunt ecclesie ... miserere nostri [T, 161r].
Sec. Lucam. In illo. Dum iret ihesus [Luke 17, 11–19; T, 161r]. *Or*., Omnipotens sempiterne [T, 161r]. *In euang. A*., Dum ingrederetur Ihesus quoddam castellum occurrerunt ei decem uiri

... miserere nostri [Luke 17,12; T 161r]. *Or.*, Omnipotens sempiterne. *Ad horam Or.*, Quesumus omnipotens et misericors deus ne nos gratia tua de- **[Fol. 2r]** -relinquat ... et noxia cuncta depellat. Per. *Alia.* Conserua domine quesumus tuorum corda fidelium ... dilectione securi. Per. *In euangelium A.* Unus autem ex illis ... magnificans dominum. Alleluia [Lk 17.15–19]. *A.* Nonne decem [T, 161r]. *Oratio.* Omnipotens.

Dominica XV. OR. Custodi domine quesumus ecclesiam tuam ... dirigatur. Per [T, 161v].

Sec. Matheum. In illo. Dixit ihesus discipulis suis, nemo potest duobus dominis seruire, et reliqua [Matt. 6, 24]. Quia non ualet transitoria simul et eterna diligere, ... non in affectu possidemus. *X.* Aut enim unum odiet et alterum diliget, ... Non potestis deo seruire et mammonae. *XI.* Audiat hoc auarus, audiat qui censetur nomine christiano ... sed qui seruit diuitiis. *XII.* Qui enim diuitiarum seruus est ... Sed qui seruit mammone ... principes huius seculi a domino deus [sic; all abbreviated in comparison with T, 161v].

Sec. Mattheum. In illo. Dixit ihesus ... **[Fol. 2v]** uobis [Matt. 6, 24–33]. *Or.* Custodi [T, 161v]. *In Eug. A.*, Nolite solliciti esse ... necesse sit, Alleluia [T, 161v]. *Or.*, Custodi. *Ad hor. Or.*, Praesta nobis quesumus omnipotens et misericors deus ut placationem tuam ... a noxiis liberemur in cursibus. Per. *Alia.* Da populo tuo quesumus domine spiritum ueritatis et pacis, ... toto corde sectetur. Per. *In Eug. A.*, Querite autem ... adicientur uobis. Alleluia [Matt. 6, 33]. *Or.* Custodi.

Dominica XVI. Or. Ecclesiam tuam domine miseratio continuata mundet et muniat ... gubernetur. Per.

Sec. Lucam. In illo. Ibat ihesus ... [Luke 7,11]. Naim ciuitas est galilee in secundo miliario tabor montis ... in quarto miliario eiusdem montis ad meridiem. *X.* Et ibant cum illo discipuli eius ... **[Fol. 3r]** ... quasi per sue ostia ciuitatis propalantem [Lk 7,11–12]. *XI.* Qui bene filius unicus matris sue fuisse perhibetur, ... rectissime fatentur [cf. T, 162r]. *XII.* Nam et electus ... per oculorum indicia profert [T, 162r].

Sec. Lucam. In illo. Ibat ihesus in ciuitatem ... [Luke 7, 11–16]. *Or.*, Ecclesiam tuam [T, 162r]. *In Eug. A.*, Accessit Ihesus et tetigit

... et cepit loqui. Alleluia [Luke 7, 14; T, 162r]. *Or*. Ecclesiam. *Ad horam. Or*., Adesto quesumus domine supplicationibus nostris ... ab omni nos aduersitate custodi. Per.
Alia. Da quesumus omnipotens deus ut qui infirmitatis ... sub tua semper pietate gaudeamus. Per.
In eug. A., Accepit autem omnis timor ... et quia deus uisitauit plebem suam [T, 162r]. *Or*. Ecclesiam.
Dominica XVII. OR. Absolue quesumus domine tuorum delicta **[Fol. 3v]** populorum, ut a peccatorum nostrorum nexibus que pro nostra fragilitate contraximus, tua benignitate liberemur. Per.
Sec. Lucam. In illo. Cum intrasset ... [Luke 14, 1–2]. Ydropis morbus ... fetido. *X*. Proprium ... exuberans aggrauat. *XI*. Comparatur ... tacuerunt. *XII*. Quod dicitur respondisse ... dixerunt uident [T, 162v–3, but subdivided differently].
Sec. Lucam. In illo. Cum intraret ... [Luke 14, 1–11]. **[Fol. 4r]** *Or*. Absolue. *In eug. A*. Dixit Ihesus ad legis peritos ... [T, 163r]. *Or*., Absolue. *Ad horam, Or*. Da quesumus domine populo tuo mentem qua tibi deuotus semper existat, ... perficiat. *In eug. A*., Cum uocatis ... discumbentibus. Alleluia [T, 163r]. *Or*., Absolue.
Dominica XVIII. Or. Omnipotens sempiterne deus misericordiam tuam ostende supplicibus ... indulgentiam sentiamus. Per.
Sec. Matheum. In illo. Pharisei audientes ... [Matt. 22, 34–6]. Conuenerunt ut [T, 163r]. *X*. Dicebant pharisei [T, 163r]. *XI*. Pharisei qui omnia ... esse confusas? Leuis est consolatio qui in se ipso confusus est quod ab aliis ignoratur [T 163r, extended]. *XII*. Magister quod est mandatum magnum in lege? ... **[Fol. 4v]** qui nec minimum obseruat [PL 186, col. 400, C–D].
Sec. Matheum. In illo. Pharisei [Matt. 22, 34–46]. *Or*., Omnipotens sempiterne. *In eug. A*., Magister ... ex toto corde tuo. Alleluia [T, 163v]. *Or*. Omnipotens sempiterne. *Ad horam, Or*., Auerte quesumus domine iram tuam ... expelle. Per. *Alia*. Protege domine quesumus dextera tua populum supplicantem, ... inuenire perpetuam. Per. *In eug. A*., Quid uobis ... dextris meis [T, 163v]. *Or*., Omnipotens.
Dominica XIX. Or. Tua nos quesumus domine gratia semper ... esse intentos. Per.
Sec. Matheum. In illo. Ascendens ihesus ... [Matt. 9, 1]. Christum

in humanis actibus diuina gessisse misteria, ... lectio hodierna monstrauit. *X*. Ascendit inquit ... **[Fol. 5r]** ... transiret. *XI*. Nonne hic est ... nautica transfretaret? *XII*. Ascendit inquit ... curare nescit [T, 163v, but differently subdivided].

Sec. Matheum. In illo. Ascendens ihesus ... [Matt. 9, 1–8]. *Or*. Tua nos. *In eug. A.*, Dixit dominus paralytico ... [T, 164v]. *Or*. Tua nos. *Ad horam Or.*, Fac nos domine quesumus prompta uoluntate tibi esse subiectos ... uoluntates. Per. *Alia*. Adesto domine fidelibus tuis ... consolationis auxilium. Per. *In eug. A.*, Videntes [T, 164r]. *Or.*, Tua nos.

Dominica XX. *Or.*, Da quesumus domine populo tuo diabolica uitare contagia, ... pura mente sectari. Per.

Sec. Matheum. In illo. Loquebatur ihesus ... [Matt., 22,1]. **[Fol. 5v]** Rex iste qui fecit nuptias filio suo ... in fine seculorum. *X*. Sed quia ex duabus personis ... personis credamus unitam. *XI*. Ex duabus quippe atque in duabus hunc ... ecclesiam sociauit. *XII*. Vterus autem genetricis uirginis huius sponsi thalamus fuit, ... et postmodum apostolos misit.

Sec. Matheum. In illo. Loquebatur ihesus [Matt. 22, 1–[14]: incomplete, breaking off at:] malos et bonos, et implete sunt nup//

Scribes and Script

The pages are the work of a single scribe who writes a clear but compressed and fairly angular, transitional late Romanesque to proto-Gothic book hand. It is characterised by relatively heavy feet and serifs, and much 'biting' of the letters. Feet are sometimes triangular (the base parallel to the horizontal ruling), but at other times they turn sharply upwards, joining the next letter. It is a moot point whether the general angularity here is best explained as a general proto-Gothic feature, or whether it echoes more specifically the earlier Kentish 'prickly' script (cf. **nos.** 19, 20–22). Rubric are written in red rustic capitals.

Abbreviation was used sparingly. Double 'i's are dashed. Accents were regularly employed. Punctuation: low point (for major and minor pauses), *punctus elevatus* (for minor pauses) and *punctus interrogativus*. Characteristic forms include a *punctus interrogativus* whose top section is like a tilting 'z' or '2', and a *punctus elevatus* which is very much a tick above a point. Word breaks across lines were invariably signalled by a sharply-rising dash.

Decoration

Although there is no decoration as such, the pages are all visually attractive owing to the many brightly coloured minor initials. The initials for the gospel readings are eight to nine lines high, slightly embellished, and done in red, yellow or green (with, on fol. 1v, small touches of a second colour); other sections are headed by one-line-high capitals in the same colours.

History

The only evidence for the history of this item is that provided by its physical fabric. The high number of sewing holes suggests that the book was rebound several times during its working life. Crude pencil sketches, on fol. 3v, of a bird and an initial show casual use in s. xv–xvi. The slit in fol. 4 presumably reflects post-medieval recycling. The liquid damage on fol. 6 evidently happened after the bifolium had been turned inside out and so postdates the dismembering of the book. The context from which the leaves were recovered is seemingly unrecorded.

32 Add. 128/31

Breviary (with notation)
England; *saec.* XII$^{3/4}$
Illustration: fragment 4

Physical Description

A series of thirteen very damaged fragments, now preserved within transparent envelopes. All the fragments are more or less imperfect – shrivelled, burnt and eroded around the edges – and the parts that survive are themselves often discoloured, weathered and perforated. Some are stained from turn-ins (e.g. nos. 2–3), others bear the perforations and scars of thongs (e.g. no. 4). They represent parts of a total of 22 folios. Nos. 4 and 5 are from one quire; nos. 7–9 are also from one quire.

The fragments themselves vary greatly in size. The original page size might be estimated at *c*. 280 × 180 mm. The written area is *c*. 200 (estimated) × 118 (certain) mm. Number of lines: uncertain. Space between lines: 8 mm. Height of minims: 3 mm (1.5 with notation). Ruled in lead.

Content

The following calendar identifies the liturgical occasions to which the principal content of the preserved portions of each leaf relates; and a short extract from one of the more legible areas is supplied. The fragments are numbered according to their likely order in the original book with the exception of 'Fragment ?'. This may well have stood very close to '2' (as indicated below) but, owing to its series of devotions to saints, there is a measure of doubt.

[Frag. 1 (fragmentary bifolium)] In die Epiphanie.
OR., Deus qui hodierna die uni[geni]tum ... ; [*V*] Reges tharsis et insule ... *V*., Re[ges arabum ...] [ad]ducent ... *G*., Omnes de saba ueniet ... *OR*. [lost]. *A*. Apertis. *Cap*. Ambulabunt gentes in lumine ...

[Frag. 2 (fragmentary bifolium)] Dominica prima post octauas Epiphanie; Ebdomada prima post octauas Epiphanie.
In III° n[octurn]o. Non sunt... *Ps*., Celi enarrant ... *A*.,

Exaudiat... *A.*, Domine in uirtute... *V.* Exaltare domine ... *Sec. Lucam* In illo tempore. Cum factus esset Ihesus annorum duodecim, et reliqua. [Lk 2, 42] Describit sanctus euangelista infantiam nostri redemptoris, ... ut ad suscipienda nostre fragilitatis infirma descenderet. *R.*, Ad te domine leuaui.

[Frag. ? (fragmentary bifolium, one side very rubbed)] Dominica prima post octavas Epiphanie; [Short devotions for SS. Michael, John the Baptist, Peter and Paul, Andrew, Stephen, Laurence, Thomas] Ebdomada prima post Octauas Epiphanie.

R., Adiutor meu[s]. *V.*, Eripe me ... *Lectio III.* Quis cognouit sensum domini... *R.*, Exaudi deus deprecationem meam ...

[Michaelis] Michael archangele ueni in adiutor // [lost]. Deus qui miro ordine angelorum ministeria hominumque ...

[Iohannis] *A.*, Inter natos mulierum ... *V.*, Fuit homo missus a deo. *OR.*, Omnipotens sempiterne deus da, cordibus nostris illam tuarum rectitudinem ... edocuit. Per.

[Petrus et Paulus] Petrus apostolus et paulus doctor gentium ipsi nos ... *OR.*, deus cuius dexte// [lost] petrum ambulantem in fluctibus ne mergeretur erexit ...

[Andreas] andreas [?Christi] famulus [damaged] ... in passione socius . *V.*, Dilex? [illegible] andream [illegible]. *OR.*, Maiestatem tuam domine suppliciter exoramus ... intercessor. Per.

[?De apostolis] *A.*, Vos amici mei estis ... *V.*, Annuntiauerunt opera dei... *OR.*, Protege domine populum tuum ... defensione conserua. Per.

[Stephanus] O beate stephane prothomartir [Christi] intercede pro nobis ... *V.*, Iustus ut palm// [lost]. *OR.*, Omnipotens sempiterne deus qui primitias martirum in beati leuite stephani sanguine dedicasti ...

[Laurentius] Laurentius ?ingestus est ... *V.*, Gloria et honor coronasti eum domine. Da nobis quesumus omnipotens [lost] uitiorum nostrorum flammas extingere ... incendia superare. Per.

[Thomas] // inpendit fac nos christe scandere ...

[Frag. 3 (fragmentary bifolium)] Septuagesima.

A., Tolle ... *A.*, Non licet ... *A.*, Sic erunt ... *A.*, Multi enim ... *A.*, Erunt primi ... *A.*, Cum autem... *Dominica.* Benedictus. *Cap.*, Benedictus. *R.*, Requieuit. [*Hymnus*, O lux] beata ... *V.*,

Vespertina ... [lost, *A.*] Loquens dominus. *OR.*, Deus qui conspicis quia ex nulla ...

[Frag. 4 (fragmentary bifolium)] Dominica in quinquagesima; dominica prima quadragesime.

R., Dixit autem dominus ad abraham, Ego ... *V.*, Ex te [lost]. Facta est autem [lost] in terra, descendit [lost] in egyptum, ... Cumque prope esset ... et te reseruabunt. Dic ergo quod soror mea ... et uiuat anima mea ob gratiam tui. *R.*, Dum staret abraham ad radicem ...

[Frag. 5 (bottom third of a fragmentary bifolium)] Dominica prima quadragesime.

R., Abscondite elemosinam ... *V.*, Honora. *Lectio VIII* [S]ed ecce cum ... si illo et alia facta pensamus. [...]

A., Cor mundum ... *Ps.*, Miserere ... *A.*, O domine, saluum me fac. *Ps.*, Confitemini. *A.*, Sic benedicam te in uita mea ... *Ps.*, Deus deus meus. *A.*, In spiritu humilitatis ...

[Frag. 6 (fragmentary bifolium – very shrivelled and lacunose)] Dominica secunda quadragesime.

A., Dextera domini. *Ps.*, Confitemini. *A.*, Factus est adiutor. [?*Ps.* lost.] *A.*, Triu[m puerorum]. *Ps.*, Benedicite. *A.*, Statuit ea. *Ps.*, Laudate. *Cap.*, [Fratres] rogamus uos et obsecramus ....

[Frag. 7 (strip from the top of a bifolium)] Dominica in Ramis palmarum; Sabbato sancto in Vigilia Pasche.

R., Attendite domine ad me ... *V.*, Recordare quod ... *R.*, Sepulto domino signatum est ... *V.*, Ait pilatus principibus sacerdotum ...

[Frag. 8 (part of a single leaf)] Parasceue.

A., Proprio filio suo ... [Lost.] *Ps.*, Domine exaudi ... *A.*, Ait latro [lost]. *Ps.*, Domine audiui ... *A.*, Memento mei ... *Ps.*, Laudate. *V.*, Christus factus ...

[Frag. 9 (lower third of one leaf, plus a sliver from its conjoint fellow)] Sabbato Sancto in Vigilia Pasche.

A., Eleuamini porte. *Ps.*, Domini est terra ... *A.*, Credo uidere ... *Ps.*, Dominus illuminatio ... *A.*, Domine abstraxisti ...

[Frag. 10 (fragmentary bifolium)] Dominica prima post Pascham; Ebdomada prima post octauas pasche.

R., In diademate ... *V.*, Corona aurea ... [Rubric lost.] Cognouit Ihesus quia uoleb[a]nt eum interrogare ... [imperfect]. *R.*, Hec est ierusalem ciuitas magna. *V.*, Porte ... [lost]. *Lectio IX.* Et contra m [lost] ... gaudebant, quando dominum occidebant ...

[Frags. 11a and b (two separate but originally adjacent fragments from a single leaf)] Historia de Job.

V., Nolo multa ... Nonne. [*Lectio III.*] Cumque in orbem ... *R.*, Utinam appenderentur. *V.*, Quasi arenam [sic] ... Et calamitas. *Lectio IIII.* Cui respondens sathan ait, Nunquid ...

Script and Scribes

The surviving portions are written in a transitional Romanesque to proto-Gothic book script of modest quality. The poor state of preservation and the distortion (through shrinkage) of much of the sample makes it difficult to evaluate in detail; however, the writing varies between a more flowing and spacious interpretation of the forms which is clearly linked to the Romanesque past (e.g. frag. 7), and a more 'colourless' laterally compressed and fully Gothic version (e.g. frag. 1). It is not impossible that two scribes with similar hands are represented, though the general consistency of letter-formation throughout might suggest rather that this is the work of one scribe who had learned to write by the middle of the century and was adapting his manner – with varying degrees of consistency – to a new aesthetic. Thus letters like 'c' and 'e' may be rounded or quite rectilinear. The chant texts are in a smaller, less elongated version of the same script.

Punctuation: low point (for major and minor pauses) and *punctus elevatus* (for minor ones). Double 'i's are dashed. Words broken across lines are signalled by long, sharply rising dashes. The notation (generally on a red four-line staff, but occasionally continuing beyond it) is the work of a single hand – though whether identical with that of the text scribe is unclear. Rubrics are in red rustic capitals or red minuscules. The ink initials within the chants are extravagantly heightened and often adorned with calligraphic flourishes. Red flourishes isolate overruns both in the margins (e.g. frag. 5) and within the written area (e.g. frag. 4).

There are s. xii jottings in the outer margins of one leaf. Further (very damaged) jottings, of s. xiv–xv date, appear in the outer margins of others.

Decoration
Red, green and blue initials (one to three lines high according to context), the more important ones modestly flourished in red or green.

History
There are some (very damaged) marginal jottings (probably liturgical rubrics) of *s.* xii date (e.g. on frags. 7–8). Much later jottings, now largely effaced, in the upper margin of frag. 8 might imply that the volume saw some limited use in *s.* xiv or xv; be that as it may, the doodles in the upper margin of the other side of the same leaf suggest a more casual attitude to the volume shortly thereafter.

Numbers were pencilled on to four of the fragments in *s.* xx (frag. 2 bears a '9' and a '12'; frag. 7 a '9', frag. 8 a '10' and frag. 10 an '8'). An informal, undated jotting, formerly kept with the leaves, stated that they had been recovered from at least three different (unspecified) contexts. Now, it will be noted that fragments 2–6 (plus, perhaps '?') all come from one portion of the original book, as likewise do fragments 7–10; and it is a reasonable hypothesis, therefore, that the individual members of these two 'groups' came from the same or related contexts. In the absence of any documentation, however, nothing more can be said.

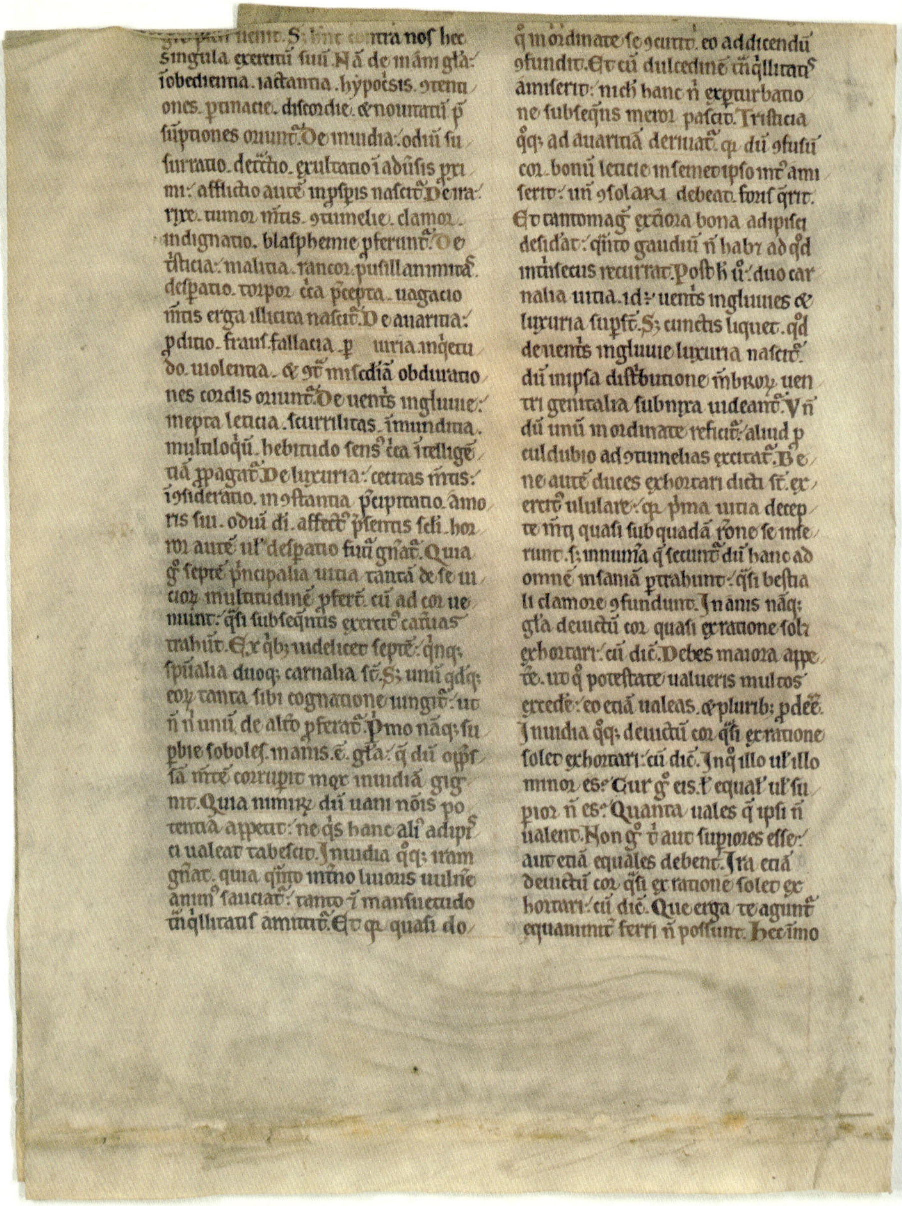

33 PRC 49/4/1–2

Gregory the Great, *Moralia in Iob*
England; *saec.* XII$^{3/4}$
Illustration: PRC 49/4/1, fol. 2v

Physical Description
Two incomplete bifolia. In the original book, PRC 49/4/2 stood – as it does now – immediately inside 49/4/1. Part of the outer column of the first half of both sheets has been trimmed away, with corresponding loss of text, and both have been further cut down to their present total size of *c.* 300 × 390 mm. Both sheets are stained, and a continuous glue scar (approximately 8 mm in width), accompanied by numerous perforations, runs horizontally across the entire lower margin of both of them. Sheet 49/4/2 is generally more weathered than 49/4/1; moreover, it has suffered significant damp-damage, bringing further loss of text (and, in places, of the parchment itself) towards the top on all faces – most severely and extensively on the first recto and verso. As the parchment was evidently well prepared and has since suffered damage to all surfaces, it is now difficult to distinguish visually between hair and flesh sides; however, the outside face of 49/4/2 is a hair-side, the inside a flesh-side; the reverse was presumably true of 49/4/1.

Size of individual page (as preserved): 300 × 200 mm. Written area (as preserved): 231 × 170 mm. The original page size and written area may be reconstructed as *c.* 355 × 245 and *c.* 245 × 170 mm respectively. Two columns (width: 75 mm). Lines: 35–36 are preserved from a probable 38. Space between lines: 6 mm. Height of minims: 3 mm. Pricked in both margins (only the inner prickings survive). Ruling: crayon – rather untidily done. The lack of any lines running across the inner margins and the obvious disjunctions between the ruling on the facing pages of the bifolia indicate that each page was ruled individually. The amount of text that is missing between the two halves of sheet 49/4/2 would fill a minimum of four folios, and possibly slightly more. There was evidently one more bifolium inside the surviving pair; there may also have been an additional singleton. If the quire was indeed a regular quaternion, the present sheets would have been the second and third bifolia therein.

Content

Gregory the Great, *Moralia in Job* (CPL 1708), Book 31, chs. 28–33 and 40–45 (incomplete). The exact details are as follows. **[Sheet 49/4/1, fol. 1r, col. 1]** // accenderat quando eum ephesi ad irrumpendas ... [PL 76, col. 605D] ... laborem quisque innoxie declinet dum // [col. 606 B/C]. **[Fol. 1r, col. 2]** // aut equatur aut uincitur labo[r–] [col. 606C] ... ymaginem rationem fungat // [col. 607A]. **[Sheet 49/4/1, fol. 1v, col. 1;** the top is rubbed and illegible; then:] // quisque deprehensis [col. 607B] ... Quia uero nec superueni[ente perc]ussione uincitur nequaquam gla[diis]// [col. 607 D]. **[Fol. 1v, col 2]** //[ui]te sese ad interitum parat. Sed quia tam [607D–608A] ... occultant. Vnde recte nunc dicitur super ipsum sona// [col. 608C].
[Sheet 49/4/2, fol. 1r, col. 1] // Hec t[un]c super equum [then very damaged; col. 608C] ... Unde bene postquam dictum est super ipsum sonabit pharetra, illico additur. Vibrabit hasta. Contra p[rae]di// [col. 609 A/B]. **[Sheet 49/4/2, fol. 1r, col. 2;** very damaged then:] //[Praedicat]ores autem [–?–] cum pro defe// [col. 609B] ... perstrepunt pharetra son[at]// [col. 609D]. **[Sheet 49/4/2, fol. 1v, col. 1]** //[ui]r enim sanctus quo maiore [very damaged; col. 609D] ... et persuasus turb[?is] lapidan// [col. 610C]. **[Sheet 49/4/2, fol. 1v, col. 2]** postero die profectus [very damaged; col. 610C] ... Neque enim ua dicere brutum animal potest, sed dum asseritur dicere quod // [col. 611B].
[Lacuna.]
[Sheet 49/4/2, fol. 2r, col. 1; very damaged] // uirgis cesus semel lapidatus [col. 617A] ... Vbi enim infirmari dei militem conspicit, // [col. 617D]. **[Sheet 49/4/2, fol. 2r, col. 2]** // firmum quempiam in carnis, illecebram [sic] uidet [col. 617D] ... Sed equus dei et ante faciem hastam superat, eum libidinem calcat, et a latere sagittam circumspicit, cum in castita// [col. 618B]. **[Sheet 49/4/2, fol. 2v, col. 1]** //diet pedem tuum ne capiaris. Pes namque [col. 618B] ... Sed feruens et fremens sorbet terram, quia nimio ardore

semet ipsum dis// [col. 619A]. **[Sheet 49/4/2, fol. 2v, col. 2]** //-one forti [obliterated] gloria nascitur [obliterated] [col. 619A] ... Longe quippe praenotat, ex una quaque re cuius uicii pugna succrescat. Vnde et sequitur procul odoratur // [col. 619 C].
[Sheet 49/4/1, fol. 2r, col. 1] //dictum est odore res non uisa cogniscitur, bellum [col. 619C] ... agit, quod hi contra se hostes per haec exsurgere // [col. 620B]. **[Sheet 49/4/1, fol. 2r, col. 2]** //tium iuste ulcisci desiderat, sagacissime cogitat, [col. 620B] ... ira, tristicia, auaritia, uentris ingluuies // [col. 621A]. **[Sheet 49/4/1, fol. 2v, col. 1]** // gratie plenus uenit. Sed habent contra nos hec [col. 621A] ... tranquillitatis amittitur. Et quia quasi do// [col. 621C]. **[Sheet 49/4/1, fol. 2v, col. 2]** // quo inordinate se concutit, eo addicendum confundit. Et [col. 621D] ... equanimiter ferri non possunt. Hec immo// [col. 622B].

Scribes and Script

The surviving fragments are the work of a single scribe. He writes a well-controlled, rectilinear book hand which represents an early phase in the transition from late Romanesque to early Gothic formal script. If the overall matrix is decidedly rectilinear, the bowls of letters are still more rounded than multangular, feet are often a curving continuation of the main stroke (as opposed to a separate, angled cross-stroke), and the 'biting' of letters is modest and is balanced by fairly generous spaces between words. This version of the script displays few idiosyncrasies, apart from an 'x' which resembles a 'j' plus a 'c'; 'us' and, above all, 'con' abbreviation marks that look like '9's; and a *punctus interrogativus* whose upper part resembles a tadpole swimming vigorously downwards. The scribe habitually placed his words well above the ruled lines. Sentences are headed by neat but bold ink capitals, whose form is Romanesque rather than proto-Gothic. Double 'i's are dashed. Punctuation: *punctus elevatus* (for minor pauses) and low point (for minor and major ones), plus *punctus interrogativus*. Marginal diples occasionally signal quotations. There is fairly regular accenting; however, while some of the accents – apparently in the same ink as the main text – were presumably supplied by the original scribe, others, in contrasting ink, may have been added at an uncertain later date. Fairly extensive use was made of the standard range of abbreviation; words are regularly broken across lines and this is signalled by a sharply-rising dash.

A late medieval hand added Roman numerals to a few of the margins. Although the sample is small, the hand is manifestly identical to that responsible for adding reference numbers to Lit. A. 8 (**no. 17**), and other Saint Augustine's Abbey manuscripts (see further **History**).

A crudely drawn, pointing 'Nota' hand was also added at an uncertain date in the intercolumnar space on the recto of the second folio of Sheet 49/4/1.

Decoration

None survives.

History

The fact that the present leaves were marked up by the late medieval hand that 'reconditioned' Lit. A. 8 (**no. 17**), a manuscript which was written at Saint Augustine's Abbey and remained there throughout the Middle Ages, – a hand, moreover, which performed similar tasks in other books from the abbey – indicates that this, too, was the provenance of the present item. Accordingly, these leaves probably come from the second part of one of the two-volume copies of the work that appears amidst a body of Gregory's writings on the second shelf of the fifth *distinctio*, as recorded in the late fifteenth-century library catalogue (James 1903, p. 232, nos. 385–8). A modern pencil annotation on PRC 49/4/2 records that it was recovered from PRC 17/38, the register of wills from the archdeaconry court for 1563–5; the same was doubtless true of its companion.

Commentary

Begun between 579x85 as discourses for a monastic audience and finally completed, after extensive revision, no earlier than July 595, the *Moralia* uses the Book of Job as the point of departure for discursive discussion of a vast range of doctrinal, ethical, and practical spiritual issues. Thus in the extracts on the present fragments, Gregory uses phrases from Job 39, 21–5 as a spring-board for exploring how an evangelist should balance bravery and discretion, might bear witness effectively while persecuted, and could endure danger in the knowledge of heavenly reward; while in the second passage he expounds the symbiotic relationship between virtue and vice, the pitfalls of good fortune, and the positive dimension of temptation.

In addition to the status of its author, the *Moralia* was valued on the one hand for its encyclopaedic content, and on the other, because of the dearth of alternative Latin exegesis on Job. In terms both of its approach and of the demands it made on the reader, it was a monastic *lectio diuina* text par excellence. Notwithstanding the difficulty of calculating exact numbers of copies from the surviving manuscripts of a text which could be subdivided into separate volumes in several ways, the evidence unequivocally shows a strong and continuous history of copying from the early to the high Middle Ages and beyond – a phenomenon which is all the more striking given the great length of the work. Unlike many patristic writings, the *Moralia* has a reasonable representation from the eighth and tenth centuries, as well as from the ninth; then, more typically, there is a rapid growth in numbers in the eleventh century (almost three times as many witnesses as from the tenth) and again in the twelfth century (approximately twice as many as in the eleventh), followed in the thirteenth by a return to eleventh-century levels.

The pattern of copying in early England is a little different. Whilst the work was known to Bede and seemingly also to Ælfric, its extant pre-Conquest witnesses are limited to a handful of fragments – which, moreover, imply greater interest before, as opposed to after, the period of Viking invasions. After a long slough during the ninth, tenth and most of the eleventh centuries, interest revived in the late eleventh century, and blossomed in the twelfth: thus, in so far as extant manuscripts are a guide, acquiring and copying the text in England was largely a post-Conquest phenomenon, and one which peaked between the end of the eleventh century and the middle of the twelfth. A steady decline in copying and acquisition from the later twelfth century is reflected in a still-reasonable representation from the thirteenth century but an exiguous one thereafter.

Given how little of the Canterbury copy survives, it is impossible to situate it precisely in relation to a tradition of presentation that is characterised by diversity, in which the division of the Books into volumes, the size, the layout, and the degree of decoration were all variables. The written area in English copies, for instance, ranges from 143 × 88 up to 360 × 235 mm, with line counts varying from 27 to 70. It must suffice to note that, on grounds of size and layout, the present copy may be loosely grouped with a cluster of other 'mid-range' twelfth-century manuscripts, including Cambridge, Pembroke College, MS 15 [Books 28–35], written area, 248 × 155 mm, lines 40 (Bury St Edmunds); Lincoln Cathedral Library, MSS 75 and 76 [Books 11–22, 23–35], written area 250 × 155 mm, lines 40 (?Lincoln); London, Lambeth Palace Library, MS 56 [Books 1–10], written area 248 × 140 mm, lines 35 (Lanthony); Lambeth, MS 109 [Books 6–10], written area 140 × 158 mm, lines 34 (Lanthony); and Oxford, University College, MS 66 [Books 21–35], written area 250 × 155 mm, lines 41. The present item is also one of a striking number of English *Moralia* manuscripts whose leaves are known to have ended up in bindings and wrappers (see, e.g., Ker 1972, n. 1): the sheer number of copies that were made, the large format of many of them (suiting their leaves for re-use as wrappers), the length of the text (implying a good store of such leaves), and – conceivably – the circumstance of a papal author may all have contributed to this phenomenon.

34 Lit. A. 13, fols. 176–9

Canticles with integral marginal and interlinear commentary (designed for a psalter)
England (?Christ Church, Canterbury); *saec.* XII$^{3/4}$
Illustration: fol. 179v

Physical Description

Four folios, bound as the endleaves (fols. 176–9) of a workaday *saec.* xiv^{1} copy of Duns Scotus on the *Sententiae* (I–III) of Peter Lombard (cf. **no.** 37). Fols. 176–7 are consecutive; the lacuna in the text indicates that two folios are missing between fols. 177 and 178; fols. 178 and 179 are probably consecutive (see further below), however the present binding of the volume makes it impossible to establish the physical relationship of these two folios to each other. The leaves are in good condition, with the exception of the first and last page (fols. 176r, 179v): the former is stained and discoloured; the latter is discoloured, has suffered surface damage, and bears prominent scars from use as a paste-down. The quality of the parchment is (or was) very even, with minimal discrepancy between hair and flesh sides. Severe damp damage afflicts the outer edges of many of the folios of the main book, particularly at front and back, but this is not mirrored on our leaves, suggesting that the Duns Scotus underwent its trauma before being joined to the present item.

Size: 326 × 225 mm. The volume was designed for interlinear and marginal glosses. Written area (main text): 218 × 100 mm. Number of lines (main text): 19. Space between lines (main text): 12 mm. Height of minims (main text) 3 mm. Space between lines (gloss): 4 mm. Height of minims (gloss): 2 mm. Ruling: lead or crayon (on each side). Prickings survive in the top, bottom and inner margin. Prickings were only supplied for the horizontal rulings of the main text – not for those of the gloss (which was ruled on an *ad hoc* basis). Nevertheless, the ruling for main text and gloss alike is very neat, and the ratio between the two sets is fairly consistent (three lines of gloss for one line of main text).

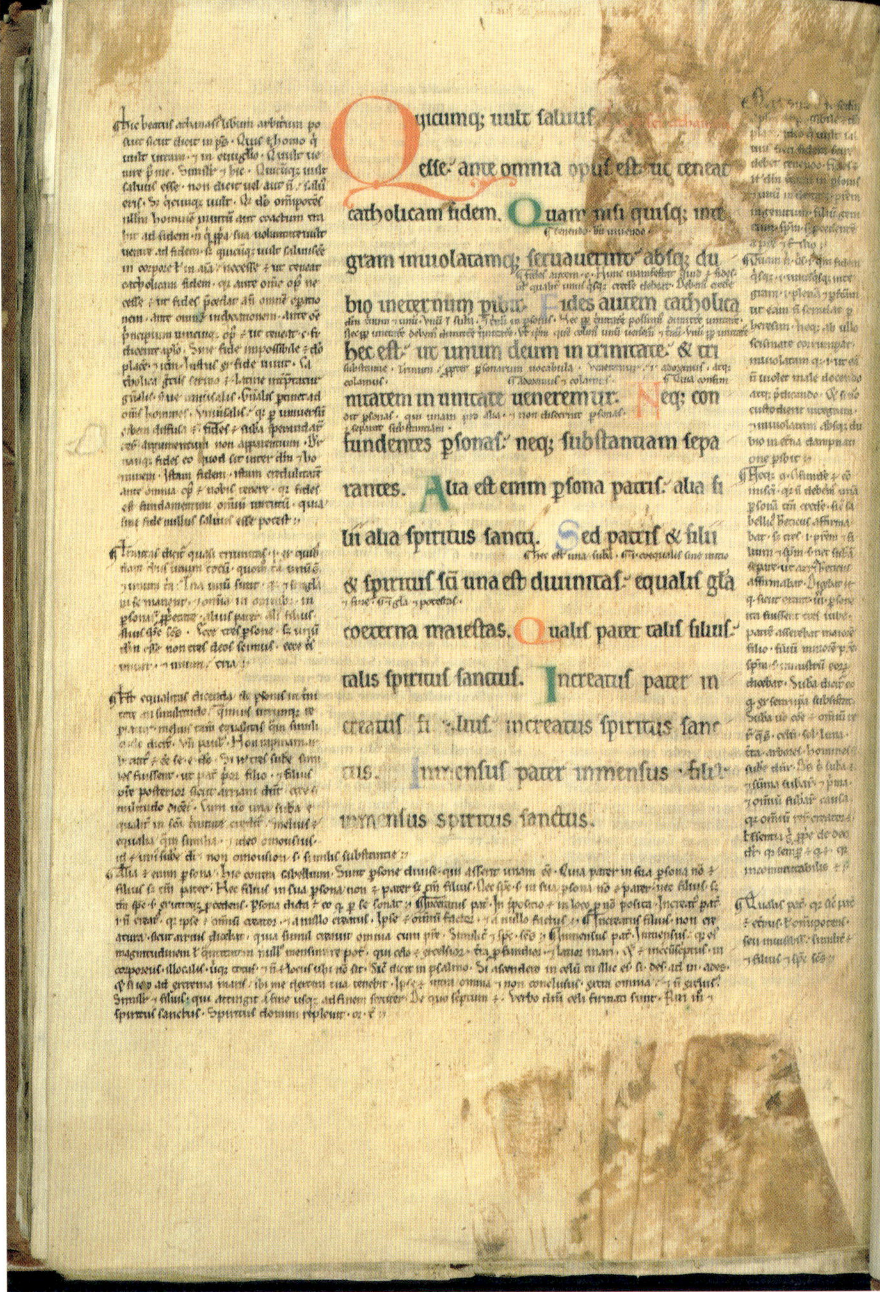
Quicumq; uult saluus
esse: ante omnia opus est ut teneat
catholicam fidem. Quam nisi quisq; inte
gram inuiolatamq; seruauerit: absq; du
bio in eternum peribit. Fides autem catholica
hec est: ut unum deum in trinitate: & tri
nitatem in unitate ueneremur. Neq; con
fundentes psonas: neq; substantiam sepa
rantes. Alia est enim psona patris: alia fi
lii alia spiritus sancti. Sed patris & filii
& spiritus sci una est diuinitas: equalis gla
coeterna maiestas. Qualis pater talis filius:
talis spiritus sanctus. Increatus pater in
creatus filius: increatus spiritus sanc
tus. Inmensus pater inmensus filius
inmensus spiritus sanctus.

Content

Old Testament Canticles (imperfect); the start of the Athanasian Creed, all with integral, contemporary marginal and interlinear commentary and glosses.

[Fol. 176r] *Canticum Ysaie prophete* [Isaiah 12, 1–6]. Confitebor tibi domine … sanctus ISRAHEL.

[First marginal gloss, fol. 176r:] [P]rophetauerat ysaias quod deus percut[er]et flumen egipti, ut sui calciati transirent in egiptum, … qui meruerunt sibi d[ominu]m fieri.

[First interlinear gloss, on 'Confitebor':] Laudabo.

[Fol. 176r] *Scriptura ezechie regis IUDE* (Isaiah 38.10). Ego dixi… [finishes on **fol. 177r:**] … in domino domini.

[First marginal gloss on right:] Ambulauit ezechias coram domino in ueritate et in corde perfecto, et fecit rectum iuxta omnia que fecit dauid pater eius, … [First marginal gloss on left:] Ego d[ixi]. Narrat q[uod] tempore angustie cogitaret, … ducuntur ad tartarum. [First interlinear gloss, on rubric:] Secundum lxx. oratio ezechie regis iuda. [First interlinear glosses to main text:] Si sic moriar. In corde meo desperationem uite. Alii in infirmitate et silentio dierum meorum, sed in imperfectione operum.

[Fol. 177r] *Canticum Anne* [I Samuel 2.1]. Exultauit cor meum in domino, … **[fol. 177v]** cornu christi sui. [NB: an error was evidently made in 'habebat' towards the end of verse 5 and only partially corrected: erroneous letters were erased but nothing was put in their place, leaving the reading: 'et quae multos ha filios infirmata est'.]

[Gloss to rubric:] Cum offerret samuhelem in templo domini. [First marginal gloss on left:] Anna, gratia dr' [?datur/dicitur] in ecclesia. Samuel postulatus prs[?]. [Second marginal gloss on left:] In Samuele figurata est mutatio sacerdotii … [First marginal gloss on right:] Per cornu, regia potestas quia reges uncturus erat, uel ipse dux populi.

[Fol. 177v] *Canticum Moysi* [Exodus 15]. Cantemus domino … [breaks off at the bottom of fol. 177v at] Electi principes submersi sunt // [verse 4].

[First marginal gloss on right:] Quia scit uictoriam gratia dei non sua uirtute factam … et nobis conuenit. [First marginal gloss on left:] Egredi te oportet de egipto, et transire mare, ut cantes primum canticum ... ut intret in sancta sanctorum. [First interlinear gloss, on 'Cantemus':] magnificatus.

[**Lost:** the remainder of Cantemus domino, the *Canticum Abbacuc* (Domine audiui), and the start of the *Canticum Moysi* (Audite caeli ...) – the equivalent of two folios.]

[Fol. 178r] // ac nouissima prouiderent Quomodo persequebatur unus mille et duo fugarent decem milia. ... [end of **fol. 178v**] Et uindictam retribuet in hostes eorum, et propitius erit terre populi sui. [*Canticum Moysis*, Audite caeli, vss 29B–43 (end)]

[Fol. 179r] [Three paragraphs of commentary (the third subdivided by a series of paraph marks), relating to the end of Audite Caeli.] [1] Alia uar[i]a suspicantur, primum peccatum, caim [i.e. cain] dicunt, quod non recte diuisit ... quod in aduentu Christi mortis et peccati aculeus fractus est. [2] IER[onymus] secundum lxx et teod' [?Theodotius], dixit dominus ei, non sic, sed omnis qui occidit caim, septem uindictas exsoluet ... quod genus suum usque ad diluuium perseuerauerit [corrected to 'perseuerauit' by expunctuation] ... [cf. Jerome, ep. 36: PL 22, cols. 453–5]. [3] IER[onymus] ad paulam et e [?eustochium], de beati immaculati [sic]. Omnis moralis locus in hoc psalmo est comprehensus. Factus est autem secundum ordinem hebreorum elementorum, ... Sicut a mandatis tuis intellexi, quod uidelicet post opera ceperit habere scientiam secretorum. [cf. Jerome ep. 30: PL 22, cols. 442–3].

[Fol. 179v] *Laus sancti Athanasii.* Quicumque uult saluus esse, ... Inmensus pater inmensus filius, inmensus spiritus sanctus. [The text stops here, although there is space for the next couple of words, 'Eternus pater'; possibly incomplete, it may alternatively have been left thus because there was not room for the marginal gloss that was to accompany the next phrase.]

[First marginal gloss on left:] Hic beatus athanasius liberum arbitrium posuit sicut dicit in psalmo. Quis est homo qui uult uitam ... quia sine fide nullus saluus esse potest. [First marginal gloss on right, partly obliterated by stain, then:] ... qui uult saluus fieri fidem scire debet tenendo ... filium genitum, spiritum s[?ed] precedentem a patre et filio.

Scribes and Script

The main text is carefully written by a single skilful scribe in a high-grade, early but well-developed proto-Gothic book hand. The letters are invariably placed just above the ruled lines. The writing is very regular and highly calligraphic; its distinctly rectilinear general aesthetic is counterbalanced by small triangular serifs, angled to rise slightly from left to right, and by the fact that down-strokes end by curling 'under' to the left. There is considerable 'biting' of letters within words, but generous spaces between words. Characteristic letter-forms include a 'g' whose tail is always finished by a cross-stroke which often touches the main bowl (assimilating the letter as a whole to an '8'); and an 'h' the leg of which curls under at the end of the stroke. The rubrics are the work of the same hand, mainly in the same script – though certain letters in personal names are distinguished by the use of a form of rustic capitals. The style is compatible with production at Christ Church, Canterbury; in terms of rectilinearity and lateral compression this formal hand is midway between the stately high-grade transitional hands used for the great mid-twelfth-century Christ Church works, the Eadwine Psalter (Cambridge, Trinity College, MS R. 17. 1) and the Dover Bible (Cambridge, Corpus Christi College, MSS 3–4), and the fully Gothic script of the late twelfth-century Canterbury Psalter in Paris (BnF, MS lat. 8846). The ink remains a rich dark black. Punctuation is by low point (for major and minor pauses) and *punctus elevatus* (for minor pauses). There is little abbreviation apart from the conventional marks for 'orum', 'bus', 'que', 'per' and 'pro'. 'Et' is represented by a rather stocky ampersand. Double 'i's are 'dashed'. There are very occasional 'acute' accents.

The gloss – which is also placed just above the lines that were ruled for it – is written by a single scribe in a smaller, lower grade book hand, with sharply angled feet which generally touch the neighbouring letter giving a cursive effect. In terms of general aesthetic, this handwriting has points of contact with the earlier Christ Church 'prickly' script. It is, as one would expect, more heavily abbreviated than the main text. Also in contrast to the main text, the Tironian 'et' was invariably used here. Punctuation is by medial point (for minor pauses), *punctus elevatus* (minor pauses) and a *positura* composed of two dots followed by a large 'comma' (for major pauses). The beginnings of sections are flagged by an ink paraph sign. It is possible that both text and gloss were written by the same scribe, but they were deliberately differentiated by script type and articulation as well as by size.

A different, much lighter-weight contemporary (*s.* xii^{med}) hand added 'Laus sci athanasíí' to the upper margin of fol. 179v.

A later (?*s.* xiii) hand entered an additional two-line gloss in the margin of fol. 177v.

At an uncertain later date, the omitted initial 'P' was supplied to '–rophetauerunt' of the first marginal gloss on fol. 176r.

Decoration

No decoration survives. Assuming that these folios were the complement to a psalter conceived at the same grade, it is highly likely that such a fine volume would have had decorated psalm initials for the major divisions at least, and possibly even full-page miniatures.

Each Canticle is headed by a two-lines-high plain coloured capital (red, green or blue) plus a red rubric in the high-grade text script. No particular emphasis is given to the 'C' of *Confitebor* – a plain (red) initial – whereas in some broadly contemporary glossed copies (e.g. York Minster Library, MS XVI.I.4) which have plain initials for the canticles, this is distinguished by an arabesque initial. Every sentence in the surviving leaves is headed by a one-line-high coloured capital (red, blue or green) with elaborate finial serifs.

History and Provenance

Written in the third quarter of the twelfth century, perhaps at Christ Church, Canterbury, the leaves were doubtless designed to follow the text of the psalms in a high-grade psalter – though whether they were actually put to this use is not entirely certain (see **Commentary**). Whatever their early status, they were patently redeployed in the later Middle Ages as endleaves for a *s.* xiv copy of Duns Scotus on the Sentences of Peter Lombard. An altered title plus *ex libris* inscription (in which the names of the author and the possessor were both re-written *in rasura*) on fol. 5v of the host book shows that, whoever was its original owner, the Duns Scotus came into the possession of *Domini Iacobi de Oxoney*/ *doctoris sacre pagine*, i.e. James de Oxeney, monk of Christ Church, by whom presumably it was conveyed to Canterbury. Professed *c.* 1328, then documented at Oxford from 1331–6, in the early 1340s and possibly also between 1355–6, James de Oxeney had obtained his D.Th. by 1358 – by which time he was penancer of Christ Church; he died *c.* 1361 (BRUO, II, p. 1416). The volume was presumably bound or re-bound in Canterbury at some point thereafter, whereupon the present folios were incorporated as endleaves. Prior to this association, the main volume had been severely damaged by damp. The present binding of the manuscript dates from s. xix; however, the fact that our leaves were indeed associated with the host book in the Middle Ages is shown by the stains from the turn-ins of its lost late medieval binding that are clearly preserved on fol. 179.

Commentary

These handsomely conceived leaves, doubtless designed to accompany a glossed psalter, were written in a skilled scriptorium which, the medieval provenance suggests, was most probably Christ Church, Canterbury. The style of the script is certainly compatible with, though hardly independent evidence for, this hypothesis.

There are anomalies in the text of the leaves which merit comment. The apparent juxtaposition of *Audite caeli* and the Athanasian Creed, though not without parallel (e.g. York Minster Library, MS XVI.I.4), is not what one would expect: normally, some or all of the *Canticum puerorum*, *Te Deum*, *Benedictus*, *Magnificat*, *Nunc dimittis*, *Gloria*, *Pater noster* and *Credo* would stand in between them. Furthermore, the erased syllables in verse 5 of the Canticle of Anna were never replaced, and the Athanasian Creed itself may have been left unfinished. Yet against the proposition that they were reject leaves *ab initio* is the early heading, the one thirteenth-century supplementary gloss, and the added initial 'P' – which imply use until at least the thirteenth century. Be that as it may, our pages were certainly recycled as endleaves in the later Middle Ages.

The marginal and interlinear commentary is distilled from Patristic and Carolingian exegesis (principally by Jerome, Bede and Hrabanus Maurus) on the biblical books from which the Canticles were taken; the commentary on the Athanasian Creed is that attributed to Bruno of Würzburg († 1045) (PL 142, cols. 561A–568D). An apparatus of this type is a familiar feature of English and French glossed psalters produced in the second and third quarters of the twelfth century, and it has been characterised as 'the continuation of the *parva glosatura*', the standard commentary on psalms 1–150 presented in the *Glossa ordinaria* (Gibson 1992, p. 110). Thus the apparatus in the present pages shares a good number of entries with other broadly contemporary copies such as Douai, Bibliothèque municipale, MS 23/II (from Anchin Abbey in Flanders), Durham Cathedral Library, MS A. III. 9, and York Minster Library, MS XVI.I.4, not to mention the Eadwine Psalter from Christ Church, Canterbury, though the precise content varies from one manuscript to the next. Whilst many of the entries are shared with Eadwine, for example, the first ones for the *Canticum Anne* are not, though they are paralleled in Douai and York. And even when entries are shared, their disposition regularly differs. Consider, for example, the commentary around 'Fel draconum uinum eorum…' from *Audite caeli* in Canterbury (fol. 178r) and Eadwine (fol. 274r): the marginal gloss in the former ('Sicut fel dracones et aspides uenena occultant …') is presented, abbreviated, as an interlinear gloss in the latter; while 'Hic reducit personam domini, nonne mihi omnia nota sunt que impie gesserunt' which is a marginal gloss in Eadwine, appears between the lines in Canterbury. Similarly, the long commentary – or series of commentaries – on the end of *Audite caeli* that in Eadwine is arranged around the margins of the text in question (fol. 275r), appears in the present manuscript – in a different order – on a discrete folio (fol. 179r), despite the fact that there was room for some of it around the end of the text itself (fol. 178v).

If these leaves were indeed made at Christ Church, they are an invaluable witness to scribal work there in the third quarter of the twelfth century. As such, they would attest to a continuity of high standards between the great mid-century projects (the Eadwine Psalter and the Dover Bible) and the Paris Psalter later in the century – the unfinished swansong of luxury book production at Christ Church Cathedral priory, albeit doubtless decorated by professional artists.

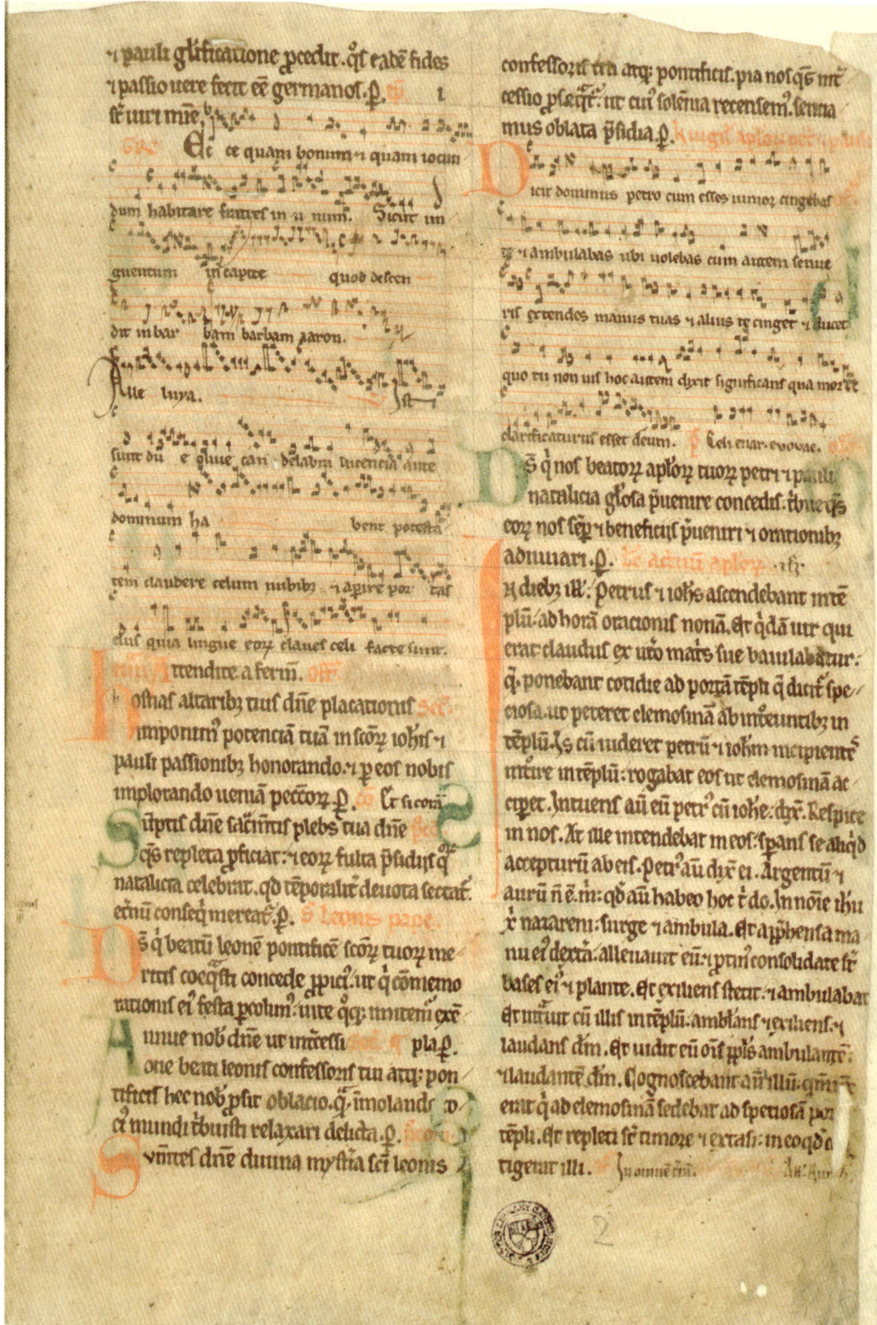

35 Add. 128/29

Missal (with notation)
England; *saec.* XII$^{3/4}$
Illustration: fol. 2r

Physical Description

Twenty-one leaves, now re-mounted as a sequence in a guard-book, interleaved with paper and foliated '1'–'21' (with errors and re-numberings). All the leaves are worn, weathered and discoloured; most have been severely trimmed round the outer edges, often with loss of text in the outer columns (modern parchment attachments reinforce the outer edge of some); a few have been perforated by verdigris. The text is substantially intact on fols. 1, 2, 5, 6, 10, 12, 13, 17, 18, and 21; it is significantly damaged or lost on fols. 3, 4, 7–9, 11, 14–16, 19, 20. Fol. 9, whose condition is particularly parlous, has more extensive modern supports, and the verso of the leaf is covered with gauze.

The following dimensions are based on fol. 10, one of the best-preserved leaves. Size: 300 x 208 mm. Written area: 250 x 160 mm. Written in two columns (width of column: 76 mm). Lines: 37. Space between lines: 7 mm. Height of minims: 3.5 mm. Ruling: lead. Pricked in both margins (see fols. 16–17). What looks like the top of an otherwise lost quire signature (seemingly composed of three strokes) is just visible in the centre of the lower margin of fol. 2v.

Content

Fols. 1–11: Sanctorale from John the Baptist (24 June) to Crisogonus (24 Nov.); fols. 12–18, Common of Saints; fols. 19–20, Votive masses; fols. 20–1, Masses for the Dead. (Notable 'omissions' amidst the portions that are preserved include Æthelwold, Mildred, Oswald and Swithun.) In the following calendar of content, major (but not minor) departures from the Westminster Missal (Wickham Legg (ed.) 1891–3: WM, cited by column) are indicated [NB: the absence of Sequences is not specifically noted on each occasion].

[Fol. 1r] [*Vigilia S. Iohannis baptiste*] [beginning acephalus at:] // multi in natiuitate eius gaudebunt. [WM 839]. [Texts as WM 839–41 except:] *Secretum*, Da quesumus omnipotens Deus, ut sicut beatus Iohannis baptista astruxit, ... peccata nostra semper emundet. Qui tecum.

In die S. Iohannis baptiste. De uentre matris ... **[fol. 1v]** [cf. WM 841–5].

S. Iohannis et Pauli officium. Multe tribulationes... [WM 845–6 except:] **[fol. 2r]** *Euangelium*, Attendite a fermento. [*Offertorium* has been thoroughly erased, and nothing substituted.]

S. Leonis pape. Deus qui beatum leonem pontificem ... [WM 846; then *Secretum* and *Postcommunio* as WM 847].

In uigilia apostolorum petri et pauli. Dicit dominus petro ... **[fol. 2v]** *Postcommunio*, Quos celesti ... [WM 847–52].

[Fol. 3r] *In commemoratione S. Pauli officium*. Scio cui credi et certus sum ... *Postcommunio*. Da quesumus omnipotens deus ut ecclesia tua ... mereatur eterna. Per. [WM 852–5].

[*In translatione S.*] *Martini*. Deus qui populo tuo eterne salutis ... *Postcommunio*. Prestent nobis ... absoluant peccatis. Per. [WM 860–1 – with erasure of ?*Epistola*].

In octaua apostolorum Petri et Pauli. Deus cuius dextera ... [WM 860–2, except:] **[fol. 3v]** *Secretum*. // tibi domine preces et munera ... and *Postcommunio*. // domine populum tuum ... conserua [both now partly lost; not as WM].

Septem fratrum officium. [Laudate] pueri ... *Postcommunio*. Refecti ... premiis. Per [very damaged; seemingly as WM 864].

Translatio S. Benedicti. Os iusti ... [WM 864–6, differing in:] *Ep*., Iustus cor suum; *Gr*., Os iusti, Alleluya, Posui; *Ev*., Nemo acc.; *Off*., Desiderium, and *Comm*., Beatus seruus.

Sancte Margarete uirginis. Oratio. Deus qui beatam uirginem margaretam hodierna die ... [WM 871, differing in:] Me expectauerunt; *Ep*., Domine deus meus exaltasti; *Comm*., Feci indicium; and *Postcomm*., Percipiat quesumus domine blebs [sic] tua beate margarete...

Praxedis uirginis officium [WM 872–3, differing in:] Loquebar de testimoniis; and **[fol. 4r]** *Comm*., Simile est.

Sancte Marie Magdalene [*officium*]. Gaudeamus. Largire nobis clementissime pater quod sicut beata maria magdelene ... beatitudinem. Per eundem. *Sapientie.* Mulierem fortem quis inueniet ... portis opera eius. *GR.* [part of the following texts are lost or damaged] Au[di ?filia; as WM 874]. *Ev.* Rogabat ihesum quidam ... [Erasure.] Benedictionem tuam ... his tibi oblatis ... exhibuit. Per eundem. [*Postcom.*] Prebeat [as WM 876].

Apoll[*inaris*]. Votiuos nos domine beati apollinaris martyris ... et tibi nos reddat ac // [then lost]. [Erasure.] *GR.* Inueni ?David. *Ev.*, Facta est contencio. [Lost.] [*Secretum.*] Hostiam [as WM 878]. *Com.* [erased.] [*Postcom.*] Sumentes [WM 878].

Vigilia beati Iacobi apostoli. Esto domine plebi [v. damaged; as WM 880, except:] *V.* Nimis.

Sanctorum [*septem*] *dormiencium officium.* Salus autem [very damaged but not close to WM 882–3].

Sanctorum martirum Felicis, Simplicii, faustini et Beatricis [partly erased, partly lost; differs from WM 885 in:] *Ep.* Lingua sapientium; *Gr.*, Sacerdotes. *Alleluya* [erased]; *Ev.*, Attendite a fermento; *Off.*, Exultabunt; *Comm.*, Ego uos elegi; *Postcomm.*, Benedictionis tue domine plebs tibi. ...

Germani episcopi officium. Exaudi nos [WM 887 differing in:] Sacerdotes domini; *Postcomm.*, Supplices te rogamus omnipotens deus ut qui percepimus ... ad uitam perueniamus eternam. Per.

Ad uinculam S. Petri officium [WM 889–91 except:] **[fol. 5r]** *Postcomm.*, Muneris diuini ... pericula cuncta depellat. Per.

Stephani prophete et martyris officium [WM 892–3 differing in:] *Ep.,* Omnis pontifex; *Gr.*, Inueni David. Alleluia. Elegit te. *Off.* Inueni David.

In inuentione S. Stephani martyris [WM 893–4, except:] Etenim; *Ep.*, Stephanus plenus gratia; *Gr.*, Sederunt principes. *Alleluya,* Video caelos. *Ev.*, Dicebat Ihesus t[unc] i[deo] Ecce ego m[itto] [Mt 23.34] *Off.*, Elegerunt. *Comm.* Video caelos. [NB: in *Secretum* and *Postcom.*, the references to Stephen's companions, 'sociisque eius' and 'nichodemi, gamalielis atque abibon' respectively were subsequently struck out.]

Sixti felicissimi et Agapiti martyrum officium [WM 896, except:] *Ep.,* Benedictus deus et pater; *Gr.,* Iustorum anime. Alleluya [Erasure]. *Off.* [Erasure]. *Com.,* Ego elegi uos.

In uigilia S. Laurentii martyris off. [WM 900–1, except:] **[fol. 5v]** *Or.*, Da quesumus omnipotens Deus ut triumphum beati Laurencii martyris ... ; *Postcom.*, Conserua quesumus domine munus tuum in nobis ...

In die officium. Confessio [WM 901–3, except:] *Ev.* Nisi granum [ends on **fol. 6r**].

Ypoliti sociorum eius. Iusti epulentur [WM 905, except:] *Ep.* Iusti ... ; *Gr.*, Iustorum anime. Alleluya. Sancti et iusti; *Com.* [erased; and] *Postcom.*, Quos tuis domine reficis sacramentis sanctorum ... moribus. Per.

In uigilia S. Marie assumptionis. Salue [WM 908–9, except:] *V.* Post partum uirgo inuiolata ... ; *Com.*, Alma dei genitrix succurre ... **[fol. 6v]**.

In die, ad missam [as WM 910–13, except:] *V.* [largely erased]; [*Lectio sapiencie*] In omnibus requiem quesiui et in hereditate domini ... suauitatem odoris [WM 914–15]; [start of *Secretum* was erased and rewritten in ?*s.* xiii]; *Comm.*, Beata uiscera.

[fol. 7r] *In oct. S. Laurentii.* Probasti [WM 913–14 except:] *Ev.* Qui parce; *GR.* Posuisti domine; [Second *Ev.*, erased and not replaced]; *Com.*, Posuisti.

In octauas S. MARIE omnia fiant sic in die sed absque Credo.

In vigilia S. Bartholomei. R. omnia –?– in die. [M]ichi autem [then as WM 922–3, except:] *Ep.* [erased]; *GR.* In [then obliterated]. Alleluya. Nimis autem. *Ev.* Facta est contentio; *Off.* [Obliterated].

Augustini episcopi officium. Statuit [much of text missing owing to loss of outer half of column; WM 926–7, except:] *Gr.*, Domine perue[nisti]; [*Postcom.*] Sumentes Domine salutaria ... gloriosa sollemnia. Per.

[*In decollatione S. Iohannis baptiste*] [outer portion of many lines lost; cf. WM 928–31, except:] *GR.* Pol// Alleluya [Lost] ... herodes spiculatore ... ; *Off.* Posuisti. *Sec.* // ... sancti iohannis baptiste et martyris ... deferimus .... Salutem. Per. *Com.*, Magna est **[fol. 7v]** [*In natali S. Egidii.*] Os iusti [substantially lost; cf. WM 933–4 except:] [*Oratio*] ... confessorem tuum atque abbatem ... *GR.* Os iusti. *Ev.* –?–. *Off.* Desiderium; *Com.*, Fidelis est; *Postcom.*, Protege domine populum tuum ...

In natiuitate S. Marie officium. Gaudeamus [WM 938–42,

except:] *GR*. Audi filia **[fol. 8r]** *Com*., Vera fides geniti purgauit … inuiolata.

[*Exultacio S. Crucis officium*.] [substantial portions lost; as WM 947–9, except:] [*Or*.] Deus qui unigeniti filii tui domini nostri ihesu christi [then imperfect] … a peccatorum suorum … ; *Ep*., Confido de uob[is]; *Postcom*. Iesu Christi domini nostri corpore saginati … deus noster, ut per hec sacrificia … salutari … //.

Eodem die Cornelii. [generally damaged; half of outer column lost] Presta quesumus omnipotens deus ut sicut// [remainder largely lost] **[fol. 8v]**.

// … *Lamberti martyris* … // Sacerdotes dei [partly lost, partly erased; but not close to WM 951].

In Uigilia S. Mathei apostoli officium. Ego autem [partly lost; WM 952–3, except:] *Ep*. –?–; *Sec*., Respice quesumus omnipotens et misericors deus munera … exequamur. Per.; *Com*., Magna est; *Postcom*. Presta quesumus omnipotens deus ut diuino … et moribus. Per.

In die officium. Michi autem [WM 954–7, except:] *Gr*. [erased]. *Alleluia*, Primus ad Syon. **[Fol. 9r**; inner column largely lost] *Off*., Posuisti; *Com*., Magna est.

[*In natali sanctorum martirum Mauricii sociorumque eius officium*.] Intret in [partly lost; cf. WM 956–7].

[*Cosmas et Damian*] [partly lost; WM 959, except] *Ev*. [erased]; *Off*. [erased]; *Com*. [erased].

Festivalis S. Michaelis. Benedicite [as WM 960–1, but only has Apoc. 1, 1–5 and Mt 18, 1–10 as readings] **[fol. 9v**, much of one column lost].

Ieronimi [*officium*] [largely lost; WM 964–5, except:] *GR*. Iurauit.

Germani [*officium*] [largely lost; WM 965]

[Leaf missing]

[fol. 10r] [*Officium Symonis et Iude*] [acephalus and imperfect] //tudo, profundum … poterit nos separare a caritate dei … [WM 984–5, except:] *Gr*., Nimis honorato. *Alleluya*, Non uos.

In uigilia omnium sanctorum. Timete [WM 986–8, except:] *Gr*. [erased]; *Ev*. [erased]; *Com*., Iustorum.

In die officium. Gaudeamus [partly lost, damaged but as WM 988–91] **[fol. 10v]**

[Very damaged] // ... Eustachii ... // [erased until] *Secretum*, Sicut beatus eustachius cum sociis suis; *Postcom.*, Sit tibi omnipotens ... prepara. Per eundem [cf. WM 992 and 991, where used as *Postcom.* and *Sec.*, respectively].

[Rubric obliterated: ?*Leonardi confessoris officium.*] Os iusti [WM 992–3, except:] *Or.*, Preces nostras quesumus domine celesti dono prosequere ... ; *Gr.* Os iusti. Alleluya. Posui; *Sec.*, Suscipe domine munera tue pietati ... accepta; *Com.*, Fidelis; *Postcom.*,, Sanctificet nos domine quesumus tui percepcio ... ad indulgentiam prosint eternam. Per.

Quatuor coronatorum officium. Intret [WM 993–4, except:] *Gr.* [partly erased]; *Ev.* [difficult to read but not as WM 994]; *Off.*, Exultab// **[fol. 11r]** *Com.* [erased].

S. Martini Episcopi. Statuit [cf. WM 996–8, except:] *GR.* Domine preuenisti; *Ev.*, Homo quidam peregre; *Off.*, Veritas; *Com.*, Beatus seruus; *Postcom.*, Auxiliare domine quesumus populo tuo ut sacramentorum tuorum uirtute proficiens ... consorcium. Per.

Bricii officium. Sacerdotes dei [WM 999, except:] *Ep.*, Iustum deduxit; *Ev.* [erased]; *Off.*, Inueni David; [large portions of *Com* and *Postcom.* missing owing to loss of large strip of outer column, but they were seemingly not as WM].

[*Octava S. Martini*] [lost or very damaged, but includes] Concede quesumus; Hec oblacio; and Sacramenta, as in WM 1003–4].

Sancti Ædmundi [very damaged; cf. WM 1004–5] **[fol. 11v]**.

[*In natali sancte Cecilie uirginis et martyris.*] Loquebar [lost and damaged; WM 1005–6, except:] *Or* [largely lost]; *Gr.* [lost] Alleluya. Veni electa.

[*S. Clementis officium*] [very damaged at start:] // meum [then as WM 1008, except:] *Ps.* Domine exaudi; *Or.*, Deus qui nos annua beati clementis martyris; *Ev.*, Homo quidam nobis; *Com.*, Beatus seruus.

Crisogoni martyris officium. [Erasure] [WM 1009, except:] *Gr.* Posuisti Domine. Alleluya [erased]; *Ev.* [erased]; *Sec.,* Oblatis quesumus domine placare ... periculis. Per.

[Rubric and text lost or obliterated] // Omnipotens sempiterne deus qui corpus g//

[Lost leaves]

[Fol. 12r] [*Commune unius martyris*. Acephalus:] // et semen eius in benedictione erit in eternum conseruabitur. *Ps.*, Noli ?emula[ri] ... Protexisti me [then WM 1042–3 except:] *Or.*, Adesto domine supplicationibus nostris et intercessione beati N martyris tui ... ; *Corinthios* [cf. WM 1060–1]; *Sapientie* [WM 1043]; *Ad Tim.* ... cum gloria celesti [WM 1043]. Then *GR.* Posuisti [as WM 1047–8] **[fol. 12v]**; Dixit ihesus discipulis suis ... nisi granum [WM 1053]; Si quis uult uenire post me **[fol. 13r]** abneget semet ipsum [WM 1053]; Si quis uenit ad me et non odit patrem suum; Nichil opertum [WM 1050]. *Off.* In uirtute [WM 1054–5]; *Off.* Posuisti; *Off.* Confitebuntur [WM 1054]; *Off.* Iustus [WM 1054]; *Off.*, Gloria; *Sec.* Presencia [WM 1055] *Comm*, Qui uult [WM 1055, etc.] **[fol. 13v]** *Postcom.*, Quos refecisti [cf. WM 968].

In natale unius martyris et pontificis. Or., Deus qui sanctam nobis huius diei letitiam pro commemoratione beati martyris tui N atque pontificis fecisiti, ... *Ad hebreos.* Fratres. Omnis pontifex ex hominibus assumptis ... melchisedech. *Ad hebreos.* Fratres. Doctrinis uariis et peregrinis... *Sec.*, Intende propicius quesumus Domine oblata tibi hec munera... *Postcom.* Sumpsimus domine in sancti martyris tui N atque pontificis ...

Plurimorum martyrum. Intret. [parts lost, cf. WM 1056–7, 1058–9] Clamauerunt ... **[fol. 14r]** Timete dominum ... Iusti epulentur ... Sapientiam sanctorum ... Salus autem ... Iudicant sancti gentes. *Ps.* Exultate. *Al.* Sancti tui. [Outer column partly cut away:] Omnipotens sempiterne // ... martyrum ... sempiternis. Per. *Ad hebreos.* Fratres [WM 1058]. [*Sapiencie*] Iustorum anime [WM 1058].

[Fol. 14v; outer edge lost] Four readings from Sapientie [WM 1062, 1059, 1061, 1061–2]; *Gr.* [as WM 1063–4].

[Fol. 15r–v; partly lost] *Gr.* and *V.* [as WM 1064–5]. [Readings from Matt. and Lk as WM 1070, 1066, 1067, 1068; one very damaged].

Off. Mirabilis deus [WM 1073]. *Off.* Letamini ... Exultabunt.... Confitebuntur. *Sec.*, Suscipe [WM 1073–4].

[?One leaf missing]

[Fol. 16r] [end of *Commune unius confessoris*] *Gr.* Iurauit [WM 1081]; [Matt. as WM 1085]. *Sec.* Munera quesumus domine tibi dicata ... intende. Per. *Postcom.,* Presta quesumus omnipotens deus ut de perceptis ... sumamus. Per.

Unius abbatis. Os iusti. [Outer half of column lost; cf. WM 1090–4] *Or.*, Deus qui beatum N confessorem tuum atque abbatem ... impetrare. Per. *Sapientie.* Iustus cor [WM 1091]. *GR.* Os iusti [WM 1093]. Nemo accendit [WM 1094]. **[fol. 16v;** damaged and imperfect] *Sec.* [damaged] //[domi]ne quod pro sancti, N, confessoris tui ... solemnitate deferimus tibi ... suffragium. Per. [*Commune*] *plurimorum confessorum.* //s induant salutari. *Ps.* Memento... *Or.* //essorum tuorum, N et N, nos ... *Ad hebreos //* facti sunt [WM 1095; then as 1096 until:] *Lucam,* In illo tempore. Dixit Ihesus discipulis suis, sint lumbi uestri ... filius hominis ueniet [Lk 12, 35–44]. *Sec.*, adesto domine precibus... *Com.*, Ego uos elegi. *Postcom.*, Fideles tui deus celestis ... delictis. Per.

[Fol. 17r] [*Unius uirginis*] Dilexisti iusticiam ... Loquebar... Me expectauerunt ... Cognoui .... [Cf. WM 1097]. *Or.*, Indulgentiam uobis domine quesumus beata N uirgo et martyr ... uirtutis. Per. *Sapientie.* Domine deus meus [Eccl. 51, 13–17; WM 1098]. *Sapientie.* Confitebor tibi ... Et liberas eos de manibus odientium te, domine deus meus [Eccl. 51; cf. WM 1098]. **[Fol. 17v]** //isti iniquitatem. Propterea unxit ... *Or.* Specie tua ...[WM 1101]. Propter ueritatem ... [WM 1101]. *GR.* Diffusa [WM 1101]. *V.* Propter ueritatem. Alleluia. *V.* Emulor enim uos ... Alleluia. *V.* Ueni electa ... Alleluia. *V.* Specie tua ... [WM 1101]. Alleluia. *V.* Diffusa est [WM 1101]. Alleluia. *V.* Hec est uirgo sapiens ... Alleluia. *V.* Loquebar [WM 1097]. *Mt.* In illo. Dixit Ihesus discipulis suis parabolam hanc. Simile est regnum celorum thesauro abscondito ... [WM 1104–5]. **[Fol. 18r]** *Off.* Offerentur...[WM 1105]. *Off.*, Filie [WM 1105]. *Secr.*, Presta quesumus domine deus noster ut sicut in tuo conspectu ... oblatio. Per. *Com.* Diffusa est [WM 1105]. *Com.* Feci iudicium [WM 1106]. *Com.*, Simile est [WM 1106]. *Com.* Principes [WM 1106]. *Postcom.* Placeat tibi quesumus misericors deus ... subministrent. Per.

Unius uirginis non martyris off. Dilexisti iusticiam. Omnipotens sempiterne deus auctor uirtutum et amator uirginitatis da nobis quesumus sancte N uirginis ... complacuit. Per. *Ad Corinthios.* Fratres, qui gloriatur [II Cor. 10, 17 etc.; WM 1107]; *Lectio*

Sapientie, Sapientia uincit maliciam, attingit [Sap. 8, 30 etc.; WM 1099]. [Rubric very damaged.] Gaudens gaudebo [WM 1109]. **[Fol. 18v]** Dicit dominus omnipotens. *GR*. Dilexisti. Alleluia. Diffusa est. *L*. Alleluia. Emulor. *Mathm*. In illo. Dixit Ihesus discipulis suis parabolam hanc, simile est regnum celorum decem uirginibius [WM 1103]. *Secr*. Offerimus [WM 1105]. *Of*., Offerentur \maior? [later insertion]/preces et munera [WM 1105]. [Damaged.] *Postcom*. [re-written] Diffusus.

Plurimarum uirginum. Uultum tuum [WM 1108, except:] *Or*., Deus qui ut humanum genus ad confessionem tui nominis prouocares; *Sapientie*., O quam pulchra est casta generatio, ... in refrigerio erit [cf. WM 1099 but longer]; *Gr*., Gloriosus Deus; *V*., Adducentur regi uirgines ...

[Lost leaves]

[Fol. 19r] [*Missa pro seipso*.] Omnipotens sempiterne deus qui me peccatorem [WM 1184]. *Sec*. Deus qui te precipis [WM 1185]. *Postcom*. Aures [WM 1186].

Pro familiaribus. Deus qui caritatis [WM 1156–7].

Contra temptationes carnis. Ure igne [WM 1154–5].

Pro pace officium [part of column lost]. Deus a quo sancta ... Deus qui credentes [WM 1149]. Deus auctor [WM 1149].

[Fol. 19v; very damaged] [*Ad pluuiam postulandum*... ; *Pro serenitate aeris*...; page ends:] *Secretum*. [E]xaudi domine preces ... misterii **[fol. 20r**; very damaged] ut qui ... correctos. Per [WM 1159]. *Postcom*. Preces populi [WM 1159].

Pro iter agentibus. Adesto ... *Sec*. Propiciare... *Postcom*. Sumpta [WM 1155–6].

Contra pestes aerias. A domo tua [WM 1310, then:] *Sec*., Offerimus tibi domine laudes; *Postcom*., Omnipotens sempiterne Deus qui nos et castigando ...

Pro peste animalium. Deus qui laboribus; *Sec*., Subueniat nobis domine ... [then (column 2) very damaged]

[*Pro fidelibus defunctis*; very damaged, includes:] *Lectio libri machabeorum*, In diebus illis. Uir fortissimos ... *Lectio apocalypsis*. In diebus illis. Audiui ... [WM 1165]. *Ad tessalonicenses*. Fratres. Nolumus [WM 1165–6] **[Fol. 20v**; first column largely lost but includes reading from John:], Dixit Martha ad Ihesum [WM

1167], [then:] Omne quod dat michi pater [WM 1168] [and] Ego sum panis uiuus [WM 1168]. *Off*., Domine ihesus christe rex glorie libera [WM 1169]. *V*. Hostias et preces [WM 1169].
[Fol. 21r] [*Pro episcopo defuncto*] Tu suscipe pro animabus [WM 1170]. *Sec*. Suscipe domine pro anima famuli\e/ tui\e/ hostiam ... qui cum patre. *Com*., Lux eterna luceat... *Postcom*. Presta quesumus domine ut anima ... perpetuo munere gratuletur. Per.
Pro episcopo oratio. Deus qui inter apostolicos [WM 1170]. *Sec*. Offerimus tibi domine oblationem ... beatitudinis porcionem. Per. *Postcom*., Proficiat domine quesumus anime famuli tui N pontificis... connumerari. Per.
Pro sacerdote. Deus cuius misericordie non est numerus [WM 1172]. *Sec*., Quesumus domine deus noster ut oblationem ... conforcia sacerdotum. Per. *Postcom*., Presta quesumus omnipotens deus per hec sancta misteria anime famuli tui, N, ... misterium. Per.
Pro quolibet defuncto. Deus cui soli competit ... aggregetur. *Sec*. Suscipe [WM 1174]; *Postcom*., Ascendant ad te domine preces ... confortem. Per.
Pro patre et matre. Deus qui nos [WM 1171–2].
Pro benefactoribus defunctis. Miserere quesumus [WM 1173–4].
[*In anniuersariis defunctorum oratio*.] Deus indulgentiarum [WM 1174]. *Sec*., Propiciare domine ... sociare digneris. Per. *Postcom*., Presta domine quesumus ut anima famuli\e/ tui\e/ ... sempiternam. Per.
Pro fratribus et sororibus. Deus uenie [WM 1172]. *Sec*. Deus cuius misericordie non est ... [imperfect]. [*Postcom*] ... recipiant beatitudinem [WM 1172–3].
Pro amico defuncto or. Deus qui proprium est miserere ... ad uitam. Per. *Sec*., Intuere quesumus omnipotens eterne deus et placatus ... sempiternam. *Postcom*., Prosit quesumus domine anime famuli tui, N .... Consorcium. Per.
Missa pro [illegible] *Or*., Inclina domine aurem tuam [WM 1175]. *Sec*., Animas famulorum [cf. WM 1175]. *Postcom*., Annue [WM 1175].
Missa pro familiaribus. Omnipotens sempiterne deus cui ... [WM 1173]. *Sec*., Propiciare [WM 1173, breaking off at:] luce in fide//.

Scribes and Script

The text (including the sections with notation and the rubric) is probably all the work of a single scribe, who used a moderately neat but not scrupulously regular, transitional Romanesque to Gothic book hand. The same scribe was probably also responsible for the small, compressed marginal guide-texts for the rubric which are done in a less formal script, and possibly also for the early correction on fol. 5r. The scribe favoured an inky pen and packed in his words to create a dense written area. Sentence capitals are generally a form of rustics, the 'A's and 'N's often being treated to calligraphic elaboration, including a double cross-bar. Punctuation: low point (major and minor pauses); *punctus elevatus* (minor pause); *punctus interrogativus*. Occasional 'acute' accents. It is impossible to say whether or not the square notation (on a red, four-line staff) is the work of the same hand.

Some corrections (e.g. fols. 4r, 5v) and additions (fols. 13v lower margin, 19v margins – now very faint) date from before *c.* 1200. In s. xiii the start of the *Secretum* for 'In die assumpcionis Marie' (fol. 6v) was erased and re-written; other erasures (fols. 9r, 10r) may date from around the same time. In s. xiv–xv, rubrics and numbers were added throughout (e.g. fols. 4r, 5v, 6r–v, 7v, 8r–v, 9v, 10r, etc.), a passage was corrected (fol. 10r), and various short additions were made in the margins (fols. 3v, 8r, 9v, 12v). Other additions, such as the elaborate inky crosses on fols. 12v, 13r and 18r, are impossible to date. As a whole, however, the various interventions attest to a long working life.

Decoration

The text is articulated with bold but plain, enlarged coloured capitals (generally two to three lines high, but occasionally more if the letter had a descender), alternately red and green. The latter pigment has attacked the parchment. Guide-letters, left by the scribe, are visible under some initials. There is no decoration in the pages that survive.

History

The various stages of annotation and erasure show that the volume had had a long working life before it was dismembered and presumably used as binding material, in the sixteenth century. The early modern context(s) from which the leaves were recovered are seemingly unrecorded. An informal note, kept with the item, states: 'Box ABC. Service Books XYZ'.

Bibliography

Orchard 1995, p. 92.

36 Add. 129/56 and PRC 49/3/3–5

Augustine, *In Euangelium Iohannis*
England; *saec.* XII²
Illustration: Add. 129/56, fol. 2r

Physical Description

Add. 129/56: one bifolium, cut down (particularly in the lower margin), its edges folded over, but with the written area intact. It is now folded inside-out in relation to its original arrangement within the book. The outside is very weathered, discoloured and dirty (with the obliteration of localised areas of text); the inside is stained (seemingly from an adhesive) but generally cleaner. The sheet has four slits, accompanied by long thread-marks, at three points in the inner margin, where thongs were laced through when it was re-used as a cover. There are faint, illegible offsets of writing, presumably from the material that it was then covering.

PRC 49/3/3: a single leaf, damaged in the upper and lower margins of the inner column, with modest loss of text. PRC 49/3/4: a single leaf damaged in the lower margin and with three small holes near the top of the written area. PRC 49/3/5: a bifolium which has been cut down, especially at the top, cropping the text; the outer margins were at one point folded over, but they have since been restored to their original form. This sheet, too, is folded inside-out in relation to its original arrangement in the book.

PRC 49/3/3 and 49/3/4 were originally contiguous; whether they were once conjugate is unclear. The sheet PRC 49/3/5 originally stood inside Add. 129/56, forming the two central bifolia of a quire.

Maximum dimensions: 310 × 250 mm. Written area 278 × 178 mm. (The original page size must have been at least: 375 × 250 mm.) Two columns (column width: 82 mm). Lines: 48. Space between lines: 6 mm. Height of minims: 2 mm. Prickings survive both in the inner margins and the (now turned-over) outer margins. Ruling: faint lead – done with an implement that has slightly scored all the surfaces. All the horizontal lines run across the intercolumnar space. Notwithstanding holes and tears caused by

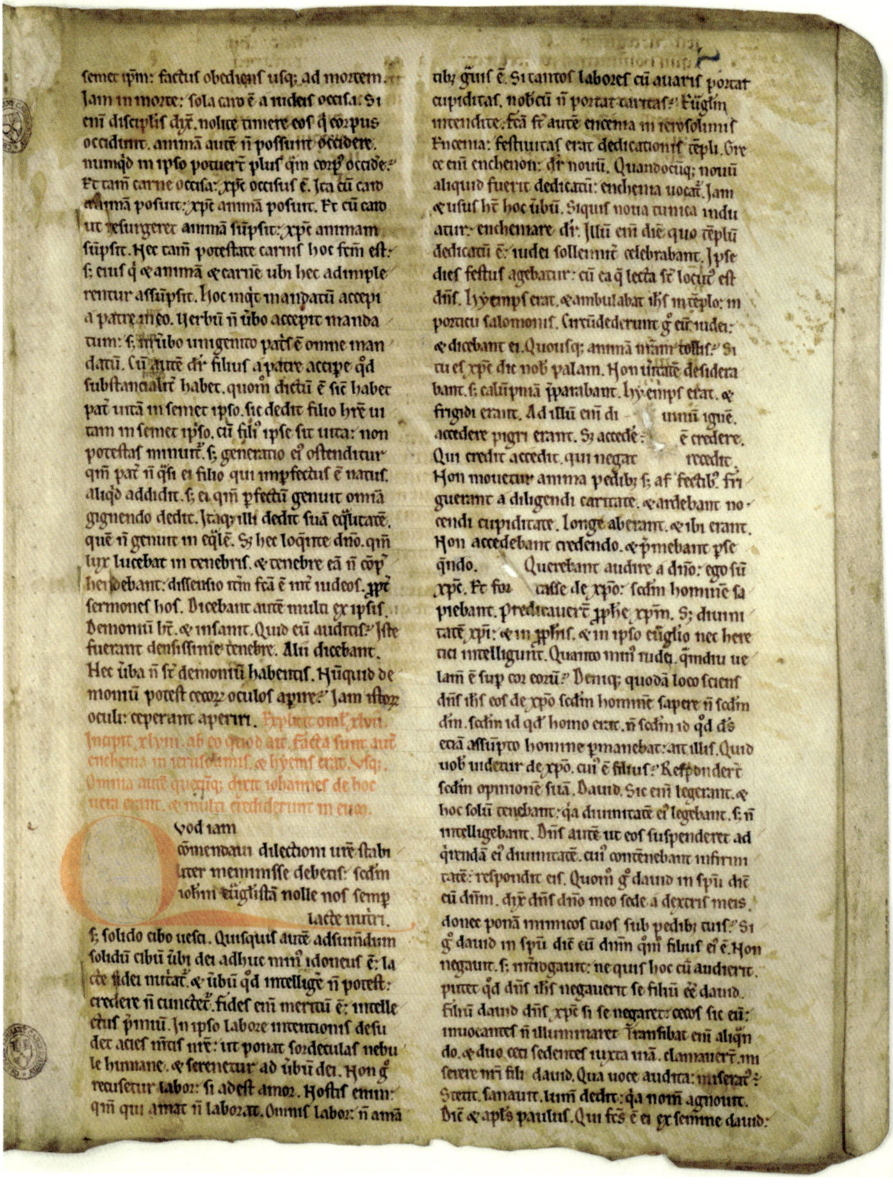

subsequent trauma, the traces of five sewing stations can be distinguished along the centre fold of the bifolium, Add. 129/56: they appear approximately 33, 90, 185, 263 and 278 mm from the top of the leaf.

Further leaves from the same manuscript ('PRC 49/3/1–2') are at Maidstone, Kent County Archives, forming the flyleaves of PRC 32/29, the register of wills in the Consistory Court for 1560–3.

Content

Augustine, *In Euangelium Iohannis* (CPL 278), the end of Tract 14 plus the start of 15; the end of Tract 47 to the start of 49. The exact content of the leaves – presented in their original order – is as follows.

[PRC 49/3/3, recto] [bearing 'xiiii' in the upper margin]: //[fort]e dictum est, illum oportet crescere me [PL 35, col. 1504, line 14] ... **[verso ends:]** Attendit infideles et ait, Qui de ce- [hole] supra omnes est et quo[d]// [PL 35, col. 1507, line. 43].

[PRC 49/3/4, recto] // uidit et audiuit loquitur, et testimonium eius nemo accepit [PL 35, col. 1507, l. 43] ... **[verso ends:]** quam iohannes, et plures baptizaret, quamquam iesus // [col. 1511, l. 12].

[Add. 129/56, fol. 2r] // semet ipsum, factus obediens usque ad mortem. Iam [PL 35, col. 1740, l. 37] ... **[fol. 2v,** ending very damaged:] // Et brachium domini cui reuelatum est [rest of line obliterated] [col. 1744, ll. 13–14].

[PRC 49/3/5] [starting on the inside recto, followed by the final verso, then the front recto, then the inside verso:] Quod non ita dictum est [PL 35, col. 1744, line 14] ... Dormit ergo omnis mortuus, et bonus et malus // [col. 1751, line 16].

[Add. 129/56, fol. 1r] // quomodo interest in ipsis, qui cotidie [PL 35, col. 1751, l. 17] ... **[fol. 1v, ends:]** Esuriuit Iesus, uerum est sed quia uoluit // [col. 1754, l. 49].

Scribes and Script

The leaves at Canterbury are all the work of a single scribe who regularly placed his writing a little above the ruled line. He has a regular, rectilinear, transitional Romanesque-early Gothic hand which, though compressed laterally, retains a Romanesque rotundity in individual letter-forms; there is some 'biting' but it is not preponderant; nor are the serifs and feet particularly angular or pronounced. Distinctive forms include an 'ur' abbreviation which looks like a rustic capital 'V' on its side (a similar form was used for the upper part of the *punctus interrogativus*); a spiralling 'us' abbreviation, rather like a slightly compressed '9'; and a fine 'x' formed from two equally-weighted crossing strokes, the left 'leg' being attractively extended. The same scribe was responsible for the running heading (preserved on PRC 49/3/3), for a series of corrections which involved rewriting some or all of a line to a slightly smaller grade (Add. 129/56, fol. 1r; PRC 49/3/4 recto), and for the rubric (written in red in normal minuscules). The text is moderately abbreviated, and regularly accented. Stylised rustics were used for sentence capitals. The ampersand is invariably used; double 'i's are invariably 'dashed'. Punctuation: low point (for major and minor pauses), *punctus elevatus* (for minor pauses), and a distinctive *punctus interrogativus* (see above). It has been stated (Parkes 1991, p. 315) that the same scribe was also responsible for the Eusebius (**no. 41**); however, in so far as the leaves at Canterbury are concerned, the identification is mistaken.

A late medieval hand added, 'Iohannis' beside the rubric on PRC 49/3/4.

Decoration

The surviving incipits (PRC 49/3/4, tract 15; Add. 129/56, tract 48; PRC 49/3/5, fol. 2v, tract 49) are headed by five- to seven-lines-high, red and blue initials, simply but competently flourished. Guide-letters (in the gutter) survive for a couple of them. That the 'Q' for homily 48 was added after the text had been written is confirmed by the fact that it overruns part of it.

History

These leaves were recycled for use as wrappers in the 1560s. Written both on the front and down the back (then the 'spine') of Add. 129/56 is 'Ex Officio Comperta & Detecta. Lib. 6. 1564,

1565'. Written on the 'front' of PRC 49/3/5 is 'Liber [the word that originally followed this has been erased and replaced (in a darker ink) by] Inventarium'; added to the side in smaller script (and now very rubbed) is 'Inventarium / Liber 1 / Hay?es / 1565 / 1566'; this covered the register of inventories from the archdeaconry court for those years (PRC 10/1). PRC 49/3/3 and 4 come from the index of inventories of the archdeaconry court for 1569–85 (PRC 48/5).

Commentary
See in general **no. 24**.

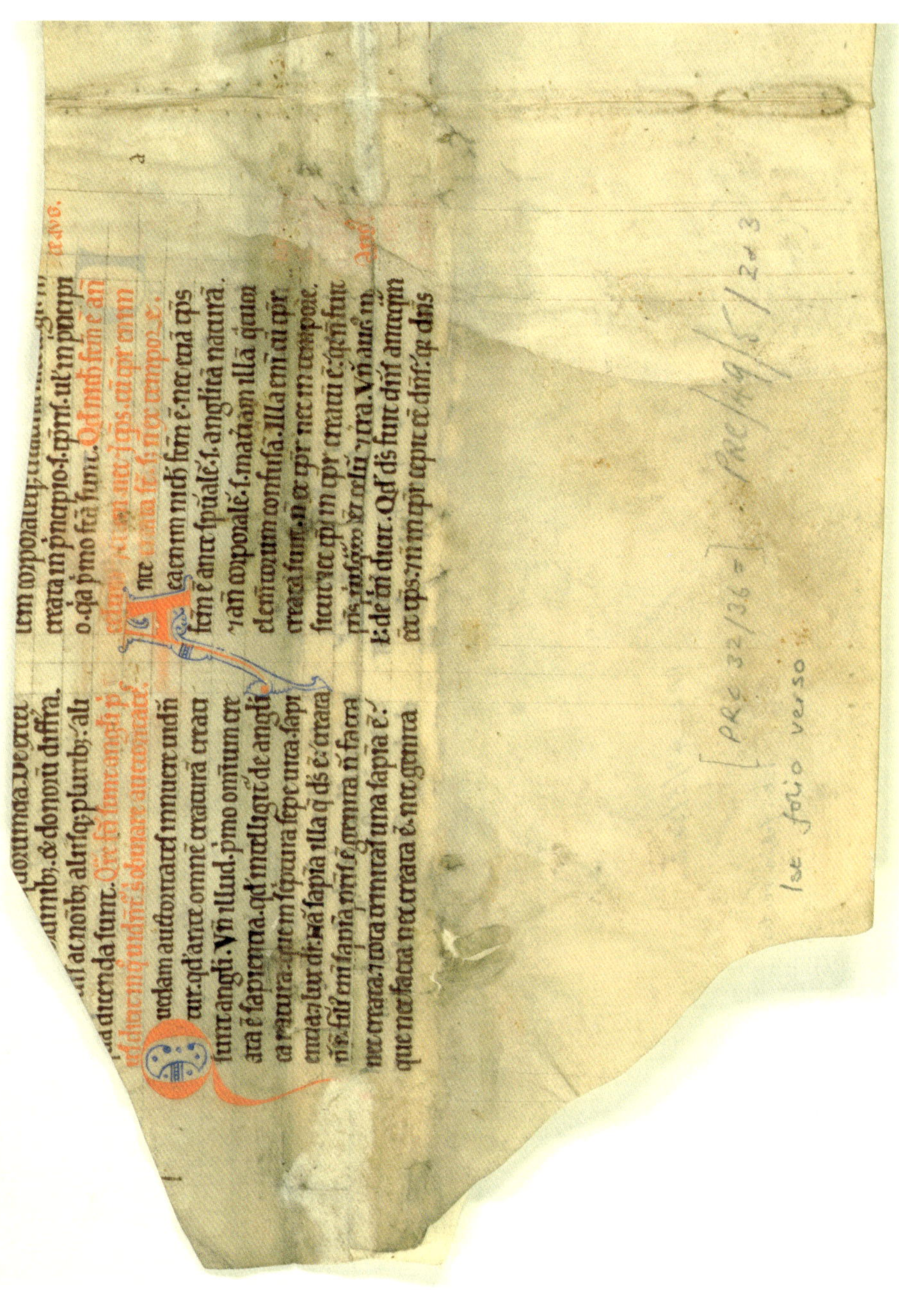

37 PRC 49/5/1–3

Peter Lombard, *Sententiae*
England or France; *saec.* XII[2]
Illustration: PRC 49/5/2 and 3, fol. 1v

Physical Description

Three thin strips from a single bifolium, including the top and bottom of the leaf; strips 2 and 3, which abut, have been joined together with gauze. All the surfaces are damaged. Fragment 1 has a glue-stain running horizontally across one side, with a matching brown discolouration on the other; one of the columns of text has been slightly cropped. Fragments 2 and 3 have both had their corners cut off with corresponding loss of parts of the outer columns of text.

Fragment 1 measures 81 × 399 mm; fragments 2 and 3 together: 170 × 398 mm. The text is set out in two columns of 68 mm, the intercolumnar space being 10 mm. The margins, as preserved, are as follows: inner, 35mm; upper, 32 mm; outer, 49 mm; and lower, 84 mm (allowing one to postulate original measurements of 35, *c.* 45, *c.* 65 and *c.* 90 mm respectively). Around 16–20 lines of text are missing (depending on the place) between the bottom of strip 1 and the top of strip 2. Space between lines: 6 mm. Height of minims: 2.5 mm. Prickings survive in the inner margins as well as in the upper and lower ones; those in the outer margin have been lost. Ruling: lead/crayon. As the parchment was evidently well prepared and the surfaces are all now damaged, it is very difficult to distinguish between the hair and the flesh sides of the leaf.

Sufficient survives to give a fairly clear picture of the original form of the pages, which must have measured *c.* 355 × 240 mm, with a written area of *c.* 220 × 140 mm, divided into *c.* 42 written lines. The amount of text missing between the end of the first half of the bifolium and the start of the second half is the equivalent of eight pages, i.e. four folios, two bifolia, indicating that the present leaf was the third from the centre of its quire. General comparison might be made with Oxford, Bodleian Library, MS

Rawlinson C.163, a well-preserved copy of the text of approximately the same date and of Lanthony provenance which is still in a medieval binding: this manuscript measures *c.* 340 × 250 mm with a written area of 208 × 140 mm, arranged in two columns of 42 lines; including the excised first leaf of Book I, it had a total of 204 folios, plus endleaves.

Content

Peter Lombard, *Sententiae* (PL 192), Liber II, parts of Distinctiones I, II and VII (all incomplete). The exact content of the fragments (presented as part of the whole-leaves they originally formed) is as follows.

[First recto; PRC 49/5/1, fol. 1r, col. 1] // Factus ergo angelus siue homo ... Positus est ergo homo in medio [PL 192, col. 653, ll. 56–66]. [Lost central portion of leaf.] [PRC 49/5/2 and 3, fol. 1r, col. 1] // [ministerium] mittuntur. *Quomodo dicitur aliquando in scriptura* ... [col. 654, ll. 8–22]. [PRC 49/5/1, fol. 1r, col. 2] // potest, Quia deus uoluit et uoluntatis eius ... qui est excellentissima creatura tam [col. 654, ll. 22–31]. [Lost central portion.] [PRC 49/5/2 and 3, fol. 1r, col. 2] // consortium terreni corporis [humiliatus est; ne forte] in hoc nimis ... [col. 654, ll. 47–60].

[First verso; PRC 49/5/1, fol. 1v, col. 1] // non caderent et isti ab eo ubi erant ad id ubi non erant ascenderent ... [marginal rubric, *Tercia*] ... in angelicam et humanam fuisse [col. 654, ll. 60–9]. [Lost central portion.] [PRC 49/5/2 and 3, fol. 1v] // quorumdam. De excellentia ... que nec facta nec creata est nec genita [col. 655, ll. 11–24]. [PRC 49/5/1, fol. 1v, col. 2] // uel procedens. De angelica igitur uita illud ... Item si in principio creauit deus coelum et terram nichil [col. 655, ll. 25–35]. [Lost central portion.] [PRC 49/5/2 and 3, fol. 1v, col. 2] //lem corporalemque ... et non in tempore cepit esse dominus quia dominus [col. 655, ll. 53–66].

[Two bifolia missing.]

[Second recto; PRC 49/5/1, fol. 2r, col. 1] // obdurati sunt ut non ualeant fieri boni et tamen ... *Quod boni post confirmationem liberius* // [col. 664, ll. 69–68]. [Missing portion.] [PRC 49/5/2 and 3, fol. 2r, col. 1] // [peccauerunt], peccare potuerunt. Et cuicumque ... *sed confirmatum* [col. 665, ll. 8–23]. [PRC 49/5/1, fol. 2r, col. 2] // Non ergo post confirmationem angeli ... enim homo et angelus creatus [col. 665, ll. 24–32]. [Missing portion.] [PRC 49/5/2 and 3, fol. 2r, col. 2] //bus rebus nosce– [lacuna] sensus partim [lacuna] –ores propter tam magna [lacuna] partim sanctis angelis quod [lacuna] deo discunt ... Unde Augustinus in// [col. 665, ll. 51–64].

[Second verso; PRC 49/5/1, fol. 2v, col. 1] // Uideo inquit infirme cogita- ... magi dicentes [col. 665, ll. 65–72]. [Missing portion.] [PRC 49/5/2 and 3, fol. 2v, col. 1; very imperfect at the start, damaged at the end] //datur quantum [lacuna] *Quod non sunt creato//* [col. 666, ll. 14–28]. [PRC 49/5/1, fol. 2v, col. 2] // formarum ab originalibus ut ita dicam regulis ... sensus corporis semi// [col. 666, ll. 28–38]. [Missing portion.] [PRC 49/5/2 and 3, fol. 2v, col. 2] // Exteriores autem [lacuna] siue occasiones ... uiribus ac facultatibus [col. 666, ll. 55–69].

[Liber II, Distinctio VII, s. 10 (PL, col. 666), on the second verso, is accompanied by a long marginal entry by the original scribe (presented on lines ruled specially for it), which is now acephalus] // q[ua]n[do] ho[mi]num [dis]positiones non solum uoce prolatas uer[um] et[iam] cogitatione conceptas, cum signa quedam ex animo exprimuntur in corpore ... Sed utrum quedam signa ex corpore ... ista cognoscant aut difficillime potest ab hominibus aut omnino non potest inueniri [Augustine, *Retractationes* I, c. 30 (*De diuinatione daemonum*): PL 32, col. 643 (this extract also cited in Gratian, *Decretum*: PL 187, col. 1345B)].

There are several interlinear glosses by a different *s.* xii$^{2\text{–}ex}$ hand (e.g. 'l[icet]] cognoscere' to 'contrahere' [PL, col. 666, l. 61]; 's[cilicet] angelorum' to 'illorum').

Scribes and Script

The surviving fragments are the work of a single scribe, writing a neat, rectilinear, formal, transitional book hand which has a Gothic matrix but retains certain Romanesque features and spacing; the bowls of letters, for instance, remain fairly plump despite the rectilinearity of their contours. The words were invariably placed about 0.5 mm above the ruled lines. The extensive red rubrics within the text were done by the same scribe in the same script. Most marginal rubrics are also presented in the same script, though one (still by the same scribe), identifying Augustine as the authority for the relevant passage, is partly minuscule, partly rustic capitals ('de AUG'). The main text is fairly heavily abbreviated. Punctuation: *punctus elevatus* (for minor pauses) and low point (for major and minor ones). Double 'i's are 'dashed'; Tironian 'et' is invariably used.

A second contemporary hand added occasional interlinear glosses.

Decoration

Each section is headed by a two- to three-lines-high red capital, lightly but competently flourished in blue (or vice versa); marginal guide-letters for a couple of these survive. There is an original, formal running heading in the upper margin of both sides of fragment 1 ('L[iber]' on the verso of the opening, 'II' on the recto). It is probable that, as in MS Rawlinson C.163 (a broadly coeval copy of the text to which the present manuscript was in many respects – including all other aspects of its visual articulation – closely comparable), the beginning of each of the four books would have been marked by a 'Channel Style' decorated initial.

History

A nondescript medieval hand subsequently added supplementary running headings to the upper margin, identifying the Distinctiones ('Distinctio 1[a]'; 'Distinctio 7', etc.): as this system of divisions was only devised in 1223x7 (in Paris), the work must be later than that, but it is otherwise undatable. Fragment 1 comes from PRC 17/47 the register of wills from the Archdeaconry Court for 1586–9; fragments 2 and 3 are from PRC 32/36, the register of wills from the Consistory Court from 1586–90/91.

Commentary

Born near Novara in Lombardy, and educated at Bologna, Reims and in the school of Saint-Victor, Peter Lombard taught in the cathedral school at Paris from 1140, becoming bishop there in 1159; he died very shortly thereafter. His four *Books of the*

Sentences, completed *c.* 1150–2, treat respectively: I) God; II) the creation and nature of angels (good and bad) and of man, including the problem of sin; III) the Incarnation and Redemption; and IV) the Sacraments and the Four Last Things – Death, Judgement, Hell and Heaven. Each book consists of a long series of related questions or issues, for and against which scriptural, canonical and patristic authorities are cited, leading to a resolution on the matter. The present fragment begins within a discussion of the purpose of making rational sentient beings, to which one answer is: to achieve knowledge, and hence love of the supreme good, God – leading on to the proposition that as man was made to serve God, so the world was created to serve man. Its second half contains part of the debate on the nature of angels. Peter Lombard reviews the time and place of their creation (they did not exist before the creation of time), their initial character, and then their good and bad (fallen) states – the former continue to fulfil their divine missions, the latter – some of whom are dispatched to Hell to torment the damned – may grow in evil, while retaining their intellect and free will.

The popularity of the *Sententiae* was immediate and lasting: it became the standard companion to matters of faith and belief, and was itself the subject of innumerable commentaries (see, e.g., Canterbury Cathedral Library, Lit. A. 13: Duns Scotus (**no.** 34)). No library of any account was without the work – often in multiple copies – and it has reasonably been said that 'no book save the Bible was copied and commented upon so often between 1150 and 1500' (Knowles 1988, p.165). The point is underlined by the late medieval library catalogue of Saint Augustine's Abbey, Canterbury, which includes nearly forty full or partial copies of the work (nos. 499–536: James 1903, pp. 253–5). The numerous entries for the *Sententiae* scattered through the early fourteenth-century catalogue of Christ Church books show equally clearly how many individuals possessed copies of the work – often alongside Peter Comestor's *Historia scholastica* (cf. **no.** 40) – which subsequently passed to their institution (e.g. James 1903, list II, nos. 601, 724, 1085, 1172, 1220, 1247, etc.). That the present manuscript belonged to a centre which had – or at least had access to – other, younger copies, against which it was 'collated' is shown by the added *distinctio* references.

Now, although this copy is fragmentary in the extreme, the extant pieces do preserve several generous margins – all of which, it should be noted, are entirely free of subsequent commentary and annotation. In this respect, the manuscript may be contrasted with the many other copies, such as Oxford, Bodleian Library, MS Bodley 695 (SC 2511) (*s.* xii/xiii; late medieval provenance ?Selby) and MS Bodley 746 (SC 2768) (*s.* xiii; late medieval provenance, Saint Augustine's Abbey), which have margins teeming with multiple layers of glossing in more or less informal hands; and once again, it may be compared with MS Rawlinson C.163, where the equally generous margins likewise remain almost completely empty, apart from the occasional late medieval reference number or short note. Whilst a lack of annotation does not show that such volumes were unused, it does imply that they were spared the generations of scholastic or pedagogical attention that was manifestly the fate of their heavily annotated, slightly younger 'cousins'. One might cautiously infer on these grounds that the present manuscript rapidly became an institutional library copy. It is impossible not to mention the fact that Christ Church had a copy of the work that was believed to have belonged to Thomas Becket: 'Sententie Longobardi' is listed under the *libri Sancti Thome* in the early fourteenth-century library catalogue (James 1903, p. 83, no. 806). Assuming the association was correct, the manuscript in question must have been written by 1170 and is unlikely to have seen heavy scholastic use. One may at least note that the appearance of the present fragments is not inconsistent with these putative circumstances, and is just compatible with the date; more than that cannot be said.

38 PRC 49/6/1–2

Canones
?France; *saec.* XII$^{4/4}$
Illustration: complete folio, hair side

Physical Description
Two substantial contiguous horizontal strips from a single bifolium which have been re-joined, thereby reconstituting a near-complete sheet: one folio is virtually intact, the other has sustained losses to the outer column of text. With the exception of the area around the cut (partly obscured on one side by a gauze support), what remains is in fairly good condition, with moderate wear and staining. The bifolium (which is preserved in an open as opposed to folded state) originally stood at the centre of its quire. The parchment is of modest quality, with a clear distinction between the hair and flesh sides, and pronounced follicle marks. Present size of sheet: 242 × 307 mm. Size of the best preserved folio: 241 × 160 mm. Written area: 187 × 122 mm. Two columns (width 53 mm). Lines: 37, 38. Space between lines: 5 mm. Height of minims: 1.8–2 mm. Pricked in both margins. Ruled in lead (all the horizontals run across the intercolumnar space). Written above top line.

Content
A seemingly unique canonical collection. The calendar of content follows the original order of the pages (which are unnumbered); *distinctio*, *capitulum* and column references are provided to Friedberg (ed.) 1879.
[Complete folio, hair side] // sexta sinodus canones fecit. Sciant ... ecclesiasticos promulgaret. Item sancta sinodus vi ... Ex his ergo colligitur quod vi sinodus bis congregata est primo sub constantino filio eius [sic] et prefatos canones promulgauit, vnde sancti patres in eadem sinodo congregati dixerunt. [Prima pars, D 16 q 6, with dp: cols. 43–4.] *Constitutiones vi sinodi.* Quoniam sancte uniuersales sinodi v, sub iustiniano augusto, vi, ... imperialem urbem sacros canones conscripsimus. Item. Placuit

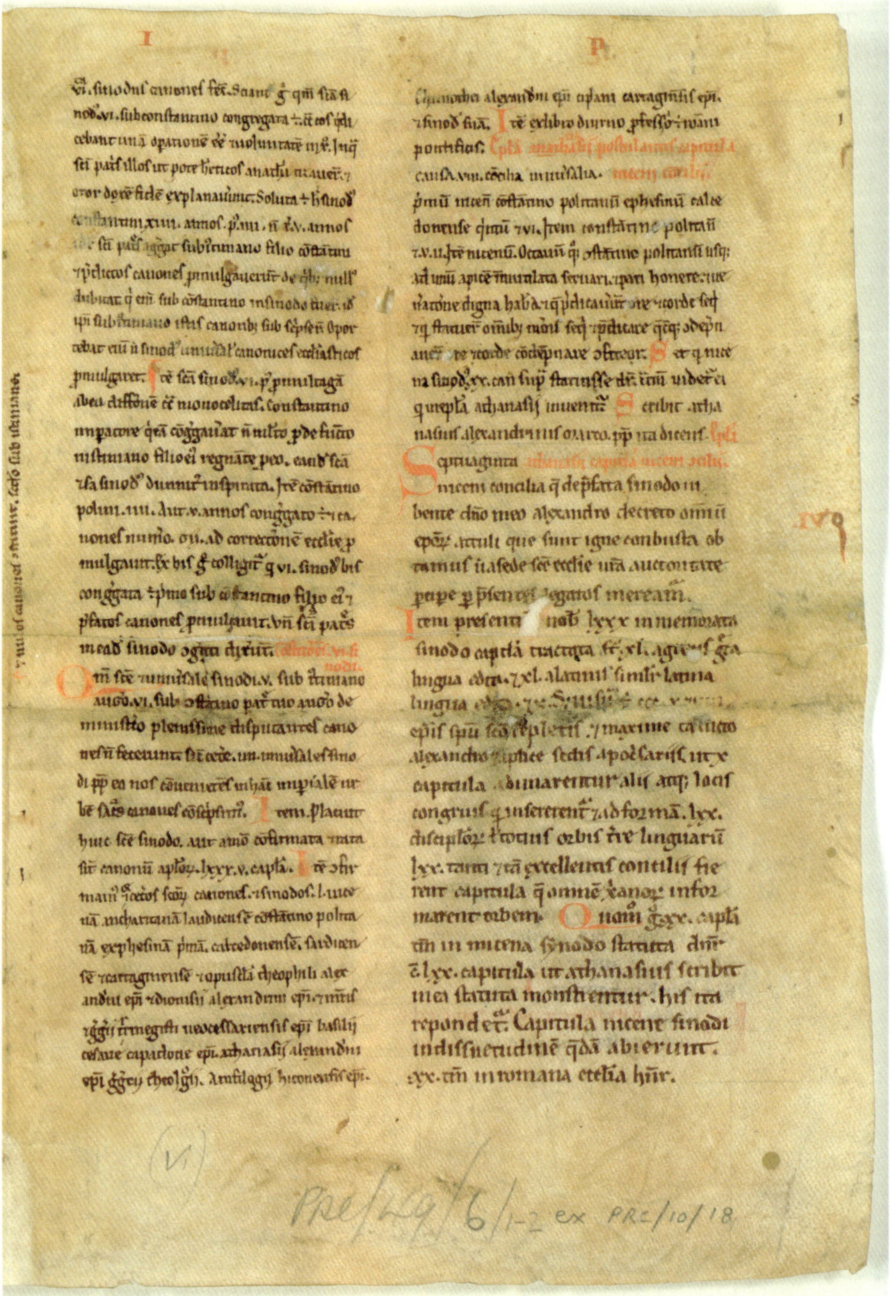

huic sancte sinodo, ... canonum apostolorum lxxx.v. capitula. Item confirmamus et ceteros sanctorum canones, et sinodos ... et sinodam suam. [D 16 c 7: cols. 44–5.]
Item ex libro diurno professio est romani pontificis. *Epistola anathasii* [corrected by original hand to *athanasii*] *postulantis capitula niceni concilii.* causa viii, concilia uniuersalia, primum ... et corde condempnare confiteor. [D 16 c 8, but rubric is from c 12: cols. 45/49.]
Set [sic] quod nicena sinodus xx ... ita dicens. [dp c 11.]
Epistola athanasii capitula uiceni niceni concilii. Septuaginta niceni concilia [sic] que de prefata sinodo iubente domino meo alexandro decreto ... per presentes legatos mereamur. Item presenti[bus] nobis lxxx [sic] in memorata sinodo capitula tracta sunt ... informarent orbem. Quomodo ergo xx capitula tantum ... in romana ecclesia habentur. [D 16 c 12 and dp: col. 49.]
[Complete folio, flesh side] Vnde stephanus papa [–?–] magun\m/tino episcopo scribit dicens. *Niceni concilii uiginti* [–?–] *capitula habentur.* Viginti tantum capitula in sancta Romana ecclesia habentur ... concilia [sic] inserta. [D 16 c 13: col. 50.]
Cardicense [sic] quoque concilium auctoritate nicholai pape recipitur. Vnde idem scribit constantinopolitano. *Auctoritate apostolica sardicensi concilii* [sic] *recipitur.* Quod dicitis neque sardicense concilium neque decretalia ... non reciperet [with 'VI' in margin] [D 16 c 14: col. 50] se non alia concilia quo tempore celebrata sunt uel quorum auctoritas certis premineat sanctorum auctoritatibus supra monstratum ... apostolicam sedem. [Jumbled version of d a D 17 c 1.]
Vnde marcellus papa [scribit] maxentio episcopo. [This section rubbed, damaged and difficult to read.] *Absque* [or: *Atque*] *romani pontificis auctoritate sinodus congregari non debet.* Sinodus episcoporum absque huius sedis auctoritate ... regulariter facere. [D 17 c 1: col. 50, without the Palaea that follows in the printed edition.]
[ ]tem iulius papa orientalibus episcopis. *Non est ratum concilii* [sic] *quod auctoritate Romane ecclesie fultum est.* Regula nostra [sic] nullos [corrected to 'nullas'] uires habet ... fultum auctoritate. [D 17 c 2: col. 51.]

Item damasius [sic]. *Nullus usurpet concessa romane ecclesie.* Huic sedi concessa nullus usurpare sine … ut [sic] contemptor iudicari. [D 17 c 3: col. 51.]
Item aug' [sic] *Absque apostolica auctoritate sinodum aliquibus congregare non licet.* Non licuit aliquando nec licebit … opprimi potestates. [D 17 c 4: col. 51] [Damaged portion] … quod in subscriptione quadam in concilio quodam habito … mediolanensis archiepiscopus ante rauennatem subscripsisse et respondisse legitur. Ex quo et sedis prerogatiuam ante eum habere colligitur. [cf d p D 17 c 6: cols. 52–3.]
Ait enim Gregorius Siagrio episcopo Augustinense. Episcopos secundum ordinationes [sic] sue tempus siue ad sidendum [sic] ordinum uendicare [sic]. Verum tempus ordinationis non ad ecclesias … euidenter apparet. Episcoporum igitur concilia ut ex premissis apparet. Episcoporum **[incomplete folio, flesh side]** igitur concilia expissis [sic] apparet, sunt inualida … specialiter obseruari preceptum. [D 17 c 7 and dp; d a D 18 c 1: col. 53, etc.]
Vnde Leo papa Thessalicensi episcopo. *Bini conuentus* … [damaged]. De conciliis autem episcopalibus non aliud uidimus [sic] … ad nostram cognitionem quicquid est illud referatur. [D 18 c 2: col. 54.]
Item ex niceno concilio. *Quo tempore episcoporum concilia sunt celebranda.* Habeatur semel concilium ante dies quadragesime … circa tempus autumpni. [D 18 c 3: col. 54.]
Item ex concilio antioceno. *Ad morum correctionem … concilium episcopale confiat.* Propter ecclesiasticas causas et que existunt … permissum iudicium. [D 18 c 4: col. 54.]
Item ex concilio Laudicensi [rubric obscured by gauze; part of text lost].
Non oportet uocatos episcopos ad … nisi forte ire non possint. [D 18 c 5: col. 55.]
Item [ex concilio cal]cedonensi. [Rubric rubbed and cropped.] Peruenit ad nostras aures quod in [outer part of each line lost] … hoc maxime cum sui corporis // **[Incomplete folio, hair side]** \\sistentes cum et [sic] ab omnibus aliis urgentibus [inner edge of each line lost] … admonitionibus corripi. [D 18 c 6: col. 55.]
[Trimmed] \\ Leo papa iiii. *Non cogantur presbiteri ad sancta*

concilia eulogias ferre. [D]e eulogiis ad sancta concilia deferendis nichil inuenimus ... delate respuende. [D 18 c 8: col. 56.]
Item [e]x concilio martini pape. *Presbiteri et diaconi et cuncti qui se lesos existimant ad metropolit[anam?] sinodum conueniant* [very rubbed]. Propter ecclesiasticas causas et altercationes' [sic] bene placuit per singulas prouincias bis in an- [outer edge of each line lost] quibus me[tropoles] sunt credite. [–lost–] inguli [sic – for 'Singuli'] uero episcoporum cli [for clericis?] [–lost–] -care studeant quod in conciliis sta// [D 18 c 15 with dp c 16: cols. 57–8.]
Unde in tol[etan]o concilio. *Que in conciliis* [–lost–] *singuli episcoporum singulis notificent ecclesiis.* [Start of each line lost] //mus ut dum in qualibet prouintia [sic] ... curriculo persistat usquequaque multatus. [D 18 c 17: col. 58.]
Idem precepta apostolica tanquam ex ore petri apostolorum principis prolata sint seruanda his auctoritatibus probantur. Ait enim agatho p[apa] omnibus episcopis. *Omnes apostolice sedis sanctiones irrefragab[il]iter sunt seruande.* Sic omnes apostolice sedis sanctiones accipiende sunt, ... firmate [cf. D 19 c 2: col. 60.]
Item ex concilio caroli imperatoris. *Tolerandum est iugum quod sancta sede inponitur licet inportabile uideatur.* In memoriam b[eat]i petri apostoli honoremus sanctam romanam ecclesiam ... uel in aliam custodiam // **[end of leaf]**. [D 19 c 3: cols. 60–1.]

Scribes and Script

The sheet appears to preserve the work of two scribes. They have similar, hasty but quite legible 'notary' book hands, the work of the first being more compressed and slightly less tidy than that of the second. Scribe 1 was responsible for the first page (i.e. the hair side of the complete folio) up to line 12 of column 2. Scribe 2 was responsible for the rest. Of the specific letter-forms that distinguish the two hands, the most noticeable is 'g' (scribe 1 invariably terminates its tail with a distinct serif or cross-stroke, whereas scribe 2 generally renders the tail as one continuous curving stroke); moreover, scribe 1 was more scrupulous in using 'dashes' to signal word-breaks across lines than was scribe 2. In both stints, the text is heavily abbreviated, double 'i' is 'dashed', and Tironian 'et' is regularly used. Punctuation in the surviving sections is limited to low point (used for major and minor pauses). Rubrics are in the same script as the main text. Some of the many minor variants from the printed edition are transcriptional errors, though how many of them should be imputed to the scribes of the present fragment, as opposed to their exemplar(s), is unclear.

Decoration

None. Each section is headed by a one-and-a-half to two-lines-high red initial set in, or projecting into the margin. Subsections are introduced by one-line-high red capitals within the written area. Guide-letters for many of the initials and capitals survive in the margins; whereas those for the former were invariably written in red ink, all those for the latter were done in ordinary (black-brown) ink. In the upper margin of each page are 'I' and 'P' in red capitals.

History

As recorded by a pencil annotation on the sheet itself, the fragment was recovered from PRC 10/18, the archdeaconry court register for 1587–8 ('Awgore'). 'VI' was also pencilled on the sheet; it is not clear to what this refers.

39 Add. 128/48

Officium/Inhumatio defuncti (presumably from a Sacramentary or Missal)
England; *saec.* XII^{ex}.
Illustration: fol. 2r

Physical Description

One bifolium and one folio, mounted thus within a modern guard-folder and foliated in modern pencil '1'–'3'. The original order of the leaves was: 2, 1, 3, i.e. the bifolium is folded inside-out; it has clearly been thus for a long time – probably since it was re-used. All the leaves are very darkened and weathered; they are particularly discoloured and dirty around what is, or was, the gutter. Maximum size: 192 × 142 mm. Written area: 135 × 88 mm. Lines: 20. Space between lines: 8 mm. Height of main text minims: 2.5 mm. Height of the minims for the cues: 2 mm. Ruling: seemingly hard point, but possibly lead, the graphite having faded away.

Content

Officium/Inhumatio defuncti. Reference is made to the Westminster Missal (Wickham Legg 1891–3) and the Missal of Robert of Jumièges (Wilson 1896): WM and RJ respectively.
[Fol. 2r] [acephalus] // eternus amator es, animam famuli tui, N., quam uera dum in corpore maneret tenuit fides ... ut segregata ab infernalibus claustris, sanctorum tuorum mereatur adunari consortiis. Per. [Per Christum amen, added in the margin in a s. xii/xiii–xiii^{in} hand] [WM, III, col. 1294].
Absolut[i]o. Absoluimus te, N, uice sancti petri apostolorum principis, ... omnium peccatorum tuorum indultor. [cf. WM II, col. 571]
De terra plasmasti me...in nouissimo die. Domine probasti me.
Oratio. Te domine sancte pater omnipotens eterne deus supplices deprecamur ... dare ei **[fol. 2v]** locum lucidum, ... immortalitatis tue uitam et regnum consequatur eternum. Per. [cf. WM III, col. 1294; also RJ, p. 297].
A[*ntiphona*]. Non intres in iuditium cum seruo tuo ... uiuens [WM III, col. 1295]. *P*[*salmus*]. Domine exaudi.

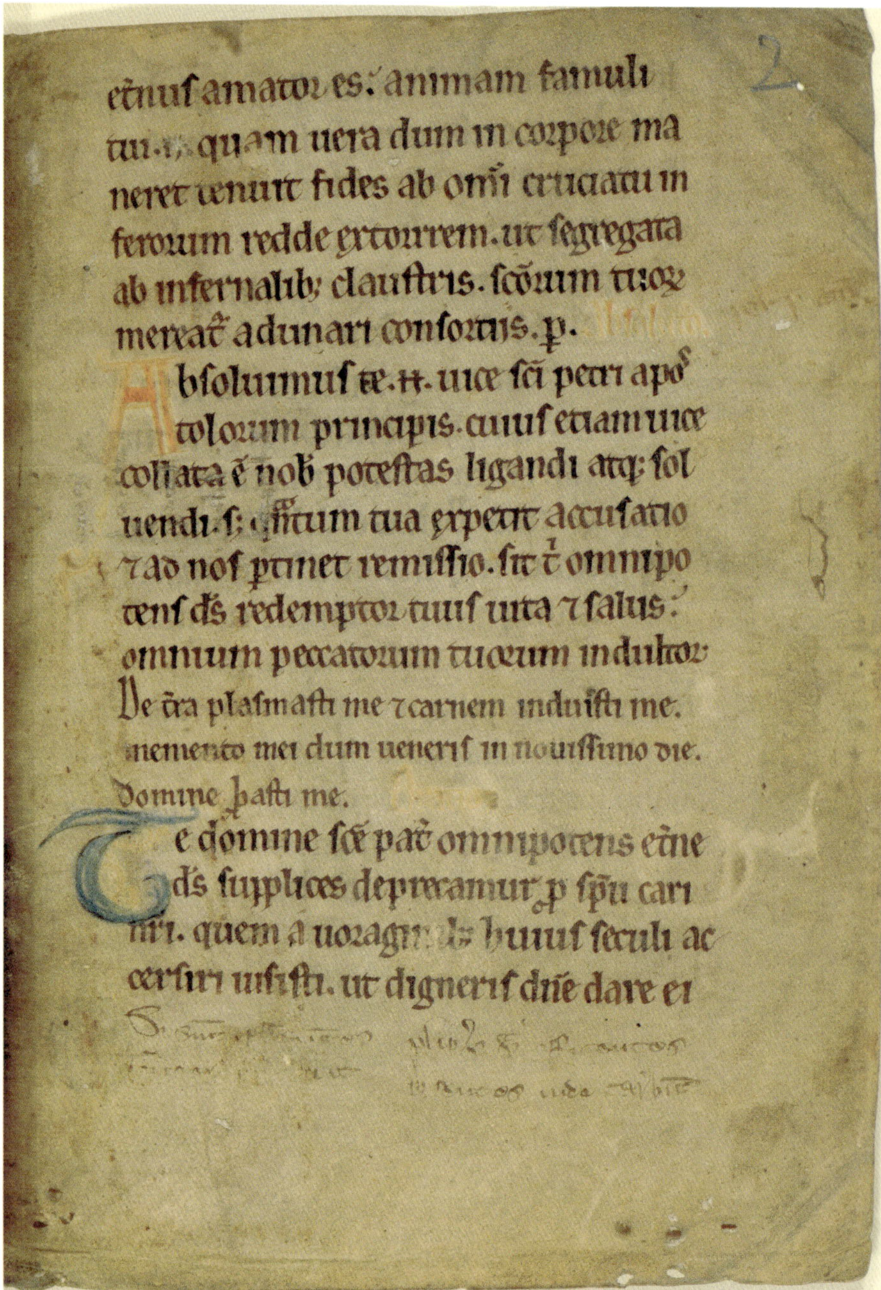

eternus amator es. animam famuli
tui .N. quam uera dum in corpore ma
neret tenuit fides ab omni cruciatu in
ferorum redde extorrem. ut segregata
ab infernalibus claustris. sanctorum tuorum
mereatur adunari consortiis. per.
Absolvimus te .N. uice sancti petri apo
stolorum principis. cuius etiam uice
collata est nobis potestas ligandi atque sol
uendi. sed quantum tua expetit accusatio
et ad nos pertinet remissio. sit tibi omnipo
tens deus redemptor tuus uita et salus.
omnium peccatorum tuorum indultor.
De terra plasmasti me et carnem induisti me.
memento mei dum ueneris in nouissimo die.
Domine probasti me.
Te domine sancte pater omnipotens eterne
deus supplices deprecamur pro spiritu cari
nostri. quem a uoraginibus huius seculi ac
cersiri iussisti. ut digneris domine dare ei

Oratio. Deus apud quem mortuorum spiritus uiuunt, ... supplicantibus nobis, ut **[fol. 1r]** anima famuli tui, N, que temporali per corpus uisionis huius luminis ... optate quietis consequatur gaudia repromissa. Per dominum nostrum. [RJ, p. 301; WM III, col. 1295]
A[*ntiphona*]. Omnis spiritus laudet dominum. *P*[*salmus*]. Laudate dominum de celis.
Oratio. Omnipotentis dei misericordiam deprecemur ... collocare dig- **[fol. 1v]** -netur, prestante domino nostro Ihesu Christo qui cum eo uiuit et regnat. [WM III, col. 1296]
Oratio. Tu nobis domine auxilium prestare digneris, ... flammasque tartari in regione uiuentium euadat. Per dominum nostrum. [RJ, p. 296; WM III, col. 1296]
V[*ersus*]. Requiem eternam dona eis domine. Et lux perpetua luceat eis. *A*[*ntiphona*]. Omne quod dat michi pater ad me ueniet et eum qui uenit ad me non eiciam foras. *P*[*salmus*]. *Benedictus*. Pater noster. Et ne nos. Non intres in iuditium. Quia. A porta inferi. Erue domine animas eorum.
Oratio. Domine sancte pater omnipotens eterne deus qui unicum filium tuum **[end of fol. 1v; fol. 3r]** dominum nostrum Ihesum Christum, incarnari constituisti, ... et beate requiei ac lucis eterne felicitate perfrui **[fol. 3v]** prestante eodem domino nostro Ihesu Christo, qui uenturus est iudicare uiuos et mortuos et seculum per ignem. [Amen – rewritten at a slightly later date] [cf. WM III, col. 1297].
Temeritatis quidem est domine ut homo hominem cinis cinerem, mortalis mortuum ... Et quae illi sunt domine cruciatibus culpe, tu // [end of page; WM III, col. 1298; RJ, p. 302].

Scribes and Script

A single scribe was responsible for all the original text, using a fairly formal yet flowing, upright, early Gothic book hand. Notable forms include the gently tapering nature of many of the downstrokes, and a 't' whose cross-strokes invariably start with a little tick. The cues are written in the same script to a smaller scale. The rubrics, done in red, have more or less faded away, but also seem to be in the same script. Stylised rustic capitals head sentences. Punctuation: low point (for major and minor pauses) and *punctus elevatus* (for minor pauses). Tironian 'et' is invariably used. Double 'i's are 'dashed'. Occasional 'acute' accents (e.g. the pair on the 'a's in Ysaac, fol. 1r).

A near-contemporary hand (?*s.* xii/xiii⁺) made a minor addition to the outer margin of fol. 2r.

A two-line addition was made to the lower margin of fol. 2r in a poor and now virtually illegible, *s.* xiv–xv cursive hand. Further jottings of approximately the same date, possibly by the same hand and now equally difficult to read, appear in the lower margins of fols. 1v and 3r.

Decoration

The principal sections are headed by two- to three-lines-high red or blue capitals which are slightly embellished; some were modestly flourished in the other colour. The workmanship is fairly crude. A couple of these initials (fol. 1v, T; fol. 2r, T) were clearly re-worked at a later date, though it is impossible to say exactly when. Small guide-letters are visible below the 'D' on fol. 2v and the 'T' on fol. 3v.

History

Written at the end of the twelfth century, these pages received minor emendation within a couple of generations (the added concluding formula on fol. 2r and the re-written 'Amen' on fol. 3v); some of the capitals were re-worked then or subsequently. Jottings were made in three of the margins in the later Middle Ages. The leaves are said to have been taken from the binding of a register of 1468 (Ker 1977) which, if correct, strongly suggests – though falls short of proving – that the volume had been broken up and its sheets were being re-cycled in the fifteenth century, by which time it was presumably imperfect and/or outdated.

40 Add. 128/10

Peter Comestor, *Historia scholastica*
England or France; *saec.* XII/XIII
Illustration: fol. 1r

Physical Description

Two consecutive folios, mounted in a modern guard-book. Both are darkened, damaged, and bear the scars of folding, as a result of being re-used as covers. The inner edges are particularly tattered and irregular, much of the inner margin being lost. Portions are missing or very abraded within the main body of the leaves; the most damaged faces (fols. 1v and 2r) have been covered in protective gauze.

Size: 440 × 330 mm. Written area: 390 × 220 mm (written above top line). Two columns (column width: 90 mm). Lines per page: 32. Space between lines: 9 mm. Height of minims: 5 mm. Ruled in lead. When complete, assuming that it contained the *Historia scholastica* alone (and none of the 'supplements' that often accompany s. xiii copies) and was not an abridgement, the volume would have comprised around 375 leaves; even if it was one part of a two- or three-volume set of the work, the total number of leaves will have been the same. This was a very substantial production.

Content

Peter Comestor, *Historia scholastica: Historia libri II Machabaeorum*, from cap. XI (acephalus) to the start of cap. XX.
[Fol. 1r] //boli, pro castellorum traditione. Post hec cum gabinus apud egyptum detineretur, alexander, aristobuli filius, iudeos, iterum ad dis[sensionem reduxit] [PL 198, col. 1530A, line 2] ... **[fol. 2v ends:]** Cumque herodem et fratres eius aliis pretulisset, hilaratus anto// [PL 198, col. 1533B, line 18].

Scribes and Script

The pages are seemingly the work of a single master-scribe, writing a monumental, very high quality, early Gothic book hand of

boli. pro castellorum traditione.
Post hec cum gabinius apud e
giptum detineretur: alexander a
ristoboli filius. iudeos. iterum ad de
[illegible]
[illegible] et pacem [illegible] et hyrcano
pontificatum confirmavit. Quo
mortuo: missus est preses syrie cras
sus: ut contra parthos quia iam ro
ma[illegible] repmuerit.
In[illegible] parthice militie [illegible]
fe[illegible] de templo tulit [illegible]
[illegible] pompeius prius abstinuerat: duo
[illegible]. Ob hoc autem in
[illegible] interiit. Cui successit
preses syrie cassius. qui in omnibus
consilio antipatris utebatur.

[illegible] aristoboli in syriam et [illegible]

[E]o tempore [illegible]
factum est dissidium inter
romanos pro pompeio et iulio ce
sare. Cesar autem post senatus et
pompei fugam transmare ioni
um. rebus omnibus romaque potitus:
[illegible]tum aristobolum cum duabus co
[hor]tibus in syriam misit. facile per
[eu]m iudeam sibi posse subici ratus.
[V]erum spes cesaris. frustrata est.
[Na]m a studiosis pompei perit aristo
[illegible] veneno. servatumque corpus eius mel
le conditum. prohibita sepultura: donec
iussu antonii in monumentis re
galibus sepultus est. Occiditur
quoque filius eius alexander antio
chie a scipione securi percussus secundum
pompeii litteras: accusatione pro bel
[illegible] que uito
riano. admiserat. Solus autem su
perstes antigonus: cum sororibus suis
ad quendam ptolomeum mennei
filium qui sub libano morabatur
confugit. acceptique ptolomeus in
nomine sororis alexandram uxorem. Ex
qua ut quidam tradunt: suscepit li
saniam abiline postea tetrarcham.

[illegible]

Post hec factum est prelium
in emathia: cui interfuit
antipater. et sub pompeio iudei.
Qui cum redisset in iudeam. ti
mens cesaris imperium: liberos su
os ad arabes cognatos eorum trans
misit. Mortuo autem pompeio: an
tipater in clientelam cesaris se con
tulit. Misit autem cesar mitri
datem pergamenum ad expugnan
dum pelusium. mittens cum eo in
colam libani ptolomeum: et anti
patrum cum tribus milibus iudeorum.
Ubi virtus antipatri plurimum e
nituit. Nam et murum primus trans
cendit. et memphitas ad obse
quendum cesari prudentia sua

formidable regularity: this is Gothic script at its most stately and legible. Framed by enormous margins, the text is spaciously presented, with (on the whole) generous gaps between individual words. Letters are characterised by a regular rectilinear matrix, and are articulated by diamond-shaped or triangular heads, and wedge-shaped, lined or rising feet. Rubrics are by the same scribe, in the same script. Sentence capitals (one line high) are emphasised by the addition of simple yet elegant calligraphic details. Abbreviation is used sparingly. Punctuation: low point (for major and minor pauses) and *punctus elevatus* (for minor pauses). Double 'i's are dashed; some vowels are stressed by very thin 'acute' accents. Occasionally, a thin comma-like stroke was inserted to indicate word separation where it might otherwise be ambiguous.

A couple of corrections were made *in rasura* by the same or a similar hand (e.g. fol. 2v, col. 1).

Decoration

Each chapter is headed by a large (three- to nine-lines-high) penwork initial done in red, green or yellow, modestly flourished in red, yellow or blue.

Given that this is a very high grade manuscript on which no expense has been spared, it might logically be presumed that each book (and the general Preface) would have been headed by a decorated initial, with particularly elaborate examples at the beginning of the work proper (*Imperatorie*) and for the start of Genesis (*In principio*). This is exactly what we find in broadly contemporary copies from English collections such as British Library, MSS Royal 2 C. i (Rochester; xiii^{in}), 4 D. vii (Saint Albans; pre 1215) and 7 F. iii (Elstow; 1191–2). Thus in the Rochester manuscript – which is much smaller and altogether more economically conceived than the present item – each chapter is headed by a modest flourished initial, each book by a 'Channel Style' letter set against a gold ground; while both the start of the work and *In principio* are marked by large decorated initials. That such was not invariably the case, however, is shown by the early thirteenth-century copy of Christ Church provenance, Cambridge, Trinity College, MS B. 15. 5: though the volume is a handsome one in general terms, the beginnings of the individual books are marked merely by red and blue flourished initials (a slightly larger version of those used for sub-sections), with a single grander initial, part-decorated, part-flourished, for *In principio*.

History and Provenance

Beyond the self-evident fact that the present manuscript was written in a major centre by a very skilful scribe and was surely destined for a high-status context, there is no evidence concerning its origin. Its medieval history is obscure: there were plenty of copies of the work in Canterbury (see **Commentary**) and it is not unlikely that this was one of them; however, it is currently impossible to demonstrate that such was the case. If the early modern history of the leaves could be established, their medieval provenance might reasonably be inferred therefrom, but unfortunately this, too, is a blank. They were evidently used as covers, and Ker (1977, p. 319) stated that they contained an (unspecified) 'document of 1541/2'. This may well be correct; however, as no date – or indeed any *s.* xvi reference – is inscribed on the leaves, nor is there seemingly (now) any other record of the document in question, it is difficult to pursue the matter further.

Commentary

Peter Comestor († 1178/9), a pupil of Peter Lombard (see **no.** 37), was dean of Troyes Cathedral (1147) and Chancellor of Notre Dame, Paris (1168); he finished the *Historia scholastica* between 1169 and 1173, after he had retired to the abbey of Saint-Victor. Although dedicated to William aux Blanches-mains, archbishop of Sens (1168–75), the work was written, the author tells us, in response to the repeated requests of his *socii* for a reference work on biblical history. Following the basic biblical narrative from Genesis to the gospels (to which a treatment of Acts was added by a *discipulus*, identified in British Library, MS Stowe 5 as Peter of Poitiers), the *Historia* provided a comprehensive commentary on events from the Creation to the Ascension, focusing on their literal/historical sense, and it rapidly became the standard work on biblical history. Events featured in the present fragment include Herod becoming prefect of Galilea, the death of Julius Caesar, and Herod and Phasaelus being made tetrarchs of Juda by Mark Antony.

The formidable number of surviving manuscripts of the work (more than 800 in total: Sylwan 2000, p. 351), along with translations and commentaries, attests to its phenomenal circulation. Possibly accorded the status of a textbook for clerks in the aftermath of the Third Lateran Council (1179) (Sylwan 2000, pp. 348–9), the *Historia* certainly received official recognition at the Fourth Lateran Council (1215), and was thereafter enshrined in university curricula. If the epicentre of its popularity was northern France, the book was nevertheless owned and used widely, and in England as much as elsewhere, as the evidence of manuscripts and book-lists underlines. We know, for instance, that by the later Middle Ages, Christ Church had at least ten copies of the text (or some part thereof), while Saint Augustine's Abbey had twice that number. A complete copy from each centre can still be identified: Cambridge, Trinity College, MS B. 15. 5 (*s.* xiii^{in}) from the former; London, British Library, MS Harley 4132 (*s.* xiv) from the latter. The library catalogues show equally clearly how frequently the work featured among the acquisitions of specific individuals, being subsequently passed to their institutions (see, e.g., James 1903, list II, nos. 1046, 1060, 1171, 1219, 1340, etc.). Manuscript and documentary evidence also reveals that, from an early date, some of the individuals in question were layfolk: Troyes, Bibliothèque municipale 290, for example, is a two-volume copy of the work that was written for the Counts of Champagne, sometime between 1185 and 1200.

The present fragment – from a copy made about a generation after the text was 'published' – is part of the considerable body of evidence for the rapidity with which it was disseminated, a phenomenon that accelerated in the thirteenth century. At the same time, the high-grade script, spacious layout and extremely generous format reflect not only the respect with which the work was already regarded in general but also, surely, the special importance of this particular manuscript. The broadly contemporary copies mentioned above, for instance, are all significantly smaller and altogether less imposing (Cambridge, Trinity College, MS B. 15. 5: 350 × 260 mm (214 × 158), 2 cols., 38 lines; British Library, MSS Royal 2 C. i: 322 × 218 mm (218 × 132), 2 cols. 52 lines; Royal 4 D. vii: 373 × 255 mm (232 × 135), 2 cols. 50 lines; Royal 7 F. iii: 350 × 250 mm (236 × 142), 2 cols. 45 lines). Even the copy that belonged to the counts of Champagne was of moderate dimensions (324 × 232 mm), albeit handsomely presented. The prodigality of the Canterbury leaves – and, correspondingly, the more economical conception of the other copies – is underlined by detailed comparison with the largest of the English manuscripts mentioned above, MS Trinity B. 15. 5, itself spaciously set out with generous margins: what in the present manuscript covers four pages, there occupies just over two (fol. 167r, col. 2, line 21 – 168r, col. 2, line 32). One of the very few manuscripts of the work that rivals ours in terms of sheer size is the copy made at Corbie in 1183 by 'One-Eyed John' (Johannis monoculus), as the colophon on fol. 190v attests, which measures 460 × 315 mm with a written area of 360 × 225 mm (BnF, MS lat. 16943). Yet with 45 lines per pages, spaced at 8 mm and with minims 3–3.5 mm high, it does not have the grandeur of the present book; nor, with its elaborate but qualitatively modest decoration, can it rival its elegance.

Whereas many copies, e.g. Bodleian Library, MS Laud. Misc. 446 (SC 1318; *s.* xiii^{in}), are broadly reminiscent in format and presentation of medium-format early Gothic Bibles (in this case measuring 315 × 220 mm, written area 243 × 160 mm, two columns of 44 lines) – to which they were, of course, companions – the present copy evokes instead the giant 'communal' Bibles of earlier generations, the supreme achievements of the best Romanesque scriptoria. Indeed, so grand is this copy that it must, surely, have been prepared for a particularly important context. In the absence of information about its history, however, the individual and/or place in question are, sadly, unknown and unknowable. The most obvious candidate for sponsor or recipient of a deluxe copy of the text of such a date with an eventual Canterbury provenance would, of course, be Stephen Langton: a great admirer of the *Historia scholastica* – on which, as a Master, he composed a gloss; he was contentiously elected archbishop of Canterbury in 1206, a post he finally held from 1213–15 and 1218–28. However, only a handful of titles in the Christ Church library catalogue are specifically associated with Langton and the *Historia* is not among them. Thus, in the absence of any information about the history of our manuscript, the identity of its recipient remains a mystery.

41 Add. 127/17

Eusebius (Rufinus), *Historia ecclesiastica*
England; *saec.* XII/XIII
Illustration: fol. 1v

Physical Description
Two non-consecutive leaves (two further leaves originally stood between them), mounted separately in a modern guard-book. Both have been irregularly cut down. All the surfaces are rubbed; the faces of fols. 1r and 2v are additionally marked and stained; the gutter of fol. 1r is glue-stained along much of its length.

Size: 296 × 200 mm. Written area: 268 × 148 mm (text written above top line). Two columns (column width: 62 mm). Lines per page: 39. Space between lines: 7 mm. Height of minims: 3 mm. Ruling: lead (all the horizontals were continued across the inter-columnar space; the 1st, 3rd, 19th, 21st, 37th and 39th were extended into the outer margins). The folio references given here refer to the present order and arrangement of the leaves; note, however, that while a '1' is pencilled on the recto of the first leaf, '2' appears on what is the verso of the second.

Two other leaves apparently from the same manuscript are in the collection of M. B. Parkes (photographs in Oxford, Bodleian Library, MS Lat. Misc. b.15; cf. Parkes 1991, p. 315).

Content
Eusebius Caesariensis, *Historia ecclesiastica* (CPG 3495) (in Rufinus's Latin translation): end of the table of contents to, and two portions from the beginning of, Book V.
[**Fol. 1r**] [end of the capitula list to Book V, comprising entries xxxvi:] De montano frige ... et multa [to lxi:] Quod quamuis scripta sua ... uerum ne quis me [followed by the explicit to the capitula and the incipit to the Book proper:] *Expliciunt capitula. Incipit historie ecclesiastice liber quintus. De eo* ...[exactly filling the remainder of column two].
[**Fol. 1v**] *Capitulum primum.* IGITUR, SOTHERI episcopo octo annis in urbe roma sacerdotio ministrante, duodecimus ab

apostolis successit eleutherius septimo decimo anno imperii antonini ueri, ... ita ut primo nobis domorum prohiberetur habitatio, tum deinde usus bal// [Schwartz *et al.* 1999, I, pp. 401, ll. 1–403, l. 22; corresponds to London, British Library, MS Royal 13 B. v, fol. 56r, l. 13–fol. 56v, l. 15].

[**Fol. 2r–v**] // supplicia mitigabat spes et corona martirii, christique caritas et spiritus sancti gratia releuabat afflictos. Istos autem ... Sed cum ferarum nulla sanctorum corpora contigisset, omnibus eorum [sic] uerberum, ceterarumque pena// [Schwartz *et al.* 1999, I, pp. 415, ll. 23–423, l. 14; MS Royal 13 B. v, fol. 58v, l. 23–fol. 59v, l. 29].

A contemporary running heading – written in red, partly in capitals, partly in minuscules – appears in the upper margins of fols. 2v (LIBER) and 2r (quintus).

Manifest differences both in the way the text itself was subdivided and in the capitula lists (see **Commentary**) make it unlikely that either of the earlier Kentish copies, Cambridge, Corpus Christi College, MSS 184 and 197 (from Rochester and Christ Church respectively), was the exemplar of the present manuscript. This is confirmed by collation of the first portion of the text of Book V. Individual errors apart (the present copy, for example, has 'intunderunt sicut' for 'intenderunt sicut' and 'ministerium celeris' for 'ministerium sceleris'), Corpus MSS 184 and 187 regularly agree with each other against the readings in the Canterbury fragment, some of whose 'variants' are paralleled in the alternative traditions represented by British Library, MSS Royal 13 B. v (St Albans) and 13 B. iv (provenance unknown).

In the following summary of notable variants, the reading from the present manuscript (Cant) is always presented first; other MSS are identified by their numbers; the reading and reference in the printed edition, Schwartz *et al.* 1999, is signalled by E

Cant, 187: Sotheri [184: Sothere [E, p. 401, l. 1: Soteri.

Cant, 184, 187: successit eleutherius [R13Biv, R13Bv, E, p. 401, l.2: succedit eleutherius.

Cant, R13Biv, R13Bv: trophea, uictorias [184, 187: trophea uictoria [E, p. 401, l. 12: tropea uictorias.

Cant, 187, R13Biv, R13Bv, E, p. 401, l. 15: absurdum non crit [184: absursum non erit.
Cant: si actus et bella describat [E, p. 401, l. 16: si bella describat.
Cant: in quibus ab aduersus [184, 187, R13Biv, R13Bv: in quibus non aduersus [E, p. 401, l. 19: in quibus non aduersum.
Cant: rodanus [184, 187 hrodanus [E, p. 403, l. 4: Rhodanus.
Cant: descripta ab eis per ordinem et ad ecclesias asie [184, 187, E, p. 403, l. 6: descripta ab eis per ordinem ad ecclesiam asie [R13Biv, R13Bv: descripta per ordinem ab eis ad ecclesias asie.
Cant, R13Biv, R13 Bv: fratribus omnibus qui per asiam et frigiam eandem quam nos redemptionis christi fidem [184, 187, E, p. 403, ll. 14–15: fratribus omnibus eandem quam nos redemptionis christi fidem.
Cant: inicium. Tribulationis nostre aiunt magnitudinem [184, 187, R13Bv, E, p. 403, ll. 14–15: initium. Tribulationis aiunt nostre magnitudinem [R13Biv: initium tribulationis. Aiunt nostre presecutionis magnitudinem ....

Scribes and Script

The fragments are entirely the work of a single scribe. The script is a low to moderate-grade, early-Gothic book hand; the scribe strove neither for conspicuous regularity nor for calligraphic effect. Notable forms include the 'x' (which looks like an 'r' with a long 'tail' heading left from the bottom of its down-stroke) and the 'ur' abbreviation (which resembles an 'm'). There is much 'biting' of the letters: most letters in the majority of words touch their neighbours. Rubrics are presented in red in the same script. The fragmentary copy of Augustine, *In euangelium Iohannis*, Add 129/56 and PRC 49/3/3–5, etc. (**no.** 36) has been attributed to the same scribe (Parkes 1991, p. 315); however, the identification – at least in so far as the leaves in Canterbury are concerned – is mistaken. The text is moderately abbreviated. Punctuation is generally by low point (for major and minor pauses) and *punctus elevatus* (for minor pauses), but there is also a single 'semi-colon' (for a minor pause). Double 'i's are 'dashed'; accents are very rare (there are 'acutes' over the 'e's on fol. 1v, col. 1, l. 25 and fol. 2v, col. 1, l. 27). Sentence capitals are stylised rustics with counter-spaces washed in yellow, green and/or red; when one happened to coincide with the beginning of a new line, it was withdrawn from the written area and placed in the inner margin. The five-and-a-half lines that comprise the first part of the long citation from the 'Acta martyrum' on fol. 1 v, col. 2 (Serui christi habitantes apud uiennam et lugdunum … et christo ihesu domino nostro [Schwartz *et al.* 1999, p. 403, ll. 9–12]) are entirely 'highlighted' with yellow and green.

The individual sections in the capitula list are headed by one-line-high red, blue or green capitals, modestly flourished in one of the other colours; while the ends of short lines therein are filled with flourishes in green, brown or red. The chapter divisions within the main text are introduced by three- to five-lines-high, red or green capitals, crudely flourished in blue or red.

Decoration

The start of Book V (fol. 1 v) is marked by a large (eighteen-lines-high) decorated initial I. Though boldly conceived and eye-catching, it is a work of modest quality. The letter-form is outlined with three bands (first green, then red, then leaf gold), while its body is filled with rather irregularly drawn zigzag patterns, rendered in green, red, blue and brown, set against a black ground, all articulated with white highlights and dots. The rest of the first line (GITUR SOTHERI) is presented in calligraphic ink capitals whose counter-spaces are coloured in green or yellow.

History

There is now no evidence bearing directly on the early history of these leaves, and the circumstances of their recovery are seemingly unrecorded. However, the presumed companion leaves (see **Physical Description**) were apparently used as wrappers for legal documents in s. xvi^{med} probably in East Kent, as they eventually came into the hands of the Hill family of Ash-next-Sandwich (from whom apparently they had passed, by 1958, to M. B. Parkes). Similar re-use as covers around the same time might very reasonably, therefore, be inferred for the present leaves.

Commentary

Arranged in ten books, the *Historia ecclesiastica* of Eusebius of Caesarea († *c.* 340) recounts the history of the christian church from its beginnings with the life and work of Christ (Book I) until its triumph under Constantine, ending with his victory over Licinus (A.D. 324) (Book X). It was translated from Greek into Latin by Rufinus of Aquilea († 411), who made various editorial changes and additions; most notably, he compressed Eusebius's Book X, conflating it with Book IX, and added two further books of his own (now Books X and XI), continuing the narrative to the death of Theodosius (A.D. 395). The beginning of Book V treats the Gallic martyrs of A.D. 177; the Canterbury fragments preserve Eusebius's introductory comments and parts of his extended quotation from an account of the martyrs, dealing with the public torments of Sanctus, Marturus, Attalus, and – the most celebrated – Blandina.

The Latin version of Eusebius's *Historia ecclesiastica* was one of the small number of 'historical' works that achieved a reasonable circulation in the early medieval west – by dint of its 'international' christian significance. The work was certainly known to – indeed was an important inspiration for – Bede, and it was re-imported into England after the Viking age, as is shown by Worcester Cathedral Library, MS Q. 28, a late ninth- or early tenth-century continental copy that had reached Worcester by the eleventh century. The number of English manuscripts of the text mushrooms in the twelfth century. One of the earliest copies of this phase (Cambridge, Corpus Christi College, MS 187, dating from *c.* 1100) belonged to Christ Church; others produced around the same time or fairly shortly thereafter can be associated with Saint Albans, Rochester and Salisbury; and the work was known to England's greatest twelfth-century historian, William of Malmesbury († c. 1143) who, indeed, transcribed a portion of it (Oxford, Merton College. MS 181, fol. 230). Library lists and extant manuscripts (including the present fragment) attest to the continuing multiplication and diffusion of the text among English collections during, and beyond, the later twelfth century.

Several traditions for organising the part of the text preserved in the Canterbury fragments appear in the pre-thirteenth-century English manuscripts. In British Library, MS Royal 13 B. v (xi^{ex}–xi/xi, St Albans), whilst all the other books are preceded by chapter lists, Book V has none. The closely related Kentish copies, Cambridge, Corpus Christi College, MSS 187 and 184 have but two chapter summaries at the head of Book V; several manuscripts (e.g. London, British Library, MS Royal 13 B. iv; s. xii^{1}, provenance unknown; and Oxford, Bodleian Library, MS Laud misc. 450 (SC 1319), s. xii$^{2/3}$, Ford Abbey, Devon) have thirty-one (there are, in point of fact, thirty-one subdivisions within the actual text of Book V in Corpus Christi MS 184), while the printed edition (Schwartz *et al.*, 1999) presents twenty-eight. The present manuscript, by contrast, has sixty-one capitula summaries; moreover, it also stands apart from the other manuscripts cited by dint of being the only one to highlight visually the *Acta martyrum*.

Bibliography

Parkes 1991, p. 315.

42 Add. 128/14

Collectar
England (?Canterbury, Christ Church); *saec.* XII/XIII
Illustration: p. 8

Physical Description

One folio, one bifolium, one folio, mounted thus within a guard-folder and paginated '1'–'8'. Pages 1–4 are consecutive, as are pp. 5–8. The two singletons were doubtless once a bifolium; and originally all these leaves formed the two outer bifolia of a quire. The intact bifolium was used as a wrapper, the two folios probably as stiffener for its covers, in s. xvi$^{3/4}$. Consequently, all the faces are stained, that which served as the outside of the wrapper (pp. 4 and 5) most severely so; three pairs of slits for laces were cut into the inner margins of the bifolium.

Size: 390 × 222 mm. Written area: 240 × 155 mm (written above top line). Two columns (70 mm). Lines: 29. Space between lines: 8 mm. Height of minims in main text: 4 mm. Height of minims in cues: 2.5 mm. Pricked in both margins (only the prickings in the inner margin remain). Ruled in lead (all the horizontals continuing across the inter-columnar space). Near-contemporary catchword and a signature ('o') under the second column, and in the centre of the lower margin respectively of p. 8, indicating that this was the final leaf of the fourteenth or fifteenth quire in the book.

Content

Collects and capitula for the Monday and Wednesday after Easter (pp. 1–4), for the fourth and fifth Sundays after Easter, and for the Monday, Tuesday and Wednesday in fifth week (pp. 5–8). The collects are as follows.

[Page 1] Deus qui solennitate [sic] paschali mundo remedia contulisti ... proficiat sempiternam. Per.

Deus qui pro nobis filium tuum crucis patibulum subire uoluisti ... gratiam consequamur. Per eundem.

Gratiam tuam domine mentibus nostris infunde, ... ad resurrectionis gloriam perducamur. Per eundem.

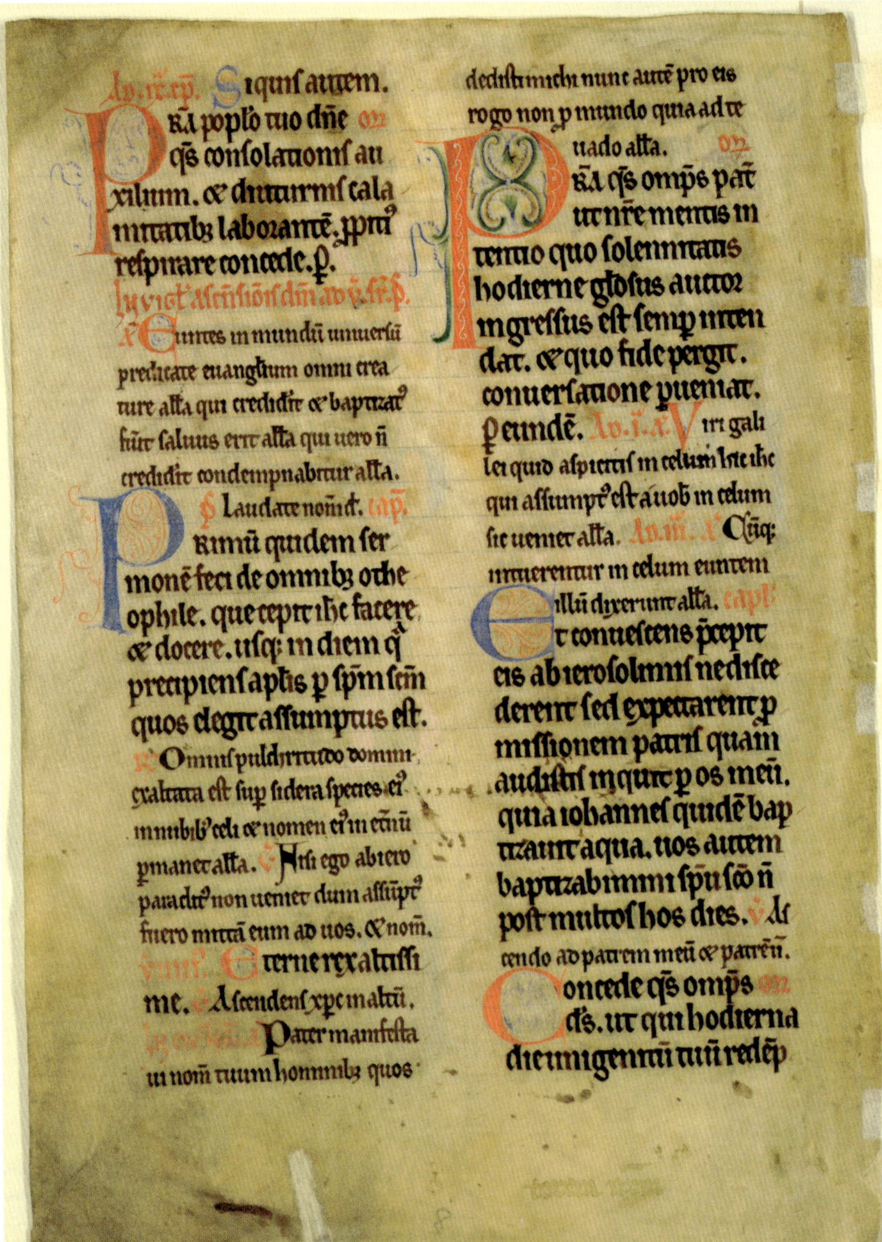

Ad .iii. cap. Siquis autem.
Presta populo tuo domine or
quesumus consolationis au
xilium. et diuturnis cala
mitatibus laborantem, propitius
respirare concede. per.
In vigilia ascensionis domini ad v. ...
Euntes in mundum uniuersum
predicate euangelium omni crea
ture alleluia qui crediderit et baptizatus
fuerit saluus erit alleluia qui uero non
crediderit condempnabitur alleluia.
Laudate nomen. cap.
Primum quidem ser
monem feci de omnibus o the
ophile. que cepit ihesus facere
et docere. usque in diem qua
precipiens apostolis per spiritum sanctum
quos elegit assumptus est.
R. Omnis pulchritudo domini
exaltata est super sidera species eius
in nubibus celi et nomen eius in eternum
permanet alleluia. V. Nisi ego abiero
paraclitus non ueniet dum assumptus
fuero mittam eum ad uos. Et nomen.
Hymnus. Eterne rex altissi
me. V. Ascendens christus in altum.
In euangelio. Pater manifesta
ui nomen tuum hominibus quos
dedisti michi nunc autem pro eis
rogo non pro mundo quia ad te
uado alleluia. or
Presta quesumus omnipotens pater
ut nostre mentis in
tentio quo solemnitatis
hodierne gloriosus auctor
ingressus est semper inten
dat. et quo fide pergit.
conuersatione perueniat.
per eundem. Ad .i. R. Viri gali
lei quid aspicitis in celum hic ihesus
qui assumptus est a uobis in celum
sic ueniet alleluia. Ad .iii. R. Cumque
intuerentur in celum euntem
illum dixerunt alleluia. capl.
Et conuescens precepit
eis ab ierosolimis ne discederent sed expectarent pro
missionem patris quam
audistis per os meum.
quia iohannes quidem bap
tizauit aqua. uos autem
baptizabimini spiritu sancto non
post multos hos dies. V. As
cendo ad patrem meum et patrem uestrum.
Concede quesumus omnipotens or
deus. ut qui hodierna
die unigenitum tuum redemp

[Then *commemorationes* of Becket, Ælphege and Dunstan: see further below.]

[P. 2] Concede quesumus omnipotens Deus ut qui peccatorum nostrorum pondere ... per hec paschalia festa liberemur. Per.

[*Feria III*]

[P. 3] Deus qui ecclesiam tuam nouo semper fetu multiplicas, ... quod fide perceperunt. Per.

Concede quesumus omnipotens deus, ut qui paschalis festiuitatis solennia ... semper sanctificatione uiuamus. Per.

Presta quesumus omnipotens deus, ut per hec paschalia festa que colimus, qui paschalis festiuitatis ... semper laude uiuamus. Per.

[*Feria IIII*]

Deus qui nos resurrectionis dominice annua solennitate ... ad gaudia eterna mereamur.

[P. 4] Presta quesumus omnipotens deus, ut huius paschalis festiuitatis mirabile sacramentum ... et uitam conferat sempiternam. Per.

[Doubtless originally:] Deus qui nos per paschalia festa letificas, ... te adiuuante fideliter teneamus. Per. [The first line was rewritten in the late Middle Ages to read: Deus cui proprium – followed by two uncertain letters.]

[*Feria V*]

Deus qui diuersitatem gentium in confessione tui nominis ad[una]sti, ... et pietas actionum. Per.

Deus qui nobis ad celebrandum paschale sacramentum ... et amare quod precipis.

Presta quesumus omnipotens deus ut qui // [breaks off at end of page].

[P. 5] [acephalus] \\ in christi resurrectione nos reparas, ... quos fecisti baptismo regenerari, facias beata immortalitate uestiri. Per eundem.

Deus a quo cuncta bona procedunt, ... et te gubernante eadem faciamus. Per.

[P. 6] Deus qui misericordie ianuam fidelibus tuis patere uoluisti, ... semitis deuiemus. Per.

[*Feria II*]

Presta quesumus omnipotens deus, ut qui in afflictione nostra de tua pietate confidimus, ... tua semper protectione muniamur. Per.

[Pp. 6–7] Pretende nobis domine misericordiam tuam, ut que uotis expetimus, conuersatione tibi placita consequamur. Per.
[P. 7] Presta quesumus omnipotens deus, ut ad te toto corde clamantes, tue pietatis indulgentiam consequamur.
[*Feria III*]
Presta quesumus omnipotens et misericors deus, ut in resurrectione domini nostri ihesu christi percipiamus ueraciter portionem. Qui tecum.
[*Feria IV*]
Presta quesumus omnipotens deus, ut qui in afflictione.
Presta quesumus omnipotens et misericors deus, ut qui iram tue indignationis agnouimus, misericordie tue indulgentiam consequamur. Per.
[P. 8] Presta populo tuo domine quesumus consolationis auxilium, ... propitius respirare concede. Per.
[*In vigilia ascensionis domini ad vesperam feria primus*]
Presta quesumus omnipotens pater ut nostre mentis intentio quo solennitatis hodierne gloriosus auctor ... et quo fide pergit, conuersatione perueniat. Per eundem.
Concede quesumus omnipotens deus, ut qui hodierna die unigenitum tuum redemp// [end of page but continued in the catchword below: –torem nostrum]
[The *commemorationes* for SS. Thomas Becket, Ælphege and Dunstan (p. 1, col. 2) are as follows:] *Commemoratio de* [erased but just recognisable as *S. Thoma*]. *Ant.* Summo sacerdotio. *Or.* Deus pro cuius ecclesia. *Commemoratio de S. Ælfego. Ant.* Ingressus celum. *Or.* Deus tuorum gloria sacerdotum. *Commemoratio de S. Dunstano. Ant.* Vir angelice. *Or.* Deus qui maxime clementiam tuam.

Scribes and Script

All the original text, including the rubrics, is the work of a single scribe, writing a high-grade, early-Gothic book hand of a fairly good quality. The collects, capitula and hymns are written to a larger gauge than the rest. The script, which is consistently positioned about 1 mm above the ruled lines, is weighty, and there is some 'biting' of the letters. The contours of 'rounded' forms are angled rather than curving, and angled serif-strokes, which, when added to the main stroke form a diamond-shape terminal, cap many minims. The ampersand is of slightly idiosyncratic form: its 'head' projects from the side rather than the top of the main body; and its 'arm' is not a continuation of the main body but rather a separate stroke which frequently ends by touching the head. Punctuation is restricted to a low point (for major and minor pauses); whatever its context, it is generally followed by an enhanced space. There is little abbreviation in the main text. There are no accents. Double 'i' is dashed (íí); y is dotted.

A contemporary or slightly younger (?*s.* xiii^{in}) and less formal hand added a catch-word ('–torem n[ost]r[u]m') and signature ('o')to the lower margin of p. 8.

A ?*s.* xv hand rewrote the first line of the second main collect on p. 4, column I in a semi-imitative script.

A ?*s* xv cursive hand added a couple of short notes (now cropped and rubbed) to the outer margin of p. 6, cued into the text by pairs of dashes; what remains of the second, appears to read, 'factores'.

Additions were made to the upper, inner and outer margins of p. I, beside the commemorations of the Canterbury saints, in a flowing cursive, almost semi-italic hand of *s.* xv–xvi; subsequently, two of them (presumably relating to Thomas Becket) were vigorously erased. The first line of the best-preserved group appears to read, 'xxviii^{o} Julii'.

Decoration

Every section is headed by – in turn – a red or blue penwork initial, flourished (rather cursorily) in the other colour. The capitals for the collects and capitula are at least twice the size of those heading other texts (two to four lines high, as opposed to one line high). The collect for Vespers on the Vigil of the Ascension (Presta quesumus omnipotens pater ut nostre mentis intentio … [p. 8]) is marked by a larger (six-lines-high) red **P**, its (still fairly cursory) flourishing shaded in green, blue and ochre, and its body articulated with fine lines in white.

History

The commemoration of the three archiepiscopal saints, Ælphege († 1012), Dunstan († 988) and Becket († 1170), points to use in Canterbury, most probably Christ Church; the inclusion of the last confirms the evidence of the script and initials, showing that the book was made after 1173, the date of Becket's canonisation. The various interventions in the margins in *s.* xv⁺ hands, along with the alteration of the collect on p. 4, indicate continuing service in the late Middle Ages. The erasure of the reference to Becket on p. 1 shows that the volume was still in 'active' use in 1538 when Henry VIII decreed that all references to him be expunged.

The volume was evidently broken up and these leaves used as wrappers by 1556, for prominently written in the gutter of pp. 4 and 5 (then the 'spine') is 'Acta curia / 37 / 1556 1559', while at the top of p. 5 (then the 'front') is written: '1556, 1557, 1558, 1559. Ad Instantiam Partium Lib. 37'. (Pages 3–6 formed the cover of Y. 2. 19; pp. 1 and 2, 7 and 8 were probably inside it.) It is highly likely, therefore, that this volume was one of the innumerable casualties of the Act of Uniformity of 1549.

ABBREVIATIONS AND BIBLIOGRAPHY

Abbreviations

B	Hughes, A. (ed.), *The Bec Missal*, HBS 94 (London, 1963)
BAV	Biblioteca Apostolica Vaticana
BHL	*Bibliotheca Hagiographica Latina Antiquae et Mediae Aetatis*, 2 vols. (Bruxelles, 1898–1901); *Supplementi* (Bruxelles, 1911); *Novum Supplementum* (Bruxelles, 1986)
BL	London, British Library
BnF	Paris, Bibliothèque nationale de France
BRUO	Emden, A. B., *A Biographical Register of the University of Oxford to A.D. 1500*, 3 vols. (Oxford, 1957–9)
CCCC	Cambridge, Corpus Christi College
CC (CM/SL)	*Corpus Christianorum* (*Continuatio Mediaevalis/Series Latina*) (Turnhout, 1954–)
CMBLC	Corpus of Medieval British Library Catalogues (London)
CPG	Geerard, M., and Glorie, F (ed.), *Clavis Patrum Graecorum*, 5 vols. (Turnhout, 1983–7)
CPL	Dekkers, E. (ed.), *Clavis Patrum Latinorum*, 3rd ed. (Turnhout, 1995)
CSLMAAG	*Clavis Scriptorum Latinorum Medii Aevi: Auctores Galliae 735–987*, 2 vols. [to date] (Turnhout, 1994–)
CUL	Cambridge University Library
HBS	Henry Bradshaw Society
MGH	Monumenta Germaniae Historica

RJ	Wilson, H. A. (ed.), *The Missal of Robert of Jumièges*, HBS 11 (London, 1896)
T	Tolhurst, J (ed.), *The Monastic Breviary of Hyde Abbey*, 6 vols., HBS 69, 70, 71, 76, 78, 80 (London, 1930–9)
TCD	Dublin, Trinity College
WM	Wickham Legg, I. (ed.), *Missale ad usum ecclesie Westmonasteriensis*, HBS 1, 5, 12 (London, 1891–3)

Bibliography

Abukhanfusa, K. 2004: *Mutilated Books: Wondrous Leaves from Swedish Bibliographical History* (Stockholm)

Aland, K. and Aland, B. 1992: *Novum Testmentum Latine*, 2nd ed. (Stuttgart)

Barré, H. 1962: *Les Homéliaires carolingiens de l'école d'Auxerre*, Studi e Testi 225 (Vatican City)

Alexander, J. J. G. 1970: *Norman Illumination at Mont St Michel 966–1100* (Oxford)

— 1978a: *Insular Manuscripts, 6th to the 9th century* (London)

— 1978b: *The Decorated Letter* (New York and London)

Barlow, F. (ed.) 1962: *The Life of King Edward the Confessor* (Edinburgh)

Barker-Benfield, B. C. 1980: 'Clement Canterbury, librarian of St Augustine's Abbey', *Manuscripts at Oxford: R. W. Hunt Memorial Exhibition*, ed. A. C. de la Mare and B. C. Barker-Benfield (Oxford), pp. 88–92

— (ed.) [forthcoming:] *St Augustine's Abbey, Canterbury*, CMBLC (London)

Bell, D. N. (ed.) 1992: *The Libraries of the Cistercians, Gilbertines and Premonstratensians*, CMBLC 3 (London)

Bischoff, B. 1981: *Kalligraphie in Bayern: achtes bis zwölftes Jahrhundert* (Wiesbaden)

— 1998: *Katalog der festländischen Handschriften des neunten Jahrhunderts I: Aachen–Lambach* (Wiesbaden)

Bishop, T. A. M. 1955: 'Notes on Cambridge Manuscripts, Part II', *Transactions of the Cambridge Bibliographical Society* 2/2, pp. 185–92

— 1960: 'Notes on Cambridge Manuscripts, Part V: Manuscripts Connected with St Augustine's Canterbury, Continued', *Transactions of the Cambridge Bibliographical Society* 3/1, pp. 93–5

Borenius, T. 1932: *St Thomas Becket in Art* (London)

Brasington, B. C. 2004: *Ways of Mercy: The Prologue of Ivo of Chartres, edition and analysis* (Münster)

Brett, M. 2004: 'Editions, Manuscripts and Readers in some Pre-Gratian Collections', *Ritual, Text and Law: Studies in Medieval Canon Law and Liturgy presented to Roger E. Reynolds*, ed. K. G. Cushing and R. F. Gyug (Aldershot), pp. 205–24

Brooke, C. (ed.) 2002: *The Monastic Constitutions of Lanfranc* (ed. and trans. D. Knowles), revised edition (Oxford)

Brooke, Z. N. 1931: *The English Church and the Papacy from the Conquest to the Reign of John* (Cambridge)

Brown, M. P. 1990: *A Guide to Western Historical Scripts from Antiquity to 1600* (London)

— 1996: *The Book of Cerne: Prayer, Patronage and Power in Ninth-Century England* (London)

Budny, M. 1997: *Insular, Anglo-Saxon and Early Norman Manuscript Art at Corpus Christi College Cambridge: an illustrated catalogue*, 2 vols. (Kalamazoo)

— 1999: 'The *Biblia Gregoriana*', *St Augustine and the Conversion of England*, ed. R. Gameson (Stroud), pp. 237–84

Carley, J (ed.) 2000: *The Libraries of King Henry VIII*, CMBLC 7 (London)

— 2004: *The Books of King Henry VIII and his Wives* (London)

Clarke, J. G. 2004: *A Monastic Renaissance at St Albans: Thomas of Walsingham and his Circle c. 1350–1440* (Oxford)

Clarke, P. D. and Lovatt, R. (ed.) 2002: *The University and College Libraries of Cambridge*, CBMLC 10 (London)

Clayton, M. 1985: 'Homiliaries and Preaching in Anglo-Saxon England', *Peritia* 4, pp. 207–42

Coates, A. 1999: *English Medieval Books: the Reading Abbey Collections from Foundation to Dispersal* (Oxford)

Cross, J. E. 1977: '"Legimus in Ecclesiasticis Historiis": a Sermon for All Saints and its use in Old English Prose', *Traditio* 33, pp. 101–35

— 1987: *Cambridge, Pembroke College MS 25* (London)

— 1991: 'Wulfstan's *De Anticristo* in a twelfth-century Worcester Manuscript', *Anglo-Saxon England* 20, pp. 203–20

— and Hall, T. N. 1993: 'The Fragments of Homiliaries in Canterbury Cathedral Library MS. Addit. 127/1 and in Kent, County Archives Offices, Maidstone MS PRC 49/2', *Scriptorium* 47, pp. 186–92

Darlington, R. R. (ed.) 1928: *The Vita Wulfstani of William of Malmesbury*, Camden Society 3rd series 40 (London)

Davril, A. (ed.) 1995: *The Winchcombe Sacramentary*, Henry Bradshaw Society 109 (London)

De Hamel, C. 1997: 'The Dispersal of the Library of Christ Church Canterbury from the Fourteenth to the Sixteenth Century', *Books and Collectors 1200–1700: essays presented to Andrew Watson*, ed. J. P. Carley and C. G. C. Tite (London), pp. 263–79

De la Mare, A. C. 1976: 'A Fragment of Augustine in the Hand of Theodericus Werken', *Transactions of the Cambridge Bibliographical Society* 6, pp. 285–90

Dewick, E. S. (ed.) 1914–21: *The Leofric Collectar*, 2 vols., Henry Bradshaw Society 45 and 56 (London)

Doane, A. N. and Pulsiano, P. 1997: *Anglo-Saxon Manuscripts in Microfiche Facsimile* 5 (Tempe, Arizona)

Dodwell, C. R. 1954: *The Canterbury School of Illumination 1066–1200* (Cambridge)

Dubois, J. (ed.) 1965: *Le Martyrologe d'Usuard: texte et commentaire* (Bruxelles)

Duffy, E. 1992: *The Stripping of the Altars: Traditional Religion in England 1400–1580* (New Haven and London)

Dugmore, C. W. 1958: *The Mass and the English Reformers* (London)

Dumville, D. N. 1992: *Liturgy and the Ecclesiastical History of Late Anglo-Saxon England* (Woodbridge)

Emden, A. B. 1957–9: *A Biographical Register of the University of Oxford to A.D. 1500*, 3 vols. (Oxford)

— 1968: *Donors of Books to S. Augustine's Abbey, Canterbury*, Oxford Bibliographical Society Occasional Publication 4 (Oxford)

Fowler-Magerl, L. 2003: *A Selection of Canon Law Collections Compiled between 1000 and 1140* (Piesenkofen)

Fournier, P. and Le Bras, G. 1931–2: *Histoire des collections canoniques en occident depuis les fausses décretales jusqu'au décret de Gratien*, 2 vols. (Paris)

Friedberg, A (ed.) 1879: *Corpus Iuris Canonici ... Pars Prior: Decretum Magistri Gratiani* (Leipzig)

Gameson, R. G. 1995: 'English Manuscript Art in the Late Eleventh Century: Canterbury and its Context', *Canterbury and the Norman Conquest: Churches, Saints and Scholars 1066–1109*, ed. R. Eales and R. Sharpe (London and Rio Grande), pp. 95–144

— 1999a: 'The Earliest Books of Christian Kent', *St Augustine and the Conversion of England*, ed. Gameson (Stroud), pp. 313–73

— 1999b: *The Manuscripts of Early Norman England c. 1066–1130* (London)

— 2000: 'Books, Culture and the Church in Canterbury around the Millennium' in R. Eales and R. Gameson, *Vikings, Monks and the Millennium: Canterbury in about 1000 AD* (Canterbury), pp. 15–40

— (ed.) 2001–2: *Codex Aureus: an Eighth-Century Gospel Book*, 2 vols., Early English Manuscripts in Facsimile 28–9 (Copenhagen)

— 2002: 'L'Angleterre et la Flandre aux Xe et XIe siècles: le témoignage des manuscrits', *Les Échanges culturels au Moyen Âge*, Publications de la Sorbonne, Série Histoire Ancienne et Médiévale 70 (Paris), pp. 165–206

— 2005: 'Recovered! On the Early Manuscript Fragments of Canterbury Cathedral', *Canterbury Cathedral Chronicle* 99, pp. 33–40

— and Gameson, F. 2005: 'From Augustine to Parker: the changing face of the first archbishop of Canterbury', *Studies in Honour of C. R. Hart*, ed. A. P. Smyth and S. D. Keynes (Dublin), pp. 13–38

Gibson, M. 1971: 'Lanfranc's Commentary on the Pauline Epistles', *Journal of Theological Studies* n.s. 22, pp. 435–450; repr. in her '*Artes' and the Bible in the Medieval West* (Aldershot, 1993), no. XII.

— 1992: 'The Latin Apparatus', *The Eadwine Psalter: Text, Image and Monastic Culture in Twelfth-Century Canterbury*, ed. M. T. Gibson, T. A. Heslop and R. W. Pfaff (London and University Park), pp. 108–22

— 1995: 'Normans and Angevins 1070–1220', *A History of Canterbury Cathedral*, ed. P. Collinson, N. Ramsay and M. Sparks (Oxford), pp. 38–68

Gilchrist, J. 1983: 'The Manuscripts of the Canonical Collection in Four Books', *Zeitschrift der Savigny-Stiftung für Rechtsgeschichte, Kanonistische Abteilung* 69, pp. 64–120

Gorman, M. 2004: 'The Oldest Lists of Latin Books', *Scriptorium* 58, pp. 48–63

Gullick, M. 1998: 'The Scribal Work of Eadmer of Canterbury to 1109', *Archaeologia Cantiana* 118, pp. 173–89

— [forthcoming:] 'A Transitional Binding (Anglo-Saxon to Romanesque) at Canterbury Cathedral'

— and Pfaff, R. W. 2001: 'The Dublin Pontifical (TCD 98 [B.3.6]): St Anselm's?' *Scriptorium* 55, pp. 284–94

Günzel, B. (ed.) 1995: *Ælfwine's Prayer Book*, Henry Bradshaw Society 108 (London)

Halporn, J. W. 1981: 'The Manuscripts of Cassiodorus' *Expositio psalmorum*', *Traditio* 37, pp. 388–96

Hecht, H. (ed.) 1900: *Bischofs Waerferth von Worcester Übersetzung der Dialoge Gregors des Grossen*, Bibliothek der Angelsächsischen Prosa 5 (Leipzig)

Hughes, A. (ed.) 1963: *The Bec Missal*, Henry Bradshaw Society 94 (London)

Hunt, R. W. 1943: 'Studies on Priscian in the Eleventh and Twelfth Centuries', *Medieval and Renaissance Studies* 1, pp. 194–231

Hussey, A. 1909: 'Appendix to Visitations of the Archdeacon of Canterbury', *Archaeologia Cantiana* 28, pp. 75–82

James, M. R. 1903: *The Ancient Libraries of Canterbury and Dover* (Cambridge)

— 1912: *A Descriptive Catalogue of the Manuscripts in the Library of Corpus Christi College, Cambridge* (Cambridge)

— 1932: *A Descriptive Catalogue of the Manuscripts in the Library of Lambeth Palace* (Cambridge)

Kauffmann, C. M. 1975: *Romanesque Manuscripts 1066–1190* (London)

Keil, H. 1855–80: *Grammatici latini*, 7 vols. (Leipzig)

Ker, N. R. 1946, 'Un nouveau fragment des miracles de S. Ouen à Cantorbéry', *Analecta Bollandiana* 64, pp. 50–3

— 1957: *Catalogue of Manuscripts containing Anglo-Saxon* (Oxford)

— 1960: *English Manuscripts in the Century after the Norman Conquest* (Oxford)

— 1964: *Medieval Libraries of Great Britain: a list of surviving books*, 2nd ed. (London)

— 1977: *Medieval Manuscripts in British Libraries II: Abbotsford-Keele* (Oxford)

— 1979: 'Copying an Exemplar: Two Manuscripts of Jerome on Habakkuk', *Miscellanea Codicologica F. Masai Dicata*, ed. P. Cockshaw, M.-C. Garand, P. Jodogne, 2 vols. (Gent), I, pp. 203–10

Kéry, L. 1999: *Canonical Collections of the Early Middle Ages (ca. 400–1140): a bibliographical guide to the manuscripts and literature* (Washington)

Knowles, D. 1988: *The Evolution of Medieval Thought*, 2nd ed. revised by D. Luscombe and C.N.L. Brooke (Harlow)

Langefeld, B. 2003: *The Old English Version of the Enlarged Rule of Chrodegang* (Frankfurt-am-Main)

Lapidge, M. 1985: 'Surviving Booklists from Anglo-Saxon England', *Learning and Literature in Anglo-Saxon England: Studies presented to Peter Clemoes*, ed. M. Lapidge and H. Gneuss (Cambridge), pp. 33–89

Light, L. 1987: 'The New Thirteenth-Century Bible and the Challenge of Heresy', *Viator* 18, pp. 275–88

— 1994: 'French Bibles c. 1200–30: a new look at the origin of the Paris Bible', *The Early Medieval Bible: its production, decoration and use*, ed. R. G. Gameson (Cambridge), pp. 155–76

Love, R. (ed.), 1996: *Three Eleventh-Century Anglo-Latin Saints Lives* (Oxford)

Lowe, E. A. 1966: *Codices Latini Antiquiores XI* (Oxford)

— 1972: *Codices Latini Antiquiores II: Great Britain and Ireland*, 2nd ed. (Oxford)

Luard, H. R. 1865: 'A Letter from Bishop Bale to Archbishop Parker', *Proceedings of the Cambridge Antiquarian Society* 3, pp. 157–73

Marsden, R. 1994: 'The Old Testament in late Anglo-Saxon England: preliminary observations on the textual evidence', *The Early Medieval Bible: its Production, Decoration and Use*, ed. R. G. Gameson (Cambridge), pp. 101–24

— 1999: 'The Gospels of St Augustine', *St Augustine and the Conversion of England*, ed. R. Gameson (Stroud), pp. 285–312

Milfull, I. 1996: *The Hymns of the Anglo-Saxon Church* (Cambridge)

Morgan, N. 1983: *Early Gothic Manuscripts I: 1190–1250* (London and Oxford)

Moricca, U. (ed.) 1924: *Gregorii Magni Dialogi, Libri IV* (Rome)

Mynors, R. A. B. 1950: 'A Fifteenth-Century Scribe: T. Werken', *Transactions of the Cambridge Bibliographical Society* 1/2, pp. 97–104

Napier, A. S. 1916: *The Old English Version, with the Latin original, of the Enlarged Rule of Chrodegang*, Early English Text Society, o.s. 150 (London)

O'Brien O'Keeffe, K. (ed.) 2001: *The Anglo-Saxon Chronicle, a collaborative edition 5: MS C* (Cambridge)

Orchard, N. 1995: 'The Bosworth Psalter and St Augustine's Missal', *Canterbury and the Norman Conquest: Churches, Saints and Scholars 1066–1109*, ed. R. Eales and R. Sharpe (London and Rio Grande), pp. 87–94

— (ed.) 2002: *The Leofric Missal*, 2 vols., Henry Bradshaw Society 113–14 (London)

Pächt, O. and Alexander, J. J. G. 1973: *Illuminated Manuscripts in the Bodleian Library, Oxford 3: British, Irish and Icelandic Schools* (Oxford)

Page, R. I. 1993: *Matthew Parker and his Books* (Kalamazoo)

— and Bushnell, G. 1975: *Matthew Parker's Legacy* (Cambridge)

Pantin, W. A. 1947: *Canterbury College, Oxford*, 3 vols., Oxford Historical Society, new series VI–VIII (Oxford)

— 1985: *Canterbury College, Oxford* IV, Oxford Historical Society, new series XXX (Oxford)

Parkes, M. B. 1991: *Scribes, Scripts and Readers: Studies in the Communication, Presentation and Dissemination of Medieval Texts* (London)

— 1997: 'Archaizing Hands in English Manuscripts', *Books and Collectors 1200–1700: Essays Presented to Andrew Watson*, ed. J. P. Carley and C. G. C. Tite (London), pp. 101–41

Partoens, G. 2001: 'La collection de sermons augustiniens *De verbis apostoli*. Introduction et liste des manuscrits les plus anciens', *Revue bénédictine* 111/3 and 4, pp. 317–52

— 2003: 'Le sermon 151 de Saint Augustin. Introduction et édition', *Revue bénédictine* 113/1, pp. 18–70

Passalacqua, M. 1978: *I Codici di Prisciano*, Sussidi Eruditi 29 (Rome)

Procter, F. and Wordsworth, C. (ed.) 1886: *Breviarium ad usum insignis ecclesie Sarum* (London)

Ramsay, N. 1995: 'The Cathedral Archives and Library', *A History of Canterbury Cathedral*, ed. P. Collinson, N. Ramsay and M. Sparks (Oxford), pp. 341–407

— 2004: 'The Manuscripts flew about like Butterflies: the break-up of English libraries in the sixteenth century', *Lost Libraries: the destruction of great book collections since Antiquity*, ed. J. Raven (London)

Rawcliffe, C. 1999: *Medicine for the Soul: the life, death and resurrection of an English medieval hospital* (Stroud)

Richards, M. P. 1988: *Texts and their Traditions in the Medieval Library of Rochester Cathedral Priory*, Transactions of the American Philosophical Society 78/3 (Philadelphia)

Robinson, P. R. 1988: *Catalogue of Dated and Datable Manuscripts c. 737–1600 in Cambridge Libraries*, 2 vols. (Cambridge)

— 2003: *Catalogue of Dated and Datable Manuscripts c. 888–1600 in London Libraries*, 2 vols. (London)

Römer, F. 1972: *Die handschriftliche Überlieferung der Werke des heiligen Augustinus II/2: Grossbritannien und Irland, Verzeichnis nach Bibliotheken* (Vienna)

Roth, C. 1964: 'Pledging a book in Medieval England', *The Library* 5th ser. 19, pp. 196–200.

Schmitt, F. S. (ed.) 1946–61: *S. Anselmi Opera Omnia*, 6 vols. (Edinburgh)

Schwartz, E., Mommsen, Th., and Winkelmann, F. (ed.) 1999: *Eusebius Werke II: Die Kirchengeschichte*, 3 vols., 2nd ed. (Berlin)

Sharpe, R *et al.* (ed.) 1996: *English Benedictine Libraries: the shorter catalogues*, CMBLC 4 (London)

Sheerin, D. J. 1974: 'An Anonymous Verse Epitome of the Life of St Anselm', *Analecta Bollandiana* 92, pp. 109–24

Southern, R. W. 1963: *St Anselm and his Biographer* (Cambridge)

— 1990: *Saint Anselm: a Portrait in a Landscape* (Cambridge)

Statutes 1925: *The Statutes of the Cathedral and Metropolitical Church of Christ, Canterbury, with other Documents, privately printed for the Dean and Chapter of Canterbury* (Canterbury)

Stoneman, W. P. (ed.) 1999: *Dover Priory*, CBMLC 5 (London)

Sweet, H. (ed.) 1871: *King Alfred's West Saxon Version of Gregory's Pastoral Care*, Early English Texts Society, o.s. 45 (London)

Sylwan, A. 2000: 'Petrus Comestor, *Historia Scholastica*, une nouvelle édition', *Sacris eudiri* 39, pp. 345–82

Szirmai, J. 1999: *The Archaeology of Medieval Bookbinding* (Aldershot)

Talbot, C. H. 1955: 'The *Liber Confortatorius* of Goscelin of Saint-Bertin', *Studia Anselmiana* 37, pp. 1–117

Tanner, J. R. 1930: *Tudor Constitutional Documents A.D. 1485–1603*, 2nd ed. (Cambridge)

Temple, E. 1976: *Anglo-Saxon Manuscripts 900-1066* (London)

Thompson, E. M. (ed.) 1902–4: *Customary of the Benedictine Monasteries of St Augustine Canterbury and St Peter Westminster*, 2 vols., Henry Bradshaw Society 23 and 28 (London)

Thomson, R. M. 1982: *Manuscripts from St Albans Abbey 1066–1235*, 2 vols. (Woodbridge)

Tolhurst, J. B. L. (ed.) 1930–42: *The Monastic Breviary of Hyde Abbey*, 6 vols., Henry Bradshaw Society 69, 70, 71, 76, 78, 80 (London)

Urry, W. 1967: *Canterbury under the Angevin Kings* (London)

Verbraken, P.-P. 1967: 'La collection de sermons de saint Augustin, *De verbis Domini et Apostoli*', *Revue bénédictine* 77, pp. 27–46

— 1976: *Études critiques sur le sermons authentiques de Saint Augustin,* Instrumenta Patristica 12 (Steenbrugge)

Watson, A. G. 1963: 'A sixteenth-century Collector: Thomas Paclomb 1496–1572', *The Library* 5th ser. 18, pp. 204–17

— 1984: *Catalogue of Dated and Datable Manuscripts c. 435–1600 in Oxford Libraries*, 2 vols. (Oxford)

— (ed.) 1987: *Medieval Libraries of Great Britain, a List of Surviving Books: Supplement to the Second Edition* (London)

Weber, R. (ed.) 1983: *Biblia Sacra iuxta vulgatam versionem*, 3rd ed. (Stuttgart)

Webber, T. 1995: 'Script and Manuscript Production at Christ Church, Canterbury, after the Norman Conquest', *Canterbury and the Norman Conquest: Churches, Saints and Scholars 1066–1109*, ed. R. Eales and R. Sharpe (London and Rio Grande), pp. 145–58

Wheeler, G. W. (ed.) 1927: *Letters of Sir Thomas Bodley to the University of Oxford 1598–1611* (Oxford)

Wickham Legg, I. (ed.) 1891–3: *Missale ad usum ecclesie Westmonasteriensis*, Henry Bradshaw Society 1, 5, 12 (London)

— and StJohn Hope, W. H. (ed.) 1902: *Inventories of Christ Church, Canterbury* (London)

Wilmart, A. 1931: 'La tradition des grands ouvrages de S. Augustin, IV: Les *Enarrationes*', *Miscellanea Agostina* II (Rome), pp. 257–315

— 1933: 'Les Reliques de S. Ouen à Cantorbéry', *Analecta Bollandiana* 51, pp. 285–92

Wilson, H. A. (ed.) 1894: *Liber Sacramentorum Romanae ecclesiae* (Oxford)

— (ed.) 1896: *The Missal of Robert of Jumièges*, Henry Bradshaw Society 11 (London)

Woodcock, A. M. (ed.) 1956: *Cartulary of the Priory of St. Gregory, Canterbury*, Camden Society 3rd series 88 (London)

Woodruff, C. E. 1911: *A Catalogue of the Manuscript Books (which are preserved in Study X. Y. Z. and in the Howley-Harrison Collection) in the Library of Christ Church, Canterbury* (Canterbury)

— 1935: 'An Archidiaconal Visitation of 1502', *Archaeologia Cantiana* 47, pp. 13–54

Wright, C. E. 'The Dispersal of the Libraries in the Sixteenth Century', *The English Library before 1700*, ed. F. Wormald and C. E. Wright (London), pp. 148–75

Wright, D. F. 1972: 'The Manuscripts of St Augustine's *Tractatus in Evangelium Iohannis*', *Recherches augustiniennes* 8, pp. 55–143

— 1981: 'The Manuscripts of the *Tractatus in Iohannem*: a supplementary list', *Recherches augustiniennes* 16, pp. 59–100

Yerkes, D. 1977: 'The Text of the Canterbury Fragment of Werferth's Translation of Gregory's *Dialogues* and its Relation to the Other Manuscripts', *Anglo-Saxon England* 6, pp. 121–35

— 1979: *The Two Versions of Waerferth's Translation of Gregory's Dialogues: an Old English Thesaurus* (Toronto)

— 1986: 'The Translation of Gregory's *Dialogues* and its Revision: Textual History, Provenance, Authorship', *Studies in Earlier Old English Prose*, ed. P. E. Szarmach (Albany, NY), pp. 335–43

INDEX OF MANUSCRIPTS

(excluding those catalogued in the present publication, for which see the **Concordance**, p. 17)

'I' plus a number indicates a page in the Introduction; all other numerals refer to catalogue numbers.

INDEX OF PEOPLE AND PLACES

'I' plus a numeral indicates a page in the Introduction; all other references are to catalogue numbers. Medieval people are indexed by Christian name, post-medieval people by surname.